'Lyndall Ryan's new accoun ,tory
of the Tasmanian Aborigine: , ... and eloquence. It is a
book that will inform and move anyone with an interest in Australian
history.'

Professor Henry Reynolds, University of Tasmania

'A powerful and insightful historical account about a unique island
and its First peoples, their dispossession and their struggle for survival
and cultural birth right/heritage that reaches from the deep past to the
present day.'

Patsy Cameron, Tasmanian Aboriginal author,
cultural geographer and cultural practitioner

TASMANIAN ABORIGINES

FANNY COCHRANE SMITH (1834-1905)

Fanny Cochrane Smith was the only Tasmanian Aborigine from the Wybalenna Aboriginal Establishment on Flinders Island to leave descendants. Born in 1834, she was brought up at Wybalenna by her mother Tarenootairrer (Sarah) and stepfather Nicermenic (Eugene) along with her older sister, Mary Ann, and younger brother, Adam (b. 1838). She learned their Aboriginal languages, songs and stories and how to hunt for bush foods and to make baskets and dive for shellfish.

At the age of seven, the government despatched her to the Queen's Orphan School in Hobart. Desperately homesick, she returned home two years later and entered domestic service in the catechist's household. But she rebelled and was finally permitted to rejoin her own family in 1847 when the Aboriginal Establishment relocated to Oyster Cove. A year later she entered domestic service in Hobart and when Nicermenic died in 1851, she appears to have returned to Oyster Cove to live in her sister Mary Ann's household along with her widowed mother.

On 27 October 1854 in Hobart, Fanny married William Smith, an English sawyer and former convict. In recognition of her Tasmanian Aboriginality, Fanny received a $48 annuity from the government. Fanny and William then took responsibility for her brother Adam and until his untimely death in 1857 they ran a boarding house in Hobart. They then took up land near Oyster Cove where their son Henry was born in 1858; five more boys and five girls followed. Her mother, Tarenootairrer, often stayed with them until her death in 1861 and Truganini and other women from the Oyster Cove station were regular visitors.

After Truganini's death in 1876, the Tasmanian parliament recognised Fanny's claim as a Tasmanian Aborigine and increased her annuity to $100; in 1889 it granted her 121 hectares (300 acres) of land. She continued to hunt and gather bush foods and medicines, make baskets, dive for shellfish and carry out Aboriginal religious observances. A photograph at the time (used on the cover of this book) shows her as a proud Tasmanian Aboriginal woman wearing a magnificent headdress of native bird feathers and native flowers and an apron belt made of wallaby skins. In 1899 and 1903 she recorded Tasmanian Aboriginal songs on wax cylinders, thus ensuring that some of her people's musical culture would be preserved for posterity.

Fanny Cochrane Smith died on 24 February 1905 at the age of 71 and was buried in the cemetery at Port Cygnet. Her descendants form part of the Tasmanian Aboriginal community today.

TASMANIAN ABORIGINES

A history since 1803

LYNDALL RYAN

ALLEN&UNWIN
SYDNEY • MELBOURNE • AUCKLAND • LONDON

First published in 2012

Allen & Unwin
Sydney, Melbourne, Auckland, London

83 Alexander Street
Crows Nest NSW 2065
Australia
Phone: (61 2) 8425 0100
Fax: (61 2) 9906 2218
Email: info@allenandunwin.com
Web: www.allenandunwin.com

Cataloguing-in-Publication details are available
from the National Library of Australia
www.trove.nla.gov.au

ISBN 978 1 74237 068 2

Maps by Robert J. Anders
Index by Trevor Matthews
Set in 11/15 pt Granjon by Midland Typesetters, Australia
Printed in China at Everbest Printing Co

10 9 8 7 6 5 4 3 2 1

This book is dedicated to two very fine scholars, Irynej Skira (1950–2005) and Bill Thorpe (1943–2009), and to my cat Mishka (1994–2011). Although they did not live to see the outcome, they never lost their belief in the project.

Contents

Acknowledgements

A project of this magnitude would not have been possible without institutional support, practical help and critical advice of many friends and colleagues. At the University of Newcastle I would like to thank Terry Lovat, former Pro-Vice Chancellor of the Faculty of Education & Arts, for providing substantial resources for the project and Hugh Craig, Director of the Humanities Research Institute, and Philip Dwyer, Head of the History Discipline, for enabling Nadine Kavanagh to prepare the bibliography and Luke Clarke to provide last-minute research assistance. Tony Marshall and the staff at the Tasmanian Archive and Heritage Office in Hobart provided unfailing help in chasing up last-minute references and gave permission to reproduce maps and illustrations. The State Library of New South Wales, the British Museum, the National Library of Australia, the Queen Victoria Museum and Art Gallery, and Ian McFarlane and Anne Bickford gave permission to reproduce illustrations. Above all I would like to thank Robert Anders, cartographer extraordinaire at the University of Tasmania, for preparing the maps based on source data provided by Geoscience Australia.

In Tasmania, Alison Alexander, Anna Diacopolous, Barbara Baird and Vicki Rich, Shayne Breen and his partner Sue, Chris and Leigh Dole, Jean Elder, Julie Gough, George and Joan Masterman, Cassandra Pybus, Ian and Vicki Pearce, Edwina and Michael Powell, Margaret Sing and Suzanne Skira provided famed Tasmanian hospitality and the opportunity to discuss Tasmanian history. Ian McFarlane, Shayne Breen, Robert Cox, John Lennox and Rex Hesline organised visits to sites of historical significance, thus enabling me to gain new insights into the settlers' war against the Tasmanian Aborigines. In Canberra, my brother, Patrick, sister-in-law, Margaret, and sister, Julia, also offered their warm hospitality as did Anne Bickford, Ann Curthoys and John Docker, and Juliet Richter did likewise in Sydney. Ben Kiernan invited me to Yale as a Visiting Fellow in September 2007 to explore the international dimensions of settler colonialism, and at Newcastle Philip Dwyer encouraged me to reconsider settler activism within the long history of violence. Anne Bickford, Sandra Bowdler, Peter Bowen, Patsy Cameron, Robert Cox, Ann Curthoys, John Docker, Raymond Evans, Rex Hesline, John Lennox and Ian Pearce provided critical advice on draft chapters. At Allen & Unwin, Elizabeth Weiss provided outstanding support, with Karen Ward as copyeditor and Ann Lennox, Jo Lyons and Angela Handley as in-house editors. I thank them all for their generosity and support. I would like to stress, however, that responsibility for errors and inadequacies in the text rests with me alone.

Terrigal
September 2011

List of illustrations

List of maps

Preface

My first book on the Tasmanian Aborigines was published in Australia and North America in 1981, with a paperback edition in 1982.[1] A second edition appeared in Australia in 1996 with two added chapters.[2] Since then, new approaches have developed, new information has emerged and so much controversy has arisen about the history of the Tasmanian Aborigines that an entirely new book was required—hence the new title. The original argument of the first book, that the Tasmanian Aborigines resisted British colonisation and 'did not die out in 1876 or in any other period of Tasmania's history', still remains cogent, but the framework of race relations that underpinned it has been replaced by one of settler colonialism, which offers a more encompassing approach to understanding how the Tasmanian Aborigines were nearly wiped off the face of the earth within a generation and how they survived, stronger than ever, into the twenty-first century.

Settler colonialism considers the white settler occupation of lands of native peoples as a structured process whereby the settlers could achieve their objective—the production of a major staple for export—only by completely dispossessing the native peoples, in particular hunter-gatherers, from their land and then subjugating and partially or fully eliminating them as a distinctive group.[3] In Tasmania, the British occupation of the island, which originally began in 1803 to forestall a possible French claim, was a prelude to the massive pastoral settler invasion in the 1820s. This new group of settlers worked with the colonial government to either exterminate or forcibly remove the Tasmanian Aborigines from the island so that they could run vast numbers of sheep and produce fine wool for export to the textile mills in northern England. By the time most of the Tasmanian Aborigines had been exterminated, many of the settlers were leaving

Tasmania in search of even larger tracts of land on mainland Australia in present-day Victoria, where they continued their exterminatory practices among the Victorian Aborigines. Even so, the few surviving Tasmanian Aborigines who were incarcerated on Flinders Island in Bass Strait were now expected to die out. The death of Truganini in 1876 and the public exhibition of her skeletal remains in the Tasmanian Museum in Hobart from 1904 until 1947 were considered by the settlers as incontrovertible proof of that extinction.[4]

As this book—just like *The Aboriginal Tasmanians*—will show, the Tasmanian Aborigines did not die out in 1876 or in any other period of their history. Rather, they actively opposed every facet of settler colonialism. They resisted the first colonial invaders, conducted a long guerilla war against the settlers, resisted incarceration on the island in Bass Strait and then succeeded in persuading the British government to allow them to return to their homeland, albeit to Oyster Cove, where a new Aboriginal community was forged. Another community emerged on the eastern Bass Strait islands that resisted dispersal and gained recognition as an Aboriginal community with the establishment of a special reserve in the 1880s. In the twentieth century, the 'Islanders', as they were known, contested settler government policies of protection and assimilation until the 1970s, when they joined with the descendants of the Oyster Cove community and others to campaign for the return of land, the return of the remains of their stolen ancestors and an apology and financial compensation for their stolen children. In using settler colonialism to juxtapose the ideas, policies and practices of settler activism with the extraordinary variety of Tasmanian Aboriginal resistance since 1803, this book offers a more encompassing narrative of the Tasmanian Aborigines' historical experiences.

In taking this approach, it is now possible to consider the story of the Tasmanian Aborigines' near extinction as a case study in the wider history of the violent dispossession and subjugation of hunter-gatherer communities by European settlers in the process of colonial conquest. The tactics used by the British settlers in Tasmania bear similarities to those used by the Dutch settlers to dispossess and violently subjugate the Khoisan on the Cape Colony's northern frontier in South Africa in the late eighteenth and early nineteenth centuries and the strategies used by colonial settler Americans to eradicate Native American communities in the Old Northwest of the United States in the decades immediately following the American War of Independence.[5] In each case, the settlers' determination to violently remove Indigenous peoples from their land so they could occupy it to produce staples such as wheat and wool for export to markets in Europe or in other parts of the United States led them to develop genocidal ideologies to justify their violent extermination of the indigenous landowners.[6]

In Tasmania, the British settlers initially invoked eighteenth-century religious and scientific beliefs in 'savagery' and 'fatalism' to explain the near extinction of what they believed were at least 6,000 to 8,000 Tasmanian Aborigines within a generation of invasion.[7] This explanation enabled the settlers to justify their genocidal behaviour by claiming that the Aborigines themselves were responsible for their near demise by virtue of their 'innate inferiority' and inability to 'compete successfully with Europeans'.[8] This belief was modernised in 1859 when Joseph Milligan, the Secretary of the Royal Society of Tasmania, applied new scientific methods of population density and report discounting to a very limited range of data and estimated that the Tasmanian Aboriginal population in 1803 was never more than 2,000 and thus far too low for long-term survival.[9] At this point the belief that the Tasmanian Aborigines were always a 'doomed race' took off. This new doctrine, which was in fact a refinement of the old religious doctrine of 'savagery' and 'fatalism', was first conferred the name of Social Darwinism and is now known as scientific racism, that is, the use of scientific techniques to sanction belief in white racial superiority.[10] It proclaimed that, by virtue of their 'extreme primitivism' and their low estimated population, the Tasmanian Aborigines were already on the road to extinction before the British arrived in Tasmania in 1803 and thus they were responsible for their own virtual disappearance within a few decades.

For the next 150 years, the doctrine proved extraordinarily resilient in denying settler responsibility for the near extinction of the Tasmanian Aborigines. Every now and then historians such as James Bonwick in 1870, James Fenton in 1884, Clive Turnbull in 1948 and Lloyd Robson in 1983 would raise the question of settler responsibility.[11] But in each case their claims would be firmly dismissed by the leading proponents of scientific racism. They included osteologist Joseph Barnard Davis in 1874, historian James Erskine Calder in 1875, anthropologist Edward Tyler in 1894, historians James Backhouse Walker in 1899 and Robert Giblin in 1939, museum director William Bryden in 1960, archaeologist Rhys Jones in 1977 and anatomist Brian Plomley in 1993.[12] Each in their own way declared that the Tasmanian Aborigines were either too 'primitive' in their technical abilities, including an apparent inability to make fire by artificial means, or were too few in number in 1803, or were unable to reproduce themselves effectively, or were too susceptible to inadvertently introduced exotic diseases, to survive settler colonialism and so had simply 'faded away'.[13]

In my earlier book, I called this doctrine the 'myth of extinction' and countered it with the framework of Aboriginal resistance. This included renaming the Tasmanian Aborigines as 'Aboriginal Tasmanians' as a way of liberating them from the shackles of scientific racism.[14] The book showed how the Tasmanian Aborigines had resisted the violent settler occupation of their land in the 1820s in which they were killed at four times the rate of the settlers, that they had not died out in 1876, and that in the mid 1970s they had regrouped as a potent political force and openly questioned the legality of settler dispossession and campaigned for their rights and the return of stolen land. Today the doctrine appears to have been overturned in Tasmania. It is now widely recognised that the Tasmanian Aborigines have occupied Tasmania for at least 40,000 years, that their population at the moment of British invasion in 1803 was probably between 6,000 and 8,000, that they could make fire by artificial means and that they were violently and unjustly removed from their land.

Even so, the doctrine still retains many powerful adherents. The best known is the polemicist Keith Windschuttle. In 2002, he self-published a book in which he drew on the long-outdated work of the key proponents of scientific racism outlined above, to claim that there were only 2,000 Aborigines in Tasmania at the moment of British colonisation, that they were an internally dysfunctional society that had survived for tens of thousands of years more from 'good fortune than good management' and that when the British arrived, 'this small, precarious society quickly collapsed under the dual weight of the susceptibilities of its members to disease and abuse and neglect of its women'.[15] He further claimed that they had no connection to the land and were politically incapable of conducting a guerilla war with the settlers. Rather, they were more like 'black bushrangers' who attacked settlers' huts for plunder, were led by 'educated black terrorists' disaffected from white society, and two colonists were recorded killed for every recorded Aboriginal death. He also claimed that he could find only one genuine incident of settler massacre of Aborigines, and that, even then, he was the first historian to identify it.[16] As a consequence of his findings he concluded that governments today do not owe the present-day community any form of reparation or apology for their dispossession or other claims of subjugation and repression.

Although many critics, including one reviewer who shared Windschuttle's conservative brand of politics, summarily dismissed these extraordinary claims,[17] the book found a ready audience with certain white Australians sceptical of stories of settler frontier violence. In this context it was designed to undermine the work of historians of the Tasmanian Aborigines such as myself, on the grounds that they had deliberately misled a generation of Australians about what happened in the past. For example, Windschuttle alleged that in *The Aboriginal Tasmanians* I had fabricated footnotes to invent settler massacres of Aborigines in the Black War in the 1820s. He then charged that I had invented these massacres as part of a well-orchestrated campaign to 'disparage the character' of the Australian nation and, ultimately, the 'calibre of the civilisation Britain brought to these shores'.[18]

A fabrication is a deliberate act of lying, employed for propaganda purposes and designed to deceive an unwary public. This is a very serious allegation to make about any historian's work. I was certainly prepared to acknowledge, as any historian would, that *The Aboriginal Tasmanians* might have contained inadvertent minor errors, but I had certainly not engaged in any wilful act of fabrication. The mainstream media, however, and *The Australian* newspaper in particular, decided that I was the historian at fault.[19] From that moment I became the key target in what became known as the Aboriginal history wars. Over the summer of 2002–03, nearly every right-wing columnist in the country attacked my credibility as a historian, although there is no evidence that any of them had read my book.[20] After checking Windschuttle's allegations by going back to original sources in the archives in Hobart I prepared my riposte for publication in Robert Manne's *Whitewash: On Keith Windschuttle's Fabrication of Aboriginal History.*[21]

In that essay I readily conceded that there were indeed some minor errors in *The Aboriginal Tasmanians*. They included transposing two endnotes; apparently using three inaccurate newspaper references for information that was otherwise correct and quickly discoverable in the only other newspaper published in Hobart at the time; using one source that had retrospectively been shown to be unreliable; omitting five references to information that exists in the historical record; and misplacing the site of a massacre that actually did take place. In each case the mistakes could be readily identified and rectified, as they were in that essay. It was also clear that none of the errors changed the story of what happened to the Tasmanian Aborigines during the Black War in any fundamental way. I concluded that, 'when one takes into account that this pioneering research was undertaken over thirty years ago when primary sources were in a much less accessible form than they are now, and that I was the first trained historian to use them in any consistent way, these kinds of errors are not only understandable, there are also remarkably few of them'.[22] Historian Inga Clendinnen agreed. As the first mainland Australian historian with a working knowledge of the Tasmanian sources to enter the debate, she concluded that the errors in my book were 'few, explicable and trivial'.[23] How, then, had the history wars generated so much heat from so little tinder, and how had the Tasmanian Aborigines emerged as the central focus?

One view is that the history wars were a conservative response to the overturning of the doctrine of scientific racism, which for more than 170 years had conveniently underpinned the myth of the Tasmanian Aborigines' self-extinction. This overturning began in 1983 in the Franklin Dam case before the Australian High Court. In that case, at least one of the judges acknowledged that he had been influenced in his decision to oppose the dam by the evidence provided by counsel for the Tasmanian Aborigines. The evidence said that they had survived into the present and had strong spiritual connections with the area that would be flooded by the proposed dam.[24] Nine years later, the High Court's Mabo judgment overturned *terra nullius*, one of the central justifications for denying Aboriginal land rights and sovereignty, in favour of recognising native title.[25] The judgment laid the groundwork for the return of land to the Tasmanian Aborigines in 1995. A year later, the report of the Human Rights Commission into the government policy of forced removal of Aboriginal children from their parents in the twentieth century described the policy as a form of genocide, in that it sought to eradicate the children's Aboriginal identity and to eliminate the Aboriginal people as a distinctive group.[26] In each case, the conservative political establishment, including the then federal minister for Aboriginal Affairs, Senator John Herron, as well as key sections of the mainstream print media, openly contested the growing recognition of Aboriginal rights and claims of government responsibility for Aboriginal dispossession and subjugation.[27] They also reacted strongly to the use of the word 'genocide' to describe the violent process of settler dispossession of the Aborigines and Aboriginal child removal.[28]

In Tasmania, however, the Liberal government took a different view. In 1995 it responded positively to the Mabo judgment and the work of the Council for Aboriginal Reconciliation by negotiating with the Tasmanian Aboriginal community for the return of some parcels of land, and two years later it was the first government in Australia to make an apology to the Stolen Generations.[29] In taking this approach, the Tasmanian government was far ahead of the other Australian states. Is it possible, then, that in selecting the Tasmanian Aborigines as the subject for the first volume of his projected trilogy, Windschuttle may have wanted to demonstrate that in taking these momentous decisions the Tasmanian government had been misled by 'black armband' historians like Henry Reynolds and myself?

Our key texts on the Tasmanian Aborigines had argued for a new approach to understanding their historical experiences and in making restitution for the past. I had already argued in the first edition of *The Aboriginal Tasmanians* that they had not died out in 1876 or in any other period of their history. In *Fate of a Free People*, published in 1996, Reynolds had further shown that in 1831 a verbal treaty had been made by

Lieutenant-Governor George Arthur with the Aboriginal chief Mannalar-genna guaranteeing government responsibility for their future welfare.[30] Put together, our books made a powerful and compelling case for the Tasmanian government to make some restitution to the Tasmanian Aborigines of the present. If such scholarship was contested, then the case for recognition and restitution would be substantially undermined.

Our books, however, had been deeply influenced by the campaigns for their rights conducted by the Tasmanian Aborigines themselves. Over the last forty years, through their peak organisation, the Tasmanian Aboriginal Centre (TAC), and the political finesse of their spokespeople such as Michael Mansell and Trudy Maloga, the Tasmanian Aborigines have transformed their position from a disparate group of people who allegedly did not exist to one of the best known and most politically active Aboriginal communities in Australia today. As this book demonstrates, they not only have had historically significant parcels of land returned to them; they remain the only Aboriginal group in Australia to receive financial compensation for their stolen children.[31] They were also among the first Aboriginal groups to regain control of some of their ancestral remains and other cultural property from museums in Australia and overseas. A possible outcome of *The Fabrication of Aboriginal History* was the targeting of the Tasmanian Aborigines as inauthentic, thus undermining the claims for restitution made by other Aboriginal groups in settled Australia.

Yet, despite the media frenzy that Windschuttle's book generated on the Australian mainland, it had a lesser impact in Tasmania. Many Tasmanians who had lived with the burden of the past about the fate of the Tasmanian Aborigines now wanted to make amends. Further, a new generation of Tasmanian scholars was well placed to question Windschuttle's use of the sources. James Boyce for example called Windschuttle's construction of Tasmania's colonial past 'fantasy island', and Shayne Breen considered that the book's purpose was to reimpose the doctrine of scientific racism as objective fact.[32] Others, such as Phillip Tardif and Ian McFarlane, questioned his methods of investigating the best known massacres, at Risdon Cove and Cape Grim, and concluded that he had discarded key evidence simply because it did not suit his argument.[33] Since then North American scholars Ben Kiernan and Benjamin Madley, in their separate surveys of violent frontier conflict in colonial Tasmania, and Tasmanian historian Ian McFarlane, in his study of the Aborigines in north-west Tasmania, have placed renewed emphasis on settler massacres as a way of verifying that what happened was, *contra* to Windschuttle's argument, in fact the violent destruction and dispossession of Tasmanian Aborigines.[34]

Where, then, does Windschuttle's work stand today? By an odd irony, his key argument that settler massacres were largely invented has become the starting point for important new countervailing work in the field.[35] His deeply flawed approach to investigation of the sources for massacre, which largely consists of dismissing or ignoring the evidence of key witnesses, has prompted a renewed interest in the ubiquity of settler massacres and the methods we use to assess whether, when, how and why they took place. To this end the interpretive framework developed by historical sociologist Jacques Semelin offers a fresh approach to the subject.[36] He points out that the act of massacre tends to be carried out in secret, it tends to suppose a relationship between the assassins and their victims, and, above all, it is intended that no witness should be present. It is here that the key question of a witness arises:

> If no witness is intended or present, who will be believed? This problem is of central importance to historians. The nature of the event often leads to silence in the immediate aftermath. However, witnesses and perpetrators sometimes speak about massacre long after it is over, when they are immune from prosecution or removed from fear of reprisal from other perpetrators.[37]

Semelin's framework readily proved its worth in my investigation of the possible massacre of Tasmanian Aborigines at Mount Augustus near Campbell Town in April 1827, which Windschuttle had strenuously denied had taken place.[38] In that case, I found that the later account of a settler who was one of the perpetrators corroborated contemporary newspaper evidence that the incident was indeed a massacre.[39] In another project, the compilation of a list of multiple killings of Tasmanian Aborigines in the period 1804–35, I found that most settler massacres of Aborigines took place in the second phase of the Black War, before martial law was declared.[40] In a further project that focused on a specific region in Tasmania in this period, I found that settler massacres of Aborigines were, in historian Shayne Breen's words, 'an established pattern of conflict'.[41] These findings, as this book reveals, have fundamentally changed the way in which the Black War, which should be renamed the Tasmanian war, has been perceived. It now appears that many more Tasmanian Aborigines were killed in the period before the declaration of martial law than previously realised, thus substantially increasing the number estimated to have been killed in the entire war from 700 to nearly 900. Windschuttle's response to date in relation to this vast new corpus of research has been a resounding silence.

So this book is vastly different from its predecessor. It uses a new framework of settler colonialism, which combines settler activism *and* Aboriginal resistance to explore the experiences of the Tasmanian Aborigines from the British invasion of their island in 1803 over the next 200 years to the end of the first decade of the twenty-first century. It also incorporates extensive new research on the Tasmanian Aborigines and foregrounds where possible their voices in contesting settler activism and asserting their rights and identity. Further, at the request of the Aboriginal community, it also restores the name 'Tasmanian Aborigines' to reflect their distinctive relationship to their own country and their indigenous rights that flow from it.

To draw out the richer and more complex narrative, the book is divided into six parts. Part I, 'Invasion', comprises four chapters. Chapter 1 provides a detailed portrait of the Tasmanian Aborigines and their society immediately before British invasion in 1803 and highlights the fact that they had arrived in Tasmania at least 40,000 years ago, that they could make fire by artificial means, that they were organised into nine separate nations and that their estimated population of 6,000 to 8,000 in 1803 was probably increasing. Chapter 2 sets out their relations with the colonists in the first years of British occupation, from 1803 to 1808, with particular focus on the founding massacre at Risdon Cove in May 1804. Chapter 3 explores their relations with the different groups of colonists between 1808 and 1820, including convicts, soldiers, sailors, whalers and sealers, and how the basis of a creole society was formed. The final chapter in this section shows how the mass arrival of free settlers in the aftermath of the Napoleonic Wars dramatically changed the fabric of relations between Aborigines and colonists and how the new settlers' ever-increasing demand for vast tracts of Aboriginal land to graze their sheep and cattle became the lightning rod for war.

Part II, 'War', consists of five chapters and analyses the two key phases of the Black War from November 1826 to February 1832. Chapter 5 shows how Lieutenant-Governor George Arthur put in place in November 1826 violent measures including massacre to destroy Aboriginal resistance and force their surrender and how, after failing to achieve this outcome, he declared martial law in November 1828. Chapter 6 follows the attempts by Arthur to force Aboriginal surrender under the rubric of martial law until February 1830. Chapter 7 focuses on the settler response to martial law, Arthur's decision to hold an inquiry into the war and finally his decision to conduct a spring offensive, now known as the Black Line, to drive the Oyster Bay and Big River nations from their country. Chapter 8 explores the origins of the idea of the Black Line, how it was carried out and how it forced the surrender of the Big River and Oyster Bay nations in December 1831. Chapter 9 considers the casualty statistics on both sides in each phase of the war. It finds that more than 850 Aborigines and an estimated 200 colonists were killed in the conflict or later died from their wounds and that Tasmania still awaits a memorial to honour the fallen.

Part III, 'Surrender', comprising four chapters, traces the missions conducted by government agent George Augustus Robinson to force the surrender of the Aboriginal nations across Tasmania between 1829 and 1834. Chapter 10 explores the experiences of the Nuenonne clan on Bruny Island in its first encounter with Robinson and his decision to undertake the first mission to the Aboriginal nations on the west coast. Chapter 11 follows the first mission to the west, from February to October 1830, and the emergence of the group known as the 'mission Aborigines', who underpinned Robinson's enterprise. Chapter 12 follows Robinson's first meeting with Mannalargenna in north-eastern Tasmania in November 1830, his mission to the sealing community in Bass Strait in 1831, his long trek in search of Umarrah in July and August 1831, and finally his search for Montpeliater and Tongerlongter, the chiefs of the Big River and Oyster Bay nations, and their surrender on 31 December 1831. Chapter 13 follows the three further missions to the west between 1832 and 1834 to force the surrender of the North, North West and South West nations. It discusses Robinson's relations with the key mission Aborigines such as Truganini and Woorraddy, as well as Umarrah, Kickerterpoller and Pevay, and his relations with the chiefs of the western nations such as Heedeek, Wymurrick and Towterrer. The chapter ends with a discussion of Arthur's removal policy and whether it constituted genocide.

Part IV, 'Incarceration', comprising three chapters, follows the experiences of the Tasmanian Aborigines at the Aboriginal Establishment at Wybalenna on Flinders Island from 1835 to 1847 and at the Oyster Cove Aboriginal Station from 1847 to 1905. Chapter 14 analyses G.A. Robinson's increasingly fraught relations with the Aborigines at Wybalenna and his failed attempts to relocate them in Victoria. Chapter 15 explores the emergence of a new generation of Aboriginal leaders on Flinders Island such as Walter George Arthur and Davy Bruny and how they organised the petition to Queen Victoria for the return of their people to the Tasmanian mainland. Chapter 16 follows Aborigines' experiences at Oyster Cove from 1847 to 1905 and discusses how leaders such as Walter George Arthur and his wife, Mary Ann, William Lanney, Truganini and Fanny Cochrane Smith resisted the attempts by the proponents of scientific racism to make them into the missing link between ape and man.

Part V, 'Survival', comprising two chapters, explores the experiences of the Islander community on the eastern Bass Strait islands between 1840 and 1973. Chapter 17 traces the emergence of the community and the campaigns by its leaders, such as Lucy Beeton and H.G. Everett, for a reserve on Cape Barren Island and the attempts by Bishop Montgomery to turn the community into small crop farmers. Chapter 18 follows the twentieth-century contest between the Islanders and the government, which tried to assimilate the Aborigines, leading to the reserve's abolition in 1951 and the 'stubborn refusal' by some Islanders to leave their homes.

Part VI, 'Resurgence', comprising three chapters, follows the political fortunes of the Tasmanian Aboriginal community from 1973 to 2010. Chapter 19 explores the formation of the TAC, the emergence of a new generation of leaders such as Michael Mansell, Rosalind Langford, Jim Everett, Trudy Maloga and Rodney Dillon in asserting their rights as Tasmanian Aborigines and their clashes with the Tasmanian government over the return of land and of their ancestral remains. Chapter 20 follows their negotiations with the government for the first return of land in 1995. Chapter 21 explores key issues that have defined Tasmanian Aboriginal politics between 1996 and 2010. They include the apology and financial compensation to the Stolen Generation, federal and state court cases about Tasmanian Aboriginal identity, the return of Wybalenna and Cape Barren Island to Aboriginal ownership, and the long battle by the TAC for the return of ancestral remains and other cultural property from museums around the world. The epilogue notes the political issues surrounding recent archaeological findings that indicate Aboriginal occupation in eastern Tasmania for 40,000 years.

As a study of Tasmanian Aboriginal resistance to settler activism, the book offers new insights into how settler colonialism defined the course of Tasmanian Aboriginal history over a period of more than 200 years and confirms the view of my earlier book that Tasmania is the best place to understand the dreadful impact of settler colonialism on Aborigines across Australia. Above all, in telling the story of how the Tasmanian Aborigines nearly disappeared during a 200-year period of their 40,000-year history, it argues that their survival against the odds surely demonstrates their resilience as a people with a very long history indeed.

PART I

INVASION
1803–26

I

Trouwunna

Tasmanian Aborigines tell several stories about their origins. One ascribes the creation of the first woman, who had a tail like a kangaroo, to a star god who tumbled to earth at Toogee Low (Port Davey) and who was turned into a large stone. Another says they came to Tasmania by land and that the sea was subsequently formed.[1] Both stories are supported by current Western research which suggests that they arrived in Tasmania at least 40,000 years ago when the island was linked by a land bridge to mainland Australia. Like all other human groups they had originally come from Africa and had made the long journey to Tasmania over many thousands of years.[2]

The Aborigines inhabited most areas of what was then a much larger land mass of Tasmania and were the most southerly occupants of the globe in the Pleistocene era. They appear to have clustered in family groups in caves like Kuti Kina and Deena Reena near the Franklin River, at Warragarra on the Upper Mersey River and at Cave Bay Cave on Hunter Island, at sheltered sites in the forests and on river banks such as on the Jordan River near present-day Brighton.

The women used wooden digging sticks to search for a wide variety of vegetable roots. They collected berries, and caught possums and wombats and shellfish, which they carried in kelp, animal skins or tightly woven grass and reed baskets. They used stone tools to grind their food and to make fire by percussion. The men used wooden spears and waddies to regularly hunt wallabies and to spear scale fish and used bone tools made from wallabies and stone tools manufactured from chert, crystal quartz, quartzite and spongelite to skin the animal carcasses and to make their wooden tools.

Both men and women smeared wallaby fat on their bodies for warmth and used charcoal and ochre for body decoration and making hand stencils on cave walls. It appears that they highly prized ochre as a sacred and ceremonial item and for gift and exchange.[3]

At this time the climate was cool and moist, especially in the west, and much of the region was covered with rainforest. Then, about 18,000 years ago, with the onset of drier, colder conditions, some of the region was transformed into open grassland, and in the higher areas glaciers appeared. It seems that the Aborigines adapted to these new conditions by abandoning the higher areas, like the caves at Kuti Kina and Cave Bay Cave, to concentrate on resource-rich areas along the coasts and inland rivers.[4]

Ten thousand years ago, the sea rose to form Bass Strait, and the Tasmanian Aborigines were separated from other Aboriginal groups on the Australian mainland (see Map 1). About 6,000 years ago they began

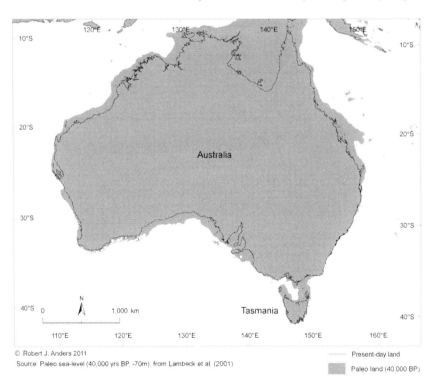

© Robert J. Anders 2011

Source: Paleo sea-level (40,000 yrs BP, -70m), from Lambeck et al. (2001)

Present-day land

Paleo land (40,000 BP)

Map 1 Australia in the Paleolithic era

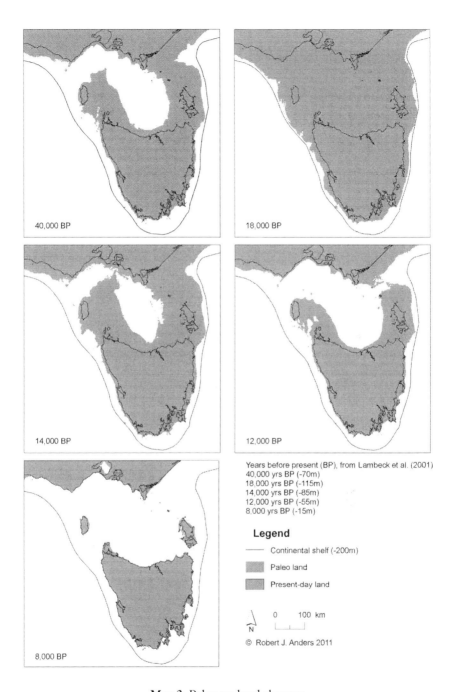

40,000 BP

18,000 BP

14,000 BP

12,000 BP

8,000 BP

Years before present (BP), from Lambeck et al. (2001)
40,000 yrs BP (-70m)
18,000 yrs BP (-115m)
14,000 yrs BP (-85m)
12,000 yrs BP (-55m)
8,000 yrs BP (-15m)

Legend

Continental shelf (-200m)

Paleo land

Present-day land

0   100 km
N

© Robert J. Anders 2011

Map 2 Paleo sea level changes

to expand their occupation along the east coast and hinterland and especially to the western half of the island in areas of marginal and peripheral rainforest, which they managed with the use of firestick farming. They also occupied new sites to exploit fat-rich foods such as seals, shellfish and mutton-birds and appear to have introduced techniques like stone traps for shallow-water fishing. These changes may have coincided with the period of territorial expansion, including the reoccupation of earlier sites like Hunter Island, the use of multi-resource sites like West Point and Rocky Cape, the increasing seasonal use of offshore sites like Maatsuyker Island for sealing and the use of firestick farming to manage the plains around the Jordan River for kangaroo hunting. Their development of watercraft over the last 2,000 years, in the north-west, south-west and south-east, to exploit seals, would have aided such expansion.[5]

By then, some Tasmanian Aborigines called their island Trouwunna.[6] With a land mass of 67,870 square kilometres—almost the same size as Sri Lanka and a little smaller than Ireland—the island lies between 40 and 43 degrees south of the Equator, which places it within the influence of the roaring forties and produces what is, for the region, a temperate marine climate of abnormally mild winters and cool summers. Trouwunna is a mountainous island. In the centre, east and south-east the mountains are plateau-like; in the west they are ridge-like. Very little of the island's surface lies close to sea level, and continuous lowland plains are limited to the extreme north-west and north-east and to the northern Midlands between present-day Launceston and Tunbridge. With these exceptions, the mountains and hills directly adjoin the coast and rise from there to heights of over 1,524 metres, forming a rugged landscape that includes some of the most spectacular mountain scenery in Australia. Trouwunna contains thousands of lakes—the north-east section of the Central Plateau alone has about 4,000. On the west coast the annual rainfall varies between 127 and 381 centimetres, but the high ridge of mountains along the western spine of Trouwunna provides a buffer against the roaring forties in the central and eastern part of the island, where the annual rainfall is between 38 and 152 centimetres. With such topography the island abounds in swift-flowing rivers.[7]

The Tasmanian Aborigines' physical appearance differed somewhat from that of Aboriginal groups on the Australian mainland; in particular, they possessed distinctive woolly hair and reddish-brown skin. Their physical size and other physical characteristics, however, varied among themselves as much as in any other Aboriginal group in Australia and 'diverged no more than might be expected if Tasmania were still attached to the mainland'.[8] As an uncircumcised people and largely monogamous they can be likened to the Aborigines who arrived on mainland Australia more than 40,000 years ago.[9]

Their spiritual beliefs and practices were so complex that the agents of British colonialism who tried to record them in the early nineteenth century confused them with notions of nationalistic animalism and neglected to note important cultural variations between each of the nine major national groups.[10] Their cosmologies involved the intertwining of landscape, ritual, music, art and law so that none formed a truly separate domain. Thus the men were associated with the sun spirit and the women with the moon, and their customs were based upon totems (each of the 100 or so clans that may have inhabited Tasmania in 1803 taking a designated species of bird or animal as a totem) and taboos, especially concerning whether an individual ate the male or female kangaroo and wallaby. Their spiritual practices appear to have been based upon the idea of the good spirit (Noiheener or Parledee), who governed the day, and the bad spirit (Wrageowrapper), who governed the night. These and other spirits were associated with the creation, fire, rivers, trees and the dead. When a person died, their relatives usually decorated the body with ochre and clay, wrapped it in leaves with items from their totem such as bird feathers or animal skins and then cremated it, in a sitting position either on a specially prepared wooden platform or in the hollowed-out base of a tree, amid intense ceremonies to farewell them on their journey to join their relatives in the spirit world. A guardian spirit or 'soul' that lived within their left breast went to live elsewhere—such as the islands in Bass Strait. After the body was cremated, female relatives might extract small bones from the charred remains, wrap them in kangaroo fur and use them as amulets to ward off evil spirits of harm and illness. Sometimes the women lit fires during bad weather, or when rivers were in flood, to appease malignant spirits.

Tasmanian Aborigines made bark drawings and stone and rock carvings or petroglyphs of geometric designs. Their significance remains unclear, although they could possibly represent the sun-male and the moon-female deities associated with particular Aboriginal groups, formations, and numbers or movements in a similar context to their myths and legends.[11]

Recent research by John A. Taylor into Aboriginal place names in Tasmania suggests that each group of Aborigines on the island spoke at least one of four major languages, all of which had very close connections with Aboriginal languages in south-eastern, central and western Victoria and parts of South Australia.[12] I have called them the north eastern, southern, central and north western Tasmanian languages. If one puts together the similarities in these languages and the findings by osteo-archaeologist Colin Pardoe that there is only a small degree of genetic divergence between Tasmanian and Victorian Aborigines, it would appear that the Tasmanian Aborigines shared important physical and cultural characteristics with the Victorian Aborigines.[13]

In their daily lives, the men usually carried fire as a lighted torch of sticks and leaves, and the women carried flints in their baskets to make fire. Both men and women could make fire by friction with two pieces of wood, by the percussion method of briskly rubbing two stones with tinder from the bark of a tree, or by striking a flint on stone.[14]

Women carried water containers made of kelp as well as grass and animal skin baskets to hold stone and shell tools, flints, amulets of the dead and ochre. They also carried their newly born children in kangaroo skins on their backs. The women's hair was closely cropped into a short coronet. Each arrangement may have had significance in the identification of their particular clan or nation. They may have used a 'black glittering mineral', perhaps an ore of antimony, 'to enhance the appearance of the eyes'.[15] They used grinding and mortar stones to grind seeds and made wooden chisel-like digging sticks to find plant roots and small animals like bandicoots and rats, to prise wombats, mutton-birds and penguins from their burrows as well as oysters from the rocks and to strip bark from the trees to make cata-marans and build shelters. They were very strong swimmers and dived to prodigious depths for shellfish like abalone, mussels and crayfish, used their agility to hunt larger sea mammals such as seals and used long ropes made from tough grass to clamber up trees for possums. They used spatulate and pointed sticks to extract small molluscs from their shells after cooking and twisted plant fibres to make handles for water containers and as binding for their 'relics of the dead'. They usually cropped their hair with sharp flints and made necklaces from tiny shells and plant fibres, used stone tools to cut kelp and animal skins, and grass and reeds to weave baskets, and twisted animal sinews to make holders for ochre, which some of the men wore around their necks.

The men regularly hunted kangaroos, wallabies, emus, potoroos and stingrays with wooden spears and waddies. They selected the wood from slender trees to make their spears, which were about 2.4 to 5.4 metres long and about 1 to 2 centimetres thick, tapering back from a robust point. They threw their spears in such a way that they spun in flight and were a lethal weapon at 60 to 70 metres. Their waddies were thick wooden sticks about 60 centimetres long and 2 to 3 centimetres in diameter, one end bluntly pointed and the other roughened for holding—either to strike a blow or to throw with a rotary motion. They used stone tools made from striking flakes of stone off a larger mass, to make the spears and waddies and to cut up their catch before braising it on the fire. They also used stone tools to make bark canoes and trap waterbirds like swans and ducks, which the women prepared for cooking with sharp shells, and to make fish traps in shallow waters.

Men loaded their scalp hair with a mixture of bird and animal fat, charcoal and ochre, twisting the individual ringlets into tubular masses which hung around the head and almost concealed their eyes. They either allowed their beards and moustaches to grow naturally or used sharp shells to trim or cut them short. If they wore beards, these would also be greased. Sometimes they wore feathers or flowers in their hair for ornamentation. They also wore loops of twisted sinews loaded with ochre around their necks and sometimes suspended the jawbone of a dead friend from their neck, bound with string made from a plant fibre.[16]

Both men and women incised their bodies and rubbed into their wounds powdered charcoal and red ochre mixed with animal and marine bird fat, in order to raise high weals on the skin. These cicatrices took the form of lines, dashes and circles and were to be found principally on the upper arms, chest, shoulders, back and buttocks. They had deep spiritual significance and in the case of the women they appear to have signified clan affiliation. Both men and women sometimes wore kangaroo skins draped over their shoulders for warmth and might use a skin to dress a wounded foot.[17]

They took shelter in at least four different types of dwellings, found in different parts of Trouwunna. In the east, men and women constructed temporary open lean-to shelters with several sheets of bark placed vertically and held together horizontally with tree branches; cupola-shaped windbreaks, which they also made from sheets of bark in the shelter of two trees; or vertical one-sided windbreaks, which they also made from sheets of bark. Each dwelling could hold up to eleven people, and such constructions were often seen clustered around creeks and lagoons near the coast in the east and south-east. English and French explorers who visited the region in the decade before British invasion made visual records of these dwellings and were surprised to find that they offered very good protection from wind and rain. In central and eastern Trouwunna, Tasmanian Aborigines often utilised the hollow of a tree or a cave in which a single family of up to eleven people might have sheltered on a regular seasonal basis. The third type of dwelling was a large hut, found in the north-east and the central highlands and made by men and women from sheets of bark and tree branches, accommodating up to forty people, possibly for major ceremonial gatherings. The final type was found on the west coast, where people faced the full force of the roaring forties and higher rainfall. Here, behind the dunes but with close access to the sea, they built permanent beehive-shaped huts of at least 3 to 3.5 metres in diameter, which, at 1.8 metres high, could hold up to fourteen people. They constructed these huts from tree branches which they steamed and bent by the fire and then packed closely together. The entrance, according to one description, was less than 1 metre high. These huts were clustered in a village and were used all year round. Inside, the Aborigines decorated the huts with bird feathers and shell necklaces and lit small fires. In their sheltered location, the huts offered excellent protection from the weather. At least one colonial observer, Charles Jeffreys, considered that 'the houses or huts, are much better formed than those of the Port Jackson natives' and 'the huts made by the natives of Van Diemen's Land approach nearer the principles of regular architecture'.[18]

How, then, did the Tasmanian Aborigines organise their social relations at the time of British invasion in 1803? Like most other hunter and forager peoples, they appear to have operated in a complex social system of three units: the domestic unit, or *family group*; the basic social unit, or *clan*; and the political unit, or *nation*. The family group camped and cooked around a single fire and, on the west coast, occupied a single hut. Its core consisted of husband, wife, children and relatives, and sometimes friends and other relations; the number of people in the group appears to have ranged from two to eleven. Families were 'invariably monogamous'. Men and women married in their late teens, the husband and wife being about the same age. They remarried quickly on the death of a spouse, and the new partners assumed responsibility for the children of previous unions. There were parental prohibitions and punishments for 'wrong' marriages and adultery, and although 'divorce' took place, infidelity, jealousy, and raids for women were the chief causes of violent conflict. They sometimes resulted in the death of some of the principal parties, although few cases were observed by either English or French explorers before British invasion and they could have escalated in the early colonial period. Even so, in several respects, Tasmanian Aboriginal marriage customs seem to have been significantly different from some of those practised by Aborigines on the Australian mainland.[19]

The basic social unit, or clan, the name preferred by Tasmanian Aborigines today, was 'a group of people who called themselves by a particular name, and were known by that or other names to other people'.[20] Like the family group, the clan was exogamous; the wife usually moved to her husband's clan and claimed it as her own, although occasionally the reverse happened, particularly if there had been a quarrel. Each clan was usually led by a man, invariably called a 'chief' in the colonial period. In the eastern part of Tasmania, the Aborigines widely used the word *bungana* to denote a chief.[21] He was usually older than the others and had a reputation as a formidable hunter and fighter; he may have had considerable temporal powers, possibly by legal sanction and through force of personality and martial prowess. Some of the chiefs in the colonial period, like Woorraddy, Mannalargenna, Tongerlongter, Umarrah, Montpeliater, Heedeek, Wymurrick and Towterrer, played pivotal roles in the Aborigines' confrontations with the British. One woman, Walyer, who led a clan on the north coast, played a similar role. The chief formed the clan's core, to which were added his or her own and other family groups, who always came from the territory encompassed by the clan. Leadership customs among the Tasmanian Aborigines appear to have been similar to those among Aborigines on the Australian mainland.[22]

Each clan 'owned' territory, the core of which was often a rich foraging zone whose boundaries coincided with well-marked geographical features like rivers, lagoons and mountain ranges. Clan ownership of land was probably formal, but this did not mean that a clan foraged only in its designated area. Rather, each clan foraged widely in the lands of other clans, sometimes with permission, sometimes without. Thus, foraging depended very much on relations with other clans.[23]

Along the coasts, the clans were regularly spaced, each occupying some 25 to 30 kilometres of coastline, with shorter distances in the rich north-western corner of the island and longer ones along the extreme south-west, where smaller supplies of food were available. Where coast and inland areas were combined, each clan's territory occupied about 500 to 750 square kilometres, and their number and size appear to have been determined by the nature of the food supply. Several clans came together for seasonal visits at places like the north-west coast for sealing and mutton-birding, at Mount Housetop and Mount Vandyke for mining ochre, which was of immense cultural significance, at Moulting Lagoon for gathering swan and duck eggs, at present-day Campbell Town and Ross for kangaroo hunting, and at Recherche Bay for sealing. Such meetings were celebrated with ceremonial singing and dancing, as an expression of their social, political and cultural relations.

Each clan's year appears to have been divided into 'private' and 'public' periods. No local clan maintained exclusive rights to the resources within its boundaries, so that visiting patterns created inter-clan relations. Thus, hosts in one season became guests in another. In this way, most clans seem to have had at least two names, one of which they gave to themselves and others given to them by various other clans. Their movements were largely seasonal, but they were also determined by spiritual and political obligations such as collecting ochre, arranging the exchange of women for marriage, settling feuds or making war with other clans by ambush or individual combat. No clan had a food surplus, for the environment itself was a storehouse and each knew where food sources were in abundance at any time of year.[24]

At British invasion in 1803 there may have been up to 100 clans in Trouwunna. Forty-eight have been identified by physical anthropologist Brian Plomley (see Table 1 and Map 3).[25] Archaeologist Rhys Jones, whose

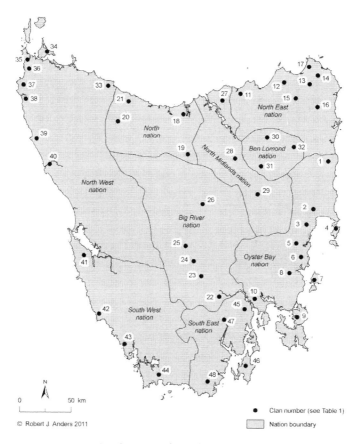

Map 3 Nation boundaries and clans

groundbreaking portrait of Tasmanian Aboriginal society before British invasion forms the basis of this account, estimates that there were originally seventy to eighty-five clans. If, as he assumes, the average clan contained between forty and fifty people, the population in 1803 would have been between 3,000 and 5,000.[26] More recently, Plomley has used newly available sources to suggest that the population could have been as high as 6,000.[27] This figure matches the minimum estimate of 6,000 to 8,000 made by the leading colonial ethnographer G.A. Robinson, which in turn agrees with two other independent estimates of 7,000 and 10,000 that were also made in the colonial period.[28] The remarkable similarity between these four estimates, each reached independently, indicates that Jones's estimate is a very conservative minimum, as he himself points out. When considered alongside the finding by osteo-archaeologist Colin Pardoe that the Tasmanian Aboriginal population before 1803 has been seriously underestimated and the suggestion by archaeologist Harry Lourandos that it was increasing at the moment of British invasion, it seems likely that the population was much higher in 1803 than previously estimated.[29]

Each clan was associated with a wider political unit, which the colonial ethnographer G.A. Robinson called a 'nation', the name preferred by Tasmanian Aborigines today.[30] Jones defines this unit as 'that agglomeration of |clans| which lived in contiguous regions, spoke the same language or dialect, shared the same cultural traits, usually intermarried, had a similar pattern of seasonal movement, habitually met together for economic and other reasons, the pattern of whose peaceful relations were within the agglomeration and of whose enmities and military adventures were directed outside it'. Its territory consisted of all the land owned by the constituent clans so that movement outside the territory, and of alien clans inside it, was carefully sanctioned. Such movements usually had reciprocal economic advantages to clans concerned, while trespass was usually a challenge to or punishable by war. Its borders ranged from 'a sharp well-defined line associated with a prominent geographical feature to a broad transition zone often found between two friendly' nations.[31]

Jones suggests that there were nine nations in Trouwunna in 1803. Today each is known by its English rather than its Aboriginal name—a reflection of the devastating impact of British invasion. Six of them, the Oyster Bay, the Big River, the North East, the Ben Lomond, the North and the North Midlands nations, were located in northern and eastern Trouwunna, in what became the heartland of British occupation; and the three others, the North West, the South West and the South East nations, were located in the western and south-eastern part of the island. Yet each nation had its own distinctive physical, social, cultural and economic characteristics and different ways of conducting their internal and external relations.[32] By using Jones's scholarly assessment of each nation as a starting point, I have added the clan names identified by Plomley and then included new information from recent archaeological, historical and linguistic studies to establish the following profile of the nations of Trouwunna in 1803.[33]

Table 1   Trouwunna: nations and clan locations

Nation	Clan		Clan location
Oyster Bay	1	Leetermairremener	St Patricks Head
	2	Linetemairrener	North Moulting Lagoon
	3	Loontitetermairrelehoinner	North Oyster Bay
	4	Toorernomairremener	Schouten Island
	5	Poredareme	Little Swanport
	6	Laremairremener	Grindstone Bay
	7	Tyreddeme	Maria Island
	8	Portmairremener	Prosser River
	9	Pydairrerme	Forestier and Tasman peninsulas
	10	Moomairremener	Pitt Water, Risdon
North East	11	Peeberrangner	Piper River
	12	Leenerrerter	Scottsdale
	13	Pinterrairer	Ringarooma
	14	Trawlwoolway	Mount William
	15	Pyemmairrenerpairrener	Great Forester River
	16	Leenethmairrener	Ansons River
	17	Panpekanner	Cape Portland

Nation	Clan		Clan location
North	18	Punnilerpanner	Port Sorell
	19	Pallittorre	Quamby Bluff
	20	Noeteeler	Hampshire Hills
	21	Plairhekehillerplue	Emu Bay
Big River	22	Leenowwenne	New Norfolk
	23	Pangerninghe	Clyde–Derwent junction
	24	Braylwunyer	Between Ouse and Dee rivers
	25	Larmairremener	West of River Dee
	26	Luggermairrernerpairrer	Great Lake
North Midlands	27	Leterremairrener	East Tamar River
	28	Panninher	Norfolk Plains
	29	Tyerrernotepanner	Campbell Town
Ben Lomond	30	Plangermairreenner	Uncertain
	31	Plindermairhemener	
	32	Tonenerweenerlarmenne	
North West	33	Tommeginer	Table Cape
	34	Parperloihener	Robbins Island
	35	Pennemukeer	Cape Grim
	36	Pendowte	Studland Bay
	37	Peerapper	West Point
	38	Manegin	Arthur River mouth
	39	Tarkinener	Sandy Cape
	40	Peternidic	Pieman River mouth
South West	41	Mimegin	Birchs Inlet
	42	Lowreenne	Low Rocky Point
	43	Ninene	Port Davey
	44	Needwonnee	Cox Bight

Nation	Clan		Clan location
	45	Mouheneenner	Hobart
South East	46	Nuenonne	Bruny Island
	47	Mellukerdee	Huon River
	48	Lyluequonny	Recherche Bay

Note: Numbers before clan names are the key to clan locations in Map 3.

Oyster Bay nation

The Oyster Bay nation in 1803 appears to have been the largest in Trouwunna, if not in area then certainly in population. Its territory covered 8,500 square kilometres, including 500 kilometres of 'usable' coastline along the east coast from St Patricks Head to the Derwent estuary. From there the border proceeded along the eastern bank of the River Derwent to the mouth of the Jordan River, which it followed inland to St Peters Pass in the Midlands, east past Crown Lagoon, north to the watershed of the Macquarie and Elizabeth rivers at Tooms Lake and Lake Leake and then north-east along the South Esk River back to St Patricks Head. The Oyster Bay nation consisted of at least ten clans producing, according to Jones, an estimated minimum population of between 700 and 800. Archaeological research by Steve Brown and new translations of the French expedition led by Marion du Fresne suggest a higher minimum estimate. The Oyster Bay people appear to have spoken the north eastern Tasmanian language. The clans and their locations were: the *Leetermairremener* from St Patricks Head, the *Linetemairrener* from North Moulting Lagoon, the *Loontitetermairrelehoinner* from North Oyster Bay, the *Toorernomairremener* from Schouten Island, the *Poredareme* from Little Swanport, the *Laremairremener* from Grindstone Bay, the *Tyreddeme* from Maria Island, the *Portmairremener* from Prosser River, the *Pydairrerme* from the Forestier and Tasman peninsulas, and the *Moomairremener* from Pitt Water and Risdon.[34]

Evidently, the Oyster Bay nation was divided into three clearly defined groups according to seasonal patterns of movement in their search for food and the maintenance of their ceremonial obligations. The first consisted of the four clans from St Patricks Head to Schouten Island; the second comprised the four clans from Little Swanport to the Tasman Peninsula; and the third consisted of the two clans from Maria Island and Pitt Water, Risdon. Each winter would find all three groups on the coastal areas of their territories living on shellfish and marine vegetables and hunting small animals until the end of July, when swans and ducks arrived in lagoons and riverine areas to lay their eggs and bring up their young. At the end of August the Poredareme from Little Swanport, the Laremairremener from Grindstone Bay and the Portmairremener from Prosser River moved up the Little Swanport and Prosser rivers to Rushy and Crown lagoons in the Eastern Marshes, where there were birds, kangaroos and wallabies. As summer drew near, they moved further west, hunting and firing the bush for game, travelling through St Peters Pass to Blackmans River and to the high country to the west or round the Blue Hill Bluff to Miles Opening and to the Clyde and Ouse river valleys in Big River country. The Moomairremener moved west up the River Derwent to New Norfolk, across to Abyssinia, and from there to the Clyde and the Ouse rivers. These were all well-defined routes, usually along territorial borders, designed for 'maximum access and minimum trespass'.

Not all the clans from the Little Swanport area and to the south travelled west every spring and summer. The Tyreddeme from Maria Island and the Pydairrerme from the Forestier and Tasman peninsulas were more likely to use their watercraft to forage within their own rich resource areas all year round, but they were known to make summer visits to Big River country, if not every year, then certainly for major ceremonial events. They returned to the Midlands in late February or early March, arriving back at the coast in June.[35]

Between August and October the Oyster Bay clans north of Little Swanport congregated at rich food-source areas like Moulting Lagoon and Schouten Island, where there were seasonally heavy concentrations of bird life. At the end of October they moved inland, up the St Pauls and Break O'Day rivers to the Ben Lomond plateau or up the Meredith River to the Elizabeth River at Stockers Bottom on the border of the North Midlands nation, across to Campbell Town and to the Great Western Tiers above the Isis River. They often spent part of the summer in these areas. Those on

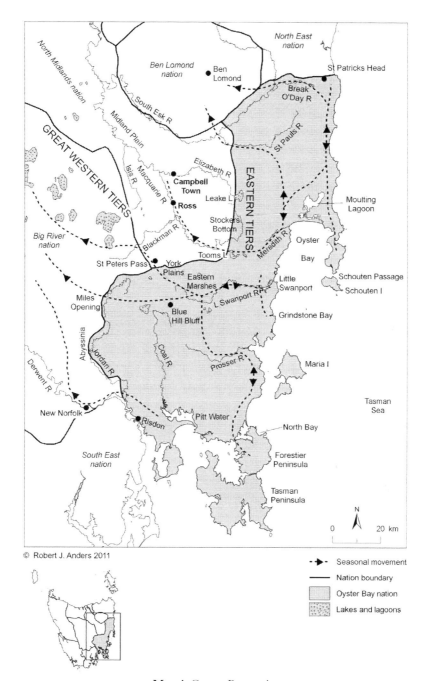

© Robert J. Anders 2011

- ▶ - Seasonal movement
─── Nation boundary
▨ Oyster Bay nation
▨ Lakes and lagoons

Map 4 Oyster Bay nation

the Ben Lomond plateau returned to the east coast at the end of January for sealing and mutton-birding, moving to Stockers Bottom in March to hunt kangaroos, wallabies and possums. There, they were often joined by other clans returning from the Great Western Tiers until they returned to the east coast in June. As with the South Oyster Bay clans, not all of the North Oyster Bay clans left their country in summer, but seasonal visits to the Ben Lomond and North Midlands nations were common. The Midland Plain also contained quarries for the fashioning of stone implements as well as important hunting and ceremonial grounds; the colonial literature contains numerous references to large concentrations of up to 500 Aborigines in the area in spring and autumn, particularly York Plains, Crown Lagoon, Ross, Campbell Town and Stockers Bottom. These places lay in the heart of what became known in the colonial period as the Settled Districts. Several clans from the Oyster Bay nation played a critical role in the Black War; at least two of their chiefs, Mannalargenna and Tongerlongter, played major roles.[36]

North East nation

To the north of the Oyster Bay nation lay the North East nation, which Tasmanian Aboriginal historian Patsy Cameron calls the Coastal Plains nation. Its territory encompassed the north-east coast from the Piper River to Cape Portland and then south to St Patricks Head. Here, the border turned inland, along the Break O'Day and North Esk rivers and past Mount Saddleback and Mount Barrow to Launceston, where it turned north to Piper River again. The area comprised 5,000 square kilometres and included 260 kilometres of coastline. In 1803 there may have been at least ten clans, seven of which have been identified by Plomley and each comprising fifty to eighty people. Jones estimates their minimum population at between 400 and 500 people, which is supported by archaeological research by Sue Kee. They appear to have spoken the north eastern Tasmanian language derived from south-eastern Victoria. The seven clans identified by Plomley have now been further clarified by Patsy Cameron. They were the *Peeberrangner* at Piper River, the *Leenerrerter* at Scottsdale, the *Pinterrairer* at Ringarooma, the *Trawlwoolway* at Mount William, the *Pyemmairrenerpairrener* at Great Forester River, the *Leenethmairrener* at

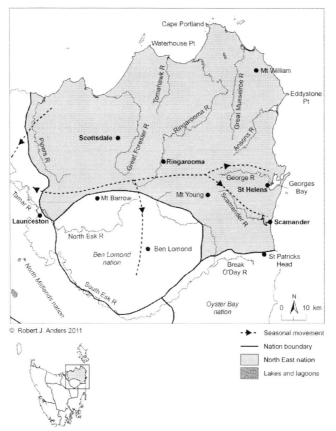

Map 5 North East nation

Ansons River and the *Panpekanner* at Cape Portland. Patsy Cameron has since identified another clan located between the George and Scamander rivers on the east coast but has not given it a name.[37]

The coastline of the North East nation and the associated lagoons and estuaries provided abundant seasonal food resources, such as mutton-birds, swans, ducks and seals. From late July to early September the egging season enticed several clans to congregate around these lagoons and estuaries to collect swan and duck eggs. In summer they hunted fur seals and in autumn mutton-birds. On the heaths and plains behind their coast, which they kept open and clear by firing, the men hunted kangaroos, wallabies and emus, and the women hunted possums and other small mammals. The north-east coast and its immediate hinterland were capable of supporting a high Aboriginal population during most seasons of the year, including summer visits from the Ben Lomond and North Midlands nations. In return, some clans visited Ben Lomond for ochre and the Tamar Valley.[38] They also used well-marked tracks and chains of small plains running east–west near the southern border. To the south the rugged mountainous rainforest formed a strong physical barrier with the Ben Lomond and North Midlands nations. One track began at the Scamander River on the east coast, turned west to the upper reaches of the Ringarooma River and to Mount Barrow, and ended at the eastern bank of the Tamar River. Within this wet forested country the Pyemmairrenerpairrener clan lived on wombats, possums, echidnas and vegetable food: ferns, roots and fungi of various types.

Of all the nations in Aboriginal Tasmania, the North East or Coastal Plains nation travelled least. A mild climate and abundant resources on both the coast and hinterland gave them insularity comparable only to the South East nation. However, they had regular summer visits by clans from the Ben Lomond and North Midlands nations.[39]

North nation

The territory of the North nation extended along the north coast from the eastern side of Port Sorell to west of Emu Bay, inland west of the Hampshire Hills to the south-west corner of the Surrey Hills, and then south of Black Bluff, Middlesex Plains and Mount Roland to the base of the Great Western Tiers. The border then swung north at Quamby Bluff past Deloraine to the ridge of the Asbestos Range on the coast, west of the Tamar River. The area was 4,500 square kilometres and included 100 kilometres of coastline. The nation consisted of four known clans, which are likely to have spoken at least three languages: the north eastern, north western and central Tasmanian languages. The known clans were the *Punnilerpanner* from Port Sorell, the *Pallittorre* from Quamby Bluff, the *Noeteeler* at the Hampshire Hills, and the *Plairhekehillerplue* at Emu Bay, with perhaps one or two more along the coast and associated with the Mersey River. Rhys Jones estimates that their population in 1803 could have been 200 to 300

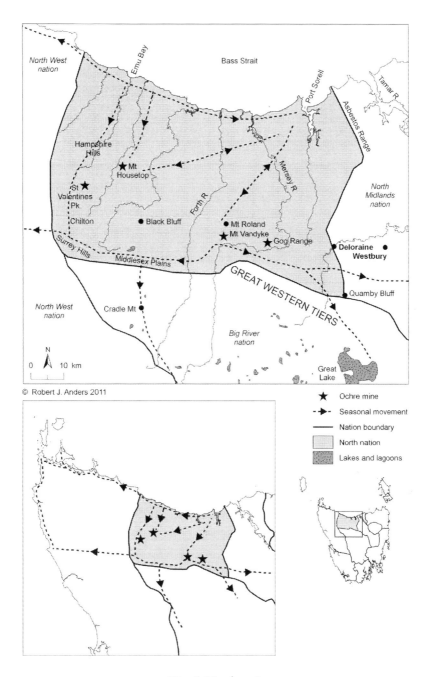

© Robert J. Anders 2011

★ Ochre mine
‑‑►‑ Seasonal movement
— Nation boundary
▨ North nation
▨ Lakes and lagoons

Map 6 North nation

people. Recent archaeological research by Greg Dunnett, however, suggests that the area had intense Aboriginal occupation, and historian Shayne Breen estimates that at least 300 Aborigines were killed by the settlers in this area between 1826 and 1834 alone and that there was probably another clan located at Westbury which extends the nation's eastern boundary. From this new information, Breen suggests that the population of the North nation was more likely to have been closer to 600, that is, twice that of Jones's upper estimate.[40]

The North nation 'owned' the ochre mines at Mount Vandyke, Mount Housetop, Gog Range and St Valentines Peak, which formed the most important sources of ochre in Trouwunna. To access them, Jones considers that the Aborigines maintained a system of well-defined tracks which they kept open by firing and that all the nearby nations visited the mines on a seasonal basis to hold important ceremonies. A major route ran east–west along their southern border from Norfolk Plains past Quamby Bluff to the Mount Vandyke mine, and then on to the Surrey Hills and eventually across the Norfolk Range to the west coast at Sandy Cape in the country of the North West nation. From two of the ochre mines, two routes ran northwards, one from Mount Vandyke to the sea at Port Sorell, the other from Mount Housetop to Port Sorell, and another ran from the Surrey Hills to Emu Bay. Running southwards were the tracks to the Big River country, one past Quamby Bluff to the Great Lake, and the other past Cradle Mountain to Lake St Clair. There was also a track along the north coast. In summer the clans kept the inland plains open by firestick farming, so they could hunt wallabies, wombats, possums and emus and gather a variety of vegetable foods. But it seems they did not occupy the area in winter because of the cold conditions and heavy falls of snow. This changed in the colonial period, when they foraged in the Surrey Hills and the upper reaches of the Forth River.

In early spring, between August and September, the North nation people would meet other clans at Port Sorell and at the mouths of the north coast rivers to collect shellfish and the eggs of swans, ducks and other waterbirds. To the west the clans from the Surrey Hills and Emu Bay paid regular visits to the coast along the Norfolk Range track. They could make the journey from Chilton in the Surrey Hills to Cape Grim in the country of the North West nation in forty-eight hours, usually in summer, possibly to take advantage of the sealing season. They made excursions to Robbins Island, also in the country of the North West nation, where, in addition to food, they collected shells for making necklaces. In return, some of the clans from the North West nation obtained ochre from their visitors as well as rights to visit the inland plains and ochre mines.

To the south-east some of the clans had access to the high plateau country belonging to the Big River nation, travelling there along the Cradle Mountain or Great Lake 'roads'. In return they permitted some of the Big River clans to visit the ochre mines at Mount Vandyke and Mount Housetop. Jones suggests that the lack of a definite pattern of seasonal movement to the North nation's eastern border indicates that relations between the clans of the North and the North Midlands nations were cool or even hostile. But, as Breen points out, the intense warfare between settlers and Aborigines in this region during the colonial period, leading to the probable disappearance of an entire clan at Westbury, suggests a more complex story. What is clear is that the clans of the North nation had an important localised source of ochre with which to bargain for reciprocal arrangements with clans from neighbouring nations. This may account for the fact that they could speak at least three languages. One of the best known members of the North nation was Walyer, the remarkable female chief who came from St Valentines Peak.[41]

Big River nation

The Big River nation occupied the largest territory in Trouwunna, more than 8,000 square kilometres largely consisting of mountain plateau country over 600 metres above sea level. To the immediate north-west lay the highest mountains in Trouwunna, while the country to the south-west was extremely rugged. Although the Big River people had no coastline, they had several lakes, including the Great Lake, which is the largest natural freshwater lake in Australia. Their shorelines totalled more than 240 kilometres, which, put together with the banks of four rivers, provided a plentiful supply of bird life. The Big River was the colonial name for the

River Ouse, whose tributary, the Shannon River, connected the Great Lake, 1,035 metres above sea level, to the Derwent Valley.

The Big River territory began near New Norfolk on the River Derwent and moved south along the border of the South East nation across very high rugged mountains to the border of the South West nation, north through the western mountains to the south-west corner of the Surrey Hills on the boundary of the North and North West nations, east through the extreme western mountains to Quamby Bluff, enclosing all the lake country, and then south along the Great Western Tiers to St Peters Pass and along the Jordan River back to the River Derwent at Herdsmans Cove. Most of their country was clothed in eucalypt woodland that contained several endemic sub-alpine species such as *E. gunnii* and *E. robertsonii*. Jones considers that the Big River nation comprised at least seven or eight clans, of whom five have been identified by Plomley: the *Leenowwenne*, whose country was on the west bank of the River Derwent above New Norfolk; the *Pangerninghe*, also on the west bank of the Derwent, opposite its confluence with the Clyde River; the *Braylwunyer*, whose country lay between the Ouse and Dee rivers; the *Larmairremener*, who came from the high country west of the River Dee; and the *Luggermairrernerpairrer*, who came from the country near the Great Lake. It is likely that they spoke the central Tasmanian language.

Jones estimates their population at between 400 and 500 people, but more recent archaeological research by Richard Cosgrove suggests a higher population. The Central Plateau was an area of intense Big River occupation and the border extended much further to the west than Jones indicates.[42]

Within their country, the clans appear to have camped along lake shores, particularly those of the Great Lake, Arthurs Lake and Lake Echo, and along the Shannon, Dee, Ouse and Clyde rivers, which connect the lakes to the River Derwent. All of these places were rich in bird and fresh-water marine life and opened out onto kangaroo hunting grounds. They also used well-marked tracks that gave access through rough country to Lake Augusta in the highest moorland of the Central Plateau, 1,200 metres above sea level, and they appear to have made periodic excursions into the densely wooded valleys south-west of the Derwent.

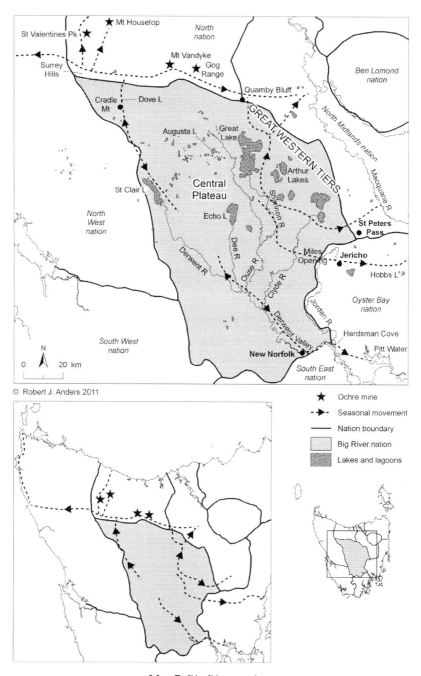

St Valentines Pk

Mt Housetop

North
nation

Surrey
Hills

Mt Vandyke

Gog
Range

Ben Lomond
nation

Quamby Bluff

Cradle
Mt

Dove L

GREAT WESTERN TIERS

North Midlands nation

Augusta L

Great
Lake

Macquarie R

Arthur
Lakes

St Clair L

Central
Plateau

Shannon R

North
West
nation

Echo L

St Peters
Pass

Dee R

Derwent R

Miles
Opening

Jericho

Ouse R

Hobbs L

Clyde R

Oyster Bay
nation

South West
nation

Jordan R

Herdsman Cove

Derwent Valley

Pitt Water

N

0   20 km

New Norfolk

South East
nation

© Robert J. Anders 2011

★   Ochre mine

- ▶ -   Seasonal movement

——   Nation boundary

    Big River nation

    Lakes and lagoons

Map 7 Big River nation

Outside their country, to the east, clans from the Big River nation enjoyed amicable and co-operative arrangements with some clans from the Oyster Bay nation; they foraged together in each other's territory and regularly used three seasonal routes: down the Derwent to Pitt Water; past Jericho and Hobbs Lagoon then through the Eastern Tiers along the Prosser River to Oyster Bay; and north-eastwards through St Peters Pass to the Macquarie River. To the north some of the Big River clans used two routes leading out of their country. The route they most commonly used went past the Great Lake and through a pass in the Great Western Tiers near Quamby Bluff where the present-day Lake Highway makes its descent. There, it connected with an east–west track running to the ochre mines near Mount Vandyke. The clans also went further westwards to the open plains at the Surrey and Hampshire hills and to the ochre mines at Mount Housetop, where they sometimes met clans from the North West nation. Some Big River clans even went as far as Cape Grim on the west coast, a distance of 240 kilometres from the Great Lake. On these journeys they used either the Norfolk Range track or the track to Emu Bay. The other route to the north led from near Lake St Clair, past Cradle Mountain and Lake Dove, to south of Black Bluff. Much of this track was between 900 and 1,200 metres above sea level, but it would have given convenient access from the western side of the Big River country to the Surrey Hills plains, the ochre mines at Mount Housetop and the western end of the Norfolk Range road to the west coast.

The ochre mines and the northern roads formed part of the southern border of the North nation, with whom some of the Big River clans seem to have had amicable relations. They allowed some clans from the North nation into their country as far as the Ouse Valley, while some of them could have gone as far as Pitt Water. To their north-east, relations with the North Midlands nation were often hostile, but they appear to have allowed some clans seasonal access to the high country around the northern part of the Great Lake and the Great Western Tiers. It seems they had little contact with the South West nation even though on a clear day in the high country they could see its smoke.

The Big River nation was the only nation to have regular access to both the east and the west coasts and to have contact with clans from six of the other nations. It was also among the few Aboriginal nations in Australia to have gained its living in a highland and sub-alpine zone. The story of its resilience under pressure from the colonial invaders forms a critical part of this book.[43]

North Midlands nation

The North Midlands nation occupied both coastal and inland country. Its western border ran from St Peters Pass in the Great Western Tiers to Quamby Bluff, northwards to the western edge of the Tamar Valley and the north coast, eastwards to the mouth of the Piper River, where it turned south to Launceston, eastwards again along the South Esk River valley to St Pauls Dome, south-west along the watershed of the Eastern Tiers and then west across the Midland Plain back to St Peters Pass. Its country comprised 6,500 square kilometres, with 160 kilometres of coastline, including both sides of the Tamar estuary. This region forms the driest in Tasmania, particularly in the Campbell Town area of the Midland Plain, which before British invasion comprised eucalyptus woodland.

It is likely that the North Midlands nation consisted of at least five clans, but Plomley could only identify three of them: the *Leterremairrener* (or Port Dalrymple people) at the east Tamar, the *Panninher* (or Norfolk Plains people) at Norfolk Plains, and the *Tyerrernotepanner* (or Stoney Creek people) at Campbell Town. There was possibly a further clan located at York Town on the western side of the Tamar River and another along the Isis River. They appear to have spoken both the north east and central Tasmanian languages. Since the North Midlands was among the first nations to experience British invasion in northern Tasmania in 1804, there is insufficient ethnographic information about the actual location of each clan. With at least five clans of between sixty and eighty people, Jones estimates their population at between 300 and 400, although, as he points out, 'there is much indirect archaeological and documentary evidence to indicate that the Aboriginal population in the Midlands regions was originally as high as anywhere else in Tasmania'. My own research suggests that at least 300 were probably killed outright by the settlers between 1820 and 1830, and recent archaeological research by Sue Kee indicates a much higher population overall.[44]

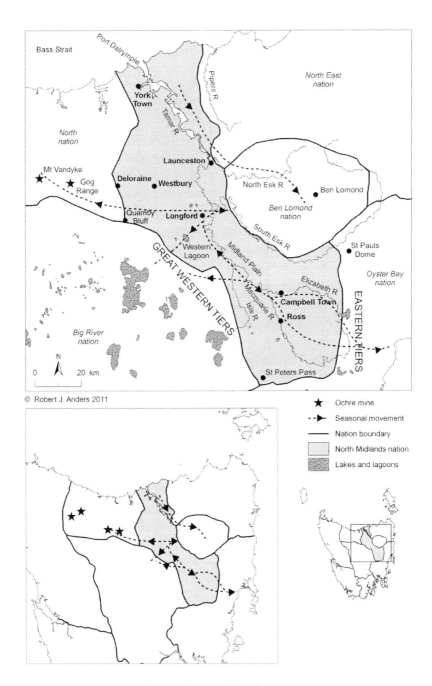

© Robert J. Anders 2011

Map 8 North Midlands nation

The North Midlands nation had extensive relations, not always harmonious, with the North, North East, Big River, Ben Lomond and Oyster Bay nations, for the largest kangaroo hunting grounds on the island lay in the heart of their country at Campbell Town, Norfolk Plains and Launceston together with the incredibly rich marine and bird life along the Tamar River. Jones notes that the colonial literature reports spring and summer concentrations of large numbers of Aborigines in all these areas. In winter the Stoney Creek clan had foraging rights among the clans at North Oyster Bay and then in spring returned to its own country for extensive kangaroo hunting. It spent the summer in the Great Western Tiers, sometimes moving along the road to Mount Vandyke for ochre. In autumn the clan returned again to the Campbell Town area for kangaroos and perhaps for an exchange of ochre with Ben Lomond and Oyster Bay people. One of the Stoney Creek chiefs, Umarrah, became well known to the colonists and played a critical part in the Black War.[45]

The Panninher clan spent the winter on the lower reaches of the west bank of the Tamar, where it gathered shellfish and swan eggs. In spring it returned to the kangaroo hunting grounds in its own country. In the summer the clan visited the Great Western Tiers, from where it could use the 'ochre road' to Mount Vandyke, and returned to its own country in the autumn. It had extensive relations with clans from the North and Big River nations, the former often visiting the Norfolk Plains area to hunt and to catch birds in the marsh area west of the Liffey River.

The Leterremairrener clan spent its winter in its own territory along the east bank of the Tamar as far as the coast, moving east in spring and up to the Ben Lomond Tier in summer, then returning to its own country at the end of January to await the mutton-bird season. Clan members met to exchange shell necklaces for ochre with the Panninher and the Ben Lomond nation and hunted extensively in the country of the North East nation.

All three known clans of the North Midlands nation appear to have engaged in seasonal movements in more diverse ways than other nations. As Rhys Jones points out, their existence depended upon sustained relations with neighbouring nations and on the full exploitation of seasonal resources.[46]

Ben Lomond nation

The Ben Lomond nation's territory comprised the Ben Lomond mountain and its neighbourhood. The eastern and southern border ran along the South Esk River from White Hills, south-east of Launceston, to the junction of the Break O'Day River at Fingal, then north to the rainforest of the North Esk River, following the line across the peaks of Mount Saddleback, Ben Nevis and Mount Barrow, and back to the North Esk River outside Launceston. The area was 2,500 square kilometres and included no coastline except by seasonal access. Ben Lomond mountain dominated the region. Most of the area was open forest with savannah woodlands and open plains, but the northern border was dominated by rainforest. The Ben Lomond nation probably consisted of up to four clans, three of which have been identified by Plomley, albeit without their specific locations— the *Plangermairreenner*, the *Plindermairhemener* and the *Tonenerweenerlarmenne*—reaching a minimum population of somewhere between 150 and 200. They appear to have spoken the central and north eastern Tasmanian languages and probably had friendly relations with the North Oyster Bay clans and the North East and North Midlands nations, in the latter case through the Stoney Creek and Port Dalrymple clans.

One of the Ben Lomond clans had foraging rights at North Oyster Bay at Moulting Lagoon between August and October, moved to the North Midlands country at Stockers Bottom in November, and then retired to the Ben Lomond plateau for the summer. Sometimes, the same clan went with some clans of the North Midlands nation to visit clans from the Big River nation for hostile purposes. In January it was also known to visit the east coast for seals and mutton-birds, returning to the Midland Plain in autumn and then the coast for the winter. Another clan spent the winter on the north coast with some clans from the North East nation, retiring to the hinterland for kangaroos in spring and returning to its own country in the summer. In autumn at least one of the Ben Lomond clans visited coastal sites in the country of the North East nation such as Cape Portland, Waterhouse Point, and Eddystone Point for mutton-birds and seals. A third clan wintered with the Port Dalrymple clan on the Tamar coast, congregating at the Lower South Esk River in spring and autumn and spending the summer

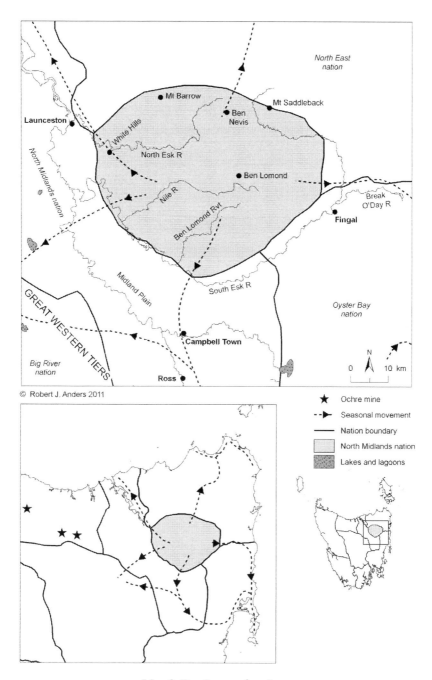

Map 9 Ben Lomond nation

on the Ben Lomond plateau. Thus, the Ben Lomond nation had access to the east and north coasts, the Midland Plain and the Great Western Tiers. Its own country was a popular summer resort. According to Jones, it was possible for a clan or a clan member to spend winter on the east coast with clans from the Oyster Bay nation, travel in spring through St Marys Pass to Schouten Passage for eggs, return to the Ben Lomond Tier for the summer, then spend autumn on the Midland Plain and the following winter at the Tamar coast.

Like other nations in the Midlands area, the Ben Lomond nation was virtually destroyed by British pastoral invasion in the 1820s, but Walter George Arthur, the son of a Ben Lomond chief, became an important leader of the Aboriginal community on Flinders Island in the 1840s and at Oyster Cove in the 1850s.[47]

North West nation

The North West nation occupied the north coast and all the islands including Robbins and Hunter islands from Table Cape to Cape Grim and down the west coast to Macquarie Harbour. It was once thought that it restricted its inland occupation to the coastal regions not more than a few kilometres from the sea, but recent archaeological research by Jim Stockton and Ingereth Macfarlane suggests that its eastern border may have extended to the mountains further east and then swung north to the coast at Table Cape just west of Wynyard. The North West country covered more than 3,400 square kilometres, with a coastline of 550 kilometres. As one of the largest nations in Trouwunna—Jones estimates its minimum population was between 400 and 600 people—it supported at least eight clans, which have been identified by Plomley: the *Tommeginer* from Table Cape, the *Parperloihener* from Robbins Island, the *Pennemukeer* from Cape Grim, the *Pendowte* from Studland Bay, the *Peerapper* from West Point, the *Manegin* from the mouth of the Arthur River, the *Tarkinener* from Sandy Cape, and the *Peternidic* from the mouth of the Pieman River. However, the more recent archaeological research referred to above suggests a much higher population. It appears that they spoke the north western Tasmanian language.[48]

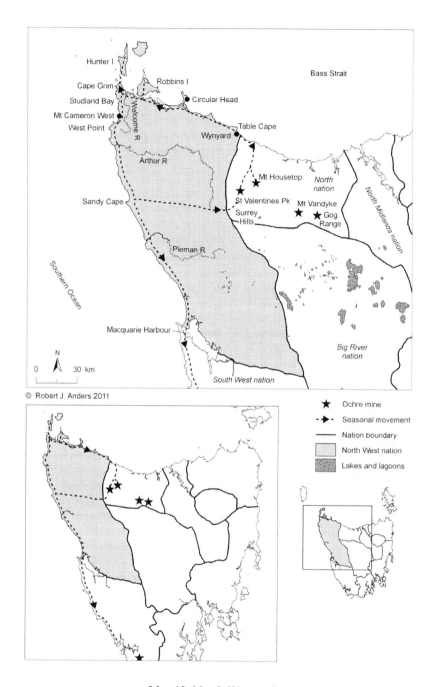

Hunter I

Robbins I

Cape Grim

Studland Bay

Mt Cameron West

West Point

Welcome R

Circular Head

Table Cape

Wynyard

Arthur R

Bass Strait

Mt Housetop

St Valentines Pk

Surrey
Hills

North
nation

Mt Vandyke

Gog
Range

North Midlands nation

Sandy Cape

Pieman R

Southern Ocean

Macquarie Harbour

N

0   30 km

Big River
nation

South West nation

© Robert J. Anders 2011

★ Ochre mine

- ▶ - Seasonal movement

—— Nation boundary

North West nation

Lakes and lagoons

Map 10 North West nation

The North West clans moved seasonally up and down the coast, travelling along well-marked footpaths or roads to gain easy access through swampy country covered with dense scrub. The Peerapper clan from West Point used to forage inland of Mount Cameron West in the swampy tea-tree and scrub country around the Welcome River and from there visit Robbins Island and Circular Head. The clans erected beehive-shaped huts in strategic locations close to foraging areas, so that as they travelled along the coast they could move from one hut to the next, occupying old huts or building new ones as the occasion demanded. They dug and kept tidy small wells and placed abalone shells near them as drinking vessels for travellers. Every September several clans would congregate at the mouths of rivers near the coastal lagoons, where swans and ducks laid their eggs. From October to the end of March they exploited the vast mutton-bird rookeries on the Hunter Group of islands and on the rocky stacks and were often joined by clans from as far south as Sandy Cape. Since these rookeries were the most extensive near the Tasmanian mainland, they were able to sustain an Aboriginal population for much longer than those near Cape Portland and at various places on the east coast and at Bruny Island. In early and mid summer the North West clans exploited the elephant sealing grounds from Sandy Cape north to Mount Cameron West. In summer the Sandy Cape and the Pieman River clans crossed Macquarie Harbour by canoe to forage on the south-west coast as far south as Port Davey. In turn, clans from the South West nation made visits in summer to Mount Cameron West and even as far as Cape Grim. The Robbins Island and West Point clans were known to have visited the South West nation, and, although they knew each other well, relations were not always friendly.

All the clans from Circular Head to Sandy Cape travelled regularly into the high inland country belonging to the North nation to collect ochre. These inland excursions were carefully sanctioned and often required the Noeteeler clan from the North nation to accompany them. Unaccompanied visits frequently led to political hostility. In return for the use of this prized resource, the coastal clans acted as host to clans from the North nation when they visited Robbins Island for mutton-birds, sealing, and shells to make necklaces. Political relations, however, were not always amicable. The

Tommeginer clan from Table Cape exploited its position in its political relations both with the other North West clans and with the North nation.

Jones believes that a North West clan, even allowing for its semi-permanent occupation of areas like West Point, still travelled about 300 kilometres a year. The Tarkinener, for example, whose local residence was at Sandy Cape, in a normal year could travel 130 kilometres north to the Hunter Islands, then 265 kilometres south to Port Davey and 95 to 130 kilometres inland to the Surrey Hills. Thus, the North West nation as an intensely maritime people exploited a wide variety of coastal resources.[49] In the 1830s, at least two chiefs from the North West nation, Heedeek and Wyne, played a critical role in resisting the forced removal of their clans from their own country.

South West nation

The South West nation occupied a coastline of about 450 kilometres, from Macquarie Harbour to somewhere between Cox Bight and South Cape, which was the border with the South East nation. Here, the border turned north until it met the south-western border of the Big River nation and continued north until due east of Macquarie Harbour, then returned to the coast. The area covered more than 3,000 square kilometres and supported at least four clans: the *Mimegin* from the southern side of Birchs Inlet, the *Lowreenne* from Low Rocky Point, the *Ninene* from Port Davey, and the *Needwonnee* from Cox Bight. With each clan comprising between fifty and seventy people, Jones estimates that their total population was between 200 and 300. However, more recent archaeological research by Ron Vanderwal and David Horton indicates an even higher population. They appear to have spoken the southern and north western Tasmanian languages.[50]

The South West nation's economy was focused on the seashore and the coastal plain immediately behind it. Its major foods were shellfish, crayfish, seals, wombats and macropods. Vegetable foods appear to have been less abundant and perhaps not as important in the diet as they were elsewhere in Trouwunna. Like the North West clans, the South West people lived in 'villages' of beehive-shaped huts situated close to fresh water and food-collecting areas. Their seasonal movements were mostly parallel to

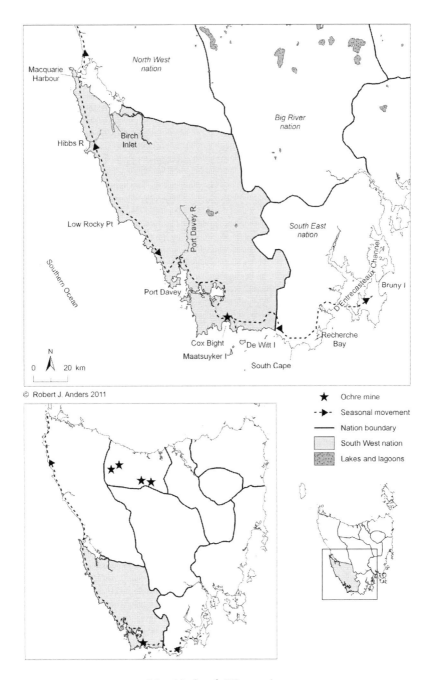

© Robert J. Anders 2011

Map 11 South West nation

the coast along well-defined footpaths where they had numerous huts; they constructed canoes to cross rivers and harbours. During the winter they tended to stay in their local residences, where they lived on shellfish until the egging season in late August. Then they moved towards Macquarie Harbour or Port Davey and obtained ochre at Cox Bight. Outside their country, the South West clans had access north across Macquarie Harbour and east along the south coast past South East Cape to the D'Entrecasteaux Channel in the country of the South East nation. They may also have used some inland routes that led to Big River country.

They had close relations with clans from the North West nation and often visited Mount Cameron West and Cape Grim during the sealing and mutton-birding seasons. To the east they used canoes to visit the Maat-suyker and De Witt islands during the summer to hunt seals and would sometimes meet the Lyluequonny clan from the South East nation. In winter they occasionally visited the Nuenonne clan of the South East nation at Bruny Island. The Ninene, or Port Davey, clan in the course of a year would travel from Recherche Bay to Mount Cameron West, a distance of 400 kilometres. Since ochre was obtained at Cox Bight they had no need to travel to the Surrey Hills.

Like their counterparts from the North West and South East nations, the South West clans were dependent on the coastal regions for basic food sources. Their ability to travel the whole extent of the west coast and to the D'Entrecasteaux Channel in the south-east suggests their need for food sources as well as ceremonial obligations. The presence of ochre at Cox Bight allowed them to take it to the clans from the South East nation in return for foraging in their area.[51] One of the South West nation's chiefs, Towterrer, led the resistance to the removal from its country in the 1830s, and his daughter Mathinna was taken into Lieutenant-Governor Frank-lin's household in the late 1830s.

South East nation

The territory of the South East nation covered more than 3,500 square kilometres, with 555 kilometres of coastline. The border ran from the west bank of the River Derwent from New Norfolk to Storm Bay, included all the D'Entrecasteaux Channel and Bruny Island as far as South Cape and extended inland north to the Huon Valley and New Norfolk. There were at least seven known clans, each consisting of at least seventy or eighty people, who probably spoke the southern Tasmanian language. Plomley has identi-fied the *Mouheneenner* clan from present-day Hobart, the *Nuenonne* clan from Bruny Island, the *Mellukerdee* clan from the Huon River, and the *Lyluequonny* clan from Recherche Bay, but there were also clans at North West Bay and at South East Cape. They operated in large groups along a coastline rich in shellfish, with ready access to birds, kangaroos and wallabies.[52]

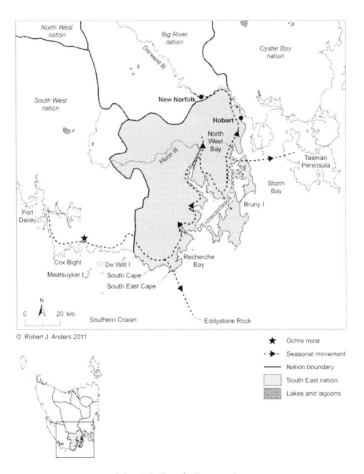

Map 12 South East nation

In winter the South East clans concentrated along the coastline for shell-fish; in November they congregated at North Bruny Island for mutton-birds and in the summer at Recherche Bay to hunt seals, seabirds, kangaroos and possums, to gather shellfish and a variety of marine and terrestrial vegetable food and to conduct shallow-water scale fishing at night with lighted torches. As the most maritime people in Trouwunna, they used their bark canoes in the sheltered D'Entrecasteaux Channel in all seasons. They made frequent short voyages between Bruny Island and the Tasmanian mainland, includ-ing journeys up the River Derwent and across the southern straits of the D'Entrecasteaux Channel to Recherche Bay and South East Cape. Woor-raddy, chief of the Nuenonne clan on Bruny Island, told G.A. Robinson that men from his clan made journeys to the Tasman Peninsula, sometimes directly across the Storm Bay passage by canoe, to visit the Pydairrerme clan from the Oyster Bay nation, to acquire women. They also used their canoes to make summer visits to the Maatsuyker and De Witt islands to hunt seals, and they may have used them to make similar visits to the Eddystone Rock, 25 kilometres off South East Cape. At the Maatsuyker Islands they some-times met the Needwonnee clan from Cox Bight and the Ninene from Port Davey. In inclement weather they constructed semicircular bark huts or windbreaks, which differed from the more permanent beehive-shaped huts made by the South West people.[53] Truganini, who became the best known Aboriginal woman in colonial Tasmania, was born in 1812 at Recherche Bay, where her father, Mangerner, was the chief of the Lyluequonny clan.

Conclusion

Over more than 40,000 years of history, at the beginning of which they were the most southerly occupants of the globe, the Tasmanian Aborigines appear to have adapted their human behaviour and technology in relation to changing climates and ecologies and, by implication, changing social and cultural strategies. Rather than their survival over this extraordinarily long period owing, according to Keith Windschuttle, 'more to good fortune than to good management', on the contrary, in the period immediately before British invasion they appear to have been physically enlarging their ecologi-cal universe. They were creating productive tracts out of non-productive vegetation and journeying to islands to the north and south in search of rich sources of food. They knew how to make fire, like all other human populations in other parts of the world, and, as in most other hunter-gatherer coastal societies, scale fish was a component of their diet. It also appears that in the decade before British invasion, in 1803, the population of the nine nations was considerably greater than Rhys Jones's conservative estimate of 4,000 and was probably closer to 7,000, taking into account estimates made by Plomley and ethnographers from the early colonial period. Indeed, it was probably increasing. It was this dynamic society that confronted the British invaders in 1803.[54]

2

Wrageowrapper, 1803–07

On a cool spring day at the end of the first week in September 1803, a family of the Moomairremener clan from the Oyster Bay nation on the eastern shore of the River Derwent saw a large white bird near the rivulet at Risdon Cove. The next day they saw another draw up alongside. They had seen such birds before and believed the human strangers they carried were Wrageowrapper, devil men's spirits. They had seen the spirits come ashore and set up camp for a few days or even a couple of weeks and then cut down trees, hunt kangaroos, catch scale fish from the river, collect water in huge round wooden enclosed baskets and then depart. But this time, the white devil men and, for the first time, some white devil women and children had come to stay.[1]

The Wrageowrapper were the advance guard of a three-pronged British invasion of Van Diemen's Land precipitated by fear of a possible French claim to the island. Indeed, had Britain not been at war with France, it is unlikely that it would have occupied Van Diemen's Land at this time. The discovery of Bass Strait in 1800 had shortened the shipping route from Cape Town to the colony at Sydney in New South Wales and thus replaced the long-used route around southern Van Diemen's Land and the known safe anchorage at Adventure Bay. But fear of the French led the British to claim the island as part of the colony of New South Wales. Within thirty years they had wiped out virtually all the Tasmanian Aborigines. The Wrageow-rapper certainly lived up to the fears that the Moomairremener may have held about them on that fateful day.

The white devils that the Moomairremener observed at Risdon Cove comprised forty-nine Britons under the command of Lieutenant John Bowen of the Royal Navy and included a sergeant and seven privates of the New South Wales Corps, Jacob Mountgarrett, who was both a naval surgeon and magistrate, three settler families and a cluster of male and female convicts. Bowen carried no instructions about how to meet with the Moomairremener. Rather, he had been told to establish a beach-head at Risdon Cove, declare that it was an integral part of the colony of New South Wales and then defend it from a possible French attack.[2]

In February 1804, on the other side of the River Derwent, some Mouheneenner and Nuenonne people saw two further large white birds, the ships *Ocean* and *Calcutta*, carrying some 200 Britons under the command of Lieutenant-Governor David Collins, anchor at Sullivans Cove at present-day Hobart. Collins's party consisted of several detachments of marines, some with their wives and children, more than 100 male convicts and some of their families, and four unmarried civil officers, including Robert Knopwood who was both the chaplain and magistrate.[3] Collins had selected the Derwent as a permanent settlement in preference to Port Dalrymple on the island's northern coast, because 'large bodies of hostile natives' from the North Midlands nation had prevented an advance party from landing there two months earlier.[4]

But Port Dalrymple, by virtue of its strategic location on the southern side of Bass Strait, was not left unoccupied by the British for very long. Towards the end of November 1804, a clan of the North Midlands nation saw a party of nearly 100 soldiers of the New South Wales Corps under the command of Lieutenant-Colonel William Paterson, lieutenant-governor of New South Wales, establish a beach-head at the mouth of the Tamar River.[5]

Each of these footholds had the standing in European law of possession by discovery and settlement. This convenient legal fiction was based on the Roman legal principle of *terra nullius*, or empty lands, which the Swiss philosopher Emmerich de Vattel had reframed in his book *Law of Nations*, published in 1759. Vattel argued that there was not enough space in the world for small nations that neither cultivated the soil nor operated a system of government recognisable to Europeans to keep hold of their country.

If this country were discovered by a 'civilised community', in reality a European power, then they could legally claim the country and 'settle' it.[6]

Vattel's revision of *terra nullius* appeared at an opportune moment. Following the loss of the American colonies in 1776, Britain was determined to found a new empire and eagerly adopted Vattel's revisionist doctrine of discovery. Captain James Cook had certainly invoked it in 1770 when he claimed the east coast of New Holland for England and named it as New South Wales. His botanist colleague Joseph Banks had reinforced the doctrine in 1785 when he was asked by a committee of inquiry in London whether land in New South Wales might be obtained from the Aborigines by 'cession or purchase'. He believed that neither was necessary. Rather, he contended that, when confronted by a settlement of 500 Englishmen, the Aborigines would 'speedily abandon the Country to the New Comers'. The message was clear: neither treaty nor land purchase would be necessary in New South Wales. Armed with these instructions, Governor Arthur Phillip had established a penal colony at Sydney in 1788.[7]

Indeed, Phillip and his judge advocate, David Collins, had expected to find New South Wales a sparsely populated and undefended country. So when the Eora people contested their unauthorised intrusion, both men refused to countenance their belligerence as ongoing resistance and hostility to their presence. Even so, they kidnapped Eora men as hostages to prevent attacks against the British settlement and when this failed they then used state-sanctioned punishment and military power to effect control. Neither of them could admit that the Eora actually owned the land.[8] When Aboriginal resistance intensified at the Hawkesbury in the 1790s and the Bediagal clans killed some farmers who had planted crops on their hunting grounds without their permission, the British carried out reprisal killings against them. A decade later, when the question was raised about whether Aborigines were 'civilized' enough to give evidence in their own defence before a criminal court, Richard Atkins, the judge advocate in Sydney, ruled that it was impossible to bring an Aborigine to trial for a crime committed against either a colonist or another Aborigine.[9]

The ruling transformed the Aborigines' legal status in New South Wales from that of British subjects to a people who lived in a 'savage state' with no

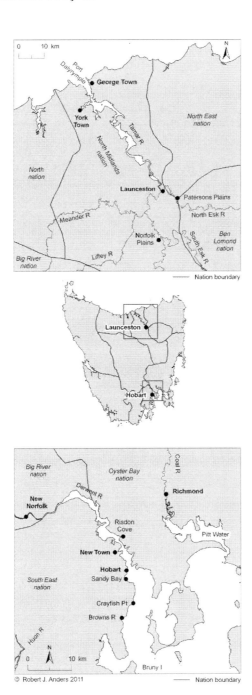

Map 13 Colonial settlement, 1803–20

enforceable legal rights. In reality it meant that if an Aborigine attacked a colonist or another Aborigine within British jurisdiction, then government forces and armed colonists could carry out reprisals against them. If they were apprehended, they could be transported without trial to another part of the colony where they would remain 'at the governor's pleasure'. This was the fate of the Sydney Aborigine Musquito, who was transported to Norfolk Island in 1806 for killing another Aborigine and later ended up in Van Diemen's Land. At the same time, it was becoming legally impossible for any colonist to be arrested and charged with the murder of an Aborigine.[10]

The Aborigines' new legal status in New South Wales coincided with the British decision to invade Van Diemen's Land. From the outset, the invaders invoked a new policy towards the Tasmanian Aborigines that Collins called 'distance and fear'.[11] It had immediate, devastating and far-reaching consequences. At Risdon Cove, for example, John Bowen tried to brush off the awful fact that he had no instructions about the Aborigines' legal status by pretending that 'few' of them 'had been sighted since his party's arrival' and that 'not apprehending they would be of any use to us I have not made any search after them, thinking myself well off if I never see them again'.[12] Nearly fifty years later, historian John West turned the oversight to colonial advantage. He said that when Bowen landed, 'a solitary savage, armed with a spear . . . entered the camp, and was cordially greeted. He accepted the trinkets which they offered, but he looked on the novelties scattered about without betraying surprise. By his gestures they inferred that he discharged them from their trespass.'[13] But there is no evidence to indicate that such a meeting, let alone the discharge of trespass, ever took place. Instead, it would appear with the benefit of hindsight that West was trying to make the Tasmanian Aborigines responsible for their dispossession and virtual elimination.

Risdon lay in the territory of the Moomairremener clan of the Oyster Bay nation and formed part of the corridor that gave the Leenowwenne and Pangerninghe clans of the Big River nation access to the kangaroo hunting grounds at Risdon and the rich shellfish and lagoon areas of the Coal River and Pitt Water. The parkland aspect of lush grasses interspersed with eucalypts that Bowen extolled had been created by firestick farming by the Moomairremener clan to flush out game. It was also one of their tool-making sites. When Bowen's outpost was strengthened in November by ten more soldiers from the New South Wales Corps led by Lieutenant William Moore and forty more convicts, two or three kangaroo hunting dogs and two 12-pound carronades loaded with shot, the conditions were ripe for violent conflict.[14] Over the next five months, the British recorded several bloody encounters with clans from the Big River and Oyster Bay nations in the vicinity of the Risdon settlement. Surveyor James Meehan fired on several large parties of the two nations' clans near the Jordan River; others in the settlement seized an Aboriginal boy who soon escaped; and botanist Robert Brown recorded some of the words of their language—the only known attempt made by any Englishman for the next twenty-five years to do so. Brown and Meehan knew that they were trespassing on Aboriginal land, but they took the Eurocentric view that the Aborigines rather than the British were the intruders.[15]

When Collins arrived at the Derwent in February 1804, he did carry instructions from London about the Aborigines' legal status. But they were a jumble of old and new policies. One paragraph replicated some of the instructions issued to Governor Phillip sixteen years before:

> to open an intercourse with the natives and to conciliate their good-will, enjoining all persons under your Government to live in amity and kindness with them; and if any person shall exercise any acts of violence against them, or shall wantonly give them any interruption in the exercise of their several occupations, you are to cause such offender to be brought to punishment according to the degree of the offence.[16]

But Judge Advocate Atkins's ruling in Sydney about the inadmissibility of Aboriginal evidence in court made this paragraph redundant. Indeed, when Collins landed, he did not even bother to publish his instructions. Thus, neither of the British footholds at the Derwent had a clear legal framework in place to deal with the Aborigines when violent conflict arose. It was not long in coming.

On the morning of 3 May 1804, Edward White, an assigned convict servant to settler Richard Clark, was hoeing his master's garden on the eastern side of Risdon Creek when he suddenly saw about 300 men, women and children appear out of the valley nearby, driving a mob of kangaroos down the hill before them. They were probably the Leenowwenne and the Pangerninghe clans from the Big River nation on their autumn migration to the east coast. They were astonished to see Risdon occupied by strangers, for, as White later said, 'they looked at me with all their eyes'. He also noted that they carried no spears, only waddies. Unafraid, he went down to the landing at the creek to report their presence to two soldiers stationed there, and then went back to his work.[17]

Lieutenant William Moore, who was in charge of the settlement at the time, was alarmed by the Aborigines' sudden appearance. Unlike Edward White, he considered that 'their numbers were far from friendly' and that they were a war party and decided to take offensive action to protect the camp. Hostilities began at eleven o'clock, when Moore sent five soldiers to assist his gamekeeper, from whom the Big River people were trying to wrest a large kangaroo. Then he was told that another group of Big River men were 'beating Mr Birt, the Settler at his farm' on the eastern side of the creek. So he despatched two more soldiers, 'with orders not to fire if they could avoid it; however they found it necessary, and one was killed on the Spot, and another was found Dead in the Valley'.[18]

Confused and in shock, the Big River people appear to have retrieved the bodies and then retreated to the hill on the other side of Risdon Creek, directly opposite Jacob Mountgarrett's recently completed stone cottage. At this point it seems Mountgarrett persuaded Moore to make this cottage the centre of military operations. Archaeological evidence suggests that Moore stationed fifteen armed soldiers and about the same number of male convicts together with perhaps two armed settlers around it and then brought up one of the carronades loaded with grapeshot as further protection. The weapon of mass destruction that Matthew Flinders had sent to Risdon as protection against the French was now put to another use. At two o'clock Mountgarrett fired the carronade at the Big River people, and the soldiers, settlers and convicts fired their rifles, pistols and muskets in support.

Archaeological findings at the cottage include a 12-pound steel cannonball, hand-made lead shot, a hand-moulded ball, lead casting waste, two lead balls for a long-arm rifle, a group of thirteen hand-made lead bullets probably for a small-calibre pistol, a group of thirty-three hand-made lead shot, and thirteen lead shot.[19]

At this point Mountgarrett yelled at Moore to shoot 'the black devils down' and brandishing his sword he led the soldiers and convicts in pursuit of the Big River people 'some distance up the valley' near to where Risdon prison now stands. There, according to Edward White, 'a great many' of the Big River people 'were killed and wounded' and 'one was seen to be taken away by the blacks'.[20]

Across the Derwent at Hobart, the colonists heard the carronade's boom at 2 pm and Collins immediately sent a messenger to find out what was happening. At half-past seven that evening the messenger returned with Lieutenant Moore, who went straight to Collins's marquee to report on the affray. At 8 pm, he repaired to Robert Knopwood's marquee and delivered a note from Mountgarrett. It said that the Big River people had made a premeditated attack on the settlement, that their number 'was not less than 5 or 6 hundred' and that they had been armed with spears. Moore told Knopwood that the Big River people had been 'very numerous, and that they had wounded one of the settlers, Burke, and was going to burn his house down and ill treat his wife'.[21] Four days later, in his official report to Collins, Moore said that the Big River people had been the aggressors, that he had not fired at them until they had 'surrounded' the 'Camp', when two of them had been killed, and that it was not he, the soldier, but Mountgarrett as the magistrate, who had proposed to fire the carronade and then led the chase up the valley. In presenting his own actions and that of the soldiers as entirely defensive, Moore escaped reprimand.[22]

But Collins was also at fault. He had been expected to take command of the Risdon settlement in February and had failed to do so. In his despatch to Governor King ten days later, he admitted that 'three' Big River people 'had been killed on the spot' but, '[n]ot having been present myself, I must take it for granted that the measures which were pursued were unavoidable'. He also said that the colonists considered that the Tasmanian Aborigines were 'cannibals' and that, conversely, the Aborigines probably thought the colonists were cannibals too.[23] By implying that the Aborigines were responsible for British aggression, Collins had shown how the new policy was expected to work—by conveniently labelling the Aborigines as cannibals the British could then shoot them with impunity.

In the massacre's immediate aftermath, Mountgarrett abducted a three-year-old boy orphaned in the affray and recovered the body of an adult male. He later dissected the body, packed the bones in a barrel and despatched it to Sydney. A week later Robert Knopwood christened the boy 'Robert Hobart May'—in honour of himself, the official name of the outpost and the month in which the massacre had taken place. The boy was the second of many Tasmanian Aboriginal children orphaned in violent clashes with the British over the next thirty years. Thus, from the outset, the British in effect were trying to eliminate the Aborigines by killing the parents, abducting their children and transforming them into white people. Robert May was a lively boy who entertained his captors by throwing spears, dancing and tracking down kangaroos.[24]

Despite Collins's attempt to underplay the massacre, the colonists wouldn't stop talking about it. One of them, convict Edward White, was a witness to the shootings. Another, marine Sergeant Robert Evans, visited the site of devastation shortly after and was told that men, women and children were killed and some children were taken away. A week later, the youths James Kelly and John Pascoe Fawkner, along with Robert Knopwood, rowed across the river from Hobart to the site. Apart from Knopwood, all the others were in no doubt that Moore had been the original aggressor.[25] When a formal inquiry into the massacre was finally held, in 1830, it was revealed that the settler Burke had never been threatened, let alone attacked, by any of the Big River people and that their number had been less than half that estimated by Moore and Mountgarrett. Knopwood admitted to five or six Aborigines being killed; Kelly said that no fewer than fifty of them had been shot down; and Fawkner later said that 'some few crawled away, only to die a lingering death in the woods. About thirty bodies were found and burnt or buried at the choice of those sent to clear the air of the effluvia.'[26] Moore's senior army officer, Captain Anthony Fenn Kemp, also later admitted that

Moore had 'committed an outrage ... by turning on a tribe which had assembled at Cove point' and 'had improperly fired a four pounder upon a body of them'. He also said that Moore had been drinking on the morning of the massacre, leading him to overreact to the Aborigines' sudden appearance, and that he had been driven to excess by 'a brutal desire to see the Niggers run'.[27]

Whatever Moore's motives were, the massacre brought an end to the Risdon outpost. A week later, Collins finally assumed command and ordered Bowen, Moore and the soldiers of the New South Wales Corps, along with Mountgarrett and most of the convicts, to return to Sydney. Robert Hobart May was sent to live with a settler family in Hobart and eighteen months later he was vaccinated against smallpox. There is some evidence that he may have rejoined Mountgarrett at Port Dalrymple in 1806. The Moomairremener clan returned to Risdon in the summer of 1804–05 and their fires were observed each summer and autumn over the next four years.[28]

Despite the massacre and its legal ramifications for the British as an invading and occupying force, Collins still neglected to publish his own instructions about the Aborigines. When Governor King in Sydney reprimanded him for this dreadful oversight, Collins had the audacity to say:

> At present we have not had any intercourse with them, which I do
> not much regret; and not finding any disposition to straggle among
> my People, I shall wait until my Numbers are increased, when
> I shall deem it necessary to inform the whole, that the Aborigines of
> this Country are as much under the Protection of the Laws of Great
> Britain, as themselves.[29]

Yet even before he had stepped ashore at the River Derwent on 13 February Robert Knopwood had recorded in his diary that '17 of the natives were seen ... that they were all men, well made entirely naked and some of them had war weapons; they had a small boy with them about 7 years old and did not appear to flee'. Indeed, Knopwood noted several times during the first few months that 'many of the natives were about the camp'.[30]

Woorraddy, a young warrior from the Nuenonne clan from Bruny Island foraging in the area when Collins's party arrived, corroborated Knopwood's account. He later recalled that when his compatriots saw the first ship coming, they were frightened and said it was Wrageowrapper, the devil:

> that when the first people settled they cut down the trees, built houses, dug the ground and planted; that by and by more ships came, then at last plenty of ships; that the natives went to the mountains [Mount Wellington], went and looked at what the white people did, went and told other natives and they came and looked also.[31]

Even so, the Mouheneenner people were friendly to small parties of invaders they encountered in the bush and were not afraid of a musket. In March, Collins's gamekeeper, Henry Hacking, and the Sydney Aborigine John Salamander confronted a group of Mouheneenner men who 'made use of every policy to wheedle Hacking out of his booty ... Although they treated him with much affability and POLITENESS, yet they regarded his companion with jealousy and indignation; and the poor fellow, sensible of his critical and precarious situation, appeared very thankful when safely delivered from their unwelcome presence.'[32] In November, one of Collins's men brought a Pydairrerme man from Betsey Island to Hobart Town 'much covered in charcoal and he had a bag made of kangaroo skins about his neck which contained the teeth of one of the tribe'. He was then 'dressed in trousers and a shirt and jacket' but he disappeared the next day. Woorraddy later recalled that at about the same time on the Tasman Peninsula, 'white men shoot two blacks dead, when they all became frightened and run away'.[33] In January 1805 the Mouheneenner were venturing to outlying huts at present-day Kingston, Crayfish Point and New Town, where they offered settlers kelp and crayfish in return for bread and potatoes.[34]

When Collins eventually published his instructions, in January 1805, eleven months after his arrival at the Derwent, the British population had reached 481 and it remained at around this level until November 1807.[35]

After that, interaction between Aborigines and colonists became uncertain. According to John Pascoe Fawkner, in 1809 a Nuenonne man 'was taken by a party of fishermen who had landed on Bruny Island. They brought him to town, and Governor Collins thought to keep him by serving him as the prisoners were usually treated when they offended him: he put an iron with a chain to it' on the Nuenonne man's leg. 'But the poor fellow got away with it on, and it was stated he worked it off. But he or some of his tribe visited the first whites they could lay their hands on, and two or three persons were slaughtered after the ironing of this poor Aborigine.'[36] In another incident, Collins apparently ordered one of his men a 'severe' flogging for 'exposing the ears of a boy he had mutilated; and another for cutting off the little finger of a native, and using it as a tobacco stopper'.[37] Salome Pitt, the young daughter of a colonial family at New Town, later recalled being looked after by some of the Mouheneenner women and suggested that the Cock-erells, another New Town family, 'took in' an Aboriginal girl they called Mary, who was abducted a decade later by the bushranger Michael Howe.[38] At the same time the Mouheneenner had begun attacking colonists who strayed from the settlement at Hobart Town, driving off watering parties at Browns River and setting fire to corn stacks.[39] In the light of this evidence, Collins's official story that there was little interaction with the Mouheneen-ner is questionable. In failing to alert his superiors to these violent incidents Collins had created the preconditions for further violent conflict.

At the third British foothold, at Port Dalrymple in northern Van Diemen's Land, Lieutenant-Governor William Paterson proclaimed the Aborigines' legal status the moment he stepped ashore. He had full knowledge of the North Midlands people's earlier success in preventing the British from landing on their territory. He also knew about the massacre at Risdon, for it had been carried out by soldiers from his own regiment. Indeed, some of the perpetrators were in his landing party, including Jacob Mountgarrett.

Within two days of Paterson's party landing at York Town in November 1804 a group of eighty North Midlands men and women confronted them:

> From what we could judge they were headed by a chief, as every-thing given to them was given up to this person . . . from this friendly

interview I was in hopes we would have been well acquainted with
them ere this, but unfortunately a large party (supposed to be the
same) attacked the guard of marines, consisting of one sergeant and
two privates . . . the Guard was under the unpleasant act of defending themselves, and fired upon them, killed one and wounded
another; this unfortunate circumstance I am fearful will be the cause
of much mischief hereafter, and will prevent our excursions inland,
except when well armed.[40]

In keeping with the tradition he had established at Risdon, Mountgarrett then prepared 'the very perfect native's head' for despatch to Sir
Joseph Banks in England. A few days later, about fifty North Midlands
men exacted revenge by spearing the storekeeper Alexander Riley in the
back. After that they apparently became friendlier.[41] But Paterson took no
chances. He despatched a detachment of heavily armed soldiers to search
for suitable land to grow crops and depasture his increasing numbers of
cattle and sheep and appears to have given them orders to shoot at Aborigines wherever they found them. These measures could explain the virtual
absence of North Midlands clans in the region after 1806.[42]

The great tragedy in all these violent incidents is that both Paterson and
Collins had long experience of the Aborigines in Sydney and knew how to
establish formal relationships with them. Had the new policy of 'distance
and fear' not been in operation, they could have recorded their observations
of the clans located at the settlements in much the same way as Collins had
done in Sydney.[43] Instead, they imposed an official blackout on the clans'
existence, at the same time enabling violent incidents to intensify, in particular over the competition for food sources.

By the end of 1804 kangaroo had become the major source of fresh meat
for all the colonists.[44] For the Mouheneenner clan around Hobart and the
Leterremairrener clan at Port Dalrymple, British kangaroo hunting brought
complex outcomes. At first the clans sought to remove the kangaroos from
the British hunters. Then they began to spear the hunters and take their
dogs. After that they started to incorporate the dogs into their own economy
as an item of gift and exchange.[45] By February 1807, the gamekeepers began

to kill the Mouheneenner, and in reprisal the Aborigines speared several more gamekeepers. At least one other Mouheneenner man was also killed. On 19 May, Robert Knopwood reported another fatal skirmish:

> My man Richardson came home, having been absent about 19 days. He gave information that the natives had nearly killed him and his dogs. The governor's people were out and fell in with them when a battle ensued and they killed one of the natives. The natives killed one of the dogs. It is very dangerous to be out alone for fear of them. They are so hardened they do not mind being shot at.[46]

It is not surprising, then, that when John Oxley, the surveyor-general of New South Wales, reported on the settlements in Van Diemen's Land two years later, he considered that kangaroo hunting had led to a 'considerable loss of life among the natives', prevented the development of agriculture and encouraged bushranging.[47]

The first bushrangers were noted by Knopwood less than a year after the British arrived at the Derwent. The following year he reported that runaway convicts were living outside the settlement right through the winter months, and according to James Boyce they were relying on kangaroo hunting dogs to 'live independent and free in the bush'.[48] In 1807, Knopwood recorded details of fourteen bushrangers 'who were all armed with plenty of dogs', while at Port Dalrymple, Paterson bewailed the fact that many bushrangers had robbed his soldiers 'of everything'.[49] Two others, Lemon and Brown, were reported to have tortured and killed two Big River men and three women. In retaliation, clans from the Oyster Bay, Big River and North Midlands nations began to contest the British hunters and bushrangers who sought access to their remote hunting grounds.[50]

The Aborigines' appropriation of dogs, the colonists' appropriation of Aboriginal children and the bushrangers' appropriation of Aboriginal women led to fraught relations between all three groups. Indeed, one of the first historians of the Tasmanian Aborigines, Jorgen Jorgenson, suggests that their numbers were 'much reduced during the first six or seven years of the colony' because in the 'early period the country was sufficiently cleared to enable the whites to harass them with impunity'.[51] There is no doubt that the Mouheneenner clan, whose territory included Hobart, experienced a massive population decline in this period, and the absence of any information about the clan around Launceston suggests a similar outcome. Yet, paradoxically, other clans from the Big River, Oyster Bay and North Midlands nations may have improved their hunting skills with the acquisition of the British dog. So although some clans declined, others may have survived at a time when the British population, by virtue of its gross sexual imbalance, remained static.[52] But at the end of 1807, this changed.

3

Creole society, 1808–20

In November 1807 a group of colonists from Norfolk Island sailed into
Hobart. They were the first of more than 100 families, totalling more than
600 colonists, who relocated from the Sydney outpost to Van Diemen's Land
over the next six years. Having originated from New South Wales, they were
already experienced colonists, although they had little experience of Aborigines. With government support they established farms on 4- to 40-hectare
grants at New Norfolk, Brighton, Browns River, the Coal River and Pitt
Water along the River Derwent in the south and at Patersons Plains and
Norfolk Plains east and west of Launceston in the north. Between 1811 and
1814 they increased the area under cultivation from 3,332 to 12,711 hectares,
the number of cattle from 421 to 5,060 and the number of sheep from 3,573
to 38,540. By then they had occupied 10 per cent of Van Diemen's Land and
transformed it into a thriving colonial economy.[1]

Their arrival signalled a major shift in relations with the six Aboriginal
nations in the northern, eastern, central and southern parts of the island.
For the colonists not only occupied more Aboriginal land; they also assumed
control of the sealing and whaling industries on the Bass Strait islands and
the D'Entrecasteaux Channel and established a timber industry in the
Huon Valley and at Birchs Inlet at Macquarie Harbour on the west coast.
In each case they created a demand for Aboriginal labour and in some cases
reached agreements with clan chiefs for the hire of seasonal labour. At the
same time, increasing numbers of male convicts absconded to the bush,
where some of them forged alliances with clan chiefs against the settlers.

In this potent mix of cross-cultural, economic and sexual interaction, a creole society began to emerge.

The Bass Strait sealing industry had begun in 1798 when 9,000 skins were obtained at Kent Bay on Cape Barren Island by Captain Charles Bishop from Sydney. The season lasted from November to May and by 1800 companies from Sydney and the United States were sending ships to eastern and western Bass Strait with gangs of ten to fifteen men to work for the season, taking as many seals as possible. Between 1800 and 1806 over 100,000 skins were obtained.[2]

After that the number of seals declined and the big companies moved on to sealing grounds in New Zealand. The Bass Strait industry was now open to exploitation by smaller companies in Hobart and Launceston, which over time were increasingly controlled and financed by Norfolk Island families. The men they employed worked in gangs and clubbed seals on islands and rocks in eastern and western Bass Strait; the precarious nature of their work soon drove them to the north coast of Van Diemen's Land for repairs and sustenance. They landed first at Cape Portland in about 1810 and later along the entire north coast from Cape Grim in the west to Eddystone Point in the east. Their visits coincided with the summer pilgrimage by clans from the North West and North East nations to the coast for mutton-birds, seals, shellfish and other seabirds and their eggs. Initially, the clan chiefs were cautious of the intruders, but it was not long before some of them were willing to exchange kangaroo skins for seal carcasses, tobacco, flour and tea. The contact intensified when some of the clan chiefs from the North East nation attempted to incorporate the intruders into their own society by offering some of their women to hunt seals in exchange for dogs. But in the North West nation, the sealers were known to kidnap women for permanent habitation on the western Bass Strait islands.[3]

By 1812 some of the North East clans had begun to gather each November at strategic points along the north-east coast, such as Waterhouse Point, Cape Portland and opposite George Rocks, in anticipation of the sealers, who usually arrived in a whaleboat containing four to six men. A ceremonial dance would then be held, a conference would take place between the clan chief, such as Mannalargenna, and the sealers, and an arrangement would be made for the number of women who would work for the sealers, sometimes for the entire season. Some women came from the host clan, and others were abducted from other clans. They were exchanged for dogs, flour and tea. Sometimes young clansmen from the North East nation accompanied sealing parties, and some of them may have accompanied

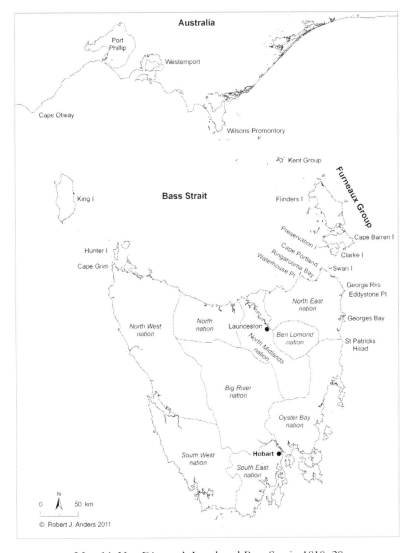

Map 14 Van Diemen's Land and Bass Strait, 1810–20

sealer George Briggs on more than one voyage to Sydney and possibly as far as New Zealand, where they would have met Aborigines from the Australian mainland as well as New Zealanders and Pacific Islanders. At least two of the women from Little Swanport—Meemelunneener, later known as Agnes, and Mirnermannerme, later known as Maria—accompanied sealing men on voyages to Sydney and to the sealing grounds at Mauritius and the Rodrigues Islands in the Indian Ocean.[4]

From 1815 some of the sealers began to establish permanent settlements on islands in eastern and western Bass Strait. George Briggs lived with Woretermoteryenna, one of Mannalargenna's daughters, on Clarke Island with their daughter, Dalrymple (Dolly) Mountgarrett Briggs. Dolly was then sent to Launceston, where she was educated by the Mountgarrett family and baptised by the colonial chaplain Robert Knopwood. She later married stockman Thomas Johnson and obtained a land grant on the Macquarie River. Later, the couple lived in the village of Perth, south of Launceston. On Clarke Island, Briggs and Woretermoteryenna had three more children, Eliza, Mary and John, the youngest of whom migrated to Victoria, where many of his descendants still live. Woretermoteryenna rejoined her daughter Dolly at Perth in the early 1840s and was grandmother to her large family of children, whose descendants form part of the Tasmanian Aboriginal community today.[5]

Another sealer, Scotsman John Smith, appears to have worked in the western Bass Strait sealing grounds before he settled on Gun Carriage Island in eastern Bass Strait with Pleenperrenner, who came from the Cape Portland clan, and their six children. They remained together until Pleenperrenner died, in 1845, and their descendants are part of the Tasmanian Aboriginal community today.[6] James Munro, a former convict from Sydney, was living on Preservation Island in 1819 with mainland Australian Aborigine Margery Munro and was still there in 1843 with Margery and their children.[7] Men like Briggs, Smith and Munro became known as 'Straitsmen'. According to historian Patsy Cameron, the Aboriginal women who lived with them called themselves *tyereelore*, or island wives, and the women who were hired on a seasonal basis to catch seals were known as *wanapakalalea*.[8] Some clan chiefs like Mannalargenna were also known to have enlisted the Straitsmen's support against other clans and accompanied them on short sealing voyages. Such interaction was possible because, unlike the Norfolk Islanders, the sealers made no claim to Aboriginal land.

The Norfolk Islanders, however, violently contested the South East, Oyster Bay, Big River and North Midlands nations for their land, by attacking their camps at night, slaughtering parents and abducting their orphaned children as their servants.[9] The first known cases were recorded in 1810 against the Mouheneenner clan at Mount Wellington:

> The natives, who have been rendered desperate by the cruelties they have experienced from our people, have now begun to distress us by attacking our cattle. Two were lately wounded by them at Collins-vale; and three, it is reported, belonging to George Guest, have been killed at Blackman's Bay. As this tribe of natives have hitherto been considered friendly, the change in their conduct must be occasioned, by some outrage on our part.[10]

Thomas Davey, the colony's second lieutenant-governor, was horrified by the practice of Aboriginal child abduction at the Coal River:

> Had not the Lieutenant-Governor the most positive and distinct proofs of such barbarous crimes having been committed, he could not have believed that a British subject would so ignominiously have stained the honour of his country and of himself; but the facts are too clear, and it therefore becomes the indispensable and bounden duty of the Lieutenant-Governor thus publicly to express his utter indignation and abhorrence thereof.[11]

The experiences of the fifty or so Aboriginal children known to have been taken into colonists' homes between 1809 and 1823 would suggest that most became domestic servants. William and Jane Dempsey, who were settlers at New Norfolk and had no children of their own, adopted an Aboriginal girl, Mary, in 1809 and trained her to become their devoted domestic servant. In the same year, an Aboriginal girl, Fanny, 'walked out on Mr Dry and had not been seen since'. Mrs McAuley, whose husband 'found' an eighteen-month-old Aboriginal boy, Robert, near Cross Marsh in 1812, told the colonial secretary in 1829 that he was 'the best servant I have about me'.[12] Robert's story continues in later chapters. Two girls, Kitty Hobart and Catherine Knopwood, were also domestic servants and joined their mistresses on return voyages to Sydney.[13] Another girl and a boy were known to have drowned, and a boy who absconded from his master was sentenced to twelve months in a chain gang. Three boys became bushrangers, and two others were convicted of theft and sentenced to transportation.[14]

Two boys later became resistance fighters. Kickerterpoller, also known as Black Tom, came from the Poredareme clan of the Oyster Bay nation and was 'taken' by Mr and Mrs Thomas Birch at Hobart in 1810; he quickly learned English. He then worked on their property, Duck Holes at the Coal River, and learned to hunt and shoot with a musket. After working as a guide for the surveyor Thomas Scott at Oyster Bay, he seems to have rejoined his clan in about 1822 and by 1826 was a well-known resistance leader. He was captured in January 1828, joined Robinson's mission in

Crossing the Mouth of the Prosser River on the Bar, East Coast of Van Diemen's Land, Sept. 1821. (Kickerterpoller guiding the party across the river.) Thomas Scott Sketchbook, State Library of New South Wales, Sydney.

January 1830 and until his death, in 1832, played a pivotal role in the concil-iation process.[15] His story continues in later chapters. Another boy, William Lyttleton Quamby, was 'found' by settler William Lyttleton near Norfolk Plains in 1810. He was also taught to hunt and shoot with a musket and rejoined his own people at puberty to lead many raids on stock-keepers and settlers. He was shot dead by 1830.[16]

In an ironical turn of events, among the last batch of Norfolk Islanders to arrive in Hobart, in 1813, was the Sydney Aborigine Musquito. His situa-tion had arisen from Judge Advocate Atkins's ruling in Sydney in 1805 that any Aborigine arrested for murdering another Aborigine within British jurisdiction could not be expected to follow the procedures of English law and thus could not give evidence in court. Rather, he should be subject to 'the governor's pleasure'. In Musquito's case this meant transportation to Norfolk Island in 1806. Upon arrival in Hobart, however, he was tech-nically a free man, and his brother in Sydney requested his repatriation. Although the governor of New South Wales, Lachlan Macquarie, agreed to his return, this never happened and he remained in Van Diemen's Land. In 1816 he successfully tracked down Michael Howe, one of the colony's more notorious bushrangers, and as a reward he was once again promised repatriation to Sydney. But when this second request failed to eventuate, he joined a clan of the Oyster Bay nation and became the colony's first known Aboriginal resistance leader.[17]

In the meantime the clans of the North East nation had developed complex relations with the Straitsmen. In the summer of 1815–16, James Kelly, the port officer at Hobart, and William Hobbs set off on a voyage around Van Diemen's Land accompanied by sealers George Briggs and James Parish. In mid January, they landed at Ringarooma Bay, where they met Mannalargenna and his clan of about 200 people. Briggs was Mannalar-genna's son-in-law and thus had obligations to him. The chief tried to elicit Briggs's assistance to fight a neighbouring clan at Eddystone Point led by Tolobunganah, with whom the bushranger Michael Howe had made an alliance. Having no wish to become entangled with Howe, Briggs promised Mannalargenna that he and his party would seek help from other Straits-men on Cape Barren Island.

The party departed but they avoided Cape Barren Island and sailed instead for George Rocks on the east coast. In breaking his obligations to Mannalargenna, Briggs knew that he faced future conflict. A few days later the party 'fell in' with Tolobunganah and his clan and they were relieved to find that Howe and his gang had departed. Howe was captured shortly afterwards by Musquito. Tolobunganah knew Briggs well and agreed to hire out six women as wanapakalalea for two days to catch seals on George Rocks. In that time the women killed fifty-four seals, and Kelly and Briggs subsequently traded 122 carcasses with Tolobunganah for 246 kangaroo skins.[18]

A decade later, Mannalargenna became a feared resistance leader in the Black War. But Tolobunganah's relations with the Straitsmen ensured that he left descendants in the Aboriginal community today. The Aboriginal children abducted by the Norfolk Island settlers had a different fate.

George van Diemen and a younger boy were found in the bush above New Norfolk, probably in 1819, 'being at the time, as it appeared, abandoned by the parents; probably in consequence of a sudden interruption from the approach of settlers' servants who discovered the children', but more likely in the aftermath of a dawn attack by stockmen on their camp. They were taken to Hobart, where the younger boy soon died. George was taught to read and write and in September 1821 he was sent to England to further his British education. In this case, perhaps, there was an expectation that, on his return, he would become a spokesman for his own people in much the same way that in New South Wales, William Charles Wentworth, the 'native born' son of a convict mother and a colonial official and sent to England for the same purpose, became a spokesman for the emancipists. This could have been the case because another Aboriginal boy, William Thomas Derwent, was also sent to England early in 1821 and placed under the care of the anti-slavery campaigner William Wilberforce, but he died soon after. George van Diemen fared a little better. After six years in England, where he was educated by a variety of schoolmasters who reported favourably on his progress, he died on his return to Hobart in December 1827.[19] Had he survived and had other boys been sent to England for a British education, they might have played a vital role in negotiating a treaty with the colonial government in 1830. But most of the abducted Aboriginal children were destined for servitude. Richard, who came from the Big River nation, was brought up on James Brumby's farm near Cressy in the 1820s and later joined G.A. Robinson's mission. It is also known that surveyor John Helder Wedge had up to four Aboriginal boys in his care.[20] But it took until the next generation for a colonial-educated Aboriginal man, Walter George Arthur, the son of a chief from the Ben Lomond nation, to assume a leadership role among his people.

Brian Plomley and Kristen Anne Henley have listed eighteen baptised Aboriginal children in settlers' homes in 1816, increasing to thirty-four in 1820. Like the settlers, not all abducted Aboriginal children were baptised, and the list does not include Kickerterpoller or Mary Cockerell, let alone John Shinall and Charley, who were 'taken in' by settlers at Pitt Water, the children known to have been 'taken in' by settlers like John Batman and Dr Temple Pearson, or those recorded by the press in other incidents.[21] However, the list does indicate that after 1816 the settlers increased their acquisition of Aboriginal children, suggesting that violent attacks on Aboriginal camps intensified as new farms were established at Pitt Water and the Plenty River above New Norfolk in the southern part of the island and at Norfolk Plains south-west of Launceston. Here, an Aboriginal girl from Piper River was 'taken in' by the Hardwicke family and baptised in 1820 with the name of Fanny Hardwicke. According to Plomley and Henley, '[a] water colour sketch of her by Charles Brown Hardwicke [made in about 1820] shows a tall, well-built girl, seemingly older than her eleven years'.[22] By 1829 she was alleged to have 'lost' her 'native tongue', and lived with a 'man of colour', the sealer John Baker. She was 'of middle stature, strong and very robust, and of quick intellect' and could also 'navigate a schooner'. She became a key player in G.A. Robinson's mission and ended her days at the Aboriginal Station at Oyster Cove.

After three years of violent conflict the *Hobart Town Gazette* reported in 1818:

> Notwithstanding the hostility which has so long prevailed in the
> breasts of the Natives of this Island towards Europeans, we now

perceive with heartfelt satisfaction the hatred in some measure
gradually subsiding. Several of them are to be seen about this town
and its environs, who obtain subsistence from the charitable and
well-disposed.[23]

These groups were known as the 'tame mobs', survivors of the Moomairremener clan of the Oyster Bay nation and Panninher clan of the North
Midlands nation, which had been displaced by settlers at the Derwent
and Norfolk Plains. The best known mob traversed the River Derwent
between Risdon and Pitt Water in the summer and retired to the east
coast in winter. Between November 1815 and November 1818, some of
the women and children called at Robert Knopwood's house for food.[24] In
May 1817, when an overseer approached their camp at Sweetwater Hills,
between present-day Sorell and Orielton, intending, so he said, to have a
chat with the women, he was attacked by one of the men, 'who threw a
stone at him, which struck him violently on the mouth and staggered him'
and was then subjected to a volley of stones which dislocated his shoulder.[25]
The man who threw the first stone could have been Musquito. By then he
and his companions openly spurned manual labour, believing that permanent reparations from the British occupiers in the form of provisions were
barely sufficient payment for dispossession.[26]

When the missionary Rowland Hassall visited Hobart in March 1819
and inquired 'Why are there no natives seen in the town?' the answer
given was: 'We shoot them whenever we find them.'[27] Yet a year earlier
the *Hobart Town Gazette* had raised pertinent questions about the colonial
government's responsibility for the Aborigines:

> Are not the Aborigines of this Colony the children of our Govern-
> ment? Are we not all happy but they? And are they not miserable?
> Can they raise themselves from this sad condition? Or do they not
> claim our assistance? And shall that assistance be denied? Those who
> fancy that 'God did not make of one blood all the natives of the earth',
> must be convinced that the Natives of whatever matter formed, *can*
> be civilized, nay be Christianized. The moral Governor of the world
> will hold us accountable. The Aborigines demand our protection.[28]

Here, it seems that the newspaper's editor, Andrew Bent, was referring to the changing conditions on the frontier. In November 1818, following the killing of a sealer at Great Swanport by a large group of Oyster Bay men in reprisal for his slaughter of hundreds of swans, a detachment of the 48th Regiment was despatched to the area, where they killed twenty-two of the Oyster Bay people.[29] Four months later, in another affray with sealers at Oyster Bay, an Oyster Bay man was shot and his children abducted. In the same month, at William Stocker's cattle run at Tea Tree Brush at the Macquarie River in the eastern Midlands, stock-keepers killed an Oyster Bay clan chief. At the same time, at Russell Falls near New Norfolk, stock-keepers killed a group of Big River people, and two or three of the children orphaned in the affray were taken to Hobart.[30]

Lieutenant-Colonel William Sorell, who replaced Davey as lieutenant-governor in 1817, was horrified by these incidents. He disparaged the popular belief held even by the chaplain Robert Knopwood that the Aborigines were a 'Hostile People' who were in league to destroy the colonists and their stock. He was even more horrified by the stories of settlers and stock-keepers chasing after Aboriginal women 'for the purpose of compelling them to abandon their Children' and warned that he would punish any colonist who had 'destroyed or maltreated any of the Native people (*not strictly in Self-defence*)' (original emphasis).[31] But the threat appears to have been more about covering himself on paper than an active desire to bring the offenders to justice. Besides, Judge Advocate Atkins's ruling about Aboriginal evidence was still in place. As Magistrate James Gordon at Sorell pointed out in 1820, convict stock-keepers in his area were allowed guns and about four or five cartridges, 'to provide a defence against the natives who would otherwise murder them'.[32]

By then Governor Macquarie in Sydney had introduced a new policy of 'civilizing' the Aboriginal children who came within the sphere of colonial settlement. Sorell followed suit and ordered that all Aboriginal children living with settlers should become the responsibility of the chaplain Robert Knopwood. By 1820 at least twelve children were in his care and seven of them had been baptised.[33] But it seems that most Aboriginal children remained with settler families, and of the fifty estimated to have survived to adulthood, very few married and produced children. Even after death they could not expect release from bondage. John Shinall was 'taken in' by settlers at Pitt Water in about 1810 and died without issue on 5 April 1839. His body was decapitated and his head was preserved in a jar of fluid. It found its way to the Royal College of Surgeons in Ireland in 1845, where it was photographed in 1896 and then featured in the second edition of Henry Ling Roth's *The Aborigines of Tasmania*.[34] After a long campaign by the Tasmanian Aboriginal community in the 1980s, Shinall's head was returned home for interment in 1990. Like so many Aboriginal children abducted by settlers in other Australian colonies, most Tasmanian Aboriginal children were rarely accorded basic human rights. Even after the abolition of slavery in the British Empire, in 1833, many colonists still considered that blackness was synonymous with slavery.

Yet at the Straitsmen's settlements at Cape Barren, King, Hunter and Kangaroo islands the tyereelore were becoming the economic backbone of a new community. They fed the community by training the dogs to track down wallabies, while they climbed trees to catch possums and dived for kelp and shellfish. To keep the settlements economically viable, they dried and cured seal and kangaroo skins and made baskets and necklaces for sale in Launceston; and to keep their own traditions alive, they sang, told stories of their people and performed ceremonial dances. In 1820 about thirty Straitsmen and fifty tyereelore and their children lived in settlements scattered across the islands in eastern and western Bass Strait. But the further decline in the number of seals led the communities in the eastern Strait to develop a more intensive exploitation of mutton-birds.[35]

The mutton-bird, or short-tailed shearwater (*Puffinus tenuirostris*), inhabits the north-east coast of Siberia between June and August, flying south in October to Bass Strait and to the north, east and west coasts of Van Diemen's Land, but most particularly to the Furneaux Group. Here, the mutton-birds develop their burrow-like nests in the rookeries at the edge of the sea. During the first week of November they leave the burrows and return between 20 and 27 November to lay their eggs, which hatch the following February. The parent birds remain for eight to ten weeks rearing their young and then depart for the long journey to Siberia. The young birds follow in the first week of May. In the early nineteenth century the mutton-bird population reached several hundred million and to the Aborigines it seemed an inexhaustible supply of seasonal food. They would gather at the rookeries along the north coast of Van Diemen's Land in early December to gather mutton-bird eggs and then again in April to harvest the young birds. Mutton-birding was probably more integral to Aboriginal society than sealing, was seasonally more reliable and was exploited by all ages and both sexes. So when the Straitsmen in the eastern Strait seized upon the economic advantages of mutton-birding, they incorporated a most important aspect of Aboriginal society into their own.[36]

One of the first Straitsmen to recognise the economic potential of mutton-birding was James Munro, who became a permanent resident on Preservation Island in 1819 with four tyereelore: Dromedeenner, Woretermoteteyer, Mirnermannerme and the mainland Australian Margery Munro.[37] He sold the feathers in Launceston for down, used the oil and fat for fuel and salted the carcasses for storage against starvation in the winter months. The tyereelore then adapted their traditional technology to increase the catch. Their digging sticks, originally used to force the birds from their burrows, were converted into spits, so that several birds could be carried at once by stringing them by their beaks along the spit,

Sketch of James Munro's Home on Preservation Island. Painted by Henry Laing, 1831, Department of Prints and Drawings, British Museum, London.

which was then slung across the shoulders. By the mid 1820s 'birding' not only provided the eastern Straitsmen and the tyereelore with a degree of economic security that ensured their survival as a new community, but it also acquired a ritual significance for their children.

By the end of 1819 the Aboriginal and colonial populations had reached parity. The Aboriginal population had fallen from an estimated 7,000 to about 5,000, and the colonial population had increased to 4,350.[38] The major difference between the two population groups, however, was a marked imbalance between the sexes, with four colonial men to every colonial woman. Yet both population groups enjoyed remarkably good health. Of the colonists who had died since 1803, it seems that scurvy, misadventure, war wounds or old age were the main culprits, rather than infectious disease, in particular influenza, which did not begin to have an impact on the Aborigines or the colonists until the late 1820s. This would suggest that the population decline among the South East, Oyster Bay, Big River and North Midlands nations after 1803 was more due to settler violence than exotic disease. The two diseases they do appear to have experienced, gonorrhoea and skin complaints, the latter of which James Boyce considers may have been an extreme reaction to their acquisition of British dogs, were not life threatening, and they are known to have responded to treatment.[39]

The year 1820 marked a turning point in Tasmanian Aboriginal–colonial relations. The clans from the Oyster Bay, Big River and North Midlands nations considered that the colonial invaders were unauthorised trespassers on their hunting grounds, but they were confident that they could be controlled by forcing them to observe the protocols of seasonal access. This state of affairs could have continued, for at this stage the colonists occupied less than 15 per cent of Van Diemen's Land. Nor was there any indication from either the invaders or the Aborigines that the latter were in terminal decline. Up to 500 of them were still seen at seasonal gatherings at Oyster Bay, and groups of up to twenty were often seen in Hobart.[40] Furthermore, the emergence of creole communities on the Bass Strait islands suggested that British and Aboriginal technologies could be combined and used to new advantage.

There is other evidence of a degree of mutual acceptance. In 1820 the
surveyor Thomas Scott and the settler Charles Brown Hardwicke made
the first drawings of the Tasmanian Aborigines since British invasion in
1803. The humanity revealed in Scott's studies suggests that he had some
knowledge of who they were.[41] Indeed, it is possible they were from the
Loontitetermairrelehoinner clan of the Oyster Bay nation, whose warriors
had burnt down William Stocker's hut at the Macquarie River the year
before. Scott may have drawn the group when he visited the site a year later
and made a sketch of the new hut that the stock-keepers had built to replace
the original.[42] James Boyce considers that the hut's mud and thatched
grass construction was influenced by Aboriginal architecture and that the
kangaroo skin clothing that so many male colonists wore also indicated a
greater cultural, social and economic overlap between the two societies than
previously recognised.[43] This is borne out by the Straitsmen and tyereelore,
who wore similar clothes made from kangaroo skins, lived in similar huts,
ate similar foods, sang similar songs and spoke Aboriginal English.

William Stocker's Hut at Tea Tree Brush, Macquarie River, 1819. Thomas Scott
Sketchbook, State Library of New South Wales, Sydney.

But, if a creole society was beginning to emerge at this time, it had little real chance of becoming dominant. Even Van Diemen's Land, one of the most remote outposts of the British Empire, could not escape the social and political upheavals that beset Britain at the end of the Napoleonic Wars. The riots by unemployed soldiers in the industrial cities and the persistent demands by de-mobbed defence force officers for adequate compensation for their war service led the British government to turn to the furthest corner of its empire for a solution. In 1819 it appointed John Thomas Bigge, a former judge of the Supreme Court of Trinidad, to explore the island's economic and social potential. He recommended that retired officers and gentlemen of means should be encouraged to migrate to Van Diemen's Land, where they could be granted land and a labour force of transported felons from Britain to assist them to graze sheep and produce fine wool for the textile mills of northern England. In this structuring of society he expected that the colonial economy would be more firmly tied to the imperial economy and that colonial society would more closely reflect the class-based ideals of English society. He failed to consider the right of the Tasmanian Aborigines to their lands. He acknowledged that they still 'cherished' a 'spirit of hostility and revenge' arising from the Risdon Cove massacre, but he could not believe they would offer resistance to the unauthorised invasion of their hunting grounds by hundreds of settler families and their convict servants, let alone the hundreds of thousands of sheep they would bring with them.[44] He could not have been more mistaken.

4

Pastoral invasion, 1817–26

From the beginning of 1817, when the colonial population stood at 2,000, to 1824, when it reached 12,643, over 1,500 free settlers and their families arrived in Van Diemen's Land. They began its transformation from a creole society based on small-scale agriculture, whaling and sealing, to a largely pastoral economy based on the production of fine wool. By 1830, when the colonial population had reached 23,500, the transformation was complete. The 6,000 free settlers and their families who formed the colonial elite consisted of retired army and naval officers from the Napoleonic Wars, sons of the English, Irish and Scottish landed gentry and the sons of colonial officials from across the British Empire. As evidence of their wealth and status, they brought letters of recommendation from the Colonial Office in London to the lieutenant-governor in Van Diemen's Land suggesting that they each receive land grants of between 400 and 800 hectares and be assigned at least one convict servant. Pastoralism, the economic term for settler colonialism, ushered in a most severe dislocation of Tasmanian Aboriginal society and resulted in a major war that ended in its dispossession.

In 1823 alone, more than 1,000 land grants totalling 175,704 hectares were made to the new settlers, the largest alienation of land in a single year in the entire history of Tasmania. By 1830 nearly half a million hectares had been granted. Between 1816 and 1823 the sheep population increased from 54,600 to 200,000 and by 1830 it had reached one million, surpassing for a short time the number of sheep in New South Wales. The Midland Plain, which was the largest Aboriginal hunting ground in Trouwunna, was admirably suited to the production of fine wool and became the centre of the pastoral economy. From there the settlers and their families fanned out west along the Clyde, Ouse and Shannon rivers and east along the Oyster Bay coast, in the centre along the Liffey, Isis, Macquarie and Elizabeth rivers and north along the North and South Esk rivers. In 1826, in a second wave of pastoral expansion, the settlers pushed along the Meander River west of Launceston. The entire area became known as the Settled Districts and by 1830 comprised less than 30 per cent of the total area of the island. By then the best grazing land on the island had been alienated.[1]

Occupation proceeded 'corridor fashion', appropriating Aboriginal hunting grounds but leaving the forested areas unoccupied. In the Clyde River area, many settler families from Scotland occupied the river flats, left the ranges unoccupied and grazed their sheep in the summer on the Central Plateau to the west. In the east, settlers dotted the Oyster Bay coastline, left the low range of mountains known as the Eastern Tiers unoccupied and in summer grazed their sheep at Crown Lagoon and Stockers Bottom located in the Eastern Marshes. The Oyster Bay, Big River and North Midlands nations were forced to use the Eastern Tiers as a base for raids on settlers' huts.[2]

The Settled Districts included the lands of the Oyster Bay nation in the centre and east, the Big River nation in the west, the North Midlands nation from Campbell Town to Launceston in the north, the Ben Lomond nation on the upper reaches of the South Esk River in the north-east, and the North nation along the Meander River west of Launceston. For these nations, the sudden appearance of settlers on their lands together with vast numbers of sheep was the greatest upheaval to their lives that they had experienced. They watched in amazement as the settlers occupied their prime kangaroo hunting grounds with vast numbers of sheep, which in turn trampled along the rivers' edges where they had usually caught birds and other small animals. They saw them build substantial dwellings and use convict servants as shepherds to tend the increasingly large flocks of sheep. They also had to contend with the gradual appearance of post and rail fences, stone walls and hedges around the homesteads and an increased presence of police and military patrols to control the convicts.

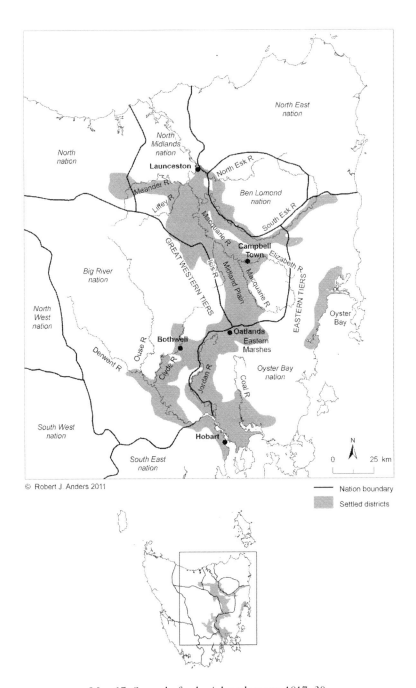

© Robert J. Anders 2011

—— Nation boundary

▓ Settled districts

Map 15 Spread of colonial settlement, 1817–30

By 1826 the settlers had occupied the heartland of Trouwunna. In this new environment the Big River and Oyster Bay nations tried to make new arrangements with them.[3]

At this stage, according to historian Sharon Morgan, most of the new settlers had 'deeply ingrained prejudices against native peoples. Englishness implied superiority; the Natives were an irrelevance.'[4] Yet in 1818 the editor of the *Hobart Town Gazette* had argued for the newly emerging humanitarian view, arising from the abolition of the slave trade in 1806, that the Tasmanian Aborigines, like the slaves, were part of 'the flesh of all nations' assigned by God and deserving of settler sympathy and support. But Australia's own 'native son', William Charles Wentworth, said that if this was the case, then the Tasmanian Aborigines were, 'if possible, still more barbarous and uncivilized than those of New South Wales', who were, he ardently believed, 'on the lowest place in the gradatory scale of the human species'. The Scottish traveller James Dixon believed that the Aborigines of both colonies were 'in the lowest scale of human beings'. Ten years later, at the height of the Black War, many of the settlers had come to the conclusion that the Tasmanian Aborigines were something akin to the 'orang-outang'.[5] It is not surprising, then, that when violent conflict broke out, in November 1823, the settlers considered that the Aborigines, rather than they themselves, were the aggressors.

In early December 1823, the *Hobart Town Gazette* reported that a couple of weeks earlier, Musquito and the Tasmanian Aborigine Black Jack had led one of the tame mobs in the murder of two stock-keepers and the wounding of another at Grindstone Bay on the east coast. A fourth stock-keeper had managed to run to his master's house and raise the alarm. The incident aroused widespread panic and was widely discussed in the press, although the reprisal massacre that Constable Adam Amos recorded in his diary was not mentioned. Four months later, in March 1824, the same mob was reported to have killed two more stock-keepers, one at the Blue Hills and the other at Salt Pan Plains on the edge of the Eastern Marshes. In July it was reported to have killed another stock-keeper at Little Swanport on the east coast.[6] A month later Musquito and Black Jack were captured with other members of the mob near the Little Swanport River and charged with murder.

This time Musquito stood trial, because the colonial authorities now took the view that Aborigines did understand English law, although they were not permitted to give evidence in their own defence. At their trial in December, Musquito and Black Jack pleaded not guilty. They were convicted by a military jury and they were hanged in February 1825.[7] No colonist was ever charged in Van Diemen's Land, let alone committed for trial, for assaulting or killing an Aborigine.

In May 1824, Lieutenant-Colonel George Arthur arrived in Hobart to succeed William Sorell as governor. He held the post for twelve years and became the colony's longest serving vice-regal appointee. From the outset he had a reputation from his previous post in British Honduras as a man of administrative vigour and an ardent opponent of slavery. But in Van Diemen's Land he had the more rigorous task of making settler colonialism work. In 1824 he simply expected that the Aborigines would voluntarily abandon their country to the settlers and joyfully accept the compensation of Christianity.[8] According to one of his biographers, M.C.I. Levy, unlike the settlers, who designated them 'the lowest order of human beings, removed but one shade from brutality', Arthur firmly believed that they were capable of 'improvement', with the helping hand of civilised and godly men. He also believed that they possessed 'a considerable amount of latent capacity' and were comparable to the 'hundreds of Irish, English and Scotch' who, until they were introduced to Christianity, were 'as wild and ignorant as they'.[9] So his brief was to promote settler colonialism *and* to civilise the Aborigines. It was some time before he realised that he had assumed a virtually impossible task.

Sir George Arthur. Drawing by Thomas Bock, State Library of New South Wales, Sydney.

In accordance with his instructions from the Colonial Office,

Arthur issued a proclamation which placed the Aborigines under the protection of British law and warned the stock-keepers on the frontier that if they continued to 'wantonly destroy' them, they would be prosecuted and brought to trial. He considered the deaths of some thirteen colonists in the previous nine months not as resistance by the Aboriginal nations against the pastoral invasion of their lands, but rather the work of individual 'civilized' Aborigines like Musquito and Kickerterpoller who had turned against the colonists. He was also convinced that other measures could be put in place to bring about their peaceful dispossession.[10]

He was in luck. In November 1824 about sixty members of the Oyster Bay tame mob, led by Kickerterpoller, arrived in Hobart in search of blankets and provisions. A month later, more than 200 North Midlands people arrived in Launceston on the same mission. Arthur hastily called a public meeting in Hobart to discuss the establishment of a 'native institution' for the children, but after rules and regulations were drawn up nothing further was done. The North Midlands clans decamped and 'were wantonly fired on by the whites' as they crossed Patersons Plains; some of their women were treated with 'indescribable brutality'. In Hobart, Kickerterpoller's tame mob was sent back to its encampment at Kangaroo Point, on the river bank opposite the town, and provisioned with food and clothing. For the next two years, the mob came and went 'as often as their convenience dictated'. Another attempt by Arthur to promote a native institution in 1825 also failed, for the colony, which had recently gained independence from New South Wales, was in economic recession and neither the settlers nor the local clergy was interested in assisting the Aborigines they had dispossessed. Rather, they considered the bushrangers a more dangerous threat to the colony's survival. Indeed, Arthur's ruthless campaign against the bushrangers between 1824 and 1826 obscured the seriousness of Aboriginal resistance.[11]

When three more colonists were speared to death in the autumn of 1826, Arthur was still convinced that individual Aborigines from the tame mob at Kangaroo Point were responsible. The capture of two of them, Jack and Black Dick, a month later, appeared to reinforce this view. So convinced was he that the two men were the last of the 'depredators' that he arranged for the chief justice, John Lewes Pedder, to appoint counsel and an interpreter on their behalf at their trial. But once again the two men were prevented from giving evidence in their own defence. Once again a military jury found them guilty and the chief justice solemnly announced that they would hang. On 16 September, the day of execution, Arthur issued a government notice which explained that hanging the two men would 'not only prevent further atrocities . . . but lead to a conciliatory line of conduct'. While some colonists thought the executions were a strange method of conciliation, others believed that they would teach the Aborigines a lesson. The tame mob got the point. They decamped from Kangaroo Point and never returned.[12]

By November the colonists had begun to wonder whether the Aborigines were teaching the lessons. Between September and November they killed six more colonists, taking the total killed for the three-year period from 1823 to thirty-six. Even though the victims were all men, mostly convict stock-keepers and shepherds, some were respectable settlers. It was the killing of George Taylor junior, a 'respectable settler' from Campbell Town in the Midlands, in mid November, whose body was found 'transfixed with many spears, and his head dreadfully shattered with blows, inflicted either with stones or waddies' that led the *Colonial Times* to demand a drastic change in policy. It advocated the immediate forcible removal of all the Aboriginal nations in the Settled Districts to an island in Bass Strait. The *Times* now believed that it was impossible to negotiate with them because they appeared to have neither a king nor a system of government with courts to dispense justice. On the other hand, the paper admitted that they did have a leader, Kickerterpoller. But he was a dangerous rebel who had abandoned his previous life as a 'voluntary member of colonial society' (a strange way to describe child abduction).[13]

The idea of forcible removal seems to have been adopted from the United States, where, as Sharon Morgan has pointed out, between 1815 and 1824 a 'white supremacist' policy of removing Native Americans from their land had begun to take shape.[14] But Arthur adopted another approach—their forcible surrender. On 29 November he issued a government notice that set out the legal conditions whereby the colonists could kill Aborigines when they attacked settlers and their property. It was based on the despatch that the Colonial Office had given Governor Ralph Darling en route to New

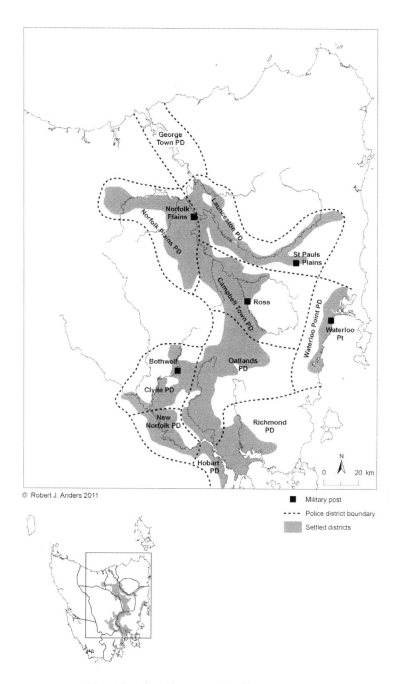

© Robert J. Anders 2011

■ Military post
- - - Police district boundary
▨ Settled districts

Map 16 Police districts and military posts, 1826

South Wales in 1825, which stated that when Aborigines 'made hostile incursions for the purpose of plunder, when such disturbances could not be prevented or allayed by less rigorous means, to oppose force by force and to repel such aggressions in the same as if they had proceeded from subjects of an accredited State'.[15] Rather than being treated as 'common criminals', like the four Aborigines who had already been hanged for murder, they were now considered as 'open enemies' of the colonial state.

The notice considered that particular Aboriginal leaders were responsible for the atrocities and their capture was 'of the first importance'. But it also accorded the colonists the right to arm and join the military to drive off with force any Aborigine who was about to attack, rob or murder them or about to commit a felony. Further:

> When a felony has been committed, any person who witnesses it may immediately raise his neighbours and pursue the felons, and the pursuers may justify the use of all such means as a constable might use. If they overtake the parties, they should bid or signify to them to surrender; if they resist, or attempt to resist, the persons pursuing may use such force as is necessary; and if the pursued fly, and cannot otherwise be taken, the pursuers may then use similar means.[16]

Arthur was confident the measures would work because he was in the process of expanding the number of police districts in the Settled Districts from five to nine and increasing the number of field police so that they could support the magistrates in containing convict unrest and Aboriginal insurgency. He also established military posts at Bothwell on the Clyde River, at Ross Bridge in the central Midlands, at present-day Longford in the north-west, at St Pauls Plains in the north-east, and at Waterloo Point on the east coast near present-day Swansea. With these new measures, Arthur was confident that the settlers' demands for assistance to expel Aboriginal insurgents or force their surrender could now be met.[17]

The editor of the *Colonial Times* was in no doubt that the government notice was tantamount to a declaration of war on the Aborigines in the

Settled Districts. 'With the murder of a Colonist still fresh in their memory, the people will kill, destroy, and if possible, exterminate every black in the island, at least so many as they fall in with.'[18]

The editor's prediction was much closer to the truth than Arthur perhaps intended. Or was it? In placing fifty-five more troops in the field, Arthur, as an experienced army officer, must have known that such an outcome was highly likely. The meaning and intention of the government notice of 29 November 1826 has been interpreted by historians in very different ways. But a close examination of its effects over the following eighteen months suggests that Arthur's intention was to use extreme measures and force the Aborigines in the Settled Districts to surrender. Then, as he later pointed out, he intended to negotiate with their chiefs to relocate them to a designated reserve in the north-east.[19] What he did not expect was that the Big River, Oyster Bay, North Midlands and North nations would employ successful guerilla tactics to keep the settlers and the army at bay. But it would come at a huge cost.

PART II

WAR
1826–31

5

Arthur's war, 1826–28

The government notice was carried into immediate effect. On the morning of Friday 8 December 1826, the Kangaroo Point mob led by Kickerterpoller appeared near Black Charlies Sugarloaf, just off today's Tasman Highway at Orielton, and called at Bank Hill farm, owned by Alexander Laing, the chief district constable at Sorell. They accosted the overseer, Robert Grimes, who gave them some bread. They appear to have remained quiet for about two hours, and then Kickerterpoller again accosted Grimes and said, 'You white bugger, give me some more bread, and fry some mutton for us'. Grimes,

> being afraid of them, commenced, and baked a peck [about 4 kilo-grams] or more of flour into bread, and cooked three-fourths of a sheep; they devoured the whole, and, in the afternoon, went out to catch opossums. On their return from the hunt, [Kickerterpoller] came to the hut by himself, and ordered Grimes to get some more bread and mutton ready by next morning.[1]

The rations were not required. While the mob was out hunting, Grimes had somehow managed to get word to the nearby town of Sorell. Around midnight, Laing and a detachment of four soldiers of the 40th Regiment arrived at Grimes's hut and just before daybreak they 'proceeded to the spot where [Kickerterpoller] and his party lay, and got upon them unperceived. They secured [Kickerterpoller] and his companions, consisting of four black men, four women, and one male child; who made no resistance.'

The *Colonial Times* reported that the 'natives were then conducted to Sorell Gaol, where they now remain'.[2]

This incident and the way it was reported set the parameters for how the war was conducted and reported over the next two years. Every time a colonist was harassed or killed by the Aborigines, Kickerterpoller would usually be cited as the ringleader, and a magistrate would authorise a joint police and military search party, assisted by armed stock-keepers and sometimes by settlers, to set off in pursuit.[3] They would surround an Aboriginal camp at night and then at daybreak shoot at the men, women and children as they lay sleeping. Sometimes, as in the incident near Bank Hill farm, in which fourteen Aborigines were killed, the party would also capture some of them. But they would neglect to officially report the death toll. In these cases newspaper reports sometimes filled in the gaps left in the official record. On other occasions, such as the reprisal that followed the killings of two shepherds at Mount Augustus near Campbell Town in April 1827, the incident would be reported in the press as a daylight ambush by a large group of Aboriginal men bristling with spears and stones forcing the small British reprisal party to shoot in self-defence, leaving 'some' Aboriginal men 'wounded' before the rest of them 'ran away', leaving behind a cache of spears and waddies and their dogs, as well as items belonging to the dead shepherds, all of which the British would carry back in triumph to the magistrate.[4] But later evidence showed that the Mount Augustus incident, at least, was a well-planned dawn attack on an undefended Aboriginal camp, in which up to forty Aboriginal men, women and children were killed.[5]

In other incidents, such as the eighteen-day campaign in June 1827 against the Pallittorre clan from the North nation in the Meander River region, including Laycock Falls, Quamby Bluff and Quamby Brook, the military would make the stock-keepers take responsibility for firing at undefended Aborigines, although it is likely that the soldiers had fired the first shots.[6]

The diverging accounts of such incidents suggest that there was considerable uncertainty on the part of the magistrates, the police, the military, the stock-keepers and the settlers about their legal right to shoot at large numbers of undefended Aborigines, although it does not appear to have stopped them. The government notice placed the military under the orders of the civil power, that is, the magistrates rather than the military officers, and it seems to have led to confusion in the field.[7]

Let us return to the incident at Bank Hill farm on 9 December 1826, when fourteen Oyster Bay Aborigines were killed and nine others including Kickerterpoller were captured and lodged in the Sorell gaol. Kickerterpoller was a problem for Lieutenant-Governor George Arthur. As pointed out in Chapter 3, he had grown up in the Birch family, a 'Christian household', and worked on their property, Duck Holes, at the Coal River. If, as the colonists expected, he were charged with the murder of John Guinea, which he was alleged to have perpetrated on 7 November 1826, then, by virtue of his Christian baptism, it could be argued by his lawyer that he should give evidence in court in his own defence. There is some suggestion that Arthur was made aware of the possibility. According to Kickerterpoller's biographer, his foster-mother, Sarah Birch, who had since become Mrs Edmund Hodgson, could have pleaded his case before the lieutenant-governor.[8] She may have indicated that she would engage Joseph Tice Gellibrand, Arthur's recently sacked attorney-general and the most experienced barrister in the colony, to defend Kickerterpoller if the case were brought to court. Arthur may have known that, in capturing Kickerterpoller and his nine compatriots, Chief District Constable Laing and the party of soldiers had killed fourteen others. This was not the kind of information that Arthur wanted known in an open court, let alone by his superiors in London. Whatever the reason, he decided not to proceed with any of the possible charges against Kickerterpoller and at the end of January 1827 ordered his release along with his nine compatriots.[9]

During the summer of 1826–27, the clans of the Big River, Oyster Bay and North Midlands nations made their intentions clear. They wanted the settlers and their sheep and cattle to vacate their kangaroo hunting grounds. In late January 1827, on the Central Plateau on the western border of the Settled Districts, a group of men from a Big River clan, possibly led by Montpeliater, speared stock-keeper George Roberts. As he lay dying they told him that they would sooner or later murder every white man on the island.[10] In early February, on the eastern side of the Settled Districts at St Pauls Plains, a group of men from an Oyster Bay clan, possibly led by Mannalargenna, speared two stock-keepers working for settler William Talbot, one of whom is believed to have later died of his wounds. Two weeks later the same clan killed another stock-keeper at Fingal. In the meantime, at Norfolk Plains, another group of men from a clan of the North Midlands nation and possibly led by Umarrah speared two stock-keepers, Abraham Spence and John Fairley, who died of their wounds.[11] From this time, these Aboriginal chiefs were becoming known to the settlers and the press.

By the end of February 1827, Arthur had established 'several of the different outposts of military and field police', which the *Hobart Town Gazette* believed would 'effectively prevent the future attacks of the natives upon the stock-keepers in the remote parts'.[12] But some settlers preferred to take the law into their own hands. Michael Steel, a settler at Macquarie Plains, told his brother, 'We fell in with [Aborigines] and poured strong fire into them and killed their leader and one more . . . [H]ad the country been even and clear we should have killed or taken the whole of them.'[13] In other cases, joint action was more effective. In March, at Great Swanport, now Swansea, on the east coast, when a group of Oyster Bay men, possibly led by Tongerlongter, killed a servant of settler James Buxton, a 'party' was 'sent out' after them, and that night they killed several Aborigines at their camp.[14] On 12 April, when another group of Oyster Bay Aborigines killed two convict servants, Thomas Rawling and Edward Green, assigned to settler Walter Davidson on his property at the Elizabeth River not far from Campbell Town, near Mount Augustus, a 'score of armed men, Constables, Soldiers and Civilians and . . . assigned Servants . . . fell in with the Natives when they were going to their Breakfast. They fired volley after volley in among the Blackfellows, they reported killing some two score.'[15] The *Hobart Town Gazette* reported that Kickerterpoller was among 'the fallen from persons who have seen the body and recognized his features, particularly a remarkable scar on his forehead'.[16] But somehow Kickerterpoller managed to escape. Perhaps he had not been there at all. Then, in early May, when Andrew Gatehouse's stock-keeper, Richard Addey, was killed by another group of Oyster Bay men at Great Swanport, Gatehouse set off with a party of field police, soldiers, neighbouring settlers and stock-keepers, including James Gumm, in search of the culprits. Many decades later, Gumm told James Bonwick that the party met Douglas Evans, who said that a large group of Aborigines were camped for the night in the gully by Sally Peak, 10 kilometres from Bushy Plains, on the border of Prossers Plains:

> They proceeded stealthily as they neared the spot; and, agreeing upon a signal, moved quietly in couples, until they had surrounded the sleepers. The whistle of the leader was sounded and volley after volley of ball cartridge was poured in upon the dark groups surrounding the little camp fires. The number slain was considerable.[17]

These kinds of reprisal killings appear to have aroused alarm among some settlers who did not believe that undefended Aborigines should be shot down in such numbers. The *Colonial Times* also acknowledged that Aborigines had legitimate grounds for bearing animosity towards the settlers, 'when it is remembered that we have taken possession of their country, and driven them from their native land'. But the editor reassured his readers:

> when we consider that they made no use of it, and their being in a state of nature, they knew no rights, but the rights of nature, we cannot so decidedly condemn the action of taking possession of their country ... where there are no laws to govern the human actions, the only right is vested in power, i.e. strength ... the right of possession always lies in the strongest to possess ... we may fairly consider, that as the Aborigines know no other ... there is less injustice in driving them from their country than at first view may appear.[18]

This view appears to have been widely shared by the settlers, for it was repeated in a host of settler tracts and underpinned the establishment of new settler colonies on the Australian mainland over the next decade.

The dramatic increase in Aboriginal resistance in the Settled Districts at this time could have been provoked by a range of lethal factors. First was

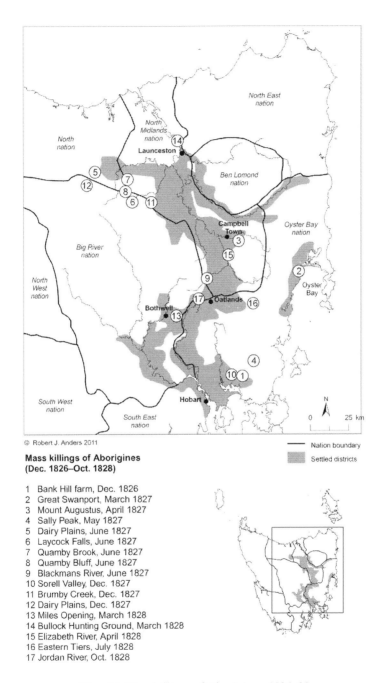

© Robert J. Anders 2011

Mass killings of Aborigines
(Dec. 1826–Oct. 1828)

—— Nation boundary

▨ Settled districts

1   Bank Hill farm, Dec. 1826
2   Great Swanport, March 1827
3   Mount Augustus, April 1827
4   Sally Peak, May 1827
5   Dairy Plains, June 1827
6   Laycock Falls, June 1827
7   Quamby Brook, June 1827
8   Quamby Bluff, June 1827
9   Blackmans River, June 1827
10 Sorell Valley, Dec. 1827
11 Brumby Creek, Dec. 1827
12 Dairy Plains, Dec. 1827
13 Miles Opening, March 1828
14 Bullock Hunting Ground, March 1828
15 Elizabeth River, April 1828
16 Eastern Tiers, July 1828
17 Jordan River, Oct. 1828

Map 17 Mass killings of Aborigines, 1826–28

the arrival of more than 3,000 convicts and settlers in the colony in 1826, the largest number in any year since 1803. The following year many of the new settlers began to occupy their land grants in the Campbell Town district and some of them started to plant hedges. 'Old hands' noted that these new properties were located on well-known Aboriginal hunting grounds and that the hedges would eventually impede Aboriginal access. Then, in May 1827, during unseasonably dry, cold weather, the first major epidemic of catarrh, more likely influenza, was reported in the colony and it probably affected some of the Oyster Bay people. Finally, the beginning of military patrols in the region appears to have provoked Aboriginal retaliation. From this time, the colonists noted that the Oyster Bay and Big River clans were often hungry, and they were increasingly reported plundering huts for bread, flour, tea and blankets, but not salted meat.[19]

In June 1827, at the Western Marshes, 70 kilometres west of Launceston, the colonists mounted a campaign against the Pallittorre clan from the North nation. The region comprised large cattle runs leased by absentee landlords in Hobart and Launceston and managed by experienced stockmen, who were armed and on horseback. Some of them had Aboriginal women as their sexual partners and all of them had interaction of some kind with the Pallittorre.[20] Violent conflict had broken out between the two groups in December 1825, and by June 1827 it was known that more than thirty Pallittorre men had been killed in at least four incidents but that no stockman had lost his life.[21]

On Tuesday 12 June 1827, a group of about 200 Pallittorre men surrounded and ransacked David Gibson's stock hut at Dairy Plains in the Western Marshes and attempted to spear the overseer, Thomas Baker, apparently in retaliation for his either killing or abducting an Aboriginal woman. Baker then rode 2 miles to the adjoining cattle run and sought assistance from another overseer, James Cubit, and Field Constable Thomas Williams. The next night they tracked the Pallittorre to their camp and at dawn the following day they 'shot nine of them'. In the official report of this incident, Baker admitted that 'one native may have been shot in pursuit'.[22]

A week later, the police magistrate at Launceston sent corporals John Shiners and James Lingen from the military post at Norfolk Plains to

Gibson's hut to assist Williams and Baker and two assigned servants, William White and Henry Smith. They did not have long to wait.

About three o'clock on a cold, wet Saturday, 23 June, the six men were in the hut when Smith heard a coo-ee. Baker went out and saw John Hurling, an assigned convict servant to T.C. Simpson, running towards them. He was wearing only his shirt and carried his trousers. He told them that he had run 3 miles [5 kilometres] across the flooded plain from Simpson's stock hut, where the overseer, William Knight, had been brutally murdered by about thirty Pallittorre men who had then plundered the stock hut of every moveable item and had burst open several bags of wheat and salt, scattering the contents in all directions and yelling: '*Rugga, rugga*', 'go away, go away'. Having viewed Knight's body, Smith and Hurling then set off for Launceston to alert the authorities. The following day, Shiners, Lingen, Williams and Baker sought help from nearby settler Thomas Ritchie's men and, having been joined by James Cubit and William White, they set off in pursuit. At about two in the afternoon, Shiners said that he noticed smoke from a fire which he judged to be near Laycock Falls, now known as Liffey Falls, at the base of Quamby Bluff, and by the end of the day the party had located the Pallittorre sitting around six campfires. That night the party quietly surrounded the camp, planning to attack at dawn, so, Shiners said, they could capture the culprits. But, just as they were about to commence the operation, the Pallittorre were alerted by their dogs and 'they ran away'. Shiners said his party set off in pursuit. He later admitted that 'three of their guns went off' and that one of the Pallittorre may have been wounded by a shot fired by one of the stock-keepers. Constable Williams also later said that 'Baker attempted to fire, but that his pistol flashed in the pan', that is, the gunpowder burnt without making an explosion in the chamber to fire the bullet.[23] Nevertheless, it seems to have hit the target because the *Colonial Times* gave a different account of the incident:

> The people over the second Western Tier have killed an immense
> quantity of blacks this last week, in consequence of their having
> murdered Mr. Simpson's stock-keeper, they were surrounded whilst

sitting around their fires when the soldiers and others fired at them about 30 yards distant. They report there must have been about 60 of them killed and wounded.[24]

The Pallittorre struck back by killing one of William Field's stock-keepers near Quamby Bluff, suggesting that he had also been part of the killing party a day or so before. Once again the two soldiers and Constable Williams, assisted by two stock-keepers, probably Baker and Cubit, set off in pursuit and found the Pallittorre's camp at Quamby Brook; in the ensuing attack, Shiners acknowledged that 'some natives were perhaps wounded'. According to the *Colonial Times*, however, 'The Military instantly pursued the blacks—brought home numerous trophies, such as spears, waddies, tomahawks, muskets, blankets—killed upwards of 30 dogs, and as the report says, nearly as many natives, but this is not a positive fact'.[25]

Seven days later, another group of Pallittorre appeared at Quamby Bluff, robbed settler William Widowson's stock hut of flour and tea and destroyed everything they could not take away. Then, a few hours later, they killed two shepherds, one employed by Widowson, and the other, John Smith, employed by settler Abraham Walker. All of these men were known to have 'interfered with' Aboriginal women. According to the *Colonial Times*, another of Widowson's men got his gun and succeeded in driving them away. Once again Corporal Shiners and his party followed them and this time they 'killed nine or ten' Pallittorre. A few days later, the Pallittorre were reported to have left the area.[26] In eighteen days, Shiners and his party appear to have killed at least 100 Pallittorre in savage acts of reprisal for the killing of three stockmen.

At the same time, Kickerterpoller and his mob were alleged to be committing 'more ravages in the interior'. The *Colonial Times* reported that his 'horde', of 'about 100 in number', had attacked two men who were splitting rails near Michael Howes Marsh at the Western Table Mountain. They both escaped and a search was afterwards 'made for the tribe but without effect'. The following morning at Blackmans River, Kicker-terpoller's mob attacked two sawyers; one got away and the other was severely wounded. This time, Mr Bennett, the chief district constable, and

Lieutenant Travers and some soldiers, as well as the settler Mr Lackey and some of his men, 'fell in with them', but they fled precipitously, 'leaving behind upwards of 300 waddies, 3 spears and many dogs. The party shot the dogs and burned the waddies.' It is hard to believe that some of Kick-erterpoller's mob did not share the same fate, for their numbers were noticeably depleted immediately afterwards, and four months later in reprisal they killed Constable Bennett.[27]

In late July, along the Clyde and Shannon rivers, a group of Big River men plundered Captain Wood's hut, chased a settler, Mr Holmes, who was on horseback, for a whole day and then wounded two sawyers working for Captain Wilson at Salt Pan Plains. In each case detachments of the 40th Regiment set off for the Great Western Tiers in pursuit, yet the outcomes were not recorded.[28] But if they matched the earlier events at the Meander River, then one can only assume that the settlers did not return until they had 'dispersed' their prey. If these incidents are added to the massacres of the Oyster Bay people in March, April and May and the Pallittorre people in June, it would appear that more than 200 Aborigines were killed in the Settled Districts in the eight months between 1 December 1826 and 31 July 1827 in reprisal for their killing fifteen colonists.[29] Arthur's aggressive measures, it seems, were making deep inroads into the popula-tions of the Big River, North and Oyster Bay nations.

That winter, during a lull in the fighting, Arthur visited every magis-trate in the Settled Districts to clarify their responsibilities. Some of them, it appears, had viewed the government notice with alarm and were unwilling to authorise violent measures. But Arthur reassured them. He told them that when Aborigines attacked, they had to take 'prompt and decisive steps . . . to repel the violence of these ignorant people'.[30]

Although the Big River nation resumed its attacks on settlers and their property in the Clyde River area in September, no killings of Aborigines or colonists were reported across the Settled Districts until the second week of November. Then, the *Hobart Town Courier* reported that at Pitt Water:

> Field Police fell in with 150 Natives who attacked them with Stones,
> one of which struck Rogers a blow to the head. The Field Police

expended 17 rounds of ball cartridges and killed two of the dogs, but are not certain whether any of the natives were hurt, on fixing their bayonets and charging, the natives retreated.[31]

One hundred and twenty-one years later, local historian Roy Bridges said that on this occasion the Oyster Bay people 'were chased by Chief District Constable Laing and his men up the Sorell Valley, overtaken, and destroyed toward the head-waters of the valley'.[32]

In the same week, the Pallittorre returned to the Meander River, where they speared three more stockmen, clubbed three to death at Western Lagoon near Brumby Creek and then killed a son of well-known settler Richard Dry. In retaliation, the police magistrates at Launceston and Norfolk Plains sent a party of soldiers and field police to patrol the left bank of the Meander River and another to patrol the left bank of the Tamar River, after which they were to cross over to the right bank of the Meander. In December they appear to have joined forces at the junction of Brumby Creek and the Lake River, where they killed a number of Pallittorre.[33] But the Pallittorre would not surrender. A few days later they were alleged to have attacked a group of settler Thomas Ritchie's stockmen who were droving eleven pairs of oxen near Dairy Plains on the road from Launceston to Circular Head. In this case, the Pallittorre were 'severely handled'.[34]

Following the killing of Richard Dry's son, sixty-eight settlers in the northern district signed a petition to Arthur, requesting that he 'adopt such measures as may be considered expedient for the purpose of putting a stop to the horrible murders and outrages'.[35] Arthur appointed twenty-six additional field police to assist the magistrates and deployed fifty-five more soldiers from the 40th Regiment and the New South Wales Royal Veteran Company to strengthen the military posts at Ross Bridge, Norfolk Plains and St Pauls Plains. He reassured the settlers that the government notice of 29 November 1826 had given the magistrates 'large scope for the exercise of their authority' and thus they had been 'thereby relieved from the doubts and apprehension which they may otherwise have entertained of the lengths to which they would be justified in going to repel the irruptions of the Aborigines'.[36]

The settler George Hobler at Patersons Plains south-east of Launceston was under no illusion about the seriousness of the situation. A few days later, after one of his servants was speared by men from the North Midlands nation, he wrote in his diary: 'I have armed four men who I hope will get sight of their night fires and slaughter them as they lie around it.' By the end of the year, magistrate Thomas Anstey at Oatlands feared that the Aborigines had devised a uniform plan of attack against the settlers.[37]

Between 1 September 1827 and 30 March 1828, at least seventy Aboriginal attacks were reported across the Settled Districts in which twenty colonists lost their lives.[38] But there is no record of how many Aborigines were killed. Yet for the first time Arthur had some intelligence of the frontier and found that the Aborigines were more interested in plundering huts for food than in killing colonists. For example, in the period from 1 December 1827 to 19 March 1828 the settlers in the Clyde police district reported twenty attacks from two Big River clans. They told of groups of six, twelve, twenty and forty Big River men harassing and spearing lone stockmen, plundering stock huts for flour, digging up potatoes and turnips from settlers' gardens, burning other crops and haystacks and setting fire to huts. They believed there were large numbers of Big River people because at least one stockman reported finding '50–60 native huts erected at the junction of the Ouse and Shannon Rivers' that could shelter between 100 and 300 Big River people, and at the beginning of the summer at least 500 Big River people were seen in the same area.[39] Some also believed that particular clans could be identified. For example, Captain William Clark, a retired army officer and a leading settler at the Clyde River, said that one group of twelve men were from the 'Hobart Town tribe', which spoke a little English. This could have been Kickerterpoller's mob, which had numbered sixty people only a few weeks earlier when he led the attack against two stock-keepers at Russell Falls in the Derwent Valley and was captured shortly after.[40] Yet of the twenty colonists killed in the Settled Districts in this period only three were from the Clyde police district. This suggests that the police and military parties in this region were quite effective in 'dispersing' the Big River clans and Kickerterpoller's mob.

But sometimes the settlers and their stock-keepers took their own revenge. On 4 March 1828 a group of about twenty Big River men ambushed settler John Franks and his stockman William Walker while they were droving cattle near Miles Opening on the Aboriginal road between Bothwell and Jericho. The Big River men then killed Walker with spears and waddies and wounded both men's horses. After seeking assistance from the men at Captain Wood's farm, Franks wrote to the colonial secretary in Hobart about Walker's horrible death and his own miraculous escape. The letter and the report of the inquest into Walker's death were published over two weeks in the *Hobart Town Courier.* But it did not report the aftermath. When G.A. Robinson travelled through the area three years later, he was told by settler Robert Barr that, in reprisal, a group of stockmen had 'killed seventeen natives; that they had first killed seven and they then followed them to the lagoon [beyond Miles Opening] and killed ten more. The natives could not get away.'[41]

Reprisal parties were also reporting their successes in other parts of the Settled Districts. Along the Tamar River in mid March, in response to the killing of a stock-keeper, 'a party of volunteers came up with the murderers at Bullock Hunting Ground, where 4 men, 9 women and a child of the Black people were killed'.[42] Two days later, after a group of Oyster Bay men killed three stock-keepers in three hit and run attacks near Ross on the Midland Plain, 'several parties went after them. One party overtook them and killed five.'[43] Then, on 2 April, in the ranges behind the Elizabeth River, the same group of Oyster Bay men killed stock-keeper Henry Beames. The magistrate at Campbell Town, James Simpson, ordered a party of field police and soldiers from the 40th Regiment to find the culprits. They were joined by some stock-keepers. In his report to the colonial secretary, Simpson said that 'it is believed that 17 Aborigines were slaughtered'.[44] Two days later a clan from the Ben Lomond nation chased one of John Batman's stock-keepers from a favoured hunting ground at the Ben Lomond Rivulet. With four of his men, Batman set out in pursuit and was joined the next day by two soldiers and three field police. At daybreak the following morning Batman found the clan asleep at its camp. With his own men he crept on his hands and knees to within 20 metres of the camp before the Aborigines noticed his presence. After an exchange of spears and gunfire, the clan escaped, leaving one man wounded and Batman in possession of a sixteen-year-old boy, who escaped the following day. A few days later the same clan killed a stockman at the River Nile.[45]

Arthur now took stock of the situation. In the sixteen months since the government notice of 29 November 1826 he knew that at least forty-three male colonists in the Settled Districts had been reported killed, even if he did not know that, in response, an estimated 350 Aborigines had been killed. He certainly believed that the Aborigines' numbers had been dramatically reduced, because he was expecting them to surrender, in the same way as the Wiradjuri nation had done following a decisive military campaign in Bathurst in New South Wales in 1824.[46]

But where would they go? To hunt them from the island altogether, he believed, would only aggravate their injuries:

> They already complain that the white people have taken posses-
> sion of their country, encroached upon their hunting grounds, and
> destroyed their natural food, the kangaroo; and they doubtless
> would be exasperated to the last degree to be banished altogether
> from their favourite haunts; and as they would be ill-disposed to
> receive instruction from their oppressors, any attempt to civilize
> them, under such circumstances, must consequently fail.[47]

In January 1828 the convict adventurer Jorgen Jorgenson, who had recently travelled across the Central Plateau, had proposed to Arthur that 8,500 hectares in that region should be set aside for the Big River people because it contained the best kangaroo hunting grounds in the colony and it could be used as a 'check' on their entering the Settled Districts.[48] But Arthur had another plan—to establish a reserve in the north-east region of the island. It was located well away from the Settled Districts, and he believed that, isolated from the settlers, the Aborigines could be 'civilized' and 'Chris-tianized'. The proposal was based on colonial policy in the British colonies in South Africa and in Canada, where special areas had been set aside to 'civilize' indigenous populations. He knew from Archdeacon Scott in New

South Wales that 'civilizing' Aborigines in defined locations outside their own country was alien to their cultural beliefs and practices, but he believed:

> It is but justice to make the attempt, for, not withstanding the clamour and urgent appeals which are now made to me for the adoption of harsh measures, I cannot divest myself of the consideration that all aggression originated with the white inhabitants, and that therefore much ought to be endured in return before the blacks are treated as an open and accredited enemy by the government.[49]

On 19 April 1828 he issued a proclamation that divided the island into two parts—one for the settlers, the other for the Aborigines. He appears to have taken this step in the belief that so many Aborigines had been killed in the Settled Districts that the remainder could be 'induced by peaceful means to depart'. But he warned them that should they resist they would 'be expelled by force'. By these 'prompt and temporary measures' he expected to open negotiations with 'certain chiefs of aboriginal tribes' with a view to their civilisation and 'leading them to habits of labour, industry and settled life'.[50]

The idea of negotiating with 'certain chiefs' and perhaps 'entering into some kind of treaty' had already been suggested by the Quaker settler W.G. Walker.[51] There is some evidence that Arthur had Kickerterpoller in mind to act as an emissary to the Aboriginal chiefs in the Settled Districts. Arthur wanted them to understand that they could pass through the Settled Districts on a seasonal basis if they applied directly to him for a pass, probably in the form of a brass neck plate.[52] It is known that Arthur had a meeting with Kickerterpoller sometime after his recapture in November 1827, without any firm conclusions being reached.[53] Perhaps he had another chief, Umarrah, from the North Midlands nation, in mind. But by the time Umarrah was captured in November 1828, it was too late. Martial law had been declared.

By the end of April 1828 Arthur had deployed nearly 300 troops from the 40th and 57th regiments at fourteen military posts located along the frontiers and in the heartland of the Settled Districts. Towards the end of

May he told Governor Darling in Sydney that the military presence had 'put a temporary stop' to Aboriginal attacks, although he admitted that the Aborigines were not usually in the area at that time of year.[54]

Had Arthur met with chiefs from the North Midlands, Oyster Bay and Big River nations, such as Umarrah, Mannalargenna, Tongerlongter, Petelega and Montpeliater, and entered into negotiations with them about their relocation to the north-east and for seasonal passage through the Settled Districts, it is possible that some agreement could have been made. But from the chiefs' perspective that outcome was highly unlikely. They could see that they were being driven out of their country by heavily armed military patrols and field police. Nor had Arthur promised them genuine access to seasonal food sources and the fulfilment of their cere-monial obligations. Arthur, it seems, had overplayed his military strength.

He also had to contend with the press.[55] Even James Ross, the editor of the *Hobart Town Courier*, the newspaper most supportive of Arthur, was opposed to the division of the colony into two parts. Like Andrew Bent, his counterpart at the *Colonial Times*, Ross believed that the situation in Van Diemen's Land was similar to that in the United States following the War of Independence. There, the settlers in states like Georgia had solved the 'problem' of occupying Native American land by forcibly removing the original owners to the 'wilderness' on the other side of the Mississippi River. Ross believed that the equivalent location for the Tasmanian Aborigines was not in the north-eastern part of Van Diemen's Land but on an island in Bass Strait. The *Colonial Times* agreed. Van Diemen's Land was simply too small, the editor argued, to support two different cultural groups, and the best solution was to remove all the Aborigines to an island in Bass Strait. The *Colonial Advocate and VDL Intelligencer* went even further: 'Shall the sons of the greatest empire in the world give way before a body of savages', it thundered, 'after having successfully repulsed the disciplined armies of all France? ... It is no vain and idle theory which dictates the removal of the blacks.'[56]

Nor was the Colonial Office of much assistance. It agreed that the Aborigines had absurd ideas about their rights over the country in com-parison with those of the settlers, but offered no real advice about how to peacefully resolve the issue. So Arthur had to confront the problem alone. He recognised that unless some Aboriginal rights were acknowledged they could not be expected to peacefully relocate to a designated area, and that unless the matter was resolved equitably in Van Diemen's Land the problem would be repeated in future settler colonies on the Australian mainland.[57]

That winter few Aborigines appeared in the Settled Districts, 'except in two or three instances, when they were immediately driven back by the military parties'.[58] This included the killing in July of at least sixteen undefended Oyster Bay people at their encampment in the Eastern Tiers by a detachment of the 40th Regiment.[59] Arthur then negotiated with Governor Darling in Sydney to keep more detachments of the 40th Regiment in the colony until 'fresh Troops had arrived from England'.[60] But if he was hopeful that an Aboriginal chief would approach a military post waving a white flag and requesting a meeting with him, he was mistaken.

That spring all hell broke loose. Between 22 August and 29 October, the Oyster Bay and Big River clans launched attacks on stock huts in the Eastern Marshes, Pitt Water, the Midlands and the Clyde River, and for the first time the Ben Lomond and North clans razed stock huts along the Nile River in the east and the Meander River in the west. In all there were thirty-nine recorded attacks, about one every two days, in which fifteen colonists were killed. But it is not known how many Aborigines were killed in the four known reprisal attacks by groups of colonists. Not even John Batman's capture of two Aboriginal boys at Break O'Day River in late August and of two young men, four women and five children of the Ben Lomond nation near George Meredith's farm at Moulting Lagoon at North Oyster Bay early in September calmed the panic.[61]

A month later, the war reached a crisis. On 9 October twenty Oyster Bay warriors killed two women, Anne Geary and Mrs Gough, and two of Mrs Gough's children near the source of the Jordan River at Lake Tiberias. When confronted by the warriors, Mrs Gough had fallen on her knees and begged them to 'spare the lives of my picaninnies'. But one of the warriors reportedly replied, 'No you White Bitch, we'll kill you all'. Two weeks later they killed the fourteen-year-old daughter of settler Mrs Langford, near Green Ponds.[62] This was the first time that the Oyster Bay people had

killed white women and their children. It was later believed that the awful
crime was in response to Anne Geary's partner, a stockman, having killed
some Aboriginal women and his having provocatively located his stock
hut adjacent to a well-known Aboriginal campsite on the northern shore
of Lake Tiberias.[63] Even though a reprisal party managed to track down
some of the warriors and avenge their atrocity by killing and wounding 'a
considerable number', Thomas Anstey, the police magistrate at Oatlands,
considered that: 'The natives have uttered their war whoop, and that it is to
be a war of extermination even of defenceless women and children. Their
disposition', he said to Arthur, 'is nearer to the cold malignity of a wicked
spirit than to the frailty and passion of a man'.[64] By then, more than sixty-
one colonists had been killed since the government notice of November
1826.

Arthur quickly sent a further sixty-eight soldiers to augment six of the
busiest military posts in the area, but he must have realised that the settlers
were now expecting more drastic measures.[65] At the end of October he
called a meeting of the Executive Council, comprising himself, the chief
justice and the colonial treasurer, to determine what to do next. They agreed
with Anstey's view that the 'outrages of the aboriginal Natives amount to
a complete declaration of hostilities against the settlers generally'. They
interviewed two magistrates from Pitt Water, who told them that it was
virtually impossible 'to apprehend the Natives with any prospect of success
after the commission of a crime amenable to the law of the realm' and that
no person 'could be found who would venture to approach' the Aborigines
alone. They then perused Bathurst's despatch of July 1825 which authorised
the use of force to repel Aboriginal aggression 'as if they had proceeded
from subjects of an accredited state'. The council advised Arthur to issue a
proclamation of martial law and regretted that it had not occurred to them
to suggest it in April.[66]

But their deliberations did not include making an estimate of the
number of Aborigines killed in the Settled Districts since the government
notice of 29 November 1826. Had they known that at least 400 of them had
been killed, they might have taken a different view of the situation (see
Table 2 in Chapter 9).

On 1 November Arthur declared martial law against the Aborigines in the Settled Districts. Martial law was that final power colonial governors could impose upon dissidents under their jurisdiction who were perceived to be engaged in an act of rebellion. In this case, martial law was tantamount to a declaration of total war. As Solicitor-General Alfred Stephen pointed out, 'the effect of the proclamation [was] to place the aborigines, within the prescribed footing of open enemies of the King, in a state of actual warfare against him'.[67] Arthur explained to secretary of state for the colonies, Sir George Murray, in London that he hoped that 'terror may have the effect which no proffered measures of conciliation have been capable of inducing!'[68] The military, though still under the command of the local magistrates, was no longer subject to the rule of law. Soldiers now had the right to apprehend without warrant or to shoot on sight any Aborigine in the Settled Districts who resisted them.[69] The settlers were still subject to the rule of law unless they acted in self-defence. But in reality martial law was further legitimation of the slaughter of the Aborigines that had begun on 29 November 1826.

Martial law had last been declared in Van Diemen's Land in 1816 against the bushrangers. On that occasion it had continued for six months. In New South Wales martial law had last been declared in 1824 in the Bathurst district and it had remained in force for four months while detachments of the 40th Regiment hunted down the Wiradjuri people. If Arthur expected that martial law would produce the same quick result against the Aboriginal nations in the Settled Districts, he was sadly mistaken. This time it remained in force for more than three years—the longest period of martial law in Australian history and almost as long as World War I.

6

Martial law, 1828–30

'Parrawa Parrawa. Go away you white buggers—what business have you here.'[1]

The proclamation of martial law on 1 November 1828 took the war into a new phase. At this stage Arthur appears to have been aware that there were at least five different clan groups operating in the Settled Districts. They comprised the remnants of the mighty nations that had lost most of their people in the preceding two years. The first group consisted of the two known remaining clans of the Oyster Bay nation. One of them was possibly led by Tongerlongter and operated in the Pitt Water area, where it had most recently killed stock-keepers John Priest and William Stringer. The other operated in the central Midlands and in early October had killed Mrs Gough and her children near Lake Tiberias. The second group, comprising two clans of Big River people, one led by Petelega and the other by Montpeliater, had most recently been seen on the upper Clyde and Ouse rivers on the Central Plateau. The third group, which was led by Umarrah, consisted of a composite clan of the North Midlands nation and operated near Oyster Bay. It had recently killed two stock-keepers, John Bailey and James Shirton. The fourth group comprised a combined clan of Ben Lomond and Oyster Bay people led by Mannalargenna in the Fingal district, where some of its members had been captured by John Batman in September. Finally, there was the Pallittorre clan of the North nation led by Quamby. Its people had recently been dispersed by Captain Ritchie's men along the Meander River, forcing them to join with another group of North Midlands people at the

Tamar. Put together, they appear to have comprised about 500 people, that is, less than half of the 1,200 that are estimated to have been in the Settled Districts in February 1826.[2]

Arthur's first response to martial law was to encourage civilian parties to capture Aborigines in the Settled Districts. One party was led by Gilbert Robertson, chief constable at Richmond, with his friend Kickerterpoller as the guide. On 7 November they tracked down Umarrah and his wife, Laoninneloonner, at their campsite in the Eastern Marshes. Both were captured, along with another couple and a young boy, Cowertenninna, or John Woodburn, who came from Little Swanport. Robertson then shot and killed another man who had tried to escape. Umarrah's capture was triumphantly reported in the press, for he was well known to the settlers, and many believed that the event signalled a major shift in the course of the war. But Umarrah had other ideas. He told Robertson 'that white people had been murdered' because they had driven his people from their kangaroo hunting grounds and he told the Executive Council that 'his determined purpose' was to destroy all the whites he possibly could, 'which he considers his patriotic duty'.[3] In response Arthur despatched him to Richmond gaol, where he languished with his compatriots for more than a year. The forced sojourn probably saved his life for a few more years. Robertson's initial success led to his appointment to 'take charge of a roving party of about 10 or 12 men to be employed against the Aborigines', under the control of the military and at a salary of £150 per annum.[4]

Arthur then established military patrols or 'pursuing parties' of eight to ten men from the 39th, 40th and 63rd regiments. They operated under the direction of the local magistrate and their orders were to scour the Settled Districts for Aborigines, whom they should capture or shoot. Each patrol was provisioned for fourteen to sixteen days at a time and assisted by one of the field police, usually a convict constable, who knew the terrain. At other times they used an Aboriginal guide from a clan outside the Settled Districts, such as the Nuenonne from Bruny Island, or recently captured Aboriginal boys, such as John Woodburn, from the Settled Districts. But they were rarely trusted by the soldiers and some were killed when patrols failed to track down their prey.

By March 1829 nearly 200 armed soldiers in twenty-three separate parties scoured the Settled Districts. Arthur also posted small detachments of one or two soldiers in settlers' homes on the remote frontiers behind the Clyde and Meander rivers. Many soldiers resisted these postings because they were deprived of their rations of rum and spirits, but Arthur believed that their presence would protect the settlers from Aboriginal attack. By then about 400 troops from three regiments were on duty in the Settled Districts, but it is unlikely that all of them were present at the same time. Over the next eighteen months the last detachments of the 40th Regiment departed for India and were replaced by further detachments of the 63rd Regiment. These changes suggest that from the declaration of martial law, in November 1828, to February 1830 the purpose of the very strong military presence in the Settled Districts was largely directed at killing rather than capturing Aborigines.[5]

On 6 December 1828, following the killing of settler Adam Wood and two stock-keepers in the Eastern Marshes by a small group of Oyster Bay men, a party of nine soldiers from the 40th Regiment and two police constables, John Danvers and William Holmes, surrounded the Aborigines' camp at Tooms Lake at daybreak. Danvers reported that: 'One of them getting up from a small fire to a large one, discovered us and gave alarm to the rest, and the whole of them jumpt [sic] up immediately and attempted to take up their spears in defence, and seeing that, we immediately fired and repeated it because we saw they were on the defensive part they were about twenty in number.' The *Hobart Town Courier* said that ten Aborigines were killed and a woman and her boy were captured.[6]

That summer, the military patrols notched up further successes. In mid January 1829, following an attack a month earlier by men from the Ben Lomond nation on settler John Allen's farm at Great Swanport, and the wounding of a stock-keeper and shepherd at Talbot's cattle run at Break O'Day Plains, a patrol from the 40th Regiment ambushed and then slaughtered nine of them. A week or so later, they killed a further nine Aborigines at St Pauls River. South of Bothwell, another military patrol surprised a group of about fifty Big River people who were robbing a settler's hut. But they 'escaped into the woods, in spite of every exertion to apprehend them'.

The Aborigines of Van Diemen's Land Endeavouring to Kill Mr John Allen on Milton Farm in the District of Great Swanport on the 14th December 1828. State Library of New South Wales, Sydney.

Believing that their guide, Black Jack, from the Nuenonne clan at Bruny Island, was responsible for the escape, two of the soldiers shot him dead 'in cold blood'.[7]

In mid February, following an attack near Launceston by the North and North Midlands people on Captain J.W. Bell's stock-keeper, who later died of his wounds, a military patrol claimed it was attacked by the same group at West Tamar and that in self-defence it shot seven of the Aborigines. The North people then moved on to Magistrate Malcolm Laing-Smith's stock run at Whitefoord Hills and killed some of his sheep. The magistrate 'immediately proceeded to the spot' with a party of soldiers and field police, but it is not known what happened next. A month later, a group of North Midlands men killed a settler's wife, Mary Miller, and two of her servants, James Hales and Thomas Johnson, at the North Esk River near Launceston, and then robbed huts of provisions and blankets near the Cataract. In retaliation the same military patrol shot four Aboriginal men, a woman and her child. At the end of March a small group of Big River people plundered some stock

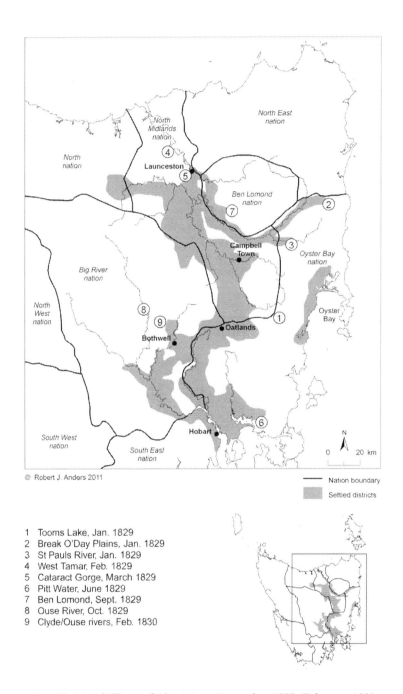

© Robert J. Anders 2011

——— Nation boundary

▨ Settled districts

1 Tooms Lake, Jan. 1829
2 Break O'Day Plains, Jan. 1829
3 St Pauls River, Jan. 1829
4 West Tamar, Feb. 1829
5 Cataract Gorge, March 1829
6 Pitt Water, June 1829
7 Ben Lomond, Sept. 1829
8 Ouse River, Oct. 1829
9 Clyde/Ouse rivers, Feb. 1830

Map 18 Mass killings of Aborigines, December 1828–February 1830

huts on the west bank of the Ouse. They turned wool out of the sacks and filled them with potatoes that they had dug out of the garden with pannikins. They were immediately pursued by a party of field police aided by some stock-keepers, who reported that they 'severely wounded an Aboriginal woman in a skirmish' and then chased the remaining Big River people for several kilometres until they crossed the Cataract at the River Derwent.[8]

By the end of March 1829 press reports alone indicated that about sixty Aborigines had been killed over the previous four months, with the loss of fifteen colonists. In May, Arthur shored up the military patrols by adding a small troop of mounted police to assist them. He then replaced Gilbert Robertson's large roving party with six smaller parties and placed them under the control of Thomas Anstey, police magistrate at Oatlands in the centre of the Settled Districts. Each party was now led by a constable from the field police and usually consisted of an Aboriginal guide and four or five ticket-of-leave men, each with a good knowledge of the bush. Three of the roving parties were under the charge of Gilbert Robertson and operated in the region south-east of Oatlands around Pitt Water, and two others were led by John Danvers and James Hopkins, who knew 'every rood of bush from Launceston Road to Oyster Bay'.[9] The other three parties, under the leadership of Jorgen Jorgenson, operated to the west of Oatlands in Big River country. Their brief was to 'look for the native fires *at night*—cautiously approach them, and wait in patience until the dawn of day, when many of the poor creatures might, thus, be captured'.[10] While Kickerterpoller was Gilbert Robertson's guide, Jorgenson was assisted by 'Mungo', who was probably Ningernooputtener of the Tyerrernotepanner clan at Campbell Town.[11] As well, other parties were formed by settlers like John Batman, who later hired Aborigines from New South Wales to assist him. But the settler parties were expected to capture rather than kill Aborigines.[12]

The military patrols and roving parties had varied success in either killing or capturing Aborigines across the Settled Districts. After his spectacular capture of Umarrah, Gilbert Robertson's own party appears to have neither captured nor killed any Aborigine, but the parties led by Danvers and Hopkins certainly did. The parties under Jorgenson's charge did not record capturing Aborigines but they are known to have killed some Big River people in 1830.[13] However, the military patrols and private settler parties seem to have had more success. They carried out dawn attacks on camps of Oyster Bay, Ben Lomond and North Midlands people and ran them down in daylight in places from which it was impossible to escape. After June 1829 the Oyster Bay people in the Pitt Water region were rarely seen in groups of more than fifteen to twenty, whereas in November the year before one group of at least sixty had been seen at East Bay Neck.[14] By comparison, the Big River people continued to congregate in large numbers. In December 1828, about seventy of them were seen crossing Black Marsh into the hills behind Bothwell, and even as late as June 1830 the *Colonial Times* reported sightings of 100 to 200 of them in the same area.[15]

By winter 1829 all the different civilian and military parties had turned the southern part of the Settled Districts into a war zone. When G.A. Robinson crossed the area in October 1831, the Aboriginal guides pointed out campsites where they had been attacked by the various parties and told horrifying stories of how their relatives had been killed and mutilated. The fifteen months following the declaration of martial law were indeed 'days of terror'.[16]

Yet the Oyster Bay people not only fought back; they made the purpose of their attacks quite plain: to acquire food and force the colonists to leave their hunting grounds. In June 1829 a group of fifteen to twenty Oyster Bay men killed five assigned servants in two separate incidents in the Pitt Water area. In each case it was reported that they were either digging up potatoes or stealing flour. The military patrol sent by the magistrate to capture them ended up shooting at them, and 'it is supposed eight or ten of the natives were severely wounded'.[17]

Gilbert Robertson told Arthur that the Aborigines were fighting for their country:

> They consider every injury they can inflict upon white men as an act of duty and patriotic, and however they may dread the punishment which our laws inflict upon them, they consider the sufferers under these punishments as martyrs of their country . . . having ideas of their natural rights which would astonish most of our European statesmen.[18]

Even so, he advised Arthur not to seek a treaty with them or to attempt to confine them to a particular part of the island. Rather, he supported the press's view that they should be rounded up by a conciliator and moved to an island in Bass Strait, where an establishment could be formed to educate the children. The adults, he said, could hunt, visit the children, and receive clothes and rations.[19]

But Arthur was not yet ready to take that step. A year before, in April 1828, five Nuenonne men from Bruny Island had complained to him about sealer John Baker, who had abducted three Nuenonne women. He ordered Baker's arrest and decided to establish a ration station on Bruny in the hope that it would attract the Aborigines from the Settled Districts. The Nuenonne accepted the rations, so in March 1829 Arthur decided to turn the ration station into a mission and to employ a suitable person to run it.[20]

The man appointed, at a salary of £100 a year, was George Augustus Robinson. He was then forty-one years of age and married with five children. He had arrived in Hobart Town in 1824 to practise as a master builder and had made a name for himself as secretary of the Van Diemen's Land Seaman's Friend and Bethel Union Society. A man of evangelical beliefs, which had been shaped by the anti-slavery discourse then sweeping the British Empire, he firmly believed that the Aborigines were his brothers in Christ and thus were entitled to know the message of God and to share in the benefits of British 'civilization'. Armed with the conviction that he could save them from destruction, he set off for Bruny Island at the end of March.[21]

With measures in place to conciliate the nations outside the Settled Districts, Arthur now returned his attention to the war zone in the Settled Districts. In February, Surveyor-General George Frankland had suggested that he could prepare a board comprising sketches of Aborigines and settlers which would 'represent in a manner as simple and as well adapted to [the Aborigines'] supposed ideas, the actual state of things'.[22] The proclamation boards, as they became known, had four panels. The first depicted a family of Aborigines in British clothes joyfully intermingling with a settler's family in complete equality. The second portrayed a chief and his family surrendering to the governor, in a gesture of conciliation, while two soldiers and a settler stood nearby. The third and fourth panels

Governor's Davey's Proclamation Board. National Library of Australia, Canberra.
The board is misnamed. It was prepared for Lieutenant-Governor Arthur in
1829 by Surveyor-General George Frankland.

showed how the rule of law worked in colonial society. One panel depicted an Aboriginal man being hanged for killing a settler and the other depicted a settler being hanged for killing an Aborigine. Arthur appears to have endorsed the boards, for about 100 of them were prepared and it is known that they were shown to Aboriginal people on two occasions in 1830.[23] But the boards represented an imagined future rather than the reality of martial law.

In April, Arthur explained to Sir George Murray in London that even though he knew that the Aborigines' 'animosity was first excited by the barbarous treatment' they had received from convicts and stock-keepers and that the 'very last degree of forbearance should be manifested' towards them, the 'pressing' need to protect the settlers had 'rendered strong measures necessary'.[24] That winter six roving parties, several military patrols and at least one settler party scoured the Settled Districts, supported by at least 200 troops who were deployed at the frontier military posts. They found that for the first time the Aborigines were continuing their offensive through the winter because they were hungry. When a group of Oyster Bay people arrived at Pitt Water in August in search of food, a 'party' was sent out after them. At least one was killed and several were wounded.[25] Arthur would have been amazed to learn that his estimate of 2,000 Aborigines at the end of July was probably less than half that number. James Ross, the editor of the *Hobart Town Almanac*, estimated at the beginning of 1830 that there were 600 Aborigines in the entire colony; James Kelly, who had sailed around the island in 1815–16, believed there were 5,000; Roderic O'Connor, one of the land commissioners, considered there were 600 or 700 left; and Jorgen Jorgenson estimated there were more than 500. A year later, G.A. Robinson estimated that only 500 to 700 remained.[26] Ross's estimates of about 350 in the Settled Districts and another 300 on the other side of the settler frontier were probably close to the mark.

Earlier in July, Arthur had instructed the colonial secretary, John Burnett, to collect all the existing correspondence about the Aborigines 'for future reference'.[27] The file formed the basis for what became the eighteen volumes of official papers on the Black War. Arthur now had an almost daily record of Aboriginal attacks on settlers at his fingertips and it deeply influenced his actions. Yet the record told only one side of the story. It may have contained the odd report of settler actions against the Aborigines, such as John Batman's sortie against the Ben Lomond nation discussed in the next paragraph, but it did not include reports of other settler reprisals or from the military patrols, although some of them were published in the press. Put together with accounts in settler diaries, memoirs, correspondence and oral histories collected by a later generation of historians, the cumulative information indicates that in the spring of 1829, the British war of attrition against the nations in the Settled Districts was proving very successful in reducing their numbers.

In August the *Hobart Town Courier* reported that a 'party' sent out after the Aborigines had killed at least one of them and wounded several others. In early September, John Batman led a dawn attack on a camp of Ben Lomond people. He estimated that fifteen had died of wounds and he executed two others, he said, to put them out of their misery. In response, the Ben Lomond people killed a shepherd at the Macquarie River by fracturing his skull with a well-aimed stone and then killed a settler at Great Swanport and horribly mutilated his body. A month later they killed another servant at Waterloo Point.[28] But many more Ben Lomond people must have been killed after these incidents, because after that, they were rarely seen again.

The main theatres of war were now located in the territories of the Big River and Oyster Bay nations, with particular focus on the Clyde, Oatlands and Richmond police districts. In September the Big River people speared and killed an assigned servant at the River Ouse and then in early October they plundered a stock-keeper's hut near Hamilton and mortally wounded the occupant, Robert Watts. On this occasion, 'an expedition was fitted out in the night and a terrible slaughter took place'.[29] Then in November, in three separate incidents, the Aborigines killed three stockmen and two women, then burnt to death a servant in the house of his master at Bothwell and speared another man at the River Ouse. At the end of the year they speared settler James Doran near New Norfolk and took his gun and two pistols. They told him, 'You white . . . we will give it to you'. Doran died later of his wounds.[30]

In September, in the Richmond and Sorell police districts, a group of Oyster Bay warriors wounded a young boy and killed Mrs Coffin, the wife of a settler, near Sorell. She had been

> rather indisposed, and had gone to bed; previous to which she had fastened the doors . . . the blacks entered the house by a window . . . Mrs Coffin got out of bed and fainted . . . one of the Blacks thrust a spear into her right and left breasts . . . and she expired on the spot! . . . They then plundered the house of 10 blankets, 6 sheets, 2 sacks of flour, 13 lbs of tea, sugar and a quantity of wearing apparel.

The magistrate, James Gordon, ordered their pursuit. They 'were fired on' and one was known to have been wounded. In retaliation they killed a shepherd near present-day Campania.[31]

Between August and December of 1829 nineteen colonists were killed by the Big River and Oyster Bay nations, bringing the total for the year to thirty-three, that is, six more than the year before.[32] Arthur had already increased the efficiency of the military patrols by providing some of the officers with horses so that they could 'constantly visit' the outstations and regularly relieve the detachments of soldiers and military parties who were stationed there. He had also ordered the officers to send in regular reports of military engagements with the Aborigines. But they rarely did so, possibly because they were still operating under the directions of the local magistrates. Arthur had significantly increased the number of field police with the purpose of driving the Big River and Oyster Bay nations from the Settled Districts, or capturing them. He told the magistrates that he regretted that he could not provide even more help, other than to encourage all the parties under their control to 'act up on the spirit of the injunctions' of martial law. He tried to prevent the last detachment of the 40th Regiment from departing for India and sought the services of another from the 63rd Regiment stationed in Western Australia, but without success. Captain Williams, the police magistrate at Bothwell, was unimpressed. He estimated that in the coming summer he would need three times the thirty soldiers already at his disposal to protect the settlers.[33]

Arthur now admitted to Sir George Murray in London that the Aborigines had become 'the most anxious subject of my Government':

> The species of warfare which we are carrying on with them is of the most distressing nature:—they suddenly appear, commit some acts of outrage, and, then, as suddenly vanish—if pursued, it seems impossible to surround and capture them, and, if the Parties fire, the possibility is that Women and children are the victims.

Indeed, they usually were. Yet he believed that their tactics were the work of the 'Chieftains of each Mob', who 'evinced much more cunning and have manifested a degree of tact which very evidently shews that this race, however barbarous, is by no means so void of intelligence as has hitherto been supposed'.[34] This information suggested to him that negotiations for the Aborigines' surrender were still possible.

Of the sixty reported Aboriginal attacks in the Settled Districts between 1 November 1829 and 31 March 1830, about the same number as the summer before, the vast majority took place in the Clyde, Oatlands and Richmond police districts. The attacks were becoming more dreadful and inexplicable. In February a group of Oyster Bay men speared and killed John Plaistow, who was a boy aged ten, while he was tending his father's herd of sheep at Constitution Hill near Bagdad.[35] A week later, a small group of Big River men burnt the dwelling hut and corn stacks of Humphrey Morgan Howells, who was district constable at Blue Hills between Bothwell and Ouse. Mrs Howells and her children narrowly escaped the flames. The hut was located on a favoured kangaroo hunting ground and the Big River people may also have burnt it down in revenge for Howells's servants having killed some of their own people a few days earlier.[36]

From there they moved on to Montacute, a farmhouse located at the bottom of three ridges that plunged down to the Clyde River south of Bothwell. The occupant, Henry Torlesse, had built a brick and stone wall to enclose the homestead and outhouses and at intervals along the wall had established positions for firing at the Aborigines.[37] After the Big River people had attacked the farmhouse at least six times, Torlesse wrote to Arthur:

As to the natives, I can assure you we all feel so fearful of their being near us, that we never move without a gun, if the cart has to go to the mill or elsewhere, we lose the service of one man at home, being obliged to send two, one as driver, the other as convoy—Mrs Torlesse is uneasy if I even go so far as the Barn, and even to that short distance I always carry a gun. The trouble and loss they cause and still will cause us is quite paralyzing.[38]

He had to admit that never more than six Aboriginal men participated in the attacks, but their use of firesticks, the surprise nature of their raids, and their ability to bamboozle the stock-keepers rendered even this small unit a formidable danger. He was not alone. A few days later, on Sunday 21 February, at three o'clock in the afternoon, John Sherwin was sitting in the front room of his house west of the Clyde River when a servant called out, 'Fire! Fire! The natives!' Sherwin described what happened next:

I immediately ran for water, and to alarm the men who were in front of the Hut at the Time—soon after which a fire broke out from the back of the men's hut—we then endeavoured to save the house, but seeing this was impossible, we began to get what things we could from the house:—during this time I never saw a native with the exception of the one who set fire to the house after which he immediately ran away—soon after this I saw smoke arise about 600 or 700 yards from the house, then saw two natives on the hillside. The smoke continued to increase and come nearer. Soon after two natives walked alongside the fences and set fire to them at every 20 or 30 yards distance—then two other Natives appeared on the Rock on the opposite side of the River, seeming to give directions whilst the other 2 still continued to communicate fire to the cross fences and another bringing fire even to the riverside. These 2 joined the others on the Rock and began to leap and use much of their language. 'Parrawa Parrawa. Go away you white buggers—what business have you here.' One of my men crossing the river with a musket I called to him to come back, when the Natives immediately cried out, 'Ah—you coward'. For some time they still continued on the Rock making use of such language as above, and constantly raising their hands and leaping.

About 2 hours after the house had been fired, I perceived one skulking round the stacks evidently with the intention of taking some of the articles we had rescued from the flames—my son seeing him first, cried out, 'Father—black fellow', he immediately ran round the stacks again and scrambled up some rocks, and on my bringing my piece to a level he immediately fell flat on the Rock— he soon got out of my sight and began shouting. I saw nothing of them afterwards ... [T]he Natives were in number about 4 or 5—one of them always had a firestick in his hand.[39]

By then the settlers along the Clyde River had had enough. The following Saturday, thirty-three of them assembled at Bothwell and drew up an address to Arthur warning that unless they were granted increased military protection and unless he abandoned his policy of conciliation they would be driven from their homes. The *Colonial Times* agreed. The dramatic change in Aboriginal tactics, the editor argued, had eroded any possibility of conciliation. The sooner they were rounded up and taken to Bass Strait, the better.[40]

But Arthur was still unwilling to take this final step. On 19 February he had offered 'a handsome reward to any individual who could affect a successful intercourse with any tribe' as no one had come forward and a week later he had introduced a bounty of £5 for every captured Aboriginal adult and £2 for every child. Now he persuaded the most senior Anglican clergyman in the Australian colonies, Archdeacon William Grant Broughton, who was then on a pastoral visit to Hobart, to become temporary chair of the 'Aborigines Committee', which Arthur had established the previous November, and conduct a special inquiry into the origin of the hostility displayed by the 'Black Natives of this Island against the Settlers, and to consider the measures expedient to be adopted with a view of checking the devastation of property and the destruction of human lives occasioned by the state of warfare which has so extensively prevailed'.[41] Arthur believed that Broughton's presence not only would lend the committee integrity and independence but that it would also recommend new measures to end the war. It had been a grim sixteen months since the declaration of martial law, and no end to the hostilities appeared to be in sight.

In the sixteen months between the declaration of martial law in November 1828 and March 1830, it would seem that there were at least 120 attacks by the Aborigines on the settlers, leading to about fifty deaths and at least sixty wounded.[42] On the other hand, at least 200 Aborigines had also been killed, many of them, it appears, in mass killings of six or more. The war was beginning to take its toll on both sides.

7

The settlers regroup, 1830

Apart from the chair, Archdeacon Broughton, the other members of the Aborigines Committee were from the civil establishment in Hobart. There were two Anglican clergy, William Bedford and James Norman; the chief police magistrate, Peter Mulgrave; the colonial treasurer, Jocelyn Thomas; the chief medical officer, James Scott; and the collector of customs, Samuel Hill. Charles Arthur, the lieutenant-governor's nephew, was the committee's secretary. On 20 February he wrote to the settlers seeking their views on possible means to conciliate the Aborigines as well as estimates of their numbers in the Settled Districts. Most respondents replied by letter, but John Sherwin, George Espie and John Brodie, whose properties had recently been burnt down by warriors from the Big River nation, made the long journey to Hobart to appear before the committee on 23 February.

Sherwin believed that the young warriors who had attacked his property were known as the 'Abyssinia mob' from the Big River nation, and, even though he had seen only four or five of them, he knew there were places beyond the River Ouse where 200 or 300 had been 'constantly seen at a time'. He was in no doubt that their object was plunder and that they wished 'to have their lands for themselves', but he knew of no white who had committed atrocities against them. Brodie, who had been speared at his hut at Meads Bottom earlier that month, also believed that plunder was the Aborigines' primary object. But he added that the women robbed huts alongside the men and took dangerous items like knives and razors as well as flour, sugar and good blankets. Espie, however, was furious that after killing his sheep the Aborigines had not eaten any of them.[1]

All three men advocated that ruthless measures should be used to capture the Aborigines. Sherwin urged that 'Sydney natives' and 'blood hounds' should be hired and that 'decoy huts, containing flour and sugar, strongly impregnated with poison', should also be used. Espie suggested that 150 prisoners should be 'sent after the Natives, who should be rewarded by a conditional pardon for every two or three they captured'. But Brodie believed that the assigned servants had 'become very much afraid of the Natives', that they would shoot more than they would capture and that the Aborigines were beyond conciliation.[2]

Another settler urged that a Maori chieftain and 150 of his followers should be employed to capture the Aborigines and remove them to New Zealand as his slaves. Still another pressed for a full-scale military campaign with high bounties for the captured, while others put their faith in the erection of huts with secret rooms, trapdoors and spring-locks which would capture Aborigines in search of plunder. One wanted Umarrah sent back into the bush with a couple of 'lifers' who would then betray the 'lurking places of the tribes'. Others wanted 'dogs to hunt the Aborigines as was done in Cuba and Jamaica with the negroes'. This started a lively discussion about whether the dogs should be 'Spanish bloodhounds from Manila' or 'pointers which would set upon the natives as if they were quail'.[3] In every case it seems the settlers were anxious to absolve themselves of responsibility for the war.

But the committee did hear stories of military violence. On 1 March settler Robert Ayton wrote to the committee about how a detachment of the 40th Regiment had attacked a camp of Oyster Bay people in July 1828 and had killed at least sixteen of them. The committee was so disturbed by this information that it arranged for Ayton to make a deposition at the Launceston police office, but he could not provide precise details of the incident except to say that Constable John Danvers had been present.[4]

Gilbert Robertson, the quixotic leader of the roving party and captor of Umarrah, was less intimidated. He appeared before the committee on 3 March and told them that twenty Aborigines had been killed for every white man; that at the massacre at the back of Hugh Murray's farm at Mount Augustus in April 1827, in which a detachment of the 40th Regiment was involved, about seventy Aborigines had been killed; and that the guides Charles Dugdale and Robert Grant had told him about it. The committee then called all the roving party guides, including Robert Morley and John Danvers, as well as Dugdale and Grant, to appear before it. Morley, who was now the overseer at a property on the Macquarie River, said that he could not attend until his employers had returned from a court hearing in Hobart. Dugdale, who held a ticket of leave and had previously worked for settler William Talbot near Fingal, did not bother to reply. His silence was rewarded eight months later with a recommendation for a conditional pardon.[5] John Danvers and Robert Grant seem to have disappeared. But Doctor Adam Turnbull and William Robertson, whose properties were located near the sites where the alleged atrocity took place, were anxious to present their side of the story.

Turnbull admitted that two parties of soldiers had killed Aborigines in crossfire at the back of Hugh Murray's farm, but that 'some of [the Aborigines] had run off'. He then referred to the massacre at the Elizabeth River in April 1828 in which seventeen Aborigines had been reported killed. He claimed that in this incident 'no bodies were found'. William Robertson agreed. He told the committee that he had gone to the site the next day with a corporal from the 40th Regiment who had told him, 'to tell you the truth, we did not kill any of them, we had been out a long time and had done nothing'. But Robertson admitted that Dugdale and Morley, who were with the party, had remained silent, implying that they had known more than they were prepared to say. He also said that he had found the bodies of three dogs near three small fires, that the Aborigines had had room to escape and that he had seen no blood.[6]

Other settlers wrote to the committee about the number of Aborigines they believed still remained in the Settled Districts. Horace Rowcroft, whose property was near Bothwell in the Clyde police district, said that over the last two years he had never seen more than forty Big River people in one group. F.D.G. Browne, from the east coast near Great Swanport, said that even six months earlier he had found the tracks of forty-two adult Oyster Bay people who had crossed the hills behind John Amos's place, but now the number had dropped to thirty. He believed that only two groups of Oyster Bay people remained on the east coast—one associated with Great Swanport and the other with Prossers Plains. Both settlers were in no doubt that many Aborigines had been shot over the last two years and that, despite the apparent increase in the number of their attacks, very few now remained. William Barnes, who had a property near Epping Forest, south of Launceston, agreed. He said that most Aborigines in the Settled Districts had been killed in 'massacres of hundreds' by the stock-keepers in the outstations.[7]

Overall, the committee heard details of at least six mass killings of Aborigines and acquired information about other atrocities. But the only incident its members mentioned in their final report was the colony's founding massacre at Risdon Cove on 3 May 1804. In their opinion, Aboriginal 'acts of violence' were 'generally to be regarded, not as retaliation for any wrongs they had endured, but as originating from a wanton and savage spirit inherent in them'. In discounting the evidence of recent massacres of Aborigines, and in failing to understand the real meaning of the 'measures of forbearance' that Arthur had implemented since November 1826, the committee absolved the government of responsibility for the war's escalation. Rather, they believed that over the last two years the Aborigines had been acting 'upon a systematic plan of attacking the settlers and their possessions' which had intensified over the last few months.

> It is manifest that they have lost the sense of the superiority of white men, and the dread of the effects of fire-arms, which they formerly entertained, and have of late conducted their plans of aggression with such resolutions as they were not heretofore thought to possess, and with caution and artifice which renders it almost impossible to foresee or defeat their purposes.[8]

They pointed out that over the previous three months more than thirty Aboriginal attacks had been recorded in the Clyde, Richmond and Norfolk Plains police districts alone, that five men and a child had been killed, and that four men and two women had been seriously wounded. These incidents suggested that the current measures had 'not been attended with success' and they now believed that the Aborigines were 'visiting injuries . . . not on the actual offenders, but on a different and totally innocent class'. In discounting the real evidence that many of the settlers had been actively engaged in killing Aborigines, the committee made it appear that the Aborigines were making random attacks rather than using defensive actions in response to specific acts of settler aggression.

The committee recommended that the measures already in place should be further strengthened by placing a detachment of mounted police with every magistrate and police station to more effectively respond to Aboriginal attacks, that the field police should be increased, the military should assist the local police magistrate, and the bounty system should be used as an incentive either to drive the Aborigines out of the Settled Districts or to capture them. It also recommended that settlers should be well armed and alert on all occasions with a 'watchful regard to the security of their dwellings and possessions' and should make sure that the stock-keepers and assigned servants understood the fatal consequences that came about from ill treatment of the Aborigines. Nor should they wantonly shoot kangaroos.[9]

Arthur agreed with most of the recommendations, in particular the warning that settlers and their families should better prepare themselves and their properties against Aboriginal attack. While the committee was in session, he visited many settlers in the Clyde police district and was surprised by their unwillingness to 'take ordinary measures of precaution'. Their tardiness suggested to him that they were 'more ready to complain of evils than disposed to exert themselves to overcome them'.[10] He discounted, on the grounds of expense, deploying mounted police beyond 'a small augmentation to convey intelligence quickly'. Rather, he believed that a more affordable option would be to bring out more English convicts who could be assigned to settlers in 'the most remote parts of the Colony' and assist troop reinforcements.[11] Yet, as military historian John Connor has pointed out, mounted police had proved extremely effective in putting down Aboriginal resistance in the Bathurst and Hunter regions in New South Wales.[12] Arthur, it appears, was still unwilling to provide the settlers with the complete police protection that they expected.

The press in Hobart and Launceston was divided about the report. The *Colonial Times* had initially welcomed the committee's inquiry, but as each week brought further news of Aboriginal atrocities and destruction of property it simply reiterated its original suggestion, that the 'whole race' should be transported to the Bass Strait islands.[13] *The Colonial Advocate* took a different view:

> The reflection that so much blood is daily spilled on both sides, must surely be very dreadful to a feeling heart. There can be little doubt that many scores of the unhappy and useless race themselves are frequently shot dead by the stock keepers and others, not only when attacked, but in revenge for the death of their fellow countrymen, who have fallen to the blacks. It is said privately that up the country, instances occur where the Natives 'are shot like so many crows', which never comes before the public.[14]

In this case, the newspaper could have been referring to unconfirmed reports from the Clyde River of at least two night attacks in April on the Big River people which had taken at least ten lives. It could also have been referring to the new military and police offensive in the same month against the Pallittorre along the Meander River in which at least ten more had been killed.[15] But by the end of July the *Colonial Times* was no longer in the mood for reflection. In its view the Aborigines were the enemy and nothing short of a full-scale military operation would 'teach them a lesson'.[16]

Arthur was more concerned by how Sir George Murray, the secretary of state for the colonies, would receive the report. Murray had already admonished him for not sending more information about his decision to invoke martial law. Murray had also been horrified to learn of the 'great decrease' in the Aboriginal population and was now concerned by the prospect that 'the whole race of these people may, at no distant period, become extinct'.[17] He told Arthur that he blamed the settlers for the 'dreadful situation' and warned that 'the adoption of any line of conduct having for its avowed or for its secret object, the extinction of the Native-race, could not fail to leave an indelible stain upon the Character of the British Government'.[18] After reading the report he was at pains to point out that, contrary to the beliefs held by the authors, the settlers and the colonial press, the British occupation of Van Diemen's Land was not sufficient reason in itself to allow the extermination of the Aborigines unless it could be demonstrated that they were the original aggressors. But, as the committee's report of the massacre at Risdon Cove had revealed, this was certainly not the case.[19]

The settlers in the Clyde police district disagreed with Murray's sentiments. They believed that they were under siege by a small group of savages who were determined to drive them out of the colony. Between 9 April and 9 August 1830 they recorded twenty-two attacks by the Big River people on their properties. A woman named Mary Daniels and her twins, Richard and Eliza, were killed and two other women and seven stockmen wounded, and fifteen huts were plundered for blankets, flour and tea.[20] Yet Arthur was also aware that each of these incidents had taken place in reprisal for atrocities by stock-keepers, military patrols and roving parties. The settlers in the Oatlands and Richmond police districts felt no less secure. How much longer, Police Magistrate Thomas Anstey wrote to Arthur, could they tolerate the daily fear and anxiety for their safety?[21]

In Hobart, Arthur was perceiving the situation in a different way. Reports from his emissaries G.A. Robinson on the west coast and Captain Welsh in the north-east said they had each made friendly contacts with Aborigines on the other side of the settler frontier. When he also heard that Anstey's son had captured four Big River people west of Oatlands on 28 July, he believed for a moment that the war had reached a turning point.[22] So, on 19 August he issued the following government notice:

> It is with much satisfaction that the Lieutenant-Governor is at length enabled to announce, that a less hostile disposition towards the European inhabitants has been manifested by some of the aboriginal Natives of this Island, with whom, Captain Welsh and Mr G. A. Robinson have succeeded in opening a friendly intercourse ... his Excellency earnestly requests, that all settlers and others will strictly enjoin their servants cautiously to abstain from acts of aggression against these benighted beings, and that they will

themselves personally endeavour to conciliate them wherever it may be practicable: and whenever the Aborigines appear without evincing a hostile feeling, that no attempt shall be made either to capture or restrain them, but, on the contrary, after being fed and kindly treated, that they shall be suffered to depart whenever they desire it.[23]

The next day he warned that the bounty would not be paid for Aborigines captured while holding a friendly intercourse with colonists in the Settled Districts. If any were shot while attempting to communicate with colonists, the colonist who was responsible would be prosecuted.[24]

The settlers at Jericho in the Oatlands police district were devastated by what they perceived as Arthur's betrayal of their interests. When a group of Oyster Bay Aborigines killed well-known settler James Hooper at Spring Hill on 22 August, they wrote to Arthur 'with inexpressible alarm':

We are convinced that Your Excellency must be deceived respecting the real state of the Colony and must labour under a mistake as respects our situation. The bringing in of a few inimical blacks—a distinct people from those in the interior and who have not had any intercourse with the European—is no criterion to judge of the character of the Aborigines generally as a people, and the events of the last week in this District must convince Your Excellency of the necessity of the most energetic measures as well as for the protection of the Colonists as for the subjection of the Aborigines.[25]

Thomas Anstey wrote that unless sufficient military protection was afforded, the spring of 1830 would be too bloody to remember. The Aborigines Committee agreed. The Aborigines in the Settled Districts, it pointed out, had now become 'too much enjoined in the most rancorous animosity to be spared the most vigorous measures against them'. Even so, at least one settler in the Bothwell region, Captain Wood, was reporting several successful skirmishes against the Big River people, in which the chief, Petelega, was alleged to have been captured and several of his people killed.[26]

On 27 August, Arthur summoned the Executive Council to consider the situation. They deliberated over the address from the settlers of Jericho, which also said that it would be 'extremely impolitic' to try settlers for killing Aborigines; they perused Anstey's letter and they took into account the most recent concerns from the Aborigines Committee. They concluded that the war being waged by the Big River and Oyster Bay nations against the colonists had so intensified during the month that unless some vigorous effort of an extended nature brought about its end there would be a great decline in the prosperity of the colony and the eventual extirpation of the Aboriginal race itself. On the grounds of humanity, the Executive Council argued, a full-scale military operation against the Big River and Oyster Bay Aborigines must take place.[27]

Arthur bowed to the inevitable. On 9 September he called on every able-bodied male colonist to assemble on 7 October, at one of seven designated places in the Settled Districts, to join in a drive to sweep the Aborigines from the region. The *levée en masse* quickly became known as the 'Black Line'.[28] The war which had now been raging for nearly four years was taking its toll on both sides. In the twenty-three months between the declaration of martial law on 1 November 1828 and the announcement of military operations on 9 September 1830, at least sixty colonists, including five women and four children, had been killed in the Settled Districts. It is estimated that 300 Aborigines were killed in the same period, with at least 100 of these losing their lives in mass killings of six or more. While most of the colonists had been killed in broad daylight at their huts, the Aborigines were more likely to have been killed at night in their encampments. In responding to public pressure, Arthur had decided to solve the problem with a sledgehammer.

8

The Black Line, 1830–31

Arthur's plan was to drive the Big River and Oyster Bay Aborigines from the Settled Districts to the Tasman Peninsula. To this end he called upon every able-bodied male in the colony, bond or free, to combine with the military and police forces to form a human chain or line to undertake the task. The Line would assemble on 7 October and stretch from St Patricks Head on the east coast to Quamby Bluff in the Great Western Tiers. At each end of the Line there would be an extra flank to prevent the Aborigines escaping to the north-east or to the Central Plateau in the west. The Line would advance for three weeks in a pincer movement south-east across the Settled Districts until it converged on 28 October into a 60-kilometre line bounded at one end by the towns of Sorell and Richmond at Pitt Water and then stretched along the Prosser River and Prossers Plains to Spring Bay on the east coast. With the Aborigines now expected to be trapped in front of the Line, the colonists would be sent home and the military and field police would drive their prey across the Forestier Peninsula to East Bay Neck and into the Tasman Peninsula, which Arthur had designated as an Aboriginal Reserve.[1]

According to military historian John Connor, 'calling for volunteers from the civilian population (a *levée en masse*) is not unusual, but Arthur's use of a human line to clear the enemy from the area, was'.[2] Yet, in June 1829, Jorgen Jorgenson had made a similar suggestion to Magistrate Thomas Anstey, and it appears that the use of civilian militia and soldiers to drive the enemy before them was not unusual at the time. Indeed, it may already have been used in other new settler colonies in the Anglophone world. For example, in the state of Georgia in the United States, in the lead-up to the 'Trail of Tears' in the

early 1830s, armed civilian militia and soldiers apparently formed in a line to
force the Cherokee to abandon their villages. Historian Ann Curthoys points
to more ancient origins in citing Herodotus's account of how the Persians
conquered the islands of Chios, Lesbos and Tenedos by joining hands 'so as
to form a line across from north to south, and then march through the island
from end to end and hunt the inhabitants'.[3] Whatever the origins of Arthur's
Line were, its purpose was clear. It was designed, as colonial historian James
Fenton has described it, as a *coup de main*, or, in the words of historian Henry
Reynolds, as a 'knockout blow that would bring the conflict to an end'.[4]

Arthur's position as the lieutenant-governor of Van Diemen's Land *and*
as 'colonel commanding' of the armed forces enabled him to make full use
of the colony's extensive civil and military infrastructure to carry out the
operation. Many of the civil officers, like the chief surveyor, George Frankland, the senior commissariat officer, Affleck Moodie, and John Montagu,
the clerk of the Executive Council, were veterans of British military operations in India, the Peninsular War in Spain and Waterloo. They played vital
parts in planning the Line, including the provision of route maps, the coor-
dination of the soldiers and civilians and the supply of food, clothing, shoes
and weapons. Arthur ordered that only two out of every five civilians should
be armed, so that the other three could carry the provisions.[5] A central depot
was established at Oatlands containing 1,000 stands of arms, 30,000 rounds of
cartridge and 300 sets of handcuffs. The military officers would take charge
of all civilians under arms and, for the first time in their insurgency operations against the Aborigines, the soldiers from the three regiments would
serve directly under their own company officers rather than the civilian
magistrates. Arthur would personally direct operations in the field.[6]

According to military historian John McMahon, the soldiers' role, 'to
advance and search the ground', was similar to that 'experienced by the
infantry in their advance' to contact the defeated French 'during the
Pyrenees phase of the Peninsula War'. Thus, 'the Black Line would have
been within the understanding of the troops as a normal soldierly duty they
were called upon to perform'.[7] But the Line's structure and tactics bore little
resemblance to the battlefield tactics of the Napoleonic period. Rather, as
Charles Esdaile, the leading historian of the Peninsular War, has pointed

out, the Line was more like 'a very large scale' Scottish Highlands shooting party: the soldiers and colonists were the beaters and the Aborigines were the prey waiting to be flushed out of the bracken.[8] Indeed, Charles Darwin compared the Line to one of the 'great hunting-matches in India'.[9] Similar kinds of settler shooting parties formed a 'battue' in southern Queensland in 1877, to flush out native game.[10]

Arthur also intended that captured Aborigines would be used as guides by every division, and it is known that Umarrah was deployed for this purpose. But, even so, afforded 'abundant shelter' the operation was unlikely to succeed. The terrain, as G.A. Robinson pointed out, was 'too friendly' to the Big River and Oyster Bay, Ben Lomond and North Midlands nations, and, as we shall see, many of them had little difficulty in getting through the Line.[11] As well, some of the guides, like Umarrah, rejoined their compatriots at the first opportunity. Further, there were at most only about 300 Aborigines from the four nations still alive at this time, with one-third well beyond the reach of the Line. At least one clan from the Big River nation was already on the other side of the River Ouse; a clan from the North Midlands nation was located along the east side of the Tamar River, where it killed two stock-keepers on 10 and 21 September; and a clan from the North nation was in the Meander River region.[12] Put together they comprised about 100 people.

The other 180 to 200 Aborigines who were inside the Line appear to have belonged to three separate groups. The first comprised sixty Big River people led by Montpeliater. At the beginning of October they were hunting near the Macquarie River and crossed the Line at Miles Opening on the road to Bothwell on 16 October. The second group, of about sixty Oyster Bay and Big River people and possibly led by Tongerlongter, was known to be in the Pitt Water area. Some of this group breached the Line at Three Thumbs in late October, with the loss of two men and the capture of two others. The final group, of at least four small clusters of North Midlands, Ben Lomond and Oyster Bay people, was led by at different times by Mannalargenna, Umarrah and Wareternatterlargener. Each of these clusters consisted of six to eight people and slipped across the Line to the north just as it moved forward in early October. Even so, two men from Wareternatterlargener's group were shot at Break O'Day Plains on 1 November.

A month earlier, a group led by Mannalargenna had boldly killed a soldier from the 63rd Regiment near Fingal and then a stock-keeper employed by George Meredith at Boomer Creek on the east coast. Then it had attacked four servants of Major Grey at St Pauls River on 24 September and managed to kill three of them. Finally, just before the Line got under way, a group of Big River people led by Montpeliater had killed assigned servant George Woodland at the Macquarie River.[13] News of all these incidents gave Arthur, the soldiers and the participating settlers every confidence that they would quickly track down their quarry.

Following preliminary patrols on 4 October, some 2,200 men assembled on 7 October at seven designated areas across the Settled Districts. They comprised 541 troops of all ranks from the 17th, 59th and 63rd regiments— a little over half of the entire garrison in Van Diemen's Land—as well as 700 convicts. The rest were free settlers or civilians. Overall, about 10 per cent of the colony's male population was involved in the operation.[14] Many prominent settlers enthusiastically volunteered and brought along their assigned servants, while ticket-of-leave convicts were ordered to take part or provide a substitute.[15] A week earlier, Arthur had extended martial law beyond the Settled Districts to the whole of Van Diemen's Land, so as to enable the 'active and extended system of military operations against the Natives'.[16]

On 7 October the Line commenced its advance on a 190-kilometre front. According to John Connor, the military force was deployed in three divisions. There were two northern divisions, one under the command of Major Douglas of the 63rd Regiment, the other under the command of Captain Wentworth, also of the 63rd Regiment; the third, or western, division was under the command of Captain Donaldson of the 59th Regiment. Each division was further divided into corps commanded by army officers. As Connor describes:

> Civilians were organised into parties of ten with leaders chosen by
> the local magistrates, but were ultimately under military command.
> The parties moved forward in extended order with no attempt
> at stealth. The aim was to 'beat the bush in a systematic manner'

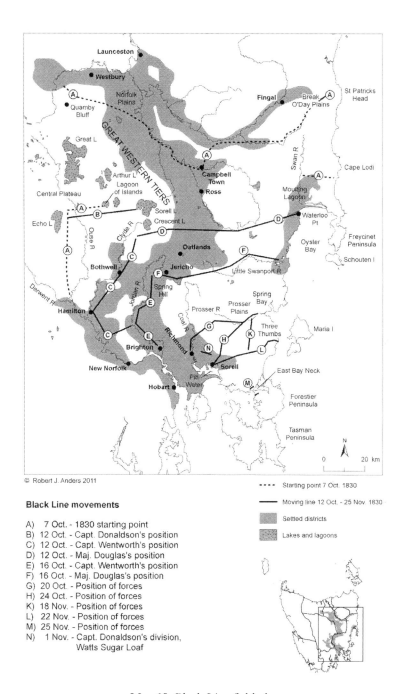

© Robert J. Anders 2011

- - - - Starting point 7 Oct. 1830

——— Moving line 12 Oct. – 25 Nov. 1830

Settled districts

Lakes and lagoons

Black Line movements

A)   7 Oct. - 1830 starting point
B) 12 Oct. - Capt. Donaldson's position
C) 12 Oct. - Capt. Wentworth's position
D) 12 Oct. - Maj. Douglas's position
E) 16 Oct. - Capt. Wentworth's position
F) 16 Oct. - Maj. Douglas's position
G) 20 Oct. - Position of forces
H) 24 Oct. - Position of forces
K) 18 Nov. - Position of forces
L) 22 Nov. - Position of forces
M) 25 Nov. - Position of forces
N)   1 Nov. - Capt. Donaldson's division,
              Watts Sugar Loaf

Map 19 Black Line field plan

and drive the Aborigines ahead of them towards the coast. To ensure that each party kept to its line of advance, Arthur allocated each a number and ordered that they continually confirm their relative position by shouting their number, firing muskets and blowing bugles.[17]

Five days later, despite the difficult terrain, the pouring rain and the uncertain route, most of the parties reached their first rendezvous points between the town of Hamilton in the west and Waterloo Point in the east. The commissariat had succeeded brilliantly in keeping the men on the Line clothed, shod and fed, which in turn reinforced the colonists' high morale.

At the end of the second week, on 16 October, the three divisions drew closer, forming a rough line from the town of Brighton in the west to the mouth of Little Swanport River in the east. But Captain Donaldson's western division failed to cut off any Big River people coming through from the Midland Plain. On 15 and 16 October, two groups of Big River people, comprising about sixty people in all and probably led by Montpeliater, were seen at Miles Opening travelling in the direction of the Great Lake. The leader of one 'skirmishing party' reported: 'Their tracks led us round the north-east side of the |Great| Lake for 5 days, and then to the westward; and we continued on their tracks until yesterday morning.'[18] But then they disappeared.

The Pitt Water district in front of the Line was now largely undefended. On 16 October, a group of about fifty warriors from the Big River and Oyster Bay nations, possibly led by Tongerlongter, plundered six houses in the Wattle Hill area for food and blankets. They speared a shepherd, Thomas Pratt, and then beat him to death with waddies, then wounded Thomas Coffin, whose wife they had killed a year earlier, and harassed Joseph Hayton's family. Two days later, eight of the same group of warriors and a woman plundered settler William Gangell's house at Forcett of food, shirts and four knives, and dangerously wounded Mr Gangell and his eleven-year-old stepson. In retaliation Gangell managed to fatally wound one of the attackers with a pitchfork. Meanwhile, thirty-five other Big River and Oyster Bay men attacked three houses at nearby Wattle Hill, plundered them of food and blankets and harassed the occupants, Mrs Walker, Mrs Brown and Mrs Lane, whose husbands had joined the Line.[19]

In just four days, the warriors had attacked thirteen houses and huts in the Pitt Water district, leaving one settler dead and three wounded, with the reported loss of only one Aboriginal life. It is not known how Arthur responded to these incidents, but he may have been reinforced in his belief that most of the Aborigines were still in front of the Line and could be driven into the Tasman Peninsula.

On 20 October, two of the three divisions met, and the Line formed a continuous 50-kilometre front from Richmond through heavily forested country behind Brown Mountain to Spring Bay on the east coast. On each hill fires were lit to ensure that contact was maintained as the Line moved forward.[20] Four days later, the Line reached Prossers Plains, where torrential rain impeded further progress. Arthur ordered the erection of brush fences and *chevaux de frise*, that is, obstacles of projecting spikes, to prevent the Aborigines from passing through. He then sent forward five skirmishing parties, each of ten men, to look for the Big River and Oyster Bay people in the expectation of capturing them at East Bay Neck.[21]

In the early morning of 25 October, in the pouring rain, a group of Oyster Bay and Big River people attempted to force their way through the Line at Three Thumbs between Sandspit River and Prossers Bay but were apparently repulsed.[22] Later that day, Edward Walpole, the leader of one of the skirmishing parties, saw them hunting in the area now known as the Wielangta Forest Reserve. He watched them for several hours until they formed an encampment for the night in a deep scrubby ravine. He then collected the rest of his party, placed them within 300 metres of the Aborigines' camp and waited until dawn to attack. He 'advanced to the first hut where he unexpectedly saw 3 blacks all fast asleep, under some blankets with their dogs'.[23] Walpole continued:

> [We] crept to one of the Natives, without being perceived by any of the others in the windbreak and there caught him by the leg. There were five men in the windbreak, and the other four rushed away, while others of the party were stooping to catch them. One, however, was caught, after he had fallen into the creek, and the two were shot. There were five other windbreaks across the creek, and in the centre of a very thick scrub.[24]

Of the two males who were taken, one of them, Ronekeennarener, was a
Big River man and the other was a boy, Tremebonener, of about thirteen
years of age, from the Oyster Bay nation. They were immediately deployed
to the skirmishing parties as guides in the rough terrain. Two days later, at
least seven other Aborigines broke through the Line and scurried north-
east to Little Musselroe River, where they joined some of Mannalargenna's
people before they surrendered to G.A. Robinson on 15 November. One
of them, a woman called Luggenemenener, told him that she had seen the
soldiers 'and had been inside the Line and had run away again, coming out
in the morning'. She 'described the soldiers as extending for a long way and
that they kept firing off their muskets' and said that there were 'plenty of
Parkutetenner, horsemen, plenty of soldiers, plenty of big fires on the hills'.[25]
She knew that she had had a lucky escape. Another woman, Woolaytopinnyer, from the Big River nation, later told Robinson 'that it had rained very
hard and they had purposed stopping two days; that the white people saw
them, that they had two fires, that they saw the soldiers and the fires', but
they 'had no trouble getting away'.[26]

The settlers and their servants returned home on 31 October, and the
next day Captain Donaldson's division arrived at Watts Sugar Loaf between
Richmond and Sorell from the Central Plateau. But some Oyster Bay and
Big River people possibly led by Tongerlongter still remained in the Pitt
Water area. On 7 November they plundered a hut on the Coal River and
speared and wounded a woman, Mary Anne Rucker. Eleven days later, as
Mr Gangell's ten-year-old stepson was looking after his father's cattle at
Forcett, 'he suddenly observed a black with his hair covered in red ochre,
peeping at him from behind a tree, and on turning his head he saw 6 or
7 more creeping among the bushes'. The boy raised the alarm and 'some
parties, led by the black boy lately taken . . . speedily pointed out the tracks',
but, once again, the Aborigines escaped.[27] For the next two weeks parties of
soldiers and field police searched the thickets around Three Thumbs, cut
new paths through the thick forests and then scoured the isthmus between
the Forestier and Tasman peninsulas. No Aborigines were found. At the
end of November the operation was officially abandoned.[28]

Although Arthur was deeply disappointed by the operation's outcome, many settlers and soldiers now believed they had a strategy in place to capture the Oyster Bay and Big River nations. In the following year they formed similar lines at Freycinet Pensinsula and the Central Plateau in attempts to force Aboriginal surrender. Further, the operation precipitated a sharp drop in the number of Aboriginal attacks on settlers and their property in the following year. The two key groups of Big River and Oyster Bay nations may have slipped through the first Line in October 1830 but they now had to break up into much smaller groups to find their compatriots. They were also more desperate, in that they were now more likely to kill settler women and children in search of food. For example, at the height of the Line on 16 November at Constitution Hill near Bagdad, three Oyster Bay and Big River men, possibly led by Montpeliater, killed Anne Peters and wounded her seven-year-old sister, Sophia.[29] Early in December another group was seen near Pitt Water and East Bay Neck, and Arthur could take comfort from the capture of a man and a woman from this group at Crown Lagoon on 19 December.[30] In the meantime the sixty or so Big River people who had slipped through the Line at Miles Opening on 16 October were once again plundering huts in the Clyde police district in parties of seven to twelve and operating in different locations on the same day. Then they disappeared into the Central Plateau, where some of them were trapped by another line formed by soldiers and stock-keepers at the River Shannon. On this occasion the Big River people killed three colonists including a woman near Thomas Shone's farm, and in retaliation 'a party of white people followed them and came upon them at night and fired in among them and killed one woman and one man'.[31]

The rest reappeared in March 1831 and plundered huts for food and blankets at New Norfolk and then St Patricks Plains and Lake Sorell. They remained on the Central Plateau for the winter and plundered huts at the River Ouse in June, where they also killed an assigned servant, Jane Kennedy, and wounded a settler, Mrs Triffett.[32] In August they plundered stock-keepers' huts at Lake Echo, and a month later they swooped down the Clyde River and plundered shepherds' huts with alacrity.[33] Then, in mid November, they were joined by the remaining clan of Big River and Oyster Bay people led by Tongerlongter. Over the previous two months this clan had just survived its seasonal journey through the southern Settled Districts. In September it had first harassed settlers and stock-keepers at White Marsh, 32 kilometres north of Pitt Water, and then early in October it had crossed to Great Swanport on its annual pilgrimage to the Freycinet Peninsula to collect swan eggs.[34] Here, settler George Meredith believed that the clan could be trapped and persuaded the police magistrate at Waterloo Point to deploy more than 200 soldiers and colonists in a line across the Freycinet Peninsula between present-day Coles and Wineglass bays to prevent its escape. But once again Tongerlongter and his people slipped through, even though they were forced to break up into two smaller groups. One group travelled north towards John Batman's property at Ben Lomond, where it was apprehended by government agent Charles Cottrell in January 1832. The other, led by Tongerlongter, crossed the Midlands to rendezvous towards the end of November with the Big River people led by Montpeliater at Den Hill near Bothwell.[35]

After combining forces, seven of this latter group robbed Clark's and Jamison's huts of flour and then disappeared towards Lake Echo.[36] But the end was near. Their numbers had by now been so severely depleted that on 31 December they surrendered to Robinson and the mission Aborigines on the western side of Lake Echo. There were twenty-six in all: sixteen men, nine women and one child. In November the year before, Montpeliater's Big River clans had comprised more than sixty people and Tongerlongter's clan had contained a similar number. In the interim at least eleven of Tongerlongter's people had been captured and at least twelve others had been shot. A similar fate had been experienced by many of Montpeliater's people. According to Robinson, Tongerlongter told him that:

> The chiefs assigned as a reason for their outrages upon the white inhabitants that they and their forefathers had been cruelly abused, that their country had been taken from them, their wives and daughters had been violated and taken away, and that they had experienced a multitude of wrongs from a variety of sources.[37]

But it seems that another Big River clan still remained. Six of its people were observed in the Abyssinia area east of the Clyde River in February

1832, and two others were seen near the River Styx on the Upper River Derwent in March 1837.[38] They may have joined some of their relatives in the North nation in the Great Western Tiers behind the Meander River, for nothing more was heard of them until 1841. Then, surveyor James Calder, who was marking the track for Sir John and Lady Franklin's expedition to Macquarie Harbour, came across some of their huts at Lake Echo, near where Robinson had captured their compatriots a decade earlier. The huts appeared of recent construction but Calder did not see any of the Aborigines. After that nothing more was heard of them.[39]

Following the surrender of the Big River and Oyster Bay clans in December 1831 and of another Oyster Bay clan in January 1832, Arthur revoked martial law, reduced the military patrols and disbanded the roving parties. The colonists in the southern, central and eastern parts of the Settled Districts were now in unfettered possession of the land.

In the period between the proclamation of martial law in November 1828 and its revocation in January 1832, at least ninety colonists in the Settled Districts were reported killed by the Aborigines. They included at least ten white women and six children. Most were killed in ones and twos, although, in three cases, three to four colonists were killed in one incident.[40] A further 180 colonists are known to have been injured.

Of the 500 Aborigines from the Big River, Oyster Bay, North Midlands and Ben Lomond nations estimated to have been in the Settled Districts in 1828, fewer than 100 of them surrendered to Robinson and his parties in 1830 and 1831. Although others were known to have died from inter-clan warfare or from disease, an estimated 350 were either killed outright or died from gunshot wounds. Of these, at least 100 were killed in nine known mass killings of six or more, and many others were killed in ones, twos and threes. Further mopping-up operations in the country of the North nation along the Meander River between 1832 and 1834 yielded forty more Aboriginal deaths and the loss of ten colonists. In defending their country against the pastoral invaders, the Aboriginal nations in the Settled Districts had indeed paid the supreme sacrifice.

9

The reckoning

How many Aborigines and colonists actually lost their lives in the Black War? How do the statistics compare with those from other Australian frontier wars? How is the war commemorated today? This chapter addresses these issues and offers some pointers for future research.

Let us begin by compiling and analysing the statistics of the Black War. By using as a starting point the estimate of 1,200 Aborigines in the Settled Districts that was made by the *Colonial Times* on 11 February 1826, it would appear that they consisted of the Oyster Bay, Big River, Ben Lomond, North Midlands and North nations. Of these nations, fewer than 150 of their people are known to have surrendered by 1834. What, then, happened to the rest?

The estimates of Aborigines and colonists killed in each of the war's four phases in the Settled Districts are set out in Table 2 on the following page.

The statistics show that most Aborigines appear to have been killed in the war's second and third phases; that is, between 1 December 1826 and 31 January 1832. In this five-year period, an estimated 808 Aborigines were killed. But there are important differences between the second and third phases. In the second phase, from December 1826 to October 1828, of the 408 Aborigines estimated killed, at least 250 of them—more than half—appear to have been killed in sixteen incidents of mass killings of six or more.[1] In the third phase, when martial law was in force and 350 Aborigines are estimated to have been killed, only about 100 of them appear to have been killed in nine mass killings of six or more. The rest were killed in ones, twos and threes. Thus, settler massacres had a greater impact on the Aborigines in the second phase. This finding supports my argument that, in this

Table 2 Statistics of the Black War in the
         Settled Districts: 1823–34

Phase	Estimate of Aborigines killed	Colonists killed	Total	Aboriginal: colonial death ratio
1. Nov. 1823 – Nov. 1826	80	40	120	2:1
2. Dec. 1826 – Oct. 1828	408	61	469	6:1.5
3. Nov. 1828 – Jan. 1832 (martial law)	350	90	440	3.9:1
4. Feb. 1832 – Aug. 1834	40	10	50	4:1
Total	878	201	1079	4:1

phase, Lieutenant-Governor Arthur implemented active measures to force the Aboriginal nations to surrender. This is further supported by the fact that fewer colonists were killed in this phase than in the martial law phase.

Few historians of the Black War appear to have understood the significance of the second phase. Henry Reynolds, in two recent accounts, acknowledges the importance of the government notice of 29 November 1826 in escalating the war but overlooks the extreme violence that followed. This has led him to estimate the Aboriginal death toll at about the same number as the settlers; that is, around 200.[2] Keith Windschuttle, in *The Fabrication of Aboriginal History*, acknowledges the possibility of the Mount Alexander massacre near Campbell Town in April 1827, but he avoids a serious discussion of the settler massacres along the Meander River in June and July 1827 and declares 'implausible' a press report of a massacre of Oyster Bay warriors following their attack on Mrs Langford and her family in late October 1828, just before the declaration of martial law.[3] James Boyce, on the other hand, contends that most Aborigines in the Settled Districts were probably killed before the declaration of martial law and that a proportion of them were 'likely to have been killed in massacres'.[4] His groundbreaking research encouraged me to carefully re-examine the wide array of known sources for the second phase. They reveal that mass killings of Aborigines were a key feature. This new information offers fresh insights into Arthur's conduct of the war in this phase and how he may have considered massacre, even though it failed, a necessary strategy to force a quick surrender.

If we accept the evidence that 878 Aborigines were killed in the Settled Districts between 1823 and 1834, and that fewer than 150 others are known to have surrendered, then at least half of the remaining 122 of the original estimate of 1,200 Aborigines can be accounted for. The evidence includes mention in G.A. Robinson's journals of thirty people killed in inter-clan disputes, of twelve others remaining in their country after 1834, and reports from the colonial press and settler diaries of the presence of about thirty Aboriginal children in settlers' homes. In the intensity of the wartime conditions, it is not unreasonable to suggest that the remaining fifty or so were either killed by the colonists and the military or died from other injuries, inter-clan disputes or malnutrition. There is very little evidence to support Windschuttle's claim that many of them died from inadvertently introduced disease.[5] It would appear that the Aboriginal nations in the Settled Districts were more likely to be mortally affected by disease after they surrendered than before.

How can we assess the statistics of the colonists who were killed? Of the 201 colonists reported killed overall, ninety of them, or nearly half, including eight women and seven children, were killed in the war's third phase, from 1 November 1828 to the end of January 1832, when martial law was in force. In this phase, it also appears that at least 180 colonists were injured. It seems extraordinary that the strong measures that were put in place to protect the colonists from Aboriginal attack resulted in more of them being killed. This may be explained partly by the fact that many more colonists were living in the Settled Districts in the martial law phase than in previous phases, and partly by the fact that, although there were then fewer Aborigines, as James Boyce has pointed out, they appear to have engaged in more desperate measures to defend their country.[6]

Overall, then, it would appear that more than 1,000 people were killed in the Black War with an Aboriginal to colonial death ratio of 4:1. This is much lower than the ratios estimated for frontier wars in two other Australian colonies. For example, in the frontier war in the Port Phillip District in 1836–51, later known as the colony of Victoria, historian Richard Broome has estimated that at least 1,000 Aborigines and eighty colonists were killed, with an Aboriginal to colonial death ratio of 12:1.[7] Yet my own research on the Port Phillip frontier indicates that more than 1,100 Aborigines were killed in settler massacres alone, suggesting that the number of Aborigines killed overall was probably closer to 2,000, which would result in a Aboriginal to colonial death ratio of 24:1.[8] Recent research by historian Raymond Evans on the Queensland colonial frontier from 1859 to 1897 suggests that more than 24,000 Aborigines and about 2,000 colonists were killed, with an Aboriginal to colonial death ratio of 12:1, which is half of that estimated for Port Phillip.[9] These statistics would suggest that the Black War had some important differences from the frontier wars in other Australian colonies.

This is indeed the case, as Henry Reynolds has pointed out. He considers that the lower Aboriginal to colonial death ratio is explained by the fact that Van Diemen's Land had an almost unlimited supply of male convicts who were deployed in great numbers on the frontier as shepherds and stockmen and thus bore the brunt of Aboriginal attacks.[10] Further, most of these men did not have access to horses, although they appear to have carried defensive weapons such as pistols, muskets and shotguns, but not breech-loading rifles. They believed that their remote locations rendered them vulnerable to Aboriginal attack. These circumstances were reversed a decade later in the new pastoral settlements of Port Phillip (now Victoria) and Moreton Bay (now Queensland) where fewer convicts, shepherds and stockmen were employed on the frontiers because of their mobility on horses and their ready access to a more formidable array of aggressive weapons, including breech-loading rifles. From this more commanding position they could initiate attacks on Aboriginal camps and thus were less likely to lose their own lives.

A further comparison of the three colonial frontiers reveals another important set of statistics: the percentage of Aborigines that were killed in relation to their estimated population. If we accept that the Tasmanian Aboriginal population in the Settled Districts in 1826 was about 1,200 and that, of these, nearly 800 were killed outright between December 1826 and 1834, this makes a death statistic of 60 per cent. If we accept that the estimated Aboriginal population in Port Phillip in 1836 was about 10,000, and that about 2,000 of them were killed outright, the death statistic is 20 per cent. On the Queensland frontier, if we accept Raymond Evans's conservative estimate that the Aboriginal population was about 35 per cent of the estimated Australia-wide population of 750,000, and that over the period from 1859 to 1897 at least 24,000 Aborigines were killed by the native police force alone, then more than 25 per cent of the Aboriginal population in Queensland was killed outright.[11] In each case, these percentages refer either to a discrete part of the colony, such as the Settled Districts in Van Diemen's Land, or to a discrete historical period, as in all three colonies, or to a particular form of settler activism, such as the native police force. Thus, the percentages represent conservative estimates. Even so, when considered alone, each percentage is startling. But the statistics become even more startling when the estimated numbers of Aborigines killed in the three colonies are put together. They reach a tally of 27,000 Aboriginal deaths, which is higher than the estimate of 20,000 for the entire Australian colonial frontier that was first made separately by Henry Reynolds and Richard Broome nearly thirty years ago.[12] These new findings would suggest that their estimate is far too low and that the data and methods they used are due for a major re-assessment.

Finally, let us return to the statistic that has particular significance in understanding the intensity of the Black War in the Settled Districts. That is, the statistic of over 1,000 lives lost overall. That number alone would suggest that a memorial to the fallen is long overdue. Ironically, the first memorial erected in Australia to commemorate the fallen in a colonial war stands in the Anglesea Barracks in Hobart. Erected by soldiers from the 99th Regiment in 1850, it lists the names of twenty-two of their comrades who lost their lives in the first New Zealand war in 1845–46. Its presence stands as a stark reminder of the absence of a memorial to the Black War, which took place over a longer period of time and took many more lives than the New Zealand conflict. Yet, unlike their New Zealand counterparts, Tasmanians today still appear unwilling to acknowledge the significance of frontier wars in shaping their destinies today. I would argue that a memorial to the fallen from both sides of the Black War would signal an important step forward on the long road to Aboriginal reconciliation. And, like the memorials to the Eureka Stockade at Ballarat, it would also signal a new understanding among Australians in general and Tasmanians in particular that violent bloodshed on home soil has been an important part of our history.

PART III

SURRENDER
1829-34

Robinson and the Nuenonne
on Bruny Island, 1829

In March 1829, at the height of the Black War, Arthur had appointed George Augustus Robinson to make some arrangements for the Aborigines captured in the conflict and to conciliate the Nuenonne people at Bruny Island.[1] Robinson's appointment marked a new policy direction for the Australian colonies. Until then, native policy in New South Wales had focused on 'civilizing' Aboriginal survivors of frontier massacres. In Governor Macquarie's time it had included the establishment of the Aboriginal school at Blacktown; and in Governor Brisbane's time it had included financial support for mission stations at Wellington Valley and Lake Macquarie. But Robinson had a different vision. He wanted to 'become acquainted with the history, manners, and language of this interesting portion of the human race, particularly as very little or nothing was known about them', because he feared that they would 'at no distant period become extinct'.[2]

He appears to have developed this approach from his knowledge of United States government policies towards Native American nations in its jurisdiction. In some cases it had appointed agents with extensive knowledge of the Native Americans' languages either to reside among nations which had treaties with the government or to ensure their deportation to somewhere else, usually the western side of the Mississippi River.[3] At first Robinson and Arthur believed that the former approach was possible, but increasingly they resorted to the latter in the firm belief that it was the only way they could save the Tasmanian Aborigines from certain extinction. As the man on the ground, Robinson met continual obstruction from many settlers, stock-keepers and government officials, not because he was a difficult person to deal with, but because they held an unmitigated hatred of the Aborigines. He also met active and sustained resistance from some Aboriginal nations. In his worst moments, he drew the strength to continue his 'friendly mission' from his deep religious convictions and his belief in the Aborigines' humanity. In one sense his ideas and beliefs formed a link to the eighteenth-century Enlightenment, which championed the Aborigines' humanity, and in another he was ahead of his time in forcing the British government to develop a humanitarian policy to ensure their survival.

Despite the contradictions in Robinson's ideas and practices, one point is clear. Had Arthur not appointed him to conciliate the Tasmanian Aborigines, they would certainly have been exterminated, probably by 1835, and as a result we would know very little about them today. Further, his journals reveal the extent of the settlers' determination to eradicate them. Indeed, he was fortunate in locating as many Aborigines as he did. This frightening fact indicates that Robinson's enterprise was 'a mission too late'. Even so, the editor of his journals, Brian Plomley, and his biographer, Vivienne Rae-Ellis, have failed to grasp this salient point. Plomley considers that Robinson was 'verbose and self praising' and that the Tasmanian Aborigines could never have survived anyway—a strange conclusion, considering that they had lived in their homeland for at least

G.A. Robinson. Benjamin Duterrau, State Library of New South Wales, Sydney.

40,000 years.[4] On the other hand Rae-Ellis considers that Robinson was far more interested in making his own fortune than in saving the Tasmanian Aborigines, but if this was the case he could have become rich far more quickly by continuing his profession as a builder.[5]

If we place Robinson and his agenda into the wider political context of the time, a different portrait emerges. As we have seen in Chapter 7, at the height of the war Sir George Murray, the British secretary of state for the colonies, raised the awful prospect that settler extermination of the Tasmanian Aborigines would leave an 'indelible stain' on the reputation of the British Empire. This is not surprising. The Beotuk in Newfoundland had 'disappeared' in 1829, and the prospect of the Tasmanian Aborigines doing the same indicated that a new approach to the problem of white settlers usurping the lands of indigenous peoples was needed. Leaving aside the obvious solution—settlers vacating indigenous lands—George Arthur, as the man in charge in Van Diemen's Land, was given the task to formulate a new policy. He was the first colonial governor to grapple with what became the great moral dilemma of settler colonies in the Anglophone world. Should the British government permit the extermination of indigenous peoples like the Tasmanian Aborigines by white settlers or should they be removed to a safe haven and 'civilized' into British ways? In searching for a solution, Arthur relied heavily on Robinson, the man in the field, for advice.

Both men were well suited to the task, for they were strong adherents of humanitarianism and ardent opponents of slavery. They placed the 'plight' of the Aborigines within this framework, considered the problem at length and believed it was their duty to find a just and equitable solution. They should be judged, then, not solely on the awful outcome, but also on their attempts to find a solution to an insoluble problem. For it must never be forgotten that they were among the first men in the British Empire to confront the issue head on and to champion indigenous rights. The next four chapters, in following Robinson's extraordinary missions to the Tasmanian Aborigines between 1829 and 1834, offer a way of understanding how the new policy was formulated and unfolded and how the Aborigines responded.

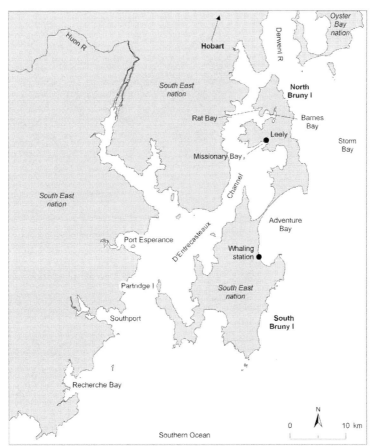

© Robert J. Anders 2011

Map 20 Bruny Island

When Robinson was appointed to take care of the Nuenonne people on Bruny Island on 15 March 1829, he wasted no time in getting there. The island is located at the head of the D'Entrecasteaux Channel, 48 kilometres south-east of Hobart. Robinson conducted his first 'interview' with some Nuenonne people on 30 March at Rat Bay on North Bruny Island. Over the next few weeks he contacted about twenty others, consisting of three families and a cluster of unattached women and men. The first family consisted of Joe, aged about forty, his two wives, one of whom was named Morley, and their two unnamed children; the second family comprised Woorraddy, then aged thirty-seven, his tall, unnamed pregnant wife and their three sons, Peter, Davy and Thomas; and the third family contained Mangerner, who was about fifty and chief of the Lyluequonny clan from Recherche Bay, his daughter Truganini, aged about seventeen, and his unnamed wife, aged about thirty, who was at the time visiting relatives at Port Davey with their adolescent son. There were also three other women: Dray, a widow from Port Davey, aged thirty, and her child; Pagerly, aged eighteen; and Nelson, aged forty, who was possibly Pagerly's sister and who had lost an arm in a man trap. The four unattached men were Catherine, Jack and two young men, Weanee and William. They were the only known survivors of the South East nation, which just six years before had comprised 160 people.[6]

Most of the Aborigines at Rat Bay had gruesome experience of the colonial invaders. Truganini's two sisters, Lowhenunhe and Maggerleede, had been abducted by black American sealer John Baker and were known to be living with another sealer, John Hepthernet, on Kangaroo Island. Truganini's fiancé, Paraweena, had been mutilated and killed in the D'Entrecasteaux Channel by two other sealers.[7] Nelson had recently returned from the Bothwell district, where she and her husband, Bruny Island Jack, had been guides to a military party in search of the Big River people. There, the soldiers had tried to rape her and had shot dead her husband when he tried to escape. On her return to Bruny Island, Mangerner's wife, was abducted by the mutineers on the brig *Cyprus*, and their son drowned.[8]

Robinson quickly made friends with Joe, who told him that he had two wives because the older one became ill and was thought to have died so he took another. But the first recovered and he was now committed to both of them.[9] Robinson learned his first Aboriginal words from Joe, and by 15 May he had obtained sixty words 'as a groundwork for a vocabulary' including *Parleva* which meant Aboriginal people.[10] By then Weanee, the seventeen-year-old boy, had died, and Robinson, in genuine distress, observed his cremation and noted that the women collected bones from the corpse, placed them in soft pouches made of kangaroo skin and used kangaroo sinew to hang them around their necks. Robinson made elaborate plans for an 'Aboriginal village' at Leely on North Bruny Island and issued notices to the nearby settlers, whalers and sealers to stay away. But all these measures came to naught, as more Nuenonne died from colds and severe chest complaints.[11] By July, Joe and both his wives had died, as well as the men Catherine and Jack, and the woman Nelson. The rest of the Nuenonne decamped to other parts of Bruny Island, including the whaling station at Adventure Bay. Despite the desperate situation, Robinson was impressed by the Aborigines' resilience and determination to survive and in particular how the men would quickly re-partner on the death of a wife. He also observed that their own food resources of freshly hunted wallabies, possums, seabirds, shellfish and wild vegetables were far healthier than British rations, although he could not deny their penchant for tea, sugar, biscuit and potatoes.[12]

In early July he was further encouraged by the seasonal visit of nine of the Ninene clan from Port Davey. Some of them were related to the Nuenonne and had walked from Port Davey to Recherche Bay, crossed to the southern tip of Bruny Island by catamaran, and then walked to the mission. But when they discovered that the Nuenonne were ill or had died, they also abandoned Leely and spent the rest of the winter hunting on South Bruny Island, where six died from illness contracted at the mission, leaving only three of them to make their way home to Port Davey. Even then one of the women died en route at Recherche Bay.[13] By 22 September, of the Nuenonne only Woorraddy and his three sons, Mangerner and his daughter Truganini, the women Dray and Pagerly, and the two orphaned children of Joe and Morley were left. By early December, Woorraddy had re-partnered with Truganini, and her father, Mangerner, had re-partnered with Pagerly.

Robinson was beginning to understand the nutritional differences between Aboriginal food and British rations, but he did not yet know that close confinement in British clothes and huts produced susceptibility to European disease. He was beginning to realise from his conversations with Joe, Mangerner and Wooraddy that their relationship to the land lay at the heart of their identity. Even so, he still believed that they would accept British ways once they had observed 'domesticated' Aborigines farming their own plots of land. To this end he was hopeful that Robert

Woureddy [Woorraddy], a Wild Native of Brune Island, One of Mr Robinson's Most Faithful Attendants Attached to the Mission in 1829. Benjamin Duterrau, State Library of New South Wales, Sydney.

Trugernanna [Truganini], a Native of the Southern Part of Van Diemen's Land and Wife to Woureddy Who Was Attached to the Mission in 1829. Benjamin Duterrau, State Library of New South Wales, Sydney.

McAuley, the 'domesticated' Aborigine whom we briefly met in Chapter 3, would lead the way. Arthur had agreed that he should receive a land grant of 20 acres near the mission so that he could begin farming.[14] But Robert came from the Oyster Bay nation and could not consider farming on Nuenonne land.

In the midst of these contradictions, Robinson began to contemplate a mission to the Port Davey people. He believed it might be a way of taking a message of peace to the Aboriginal nations on the other side of the colonial frontier. He seems to have developed the idea from discussions with the Nuenonne people, including Joe, Mangerner, Woorraddy and Dray, and from his understanding of Native American life, gleaned from his reading of Charles Adair's *History of the North American Indians* and William Robertson's *History of America*.[15] The welfare of the Tasmanian Aborigines, he wrote in his diary on 27 November, 'will ever be a paramount object on my mind. I am encouraged in the belief that the aboriginal tribes of this territory may ere long assume a more favourable cast in the scale of improvement than would be imagined from their present rude and uncultivated state.' If he could convey to the Aboriginal nations on the other side of the frontier that the government believed in their humanity and capacity for improvement, then the first step towards conciliation would have been made.[16] By the time Arthur gave him permission to undertake an expedition to Port Davey, on 1 December, 'for the purpose of endeavouring to effect an amicable understanding with the aborigines in that quarter, and through them, with the tribes in the interior', he had a clearer purpose—to meet with every Aborigine on the other side of the frontier.[17]

In planning the expedition, he provided for a party of nineteen people to accompany him. The most important were the twelve Aborigines he had met over the last few months. They included the seven Nuenonne from the Bruny Island mission: Woorraddy, his three sons and his new partner, Truganini; Dray, who originally came from Port Davey; and Pagerly, whose new partner, Mangerner, had died a month earlier. The remaining five Aborigines were men who came from the Settled Districts and included Umarrah, the wily chief of the Stoney Creek clan of the North Midlands nation who had been captured in November 1829, and two of his warrior compatriots, Parwareter and Trepanner. The others were Kickerterpoller, the former 'insurgent' leader of the tame mob who for the past year had been living on Gilbert Robertson's estate at the Coal River, and Robert McAuley, the 'civilized' Aborigine, who had lived with the McAuley family near Brighton since 1810.

The party was supported by fifteen male convicts to carry the supplies, beat their way through the bush and crew the whale boat and schooner. They included Alexander McKay and Alexander McGeary, who had previously worked for the Van Diemen's Land Company and were known as experienced bushmen, Thomas Macklow, James Platt, Jonathon Simpson and William Stansfield who remained with Robinson for several missions and the Polynesian, Joseph Maclaine from Hawaii. He quickly formed a close bond with Robinson, his seventeen-year-old son George and with the mission Aborigines, and over the next five years, he accompanied them on all their missions. But after that, his fate is unknown.[18]

Everyone in the party looked forward to the journey. The Nuenonne people had no wish to return to Leely, where so many of their compatriots had died. Dray wanted to return to her own people, the Ninene clan at Port Davey, while Umarrah and his two compatriots were ecstatic at their release from Richmond gaol. Kickerterpoller was known as an excellent translator, and Robert was to carry the message of 'civilization'. Robinson hoped to convince the Aborigines on the other side of the frontier that they could expect friendship from the government if they did not kill the settlers. On 3 February 1830 fourteen of the party and four of their dogs set off from Recherche Bay along the 'native road' to Port Davey. It was the first of six momentous journeys that Robinson and the 'mission Aborigines' undertook in Trouwunna.

II

Mission to the western nations, 1830

The clans of the South West nation were the most remote from colonial Van Diemen's Land. Even so, their seasonal visits to the D'Entrecasteaux Channel had alerted them to the British invaders since 1804, while those to the North West nation after 1810 had brought them into contact with the sealers. The invasion of their own country may have begun in 1815 with timber-getters logging Huon pine at Birchs Inlet, and it intensified in 1822, when a penal settlement was established at Macquarie Harbour, a pilot station was set up at Cape Sorell and a temporary whaling station began operations from Port Davey. From that time the Ninene at Port Davey were regularly visited by supply ships, and it is known that at least three runaway convicts died there. The Mimegin clan at Macquarie Harbour also appears to have encountered the working parties who cut down its timber and soldiers and convicts hunting its kangaroo, birds, eggs and shellfish. At the same time the soldiers stationed at the pilot station at the head of Macquarie Harbour abducted clanswomen and shot at their husbands.[1]

The inroads into the lands and lives of the four clans of the South West people—the Mimegin from Birchs Inlet on the southern side of Macquarie Harbour, the Lowreenne from Low Rocky Point, the Ninene from Port Davey, and the Needwonnee from Cox Bight—indicates that by 1830 their population had declined from between 200 and 300 to about sixty. Like the Bruny Island people, many were reported to have died from influenza and chest complaints.

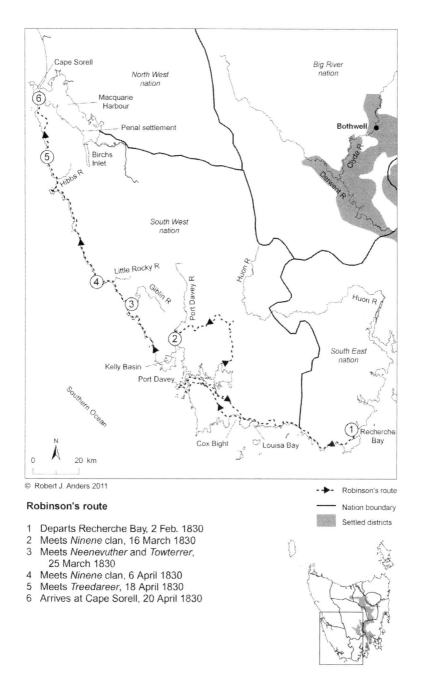

© Robert J. Anders 2011

- →- Robinson's route

—— Nation boundary

▓▓ Settled districts

Robinson's route

1 Departs Recherche Bay, 2 Feb. 1830
2 Meets *Ninene* clan, 16 March 1830
3 Meets *Neenevuther* and *Towterrer*,
   25 March 1830
4 Meets *Ninene* clan, 6 April 1830
5 Meets *Treedareer*, 18 April 1830
6 Arrives at Cape Sorell, 20 April 1830

Map 21 Robinson's search for the South West nation, 2 February – 20 April 1830

No white man had travelled the 'native road' between Recherche Bay and Port Davey before, and Robinson expected to reach Port Davey in three days. But even with Dray and the Nuenonne people as his guides, the journey took more than six weeks. Robinson was unprepared for the impenetrable mountains and extensive marshes through which the party often waded, waist deep. Game was scarce and the rivers were bare of both scale fish and shellfish. They did not find a single South East person on this part of the journey, although they saw nearly 100 of their huts. Robinson concluded that none lived in that area; rather, they used the huts for shelter during seasonal visits.[2]

It was not until 16 March, at the mouth of the Port Davey River, that the mission Aborigines 'descried the smoke of the natives' fire' and Robinson sent Woorraddy, Truganini, Pagerly and Dray to make contact. He waited anxiously for a day, and eventually Woorraddy, Truganini and Pagerly returned. They had met some of the Ninene clan and told them of his mission. Dray had stayed with them, for she had met her brother, Neennevuther, who was a chief and requested that Robinson 'should come to them in the morning'. He was most relieved when Dray returned the next morning with two young women. Leaving them at his tent as hostages, Robinson set off in search of the other Ninene, taking eight mission Aborigines and three convicts. But the Ninene were frightened by this large party of strangers and remained hidden. After two days of fruitless search, Robinson finally allowed Dray, her two companions and Woorraddy to track them to their hiding place in thick scrub. Dray called to them to come out. An elderly woman emerged and was soon followed by the rest of the women and children. They sat down by Robinson's fire and were then joined by the men, who had been hunting. Robinson counted twenty-six in all, consisting of ten couples and six children. He gave them biscuit and distributed beads and ribbons, but they were suspicious of his intentions and during the night they decamped, leaving behind three women. Thus, the first encounter had met with mixed results.[3]

On 25 March, near the Giblin River, Robinson encountered two chiefs, Neennevuther, who was Dray's brother, and Towterrer:

Robinson Meets Neennevuther and Tauterrer. Journal of G.A. Robinson, 25 March 1830, State Library of New South Wales, Sydney.

They stood on the crown of the hill, holding in their hands a waddy with which they had been hunting. Over their shoulders hung a kangaroo mantle. I made towards them with some difficulty, having a heavy pack on my back.

As soon as I came within hearing they called to the young women accompanying me who belonged to their tribe, to know if there was any NUM ('white man'), for they did not seem to heed me. A sullenness hung over their countenance and when I spoke they would not answer. As soon as the young women acquainted them that there was no NUM, they became cheerful and approached me and shook hands.[4]

The rest of the clan members, who had remained in the bush, then appeared. Among them was an old man with two wives and two daughters, one of whom discovered three pistols in Robinson's knapsack. He then had to restrain Woorraddy, whose behaviour 'had begun to excite their apprehensions'. Robinson told them that he came not to injure them but to do them good. If they wished to accompany him they were welcome; if not, they would stop and he would proceed. They stayed and invited the mission Aborigines to celebrate the meeting with a feast and singing and dancing until a late hour. The clan stayed with Robinson for four days, travelling up the coast to Little Rocky River at Elliott Bay. Then in the middle of the night it decamped. Dray said they were afraid of the mission men, Woorraddy, Kickerterpoller and Umarrah. When Robinson returned with Dray to Little Rocky River on 6 April, he was delighted to meet some of the people from the earlier encounter, but they disappeared the next morning, taking Dray with them and leaving another woman, Timemedenene, in her place.[5]

On 18 April, near a lagoon at the mouth of the Hibbs River, Robinson's party came across four more of the Ninene clan. Timemedenene knew them, for one of the men, Treedareer, was her brother. Robinson gave each of them blankets and beads and travelled on, with Treedareer joining them. About six kilometres further on, they made a fire and Treedareer went in search of others from his clan. He soon returned accompanied by an elderly woman named Pennerowner and her two sons. Robinson parted from them and the next day came across another family—a man named Leelinger and his wife, son and daughter. The daughter was so terrified by the presence of a white man that she plunged into the sea, and despite Truganini's attempts to reassure her she would not come out.[6]

Robinson had now contacted about sixty people from the South West nation and had learned something of the art of conciliation. He knew he should not carry firearms, that he should travel with only a small party of mission Aborigines rather than a large party of white men and Aborigines, and that he should try to live off the land and independent of supply depots. Although the Ninene were wary and hostile, he considered they were unlikely to make attacks in the Settled Districts and that if he returned in a year or so they would probably surrender to him.

He pressed on to Cape Sorell and then the penal station at Macquarie Harbour, where he wrote of his success to Arthur and then continued

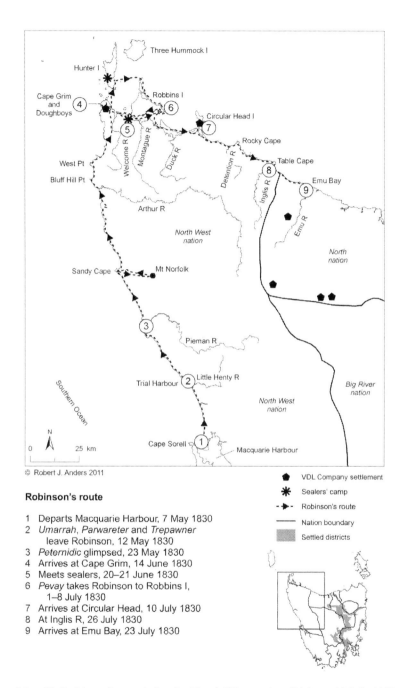

© Robert J. Anders 2011

Robinson's route

1 Departs Macquarie Harbour, 7 May 1830
2 *Umarrah*, *Parwareter* and *Trepawner*
 leave Robinson, 12 May 1830
3 *Peternidic* glimpsed, 23 May 1830
4 Arrives at Cape Grim, 14 June 1830
5 Meets sealers, 20–21 June 1830
6 *Pevay* takes Robinson to Robbins I,
 1–8 July 1830
7 Arrives at Circular Head, 10 July 1830
8 At Inglis R, 26 July 1830
9 Arrives at Emu Bay, 23 July 1830

⬠ VDL Company settlement
✳ Sealers' camp
- ▶ - Robinson's route
— Nation boundary
▨ Settled districts

Map 22 Robinson's search for the North West nation, 7 May – 28 July 1830

his journey up the coast to find people from the North West nation. But on 12 May at Trial Harbour, north of the Little Henty River, Umarrah, Parwareter and Trepanner, the three mission Aborigines who were known to have contacts with the North West clans, decamped. Their departure brought home to Robinson the precarious nature of his relationship with the mission Aborigines. The three men had used their diplomatic skills in difficult moments of contact with the clans of the South West nation. For example, when supplies of fresh meat had run low they had quickly hunted for kangaroo, and when tensions had increased they had been the first to respond to invitations by the South West people to participate in ceremonial dancing and singing. Indeed, by the time Robinson had reached Trial Harbour he placed more trust in these three men than the other mission Aborigines. Their sudden departure was a severe blow to his prestige and upset his plans for the next stage of the mission.[7]

The eight known clans of the North West nation had experienced more than twenty years of violent conflict with the colonial invaders. It had begun in 1810 with sealing parties abducting women, and in 1820 a group of sealers had hidden itself in a cave at the Doughboys near Cape Grim to ambush a group of Pennemukeer women collecting mutton-birds and shellfish. As the women swam ashore the sealers rushed out with muskets, pushed fourteen women into an angle of the cliff, bound them with cords, and carried them off to Kangaroo Island. In revenge the Pennemukeer men had later clubbed three sealers to death. By 1825 the sealers had hunted out most of the elephant seals as well as kangaroos on Robbins Island, forcing the Parperloihener clan to seek new places to forage, thus creating tension with other clans in the area.[8]

Violence had further intensified from 1822 when small groups of escaped convicts took the coastal route north from Macquarie Harbour in search of freedom. They regularly harassed the Peternidic in search of food and fire, which made the clan suspicious of other white intruders. And a detachment of soldiers stationed at the head of the Pieman River shot at the Peternidic and the Tarkinener when they were hunting.[9]

But the Van Diemen's Land Company (hereafter known as the VDL Company), which obtained a land grant of more than 200,000 hectares in 1825 to graze sheep, had the greatest impact on the North West nation.

The company represented the last phase of pastoral expansion in the colony in the 1820s and occupied key Aboriginal kangaroo hunting grounds at Circular Head and Cape Grim in 1826.[10] When the Peerapper clan from West Point visited Cape Grim in November 1827 in search of mutton-bird eggs and seals it found shepherds tending a large flock of sheep. The shepherds immediately tried to entice some Peerapper women into a hut, and, when the men objected, in the resulting skirmish one of the shepherds, Thomas John, was speared in the thigh and several Peerapper men including a chief were shot. In retribution on 31 December the Peerapper, probably led by Wymurrick, returned to Cape Grim and destroyed 118 ewes from the company's stock, spearing some and driving the remainder into the sea.

A month later, four shepherds, Charles Chamberlain, William Gunshannon, Richard Nicholson and John Weavis and Richard Frederick, the master of one of the company's ships, *Fanny*, searched for the Peerapper clan at its nearby camp at night and killed twelve of its members. A few days later, on 9 February, the same four shepherds surprised and trapped a party of Peerapper men, women and children at what is now known as Suicide Bay as they were feasting on mutton-birds that the women had caught at the nearby Doughboy Islands. Some of the Peerapper rushed into the sea, others scrambled round the cliff and the rest were 'put to death' by the shepherds. Others who had sought shelter in the cleft of the rock the shepherds forced 'to the brink of an awful precipice, massacred them all and threw their bodies down the precipice, many of them perhaps but slightly wounded'. After that the Pennemukeer called the white people at Cape Grim *Nowhummoe*, the devil, and when they heard the report of a gun they said that Nowhummoe had shot 'another tribe of blacks'. The Pennemukeer afterwards avoided the settlement at Cape Grim but plundered remote huts to obtain provisions.[11]

By then the Pennemukeer and the Parperloihener had been joined by other clans like the Tommeginer from Table Cape, the Pendowte from Studland Bay and the Peerapper. Further down the coast the inland routes that the Manegin from the Arthur River, the Tarkinener from Sandy Cape and the Peternidic from the Pieman River usually travelled to the

ochre mines at Mount Vandyke were immediately affected by the establishment of VDL Company stations at the Hampshire and Surrey hills.
By mid 1830, all the North West clans that Robinson expected to contact
were locked in a violent struggle with the VDL Company for control
of their land, and their overall population had plummeted from 700 to
about 300.

On 23 May, inland from the mouth of the Pieman River, Robinson first
saw some Peternidic people from the Pieman River clan, but they refused
to meet him. None of the mission Aborigines had relatives among them,
and Umarrah, who would have known some of them, had departed a
week earlier. The Peternidic shadowed Robinson's party along the coastline until it reached the VDL Company establishment at Cape Grim on
14 June. Disappointed by the failure to make contact, Robinson left gifts
at their campsites as a gesture of friendship. A week later, at the Welcome
River opposite Robbins Island, he met a group of sealers. With them were
six Aboriginal women they had abducted from the north-east several years
before and a young man, Pevay, or Tunnerminnerwait, aged eighteen,
from Robbins Island. He had joined them about a week before. Among
the sealers was a New Zealander called Witieye. 'He had two women and
was head man among the sealers and considered the most honourable.'[12]
The others were an Englishman, Robert Drew, who had two tyereelore,
David Kelly, and Edward Tomlins, the son of an Aboriginal mother and
an English father. Robinson considered their activities immoral and told
Witieye and Kelly that

> numerous complaints had reached the government as to the conduct
> of the sealers both in the eastern and in the western straits, and that
> numerous aggressions had been committed by them upon the abori-
> gines of the colony. I said that I was not aware that the government
> had taken measures respecting them (it would perhaps depend on
> my report), but I assured them the government would do so should
> I report the necessity of such a thing, and if such an act should be
> passed it would make their situations very irksome.[13]

Robinson also told them he intended to make contact with every Aborigine on the island and that if any told him of outrages by the sealers he would bring the offenders before the courts. But if they 'conducted themselves with propriety', they would not be harmed. They accepted Robinson's authority with extraordinary politeness, offered him provisions when his own supply boat failed to appear and then rowed him back to Cape Grim and invited him to visit their camp on Hunter Island. By then Robinson realised that Pevay and his boatman, Alexander McKay, who had previously worked for the VDL Company, would prove the best people to assist him in contacting the North West clans.[14]

After teaching Robinson the basic vocabulary of the Parperloihener language, Pevay took him to Robbins Island to locate his brother Pendow-tewer and Narrucer, a twenty-year-old widow from the Peerapper clan at West Point. But they failed to entice the other Parperloihener who were also on the island to join them.[15] Robinson decided not to force the issue. He arrived at the VDL Company's headquarters at Circular Head on 10 July and two weeks later set off with eight mission Aborigines and two assigned servants to track down the Tommeginer clan near Table Cape.

The Sealers' Camp on the Main Near Robbins Island. Journal of G.A. Robinson,
20 June 1830, State Library of New South Wales, Sydney.

On 27 July he met his supply boat, steered by Alexander McKay, at the Inglis River. On board were two men, Nicermenic and Linermerrinnecer. They had seen McKay's boat and because they knew him had signalled him to pick them up. Robinson sent Nicermenic, Pendowtewer and Linermerrinnecer to Launceston gaol, and Narrucer to Hobart Town, believing that he would be rewarded for his efforts. Instead, Arthur authorised their release because they did not come from the Settled Districts. Robinson met them all again two years later. Reaching Emu Bay on 28 July, he wrote to Arthur of the success of his journey so far, even though, in comparison with his interactions with the South West people, he had not managed to contact many of the North West clans. But he warned that, unless a plan was formulated for their quick removal, the sealers and VDL Company shepherds would exterminate them within a very short time. He also wrote to the Reverend William Bedford on the Aborigines Committee and told him that, had the opportunity existed to make this kind of contact with the Aborigines some years before, cordial relations could have been reached. But now it was a mission too late.[16]

The North nation, whose country Robinson was about to enter, was locked in a desperate war with two of the most ruthless colonising groups in the colony—the VDL Company in the west and the cattle barons in the east—for control of their country. The company's grazing establishments at Emu Bay, the Surrey Hills, Hampshire Hills and Middlesex Plains were key theatres of violent conflict with the North nation, as were the vast cattle grazing runs in the Western Marshes near the Meander River. The North nation's four known clans—the Plairhekehillerplue from Emu Bay, the Punnilerpanner from Port Sorell, the Noeteeler from the Hampshire Hills, and the Pallittorre from Quamby Bluff—were the guardians of the ochre mines at Mount Housetop, St Valentines Peak, Mount Vandyke and the Gog Ranges and were well prepared to defend their country from the invaders. When violent conflict broke out on the cattle runs between the Pallittorre and the stockmen in December 1825, it was the beginning of some of the bloodiest encounters in the Black War.[17]

In that month the Pallittorre had returned to their country from the north coast, expecting to hunt kangaroo in the Western Marshes. To their surprise they found vast numbers of cattle occupying their kangaroo hunting grounds and heavily armed and experienced stockmen like Thomas Baker and James Cubit mounted on horseback shooting their kangaroos. Baker and Cubit carried shotguns, and Thomas Johnson wore a brace of pistols and carried a musket and a bayonet. Another stockman, Paddy Heagon, who managed Gamiel Butler's cattle run at The Retreat near present-day Deloraine, had a swivel gun which he had learned to use while working at George Meredith's whale fishery at Oyster Bay. The stockmen on this frontier saw themselves as frontline troops, ready to defend themselves and their masters' cattle and with the capacity to kill numbers of Pallittorre people.[18]

When some Pallittorre men complained to James Cubit about shooting their kangaroos, he brazenly shot at them. A few days later about 160 Pallittorre men surrounded his hut and threw spears at him. He was saved by his partner, Dolly Dalrymple Briggs, who was the daughter of Wottecowiddyer and sealer George Briggs. She fought them off with a shotgun, killing fourteen of them.[19] Six months later, Cubit told Henry Hellyer, the VDL Company's chief surveyor, that on another occasion he had been obliged 'to drop 4 or 5 of them', and in a similar skirmish reported in September 1826 more were reported as 'severely wounded if not slain'.[20]

In January 1827 the Pallittorre returned to the Western Marshes to hunt kangaroo and remained there for the next six months, harassing the twenty or so stockmen stationed in huts in the area. The stockmen had no hesitation in firing back but by June they had had enough. After a group of Pallittorre men ransacked David Gibson's stock hut at Dairy Plains on 12 June and tried to spear the overseer, Thomas Baker, Gibson and the other stockmen in the region, with the assistance of a local constable and two corporals from the 40th Regiment, exacted revenge. Over the next eighteen days they slaughtered about 100 Pallittorre in four separate nighttime raids on their camps.[21]

But the North people were not without leaders. It was believed in 1827 that the Pallittorre were led by Quamby, who had been orphaned as a small boy in 1810 when his parents were killed by stockmen. He was taken into the home of the leading settler in the region, William Lyttleton, and baptised in 1811. His surname identified him with Richard Dry's estate, Quamby, and with Quamby Bluff, the prominent mountain peak in the district. Local legend suggests that he was raised first at Lyttleton's house, where he learned English and perhaps to read and write, and then at Dry's estate, where he worked as a stockman, but that he returned to his own people, the Pallittorre, in the mid 1820s. Henry Hellyer told Robinson that Quamby 'had disputed the land occupied by the whites and that he had successfully driven them off, but that he was afterwards killed with others'.[22]

At the end of 1828 the stockmen were confronted by the Plairhekehill-erplue clan, led by a woman, Tarerenorerer, or Walyer, as she was known by the sealers. As a young woman she had been abducted by men from the Port Sorell clan and exchanged for dogs and flour to the sealers. After living with them for some years she had escaped in 1828 and had become the leader of the Plairhekehillerplue clan at Emu Bay. She had taught the clan how to use firearms. Walyer would stand on a hill and give orders to her men to attack the stockmen, taunting them to come out of their huts and be speared.[23] The North people were also known to have killed stockmen trespassing on the road to the ochre mines at Mount Housetop and Mount Vandyke, systematically besieging their huts for plunder and firearms, and spearing their cattle. At the Meander River in May 1830 a party of North people entered a settler's hut during his temporary absence, even though two assigned servants were ploughing in sight of the hut, and carried off nearly all its 'moveables', recognising that only by destroying the white man's environment would they convince the invaders to leave the area. One of the North people ran from the hut with a bag of sugar weighing about 59 kilograms, while others took loaded guns. There was considerable fear among the colonists that the North people would use them.[24]

By the time Robinson entered the country of the North nation on 6 August 1830 its numbers had plummeted from about 400 in 1826 to fewer than sixty. His first foray was to the Hampshire Hills, a VDL Company grazing run on the border with the North West nation. He was accompanied by two assigned servants, the two couples, Woorraddy and Truganini and Kickerterpoller and Pagerly, and Robert and Pevay. When they arrived, some of the shepherds told them that they would shoot Aborigines

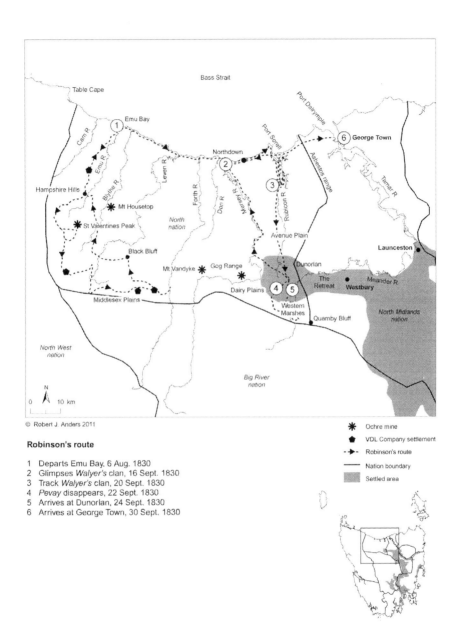

Map 23 Robinson's search for the North nation, 6 August – 30 September 1830

whenever they found them. These attitudes, Robinson realised, provided plenty of reasons for the Aborigines to retaliate. He wrote in his journal:

> The children have witnessed the massacre of their parents and their relations carried away into captivity by these merciless invaders, their country has been taken from them, and the kangaroo, their chief subsistence, have been slaughtered wholesale for the sake of paltry lucre. Can we wonder then at the hatred they bear to the white inhabitants? This enmity is not the effect of a moment. Like a fire burning underground, it has burst forth. This flame of aboriginal resentment can and ought only to be extinguished by British benevolence. We should fly to their relief. We should make some atonement for the misery we have entailed upon the original proprietors of this land.[25]

But he could not make contact with any of the North people. After more than five weeks' fruitless search in the Middlesex Plains region, Robinson headed back to the coast and turned east to the Mersey River. Then on 16 September at the Mersey River, he saw some of their fresh footprints, but he lost sight of them at Port Sorell. The following day he heard them on the other side of the water, where they had gathered to collect swan eggs. He saw them again on 20 September at the Rubicon River. He realised then that they were part of Walyer's clan, and that they were stalking him with the probable intention of killing him. He wanted to capture them, but since his earlier captives had been freed he saw no point.[26]

When Robinson and his party returned to the mouth of the Rubicon River at Port Sorell, they found that the coxswain and three of the mission Aborigines—Kickerterpoller, Pagerly and Robert—had tracked down two Aboriginal youths from Circular Head who knew Pevay. William Parker, overseer of Captain Thomas's nearby property of Northdown, said he was pleased the boys had been captured because 'he would have shot them had he seen them'.[27] (Thomas and Parker were killed by Aborigines the following year.) The boys had been found near Launceston a short time before, but, like those captured by Robinson, they had also been freed by the government. The next night they departed, taking Pevay with them, determined to join their other recently released compatriots, Pendowtewer, Narrucer and Linermerrinnecer. Pendowtewer and Pevay were quickly recaptured by some stockmen and taken to Launceston gaol, from which Robinson released them a few weeks later. He met up with Narrucer and Linermerrinnecer in their country in the west in 1832.[28]

Despite these setbacks, Robinson had learned some more protocols about meeting 'strangers'. Now he always carried tea and damper—the bushman's bread made from flour and water and baked in hot ashes—to offer any new Aborigines that he met. He reached Dunorlan, the home of police magistrate William Moriarty on the north-west frontier of the Settled Districts on 24 September and four days later at the Mersey River, he read the proclamations announcing the forthcoming military operations against the Aborigines in the Settled Districts: the Black Line. He hastened to George Town and then Launceston, where he found the colonists eagerly preparing to do battle with the Aborigines, and then to the town of Ross, in the heart of the Settled Districts, to confer with Arthur about the next phase of his mission.[29]

Robinson had completed a remarkable journey. With Dray's help he had met most of the South West nation. With Pevay's help and the assistance of his boatman, Alexander McKay, he had met seven people from the North West nation and had avoided possible aggression from Walyer's people from the North nation. He had learned several Aboriginal languages and had begun to understand the art of conciliation. But he also considered that relations between the North West and North nations and the VDL Company had become too fractured for the former to survive for much longer. This led him to believe that he could entice them to surrender in the near future and that they could be compensated for the loss of their land by placing them in a sanctuary arranged by the government, where they could learn the art of civilisation and Christianity. In the meantime the more pressing matter of the Black Line overtook all other concerns.

12

Surrender in the Settled Districts, 1830–31

When G.A. Robinson met Arthur at Ross on 6 October 1830, they agreed that Robinson should proceed first to the north-east, where they hoped he would find clans that had slipped through the Line and negotiate their surrender. Then he would take them to a temporary refuge on Swan Island, start removing the tyereelore from the sealers and search for a permanent site on one of the Bass Strait islands as an asylum for the captured Aborigines. After that Robinson would track down all the other Aborigines remaining in the Settled Districts and negotiate their surrender.[1]

The clans in the north-east of Van Diemen's Land that Robinson set out to contact in October 1830 were no longer discrete. Rather, as was pointed out in Chapter 8, they were composite groups led by very strong chiefs like Mannalargenna, Umarrah, Montpeliater and Tongerlongter. So they were unlikely to prove friendly to an unarmed government agent like Robinson when so many other white men were hunting for them. But, unlike in his expedition to the nations in the north-west, Robinson was better prepared to meet the North East clans because some of the mission Aborigines had relatives among them. He also had the support of some of the tyereelore, like Drummernerlooner, aged about nineteen, from the Cape Portland clan, who it seems had been abducted with her mother, Poolrerrener, by James Munro a decade earlier and taken to Preservation Island. Drummerner-looner appears to have known Mannalargenna and may have made some journeys back to her clan at Cape Portland. The other tyereelore supporting Robinson, Tanlebonyer, aged about twenty-four, came from Little Swanport.

She had recently been abducted by sealer John Brown, who had drowned shortly afterwards, and she had then been taken with Drummernerlooner by James Parish to Captain Donaldson, who was looking for guides to assist his army division in the Black Line.[2] Indeed, during this part of his mission Robinson was confronted with the contradictions of the Straits community and demands by some of the chiefs for the return of their kinswomen. Some of the women were delighted to return to their Aboriginal families, but others resisted capture and remained with their new families on the eastern Bass Strait islands.

The party that Robinson set off with from Launceston on the early spring day of 9 October included Drummernerlooner and Tanlebonyer, the young man Pevay, released from Launceston gaol, and four of the mission Aborigines: Pagerly, Kickerterpoller, Truganini and Wooraddy. As backup he retained the services of boatmen Alexander McKay and Alexander McGeary and three convict servants, James Lindsey, Thomas Macklow and the Hawaiian Joseph Maclaine.

In comparison with the dense forests and mountains Robinson had encountered in the winter in the west and north, the north-east coast in spring was flat, open heath country, abounding in kangaroos and small animals, with river estuaries stocked with swans and shellfish and an abundance of mutton-birds and seals. Robinson's party travelled up to 40 kilometres a day between the Piper River and George Bay, sometimes hugging the coastline, sometimes taking inland Aboriginal roads. On 31 October, near the source of the Anson River, 16 kilometres inland from the east coast, the party was rewarded by signs of Aboriginal fires. The next day they found an Aboriginal hut and as they approached it a number of very large, fierce dogs leaped out. Drummernerlooner then called out. Soon Mannalargenna approached and Drummernerlooner explained why they had come. Mannalargenna saluted Robinson with an embrace and a kiss and then introduced him to five of his compatriots, four men and one woman. Another man and a woman remained hidden in the bush.[3]

Robinson told Mannalargenna and his people about the Line by tracing in the sand with a stick its nature and formation and told him that the military parties before long would be in the north-east. 'In reply to this

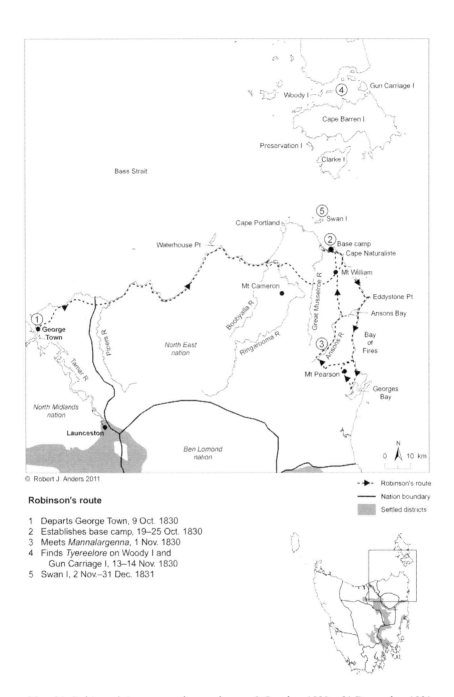

© Robert J Anders 2011

Robinson's route

- – ▶ – Robinson's route
——— Nation boundary
▨ Settled districts

Robinson's route

1 Departs George Town, 9 Oct. 1830
2 Establishes base camp, 19–25 Oct. 1830
3 Meets *Mannalargenna*, 1 Nov. 1830
4 Finds *Tyereelore* on Woody I and
   Gun Carriage I, 13–14 Nov. 1830
5 Swan I, 2 Nov.–31 Dec. 1831

Map 24 Robinson's journey to the north-east, 9 October 1830 – 31 December 1831

preamble they complained in bitter terms of the injuries to which they and their progenitors had been exposed through the medium of the whites.'[4] Robinson made some tea and then told Mannalargenna that he proposed to go to Swan Island to keep out of the way of soldiers' guns and invited him and his party to join him. Mannalargenna agreed to go with him and went to look for the other man and woman, Polelerwin and Tarnebunner. They would not come out, but they joined Robinson's party the next day.[5]

As we have seen, Mannalargenna was a chief from the Oyster Bay nation who had developed complex relations with the sealers since at least 1815 and since 1827 had conducted guerilla raids against the settlers. Now in his late sixties, he was held in awe by most of his people for his extraordinary abilities as a hunter and guerilla fighter and in maintaining social, spiritual and political relationships, which were vital to the Aborigines' survival. His party had recently comprised about twenty people from the Ben Lomond nation and the Great Swanport and Stoney Creek clans which had crossed the Settled Districts to Blackmans River to fight the Big River people, with whom they had been in conflict over women. On their return to the east coast across the Midland Plain, three of them had been shot in an encounter with a military party. In revenge the Ben Lomond people had followed their assailants, waited until they were asleep beside a campfire, and killed two of them. Then they had encountered the Line east of Campbell Town and had to separate. Three of them had gone to look for their compatriots near Piper River, another six had gone to Schouten Passage at Oyster Bay to get swan eggs, and Mannalargenna and eight others had gone to John Batman's house at Ben Lomond to free four women and a boy captured the year before. There, Mannalargenna had realised that if they were to keep the settlers' dogs and to make contact with the others who had gone to find the Stoney Creek people, they must again separate. So he and eight others had moved towards the north-east while the other four had gone towards Piper River. Mannalargenna's party had been in the George River area for about six days when Robinson's party found them.[6]

After an evening of feasting, singing and dancing, Robinson obtained the names of seventy-two other Aborigines still in the region, of whom only six were women; there were no children. The low number of women led

an to return some of the tyereelore, as a way of restoring
e and ensuring that the Aborigines in the region would

me he ferried Mannalargenna and his people across to
Swan Island and five days later left them feasting on penguins and mutton-
birds with the mission Aborigines while he set off with Drummernerlooner
and his new coxswain, James Parish, to recover the tyereelore. At that time
he believed there were about thirty sealers and twenty-five tyereelore in
the eastern strait, scattered in small communities from Preservation Island
to the Kent Group. After brief visits to the sealing camps on Preservation
and Woody islands, where he recovered Toogernuppertootener, who was
Mannalargenna's sister, he landed at Gun Carriage Island, the main sealers'
settlement. But only one sealer was in residence, the rest having fled after
hiding the tyereelore among the rocks and warning them that Robinson
would shoot if he found them. Despite this, Drummernerlooner and
Toogernuppertootener located two women, Tencotemanener from Little
Swanport and Woreterlokekoteyer from Cape Portland, and they returned
in triumph with Robinson to Swan Island on 15 November.[8]

During his absence, six more of Mannalargenna's people, a woman and
five men, had recognised the smoke from his fire on Swan Island and had
been ferried across to join him on 14 November. Robinson recognised
the woman as Luggenemenener, who had been at his house in Hobart
Town and then rejoined the Oyster Bay people when he had departed
on his mission to the west coast. Two of the men, Terlanderreenner and
Trueermermarmlenener, were her brothers and a third was their friend
Pundootternoonnenner. The fourth man, Tillarbunner, also known as
Batman's Jack, had been a guide with the military parties. Luggenemenener
had slipped through the Line at Three Thumbs a month earlier and then
gone to Batman's house at Ben Lomond. From there she had run away
with Tillarbunner to find Wareternatterlargener from Pipers River, two
of her brothers and Pundootternoonnenner. According to Robinson, they
exchanged stories of relatives and friends who had been killed by soldiers
and settlers while defending their country.[9]

Wareternatterlargener and Mannalargenna told Robinson that only
two groups of their people remained in the north-east. One of them, led by

Umarrah, was in the Tamar Valley and the other was in the Fingal Valley. This meant that only six groups remained on the periphery of the Settled Districts: the two groups in the north-east, the two groups of Big River people led by Montpeliater, the group of Oyster Bay people led by Tongerlongter and Walyer's group from the North nation at Port Sorell. The rest were on the other side of the frontier.

Robinson now sent James Parish to search for more of the tyereelore and by 19 December he returned with eleven of them, many of whom had relatives among the people on Swan Island. They included Tanlebonyer's sister, Tekartee, and Nickerumpowwerrerter, who both came from Ben Lomond; Wottecowiddyer, from the Trawlwoolway clan at Mount William, who had at least two living children by two different sealers; Emerenna, also from Cape Portland, who was Mannalargenna's daughter and was living with the sealer Thomas Beeton and had a child, Lucy Beeton, nearly two years old. Lucy became a central figure in the Straits community in the 1850s. Finally, there was Tarenootairrer, aged about twenty-five, who also came from Cape Portland and was about to play a critical role in Robinson's mission.

To celebrate the women's arrival, the Aborigines once again plunged into ceremonial feasting, singing and dancing and forged new political and social relationships which included the 'marriage' of Mannalargenna to Tanlebonyer. One of the most popular performances was the horse dance, based on the story of one of Luggenemenener's brothers having outrun a man on horseback. In their revitalised condition, they completely ignored Robinson's attempts to move them into huts or to attend his makeshift Sunday services.[10]

Robinson found that one of the tyereelore whom Parish had brought to Swan Island was Walyer, who had shadowed his party along the north coast near Port Sorell three months before. Since then, she had been captured by two sealers and taken to an island in eastern Bass Strait. There, she had refused to work for them so they had decided to isolate her on Penguin Island, but during the voyage there she had attempted to kill them, and according to Parish she would have succeeded, had he not appeared in his own boat. The sealers were very pleased to give her up. Now at Swan

Island, Walyer soon circulated a story that a boat had gone to Launceston to bring soldiers to shoot them all or send them to gaol, where they would have fetters put on their legs. To maintain order, Robinson was forced to send her away with Parish on his next trip to search for more women on the Bass Strait islands. But when she returned to Swan Island at the end of December she had, within a few hours, 'thrown the whole of the natives into a state of alarm by telling them the white people intended shooting them'. She told Robinson that she liked *lutetawin*, the white man, as much as a black snake. He was relieved when she died of influenza at the end of May 1831.[11]

On 4 January 1831, Robinson left the people feasting on Swan Island and set off for Hobart. He had been summoned to appear before the Aborigines Committee and the Executive Council to discuss the success of his mission so far and the future of the Aborigines who had surrendered. Arthur was enormously pleased with Robinson's work and accepted the Aborigines Committee's recommendation to increase his salary from £100 to £250 a year, with a gratuity of £100 as well as a maximum land grant of 1,036 hectares.[12] With the Line now in retreat, Arthur exhorted Robinson to seek the surrender of the nations remaining in the Settled Districts, particularly the Big River people. But Robinson was fearful of venturing into their country so soon after the Line, for he believed that every settler, stock-keeper and soldier in the area was 'extirpationist to a man' and would undoubtedly shoot at any Aborigine on sight, including the mission Aborigines. Besides, if the Big River people surrendered, where would he take them? The temporary asylum on Swan Island was now stretched to capacity. Surely, he told Arthur, it would be more practical if he first established a permanent asylum on one of the Bass Strait islands, and then searched for the Big River people.

When Robinson appeared before the Executive Council on 23 February, he estimated that the remaining Aboriginal population on the island did not exceed 700 and that it was divided into various nations under chiefs occupying particular districts. He knew some of the nations about Port Davey and Macquarie Harbour by name. He believed that no area on the island was safe from settler attack and that the only place where the Aborigines could survive in the long term was on an island in Bass Strait. He recommended

Gun Carriage Island as the most suitable in terms of climate and fertility and because it provided ready access to nearby Cape Barren Island, where they could hunt game. He also believed that it would take him three years to communicate with every Aboriginal nation before he could remove them.[13]

Chief Justice Pedder, a member of the Executive Council, was not convinced that expatriation to an island in Bass Strait was a just outcome. He believed they would soon 'pine away'

> when they found their situation one of hopeless imprisonment, within bounds so narrow as necessarily to deprive them of those habits and customs which are the charms of their savage life; he meant their known love of change of place, their periodical distant migrations, their expeditions in search of game, and that unbounded liberty of which they had hitherto been in the enjoyment.[14]

He agreed that Gun Carriage Island could be a temporary refuge but he also considered that, in the aftermath of the Line, it was now time to negotiate a treaty with the chiefs in the Settled Districts. It would stipulate that their nations could not enter the region and it would be monitored by government agents who would live among them and also protect them from settler attack.

Robinson disagreed. He acknowledged that a treaty could have been possible a few years earlier, but said that now it was too late. The chiefs had lost influence over their clans, and government agents like himself could not protect the Aborigines from settler attack. Perhaps the nations in the west who had never been at war with the settlers might accept government agents in their midst, but he was doubtful that nations in the Settled Districts would accept them.[15]

Arthur took a different view. He was concerned that the '200 or 300' Aborigines in the Settled Districts would be exterminated before a treaty could even be considered, let alone negotiated. Thus, it was paramount that they should be

> drawn by every mild excitement to resort to the Aboriginal Establishment ... for, even if they should pine away in the manner the

Chief Justice apprehends, it is better that they should meet with their death in that way, whilst every act of kindness is manifested towards them, than that they should fall a sacrifice to the inevitable consequences of their continued acts of outrage upon the white inhabitants.[16]

From these views, the council agreed to put the question of final expatriation on hold until Robinson had secured the surrender of the Big River people. In the interim, it agreed that Mannalargenna and his people should be relocated from Swan to Gun Carriage Island.[17] Arthur appointed Robinson as superintendent of what was now known as the Aboriginal Establishment, provided him with a detachment of soldiers to evict the sealers from Gun Carriage Island and issued him with the authority to remove other tyereelore from their clutches. He also appointed three more government agents, Daniel Clucas, Anthony Cottrell and Alexander McKay, to secure the surrender of three of the four remaining groups in the Settled Districts and urged Robinson to secure the surrender of the Big River people by the end of the year.[18]

Armed with his new authority, Robinson left Hobart Town by boat on 5 March with the four mission Aborigines, Tekartee, who later died en route at Maria Island, and ten others. They comprised a woman, Lotabrah, who came from Birchs Rocks in the south-west; a child, Mary, who died on Preservation Island on 20 March; the man Cowertenninna, or John Woodburn, who had been with Gilbert Robertson's roving party; Woorraddy's sons, David and Peter Bruny; two women, Trometehenne and Pieyenkomeyenner, who had been in the hospital, one of whom soon died; the two men taken in the Line at Three Thumbs; the Big River man Ronekeennarener and the thirteen-year-old boy Tremebonener from Oyster Bay, 'and another big man from the Big River' named Weltepellemeener.[19] Also on board were a corporal and two soldiers from the 63rd Regiment to enforce the law on the Bass Strait islands, the government agent Daniel Clucas, who was expected to track down Umarrah's people, and several new additions to the Aboriginal Establishment: a medical dispenser, Archibald Maclachlan; a clerk, Henry Laing; and Robinson's eldest son, George.

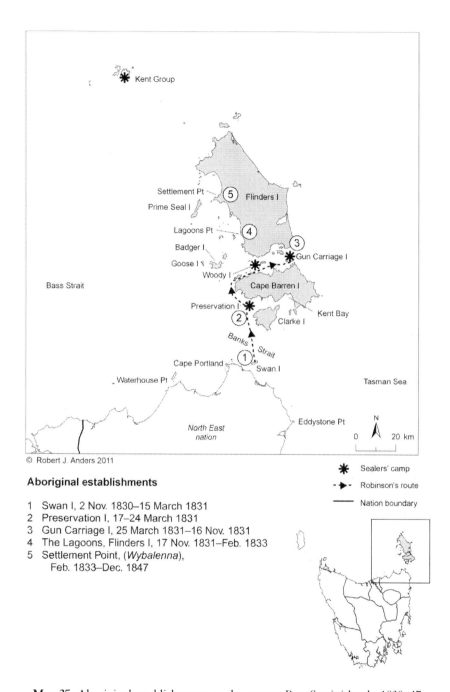

© Robert J. Anders 2011

Aboriginal establishments

1   Swan I, 2 Nov. 1830–15 March 1831
2   Preservation I, 17–24 March 1831
3   Gun Carriage I, 25 March 1831–16 Nov. 1831
4   The Lagoons, Flinders I, 17 Nov. 1831–Feb. 1833
5   Settlement Point, (*Wybalenna*),
     Feb. 1833–Dec. 1847

✱   Sealers' camp
‐▶‐   Robinson's route
─────   Nation boundary

Map 25 Aboriginal establishments on the eastern Bass Strait islands, 1830–47

Robinson's first task was to relocate the Aboriginal Establishment from Swan Island to Gun Carriage Island. Three kilometres long and almost 2.5 kilometres wide, situated between Flinders and Cape Barren islands, Gun Carriage Island, now known as Vansittart Island, is 57 kilometres from the mainland of Van Diemen's Land, which was too far for Aboriginal escape but close enough for easy transportation of stores and supplies. It also had the advantages of sealers' huts ready for immediate occupation and an abundance of mutton-birds and shellfish which were then in season. After issuing a proclamation to evict the sealers and locating two more of the tyereelore, Robinson tried to establish a British-style community by allocating huts to his three favoured couples, Mannalargenna and Tanlebonyer, Kickerterpoller and Pagerly, and Woorraddy and Truganini, in the hope that they would begin cultivating gardens, that sure sign of adjustment to British 'civilization'. He also hoped that Woorraddy's sons, Peter and Davy Bruny, would become part of Woorraddy's 'household', but this never eventuated.

After a fruitless expedition to other islands in Bass Strait to locate more tyereelore, Robinson returned to Gun Carriage Island on 30 April to find

Sketch of Gun Carriage Island Showing Fenced Gardens, Sheltered Huts and Boat Harbour with G.A. Robinson's Ship Under Sail and Straitsmen's Boats Anchored Close to the Beach. Henry Laing, Department of Prints and Drawings, British Museum, London.

that Cowertenninna and a woman, Lucceremictic from Robbins Island, had died and that fifteen others were in 'a sickly state'.[20] Confronted by Pedder's warning about the Aborigines' 'pining away', Robinson was now fearful for their survival. The medical dispenser, Archibald Maclachlan, pointed to the 'bleakness of this place and the want of proper habitation', for the Aborigines had told him that they would not sleep in their huts because 'if they slept outside the devil would cure them'.[21] But the insufficient water supply and the lack of fresh food were more likely reasons for their illness. Robinson quickly realised that an island the size of Gun Carriage could not sustain sixty Aborigines for very long. He wrote to the Reverend Bedford on the Aborigines Committee on 20 April that he would not recommend 'the outlay of any great expenditure' at Gun Carriage 'until the government are [sic] fully satisfied that it will answer all the purposes required'.[22]

Robinson tried to alleviate the overcrowding by moving fourteen mission Aborigines back to Swan Island. By the beginning of June, he had to confront two new problems. Daniel Clucas had been unable to find Umarrah, and James Munro, who had been appointed a constable in the Straits community in 1825, had complained to Arthur about Robinson's appropriation of the tyereelore. Arthur had agreed that each sealer should have the right to live with one tyereelore and Robinson was ordered to return some of them. They included Mannalargenna's daughter Emerenna, her daughter Lucy Beeton and Mannalargenna's sister, Toogernuppertootener, the last of which was returned to Woody Island even though she had an Aboriginal husband and several children among Mannalargenna's people.[23] With his prestige diminished among the male Aborigines at the Establishment, Robinson decided to conduct his own search for Umarrah.

For the next two months, from 3 June to 31 July, Robinson and seven mission Aborigines, Kickerterpoller and Pagerly, Woorraddy and Truganini, Tarenootairrer, later known as Sarah, Robert McAuley and Richard, crisscrossed the entire north-east in search of Umarrah, but without success. It soon became clear that Robinson's own party was leading him on a wild goose chase. They had tasted the horrors of institutionalised life on Gun Carriage Island and were determined never to return. Instead, they used these months attempting to incorporate Robinson into their own society of mutual reciprocity, for they knew he was dependent upon their skills and knowledge of the bush. So they hunted, held ceremonies, told stories and taught Robinson new Aboriginal languages.

By 1 August he realised that they would never find Umarrah, so he fetched four others from Gun Carriage Island to assist in the mission. They were Mannalargenna and his wife, Tanlebonyer, a youth, Maulboyheenner, all of whom knew the north-east well, and also Pevay, who had recently been with Alexander McKay's party to track down the Punnilerpanner clan at Port Sorell. To enlist Mannalargenna's support in his quest for Umarrah,

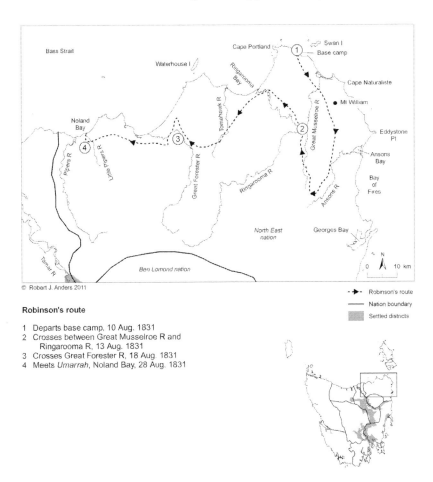

© Robert J. Anders 2011

- ▸ -   Robinson's route
——— Nation boundary
▨▨▨ Settled districts

Robinson's route

1 Departs base camp, 10 Aug. 1831
2 Crosses between Great Musselroe R and
   Ringarooma R, 13 Aug. 1831
3 Crosses Great Forester R, 18 Aug. 1831
4 Meets *Umarrah*, Noland Bay, 28 Aug. 1831

Map 26 Robinson's search for Umarrah, 10 – 28 August 1831

Robinson reversed his earlier view about Aboriginal expatriation presented to the Aborigines Committee only six months before, and appeared to accept Chief Justice Pedder's idea of a treaty. In Kickerterpoller's presence, he told Mannalargenna that, if his people

> would desist from their wonted outrages upon the whites, they would be allowed to remain in their respective districts and would have flour, tea and sugar, clothes &c given them; that a good white man would dwell with them who would take care of them and would not allow any bad white man to shoot them, and he would go about with them in the bush like myself and they then could hunt.[24]

Mannalargenna. Benjamin Duterrau, State Library of New South Wales, Sydney.

Tanlebonyer. Benjamin Duterrau, State Library of New South Wales, Sydney.

Robinson's change of heart may have occurred from spending more time in the north-east region which may have led him to seriously consider that Mannalargenna and his people could remain in their own country. Indeed, Arthur had hinted at such a possibility in June when he wrote to Robinson indicating that 'whether the natives will or will not go to the establishment they should be conciliated by every possible means and promised food, clothing and protection if they will only be pacific and desist from the outrages which they have been in the habit of committing'.[25] The high death rate at Gun Carriage Island may also have encouraged Robinson to reconsider Pedder's suggestion. But he was also in a desperate situation. He needed to capture Umarrah, who was known to have killed settler women along the Tamar River, and he may have been prepared to negotiate his surrender with Mannalargenna in return for some kind of treaty.

But Mannalargenna had little interest in finding Umarrah. It was not until 29 August, after a long walk across the north-east, that Tarenootairrer, who had a brother among Umarrah's people, finally located Umarrah and seven of his clan, including Memerlarlannelargenna and his wife, Meemelunneener, as well as Ningernooputtener, or Mungo, who had been Jorgen Jorgenson's roving party guide, Pleengkotetenner, Tootetiteyerlargener and Wattewittelargener, near Noland Bay.

In the meantime Mannalargenna had worked very hard to incorporate Robinson into his own world of social relations and obligations. He taught Robinson many of his songs and told him of his own traditions including the origins of his people in the stars. It was once again early spring and everyone in the party enjoyed the abundance of food. Although he did not realise it at the time, Robinson was gradually being incorporated into an Aboriginal world view that was far beyond his own experience to understand.[26]

Umarrah was an important prize for Robinson, because he was the best known resistance leader in the Settled Districts. As chief of the Stoney Creek clan, he had come to prominence in the period from 1826 to 1828, when he led a series of raids against the settlers in the Campbell Town area. When martial law was declared in November 1828, Umarrah and five of his people had been captured by Gilbert Robertson and Kickerterpoller near the Eastern Marshes. Arthur had met with Umarrah to discuss the possibility of a treaty and then sent him to join a roving party in the hope that he would conciliate other Aborigines in the area. But he had escaped to join his compatriots and was recaptured a few days later. On this occasion he had been sent to Richmond gaol, where he remained for the whole of 1829; he was released in January 1830 to join Robinson's mission to the west coast. But, in May 1830, together with Parwareter and Trepanner, Umarrah had left Robinson's mission at Trial Harbour, taking the Aboriginal road back to the Settled Districts. By October they had reached Launceston, where Umarrah was recaptured and assigned as a guide to one of the military parties in the Black Line. Again he had decamped and joined some of the Port Dalrymple clan along the Tamar River. They had spent the summer of 1830–31 in the Ben Lomond Tier making occasional forays into the North Esk River valley to plunder shepherds' huts for provisions. At the end of January 1831 they had attacked farms on both sides of the Tamar and North Esk rivers, spearing settlers and horses and taking provisions. Between January and July they had killed three settlers including Mrs Cunningham, wounded five shepherds and taken four muskets, two pistols and a bayonet, although there is no evidence that they ever used any of these weapons. Rather, it seems that they wanted to deprive the settlers of the means of killing Aborigines.[27]

Umarrah had made it plain on several occasions that the British were unlawfully appropriating his country. He had told Gilbert Robertson in November 1828 'that white people had been murdered' because they had driven the Aborigines off their kangaroo hunting grounds and had probably repeated this belief to Arthur a few weeks later.[28] At that stage Arthur may have considered appointing him, along with Kickerterpoller, as possible conciliators to the other Aborigines in the Settled Districts in 1829, but Arthur appears to have been concerned that Umarrah would lead an uprising against the settlers. Robinson, on the other hand, had got to know Umarrah well during his mission to the west coast between February and May 1830 and had learned from him how to negotiate with the South West people. Now Umarrah met Robinson with a hearty handshake and told him that only three of his clansmen remained in the bush.[29]

Over the next two weeks Robinson had to negotiate between the two chiefs, who were, in effect, old enemies. He had promised Mannalargenna that he would remove Umarrah and his people to Waterhouse Island, but Umarrah, who had known Robinson much longer, tried to break Mannalargenna's hold on Robinson by rekindling the obligations that he had forged during the first mission to the west. When this failed, some of Umarrah's people decamped, because they were wary of Robinson's intentions. Robinson now promised both chiefs that they could stay in their own country and that 'a white man' would be appointed by the governor to 'take care of them'. Yet he had already promised Mannalargenna that he could stay in his own country if he assisted him to put Umarrah and his clan on Waterhouse Island. And he had promised Umarrah that he would not send him to Bass Strait if he assisted in the search for the Big River people. It was not until the end of September that Umarrah agreed to spend a few weeks hunting on Waterhouse Island, where some of his Big River relatives, including his wife, Woolaytopinnyer, had arrived after their capture by Alexander McKay near Port Sorell.[30]

On 5 October, Robinson took Mannalargenna and eleven of his clan to meet Arthur at Launceston. The lieutenant-governor was clearly impressed by Mannalargenna as the most senior chief in the Settled Districts and immediately agreed to his request to retrieve his sister, Toogernuppertootener, and his daughters, Teekoolterme and Wapperty, from the sealers. Arthur then agreed to Robinson's request that Campbell Town should become the 'central situation' for the mission, 'constituting a kind of home for Mannalargenna and Umarrah and the rest of the natives who form Mr Robinson's party, and whom he considers perfectly conciliated'. He authorised that 'a hut be erected there for Mannalargenna, and accommodation also erected for the rest of the natives as well as Mr Robinson' and that the inspector of roads set aside some workmen for the purpose.[31] Yet Arthur and Robinson must have known that the settlers would never tolerate an Aboriginal refuge in the heart of the Settled Districts. Whatever their motives, the Campbell Town Aboriginal Establishment never eventuated.

Robinson set off from Campbell Town on 15 October 1831 in search of the Big River and Oyster Bay peoples with thirteen mission Aborigines: the four youths Richard, Maulboyheenner, Lacklay and Pevay, who carried supplies to the party from depots at Campbell Town and Bothwell; the four couples Kickerterpoller and Pagerly, Woorraddy and Truganini,

Mannalargenna and Tanlebonyer, and Umarrah and Woolaytopinnyer, who acted as guides in country that all but Woorraddy and Truganini knew well; and the tyereelore, Tarenootairrer. They were accompanied by three servants, Robinson's son George, a clerk, seven dogs and two horses.

At first they travelled east across to the Eastern Tiers and then south-east to the Eastern Marshes, believing that the Big River people who had gone to Oyster Bay for the winter could be intercepted in the Midlands on their return journey. Again, Robinson found the country 'peculiarly adapted' for Aborigines, consisting of thickly wooded hills and small open plains of grassy land which afforded shelter and food for kangaroos.[32]

Robinson was now in the heartland of the Settled Districts. Although he avoided the major roads and settlers' homesteads, within a week of setting out the party encountered at least six well-armed colonists and later met many more. Indeed, on at least one occasion, Robinson feared that the party would be attacked at night and they would all be slaughtered.[33] Yet Kickerterpoller, Mannalargenna, Umarrah and Woolaytopinnyer 'had often wandered over this country, many of them from childhood, and every part was familiar to them. They would often point to spots near a rill of water where they and their companions had regaled themselves on the spoils of the chase.' Woolaytopinnyer took Robinson to a place where her people had secreted firearms that the women had stolen from the settlers in the Line and then to lagoons stocked with eels and birds and their eggs. Kickerterpoller took Robinson to the site in the Eastern Marshes where he had tracked down Umarrah in November 1828 and to other favoured camp-sites where his people had held important ceremonies. Mannalargenna pretended to consult his 'devil' to find the direction of the Big River people, while Umarrah entertained the party each evening with stories, 'many of them so long as to take upwards of an hour in reciting, keeping them awake listening to his relation until twelve or one o'clock'. On another occasion, Woolaytopinnyer lit a fire and made a great deal of smoke, which Robinson realised was a signal to the Oyster Bay people to stay away.[34]

On 29 October, now infuriated by the Aborigines' stalling tactics, Robinson abandoned his search in the Midlands and turned west, convinced that the Big River and Oyster Bay peoples had joined forces and were now hiding in Big River country. Again, the mission Aborigines stalled for time. Some of them said the Big River country was cold and that many devils lived there, and Mannalargenna protested that he was an old man and he would soon die if he walked too much.[35]

Taking the Aboriginal road west towards Jericho, Robinson crossed the Launceston–Hobart road on 4 November and then the Jordan and Clyde rivers, reaching Lake Echo on 7 November, where he saw Aboriginal smoke. But none of the mission Aborigines wanted to pursue it. Instead, Kickerterpoller set fire to the bush to warn the Big River people of their presence.[36] For the next two months Robinson was reliant on Woolaytopinnyer's advice about where her people might have gone. But despite several opportunities to contact them she also appeared reluctant to find them, although she readily showed him more caches of firearms that they had stolen from the colonists and pointed out favoured campsites and other places where her relatives had been killed by colonists and other Aborigines.

G.A. Robinson with a Group of VDL Aborigines. Benjamin Duterrau, Allport Library and Museum of Fine Arts, Hobart.

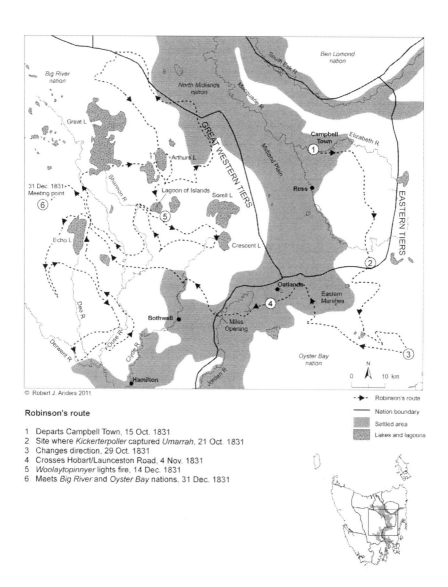

Robinson's route

1 Departs Campbell Town, 15 Oct. 1831
2 Site where *Kickerterpoller* captured *Umarrah*, 21 Oct. 1831
3 Changes direction, 29 Oct. 1831
4 Crosses Hobart/Launceston Road, 4 Nov. 1831
5 *Woolaytopinnyer* lights fire, 14 Dec. 1831
6 Meets *Big River* and *Oyster Bay* nations, 31 Dec. 1831

Map 27 Robinson's search for the Big River and Oyster Bay nations,
Campbell Town (15 October 1831) to NW Lake Echo (31 December 1831)

Tongerlongter. Thomas Bock, Queen Victoria Museum and Art Gallery, Launceston.

Then, at the Lagoon of Islands, she tried to abscond with some other mission women to join her relatives. At the same time Kickerterpoller, Mannalargenna and Umarrah employed every possible tactic to divert Robinson from meeting his objective. He found them 'less diligent, less assiduous, less obedient than on former occasions'.[37]

Eventually, on 31 December, the party came upon the Big River and Oyster Bay people a few kilometres north-west of Lake Echo. They were twenty-six in all, comprising sixteen men, nine women and a child, and were led by Montpeliater and Tongerlongter. The surrender was negotiated by Woolaytopinnyer, whose brother was with them. They formed the largest group to surrender to Robinson at any one time. The following day Montpeliater took Robinson to one of their newly erected huts, 'the interior of which was decorated with an assemblage of rude sketches representing bird, beasts, human forms &c'. Adjoining the hut was a huge hollow tree with a cavity containing six stands of firearms, and Robinson found another firearm nearby. He then suggested that they should surrender personally to the governor. Arriving at Hobart Town on 7 January 1832, they were greeted by Arthur. But it is not known what he said to them, let alone whether he made any promises about a treaty. Ten days later they were despatched to Flinders Island along with four of Umarrah's clansmen who had just surrendered to Anthony Cottrell north of Oyster Bay. Thus, it appeared that all of the surviving members of the four nations in the Settled Districts had been accounted for.[38] But this was not the case. As pointed out in Chapter 8, some Big River people may have remained on the Central Plateau, and some Oyster Bay people may have remained in the Eastern Tiers behind the Cotton family's farm at Oyster Bay.

Robinson had spent seven months in the Settled Districts with a diverse group of Aborigines who were becoming increasingly disillusioned with his promises to allow them to remain in their own country. A mutual dependence had developed between the mission Aborigines and Robinson, and from now on a certain bitterness and ambivalence emerged.

The Natives That Were Sent from Hobart Town to Great (Flinders) Island 1832. John Glover, State Library of New South Wales, Sydney.

13

Western nations:
forced removal, 1832–34

Elated by the surrender of the Aboriginal nations in the Settled Districts,
Arthur turned his attention to their counterparts on the other side of the
frontier, in the north, north-west and south-west. He believed that the rapid
spread of settlement would expose them to the settlers' guns and that unless
they were quickly 'brought in' they would soon be exterminated. Anxious
to avoid this awful outcome, he persuaded Robinson to undertake the task,
offering him £1,000 with £300 as an advance. Robinson believed there were
now about 200 Aborigines on the other side of the frontier and he was
optimistic of quick success. But the North West and South West nations
were determined to fight for their country, and for the next three years they
actively resisted his removal campaign. Unaware of their determination,
Robinson planned first to visit the Aboriginal Establishment in Bass Strait
with the new acting commandant, Lieutenant James Darling, and then
set off with the mission Aborigines to remove the western nations. He left
Hobart on 13 February 1832.[1]

Since Robinson's last visit to the Aboriginal Establishment, in June 1831,
Sergeant Alexander Wight had removed it from Gun Carriage Island to the
site known as the Lagoons on the west coast of Flinders Island. The new site
was exposed to the westerly gales, the soil was unfit for cultivation and the
wooden buildings lurched precariously on a sand dune about 45 metres from
the sea. The only fresh water came from wells dug close to the beach, and
the nearest anchorage for supply ships was at Green Island, nearly 5 kilometres away. So the new site was only marginally healthier than Gun

Carriage Island. Since then, at least twenty Aborigines had died, leaving only twenty survivors. With the surgeon, Andrew Maclachlan, six convicts and three sealers, Wight had treated the Aborigines as if they were criminals. Then, in August 1831, twenty of the North Midlands, North and North East peoples who had surrendered to Robinson and his parties a short time before arrived at the Establishment and were further supplemented in January 1832 by the arrival of the twenty-six Big River and Oyster Bay people who had surrendered to Robinson a few weeks earlier. There were now sixty-six Aborigines at the Lagoons and they congregated in three distinct groups— those identifying with the Ben Lomond nation, those with the Big River nation and those with the North and North Midlands nations. They lived in separate encampments, hunted separately and exchanged women with the convicts and sealers for dogs and flour. Before long Wight feared that they would incite the sealers to take them back to the mainland.

His fears were soon realised. On 22 January some Big River men attacked the convict boat crew for abducting two Big River women. Convinced they were about to kill him, Wight armed the three sealers and herded the Big River people into the boat and isolated them on Green Island. Two weeks later, when supplies had run short at the Lagoons and tensions of confinement had escalated, he sent the Ben Lomond and North Midlands people on a three-day hunting trip. When they returned, a North Midlands man was missing, killed, some of the sealing women said, by two of the Ben Lomond men. Wight handcuffed the two men and ordered Maclachlan and two sealers, Robert Gamble and Edward Mansell, to take them to the place where the missing North Midlands man had last been seen. But they were unable to find him. Still shackled, the two Ben Lomond men then tried to escape, and in the struggle that followed Mansell fired at and wounded both men. On their return to the Lagoons, Wight encased the men in iron hoops. Five hours later the supposed murdered man returned, but already one of the wounded Ben Lomond men had died. In panic, Wight removed the rest of the Aborigines to Green Island.[2]

When Robinson arrived at Green Island on 25 February the Aborigines were feasting on mutton-birds, but, even so, most of them had dysentery and influenza. He relieved Wight and the convicts of their duties and installed Lieutenant Darling and eight soldiers of the 63rd Regiment in their place. The Aborigines were horrified. They reminded Robinson that they had surrendered on the promise that they would be protected from the redcoats. But Robinson preferred the soldiers' regimentation to the uncontrolled behaviour of convicts and sealers. He removed the Establishment back to the Lagoons, arranged for huts to be erected and on 4 March held the first church service, with Kickerterpoller acting as interpreter. Confident that Darling would make considerable improvements, Robinson left Flinders Island on 10 March with sixteen mission Aborigines.[3]

When they arrived at Launceston three days later, four of them, Robert McAuley, Kickerterpoller, Umarrah and Woolaytopinnyer, had contracted influenza. By 24 March, Robert and Umarrah were dead. Robert was given a Christian burial by the Reverend Dr William Browne, the Anglican chaplain at St Johns Church, and two days later Umarrah was buried outside the burial ground in full body paint. His widow, Woolaytopinnyer, who had negotiated the surrender of the Big River and Oyster Bay people, died at Emu Bay on 28 May. By then Kickerterpoller had also died and had been buried at the back of the VDL Company's store at Emu Bay—an unfitting end to a man who had withstood the full force of colonial invasion. To his credit, Robinson regretted that he was not present when Kickerterpoller died and that he had been buried in a pauper's grave.[4]

The deaths of the four mission Aborigines at the beginning of the mission to the western nations confirmed for the others that Flinders Island was a place of death and that they must on no account return there. Robinson was aware of their shaken confidence and lived in increased anxiety that Pagerly and some of the others would abscond. By the time they arrived at Cape Grim in early June, there were twelve Aborigines in the mission. They were the two couples Truganini and Wooraddy, and Tanlebonyer and Mannalargenna; Pagerly, Kickerterpoller's widow; three women from the west coast, Karnebutcher, Nolleralleke and Numberloetinnare; three young warriors, Lacklay from Port Sorell, Maulboyheenner from Cape Portland and Pevay from Robbins Island; and the 'domesticated Aborigine' Richard.[5]

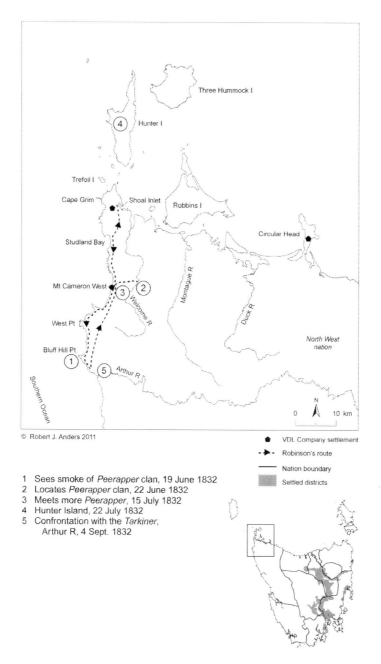

© Robert J. Anders 2011

      ⬟   VDL Company settlement

- ▶ -   Robinson's route

──────   Nation boundary

▨   Settled districts

1 Sees smoke of *Peerapper* clan, 19 June 1832
2 Locates *Peerapper* clan, 22 June 1832
3 Meets more *Peerapper*, 15 July 1832
4 Hunter Island, 22 July 1832
5 Confrontation with the *Tarkiner*,
    Arthur R, 4 Sept. 1832

Map 28 Robinson's search for the North West nation,
14 June – 28 October 1832

Robinson planned first to contact and force the surrender of all the clans in the country claimed by the VDL Company on the west coast, from Cape Grim to West Point, then to push south to the Arthur River to locate the Tarkinener clan from Sandy Cape and the Peternidic clan from Pieman River, and then to search Macquarie Harbour for the Aborigines from the South West nation that he had met two years before. For the first stage of the expedition he employed Anthony Cottrell and four Sydney Aborigines to assist him and attached his son George and his black convict servant from Hawaii, Joseph Maclaine, to his own party. On 14 June 1832, in the middle of a wet, cold winter, the entire party set off south from Cape Grim. It was to prove one of the most hazardous journeys Robinson had yet undertaken.

On 19 June at Bluff Hill Point near the mouth of the Arthur River, the mission Aborigines saw smoke from the Peerapper clan from West Point, and Robinson sent Pevay and Nolleralleke to look for their compatriots. Nolleralleke returned that afternoon with the news that they had located four men and three women and that Pevay had remained with one of the men, Pannerbuke, who was a close relative. The rest had gone to Robbins Island to make spears and when they returned they expected to fight the Tarkinener clan from Sandy Cape over the abduction of women. On 22 June, Robinson was joined by Pevay and Pannerbuke and they set off for Mount Cameron West to intercept the others. When he saw smoke from their fire the next day, Robinson again sent Pevay and Nolleralleke after them, accompanied by Mannalargenna and Woorraddy. They returned with about seven of the Peerapper, including their chief Wymurrick, who stood 2 metres tall and was Pevay's brother, together with his wife and two children. Later, five more Peerapper people joined Robinson, and Wymurrick went to find others. On 15 July about twenty more of the Peerapper people, including the young chief Heedeek, formally surrendered to Robinson. He then detained them on Hunter Island until a ship was available to deport them to Flinders Island.[6]

Robinson set up temporary encampments on each side of Hunter Island, and the Sydney Aborigines erected huts and hunted kangaroos and penguins on the nearby mainland to provide an adequate supply of food. Then, a

Peerapper woman, her infant son and an old man died, although it seems they were ill when Robinson first met them. Nevertheless, their deaths created uneasiness among the other Peerapper, and Robinson was unsettled by their intense mourning ceremonies. There were now nearly forty Aborigines in his care and he was anxious to return to the Arthur River to capture the Tarkinener clan, but, with no sign of the ship that was expected to take the Peerapper clan to Flinders Island, he was forced to stay at Hunter Island for about two months.[7]

In correspondence to his friends George Whitcomb in Launceston and the Reverend William Bedford in Hobart, Robinson acknowledged that the Peerapper, the Tarkinener and all the other clans in the west had full rights to their land. He wrote: 'Las Casas—to his dying hour maintained the right of the native Indians to make war upon their oppressors for the purpose of obtaining the restitution of their property and their freedom.' He also remembered that John Locke had said that 'no body has a right to take away a country which is the property of the Aboriginal Inhabitants without their own consent—that if they do, such inhabitants are not free men but slaves under the force of war'.[8] By what tenure, Robinson argued, did the British hold Van Diemen's Land? The colonists had neither conquered nor purchased it; they had illegally occupied it. However, in admitting to his friends that the clans from the west were rightfully fighting for their land, he was also trying to convince himself that they had to be removed from their homeland to prevent their extermination. Their compensation would be the promise of their 'civilization'. This extraordinary logic sustained him for the rest of his journey.

In the last week of August, Robinson left his captives on Hunter Island and set out again for the Arthur River with the mission Aborigines, some Peerapper people captured in June and two Sydney Aborigines to assist with the baggage. He reached the river on 31 August and sent Woorraddy, Truganini, Maulboyheenner, Lacklay and Pevay with three Peerapper men, Pannerbuke, Penderoin and Heedeek, across the river in the hope of meeting the Tarkinener. On 3 September, having heard nothing from his scouting party, he crossed the Arthur on a raft, ferried by four mission women. Shortly after, one of the women called 'that plenty of blackfellows was coming'. A large group of men armed with spears came to Robinson's fire with seven mission Aborigines. Many of them had seen him before but he observed 'that something was suspicious about them. They were shy and sullen, yet bold and full of bravado.'[9]

The men went to hunt and Robinson visited their camp, where he 'conversed freely with the women'. There were twenty-nine in the entire group, consisting of some men and women that he knew from the Ninene clan from Port Davey, some from the Peternidic clan from the Pieman River and the rest from the Tarkinener clan from Sandy Cape. Among the last group was Naruccer, whom Robinson had met two years before at Robbins Island. Then, he had despatched her to Launceston, but she had been released to rejoin her own clan and was now pregnant.

Robinson spent the night in great anxiety. He got up at dawn, put on his clothes and packed up his knapsack, expecting an attack. He told Pevay that if these people did not wish to join him they could go away, for he would not use force. Scarcely had he spoken when the men surrounded Robinson holding spears. The mission Aborigines fled. Somehow, Robinson escaped. As he ran through the scrub he overtook Truganini, who was fearful of capture, for she had relatives among the Ninene clan and they had a shortage of women. On reaching the river Robinson fashioned a makeshift raft out of two spars of wood tied together with his garters at first and then, when they broke, with his cravat. He lay on this raft and urged Truganini to push him across, for he could not swim. Arriving safely at the other side, they made for their own camp and alerted the others.

When he returned to the river Robinson found that most of the mission Aborigines had crossed with his tent and knapsack. Four young Tarkinener women had also joined them. On the other side of the river the Tarkinener men were goading the mission Aborigines to join them and eventually they enticed Heedeek back across the river. Robinson was then told that Heedeek had played a major part in the plot to kill him. After offering dogs in return for their women the Tarkinener disappeared into the bush.[10]

Robinson was shaken by the experience. He later learned that the group had gone first to the Welcome River, then to Mount Cameron West, and finally to West Point in search of Wymurrick and his people, with whom they were at war. When they found Robinson's huts they assumed Wymurrick had been captured. They told the mission Aborigines that they would not go to Hunter Island and would take the women and dogs in Robinson's party. Unable to accept that these people were fighting for their lives, Robinson in future carried firearms and used belligerent methods to force surrender. He beat a hasty retreat to Hunter Island, where he found the Peerapper people in a state of rebellion. There was still no sign of a ship.[11]

Relations between all the Aboriginal groups on Hunter Island and between Robinson and the mission Aborigines deteriorated. Woorraddy became so rebellious that Robinson had to threaten him with a gun; Mannalargenna feared the Peerapper people planned to abscond; the Sydney Aborigines complained of insufficient rations; and one of the tyereelore absconded to the sealers' camp at the southern tip of the island. When more of the women visited the sealers' camp on 22 October, Robinson knew it was time to depart.

He decided to return to Hobart to arrange for a ship to take the Peerapper and the four Tarkinener women to Flinders Island. The mission Aborigines were to remain on Hunter Island with his son, Cottrell and the Sydney Aborigines until he sent word to meet him at Macquarie Harbour. But on 28 October the long-awaited ship from Flinders Island, the cutter *Charlotte*, with Lieutenant Darling and two soldiers on board, intercepted Robinson at Circular Head. He decided not to accompany the cutter to Hunter Island, 'to avoid the unpleasant feeling at removing the aborigines', knowing that force would be used. He waited for the cutter to return to Circular Head and sailed with the twenty-seven captured Aborigines to George Town, where he disembarked and the cutter took the Aborigines to Flinders Island. Robinson then went overland to Hobart.[12]

Meanwhile, from Hunter Island, Cottrell and Robinson's son, the Sydney Aborigines and the mission Aborigines proceeded on 20 November 1832 down the west coast towards Macquarie Harbour. On 26 November they again met the Tarkinener at the Arthur River. The following morning the Tarkinener called to Cottrell and he beckoned them across, promising blankets. They refused, insisting that Robinson was with them and that he had surely planned revenge. Cottrell assured them that Robinson was in Hobart. A short time later two men crossed, explored the camp and, satisfied there were no firearms, signalled the others to join them. But the Tarkinener chief, Wyne, insisted that Cottrell's people make rafts for the women and children. Three men, one woman and a female child then crossed, but the rest remained. In the evening one of the Sydney Aborigines went across in a canoe, but he was greeted with a shower of spears. By next morning the Tarkinener had gone, so Cottrell returned to Hunter Island with the seven Tarkinener who had joined him. From there they were taken to George Town and lodged in the gaol to await a ship to Flinders Island.[13]

Cottrell returned to the west coast and on 10 January 1833 again encountered the Tarkinener people, about 50 kilometres north from the heads at Macquarie Harbour. They remained with Cottrell's party all night and agreed to accompany him to Macquarie Harbour, but when they had proceeded about 6 kilometres they disappeared into the scrub. The Tarkinener were not yet ready to surrender. Undeterred, Cottrell continued south-west and on 5 February met with some Ninene people from Port Davey. He succeeded in inducing five women, two men and a boy to join him, and these he took to Macquarie Harbour to wait for a ship to take them to Flinders Island. By the time Robinson arrived at the end of April, all Aboriginal groups in the west had been contacted and they knew that Robinson intended to bring them in. But it had been a costly operation. Two convict servants had drowned while crossing the Pieman River; three Sydney Aborigines had absconded north of Macquarie Harbour; and three of the Ninene women had escaped from the settlement by swimming across the harbour. Before returning responsibility to Robinson, Cottrell warned him that the only way to capture the remaining Aborigines was to use force.[14]

Desperate to accomplish his task as quickly as possible, Robinson ordered the four convict assistants to carry firearms and warned the mission Aborigines that they would probably have to bring in the western nations by force. The party moved south and on 19 May discovered traces of the Ninene people near Low Rocky Point. Robinson sent the mission Aborigines in pursuit. They returned the next day with twelve Ninene people; they had used force to bring them in and in the ensuing melee three women had escaped.[15] That night Robinson conceded in his journal that the use of force represented a dramatic shift in government policy from his first mission to the west three years earlier, 'but the work now is different and the case is completely altered. All the tribes with the exception of these are removed, and it is a satisfaction to know that their removal is for their own good.' He also conceded that:

> Patriotism is a distinguishing trait in the aboriginal character, yet for all the love they bear their country the aboriginal settlement will soon become their adopted country and they will find that protection which they cannot find in their own land, not only against the attack of the whites but also against the tribes in hostilities with them. With these views I purposed acting accordingly and trusted to the goodness of providence for wisdom to direct me in what I had to do.[16]

But the Ninene refused to go to Macquarie Harbour. When they began to sharpen their spears Robinson ordered the four white men in his party 'to uncover their fusees'. In shock, the Ninene then surrendered. But Robinson did not breathe freely until he reached Macquarie Harbour and embarked them on the *Shamrock* for Flinders Island on 5 June.

On 17 June the mission Aborigines located more of the Ninene, including Dray. She had been with Robinson's first mission and had left it to rejoin her people at Little Rocky River in April 1830. Among the others were the chief, Towterrer, who had met Robinson three years earlier, his wife, Wongerneep, and their new baby daughter, Mathinna. They too resisted capture, and Robinson had to use another show of force to ensure their surrender. He sent them all except Dray to Flinders Island on 23 June. Now only sixteen of the South West nation remained in their country and Robinson relied on Dray to negotiate their surrender on 12 July. On the return journey to Macquarie Harbour, they tried to escape, and for the third time Robinson had to order the white men in his party to display their guns as a show of force to get them back.[17]

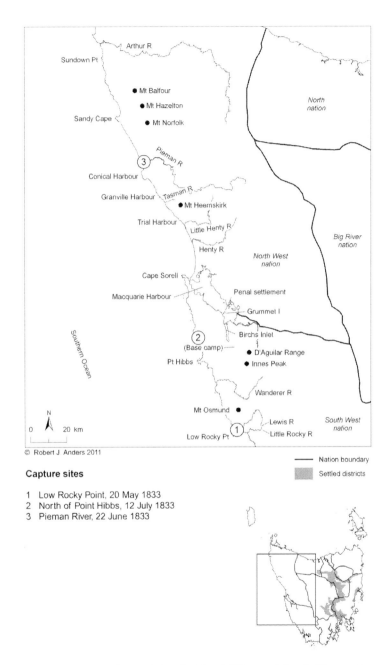

© Robert J Anders 2011

Capture sites

1   Low Rocky Point, 20 May 1833
2   North of Point Hibbs, 12 July 1833
3   Pieman River, 22 June 1833

Map 29 Robinson's search for the North West and South West nations,
11 May – 13 September 1833

Leaving this group of Ninene on Grummet Island in Macquarie Harbour, Robinson turned north, hoping for the same quick success in capturing the remaining Tarkinener and Peternidic clans. On 21 July he found traces of them at the Pieman River and hastily despatched the mission Aborigines to surround their huts for the night to prevent their escape. They returned next morning with nine captives. Among them was the chief Wyne, who had attempted to spear Robinson at the Arthur River the previous September. They were soon joined by two other men. Like the Ninene, the Peternidic were unwilling to go to Flinders Island, but they were anxious to see their

Towterrer. John Gould, State Library of New South Wales, Sydney.

relatives and friends. Robinson noted proudly: 'Providence had certainly crowned my labours with abundant success and I remarked that with me the motto, *veni, vidi, vici,* was applicable.'[18]

Upon his return to Macquarie Harbour, Robinson found the sixteen Ninene people on Grummet Island had succumbed to chronic chest complaints. One woman had already died and two men and another woman were dangerously ill. By 27 July two others had died, The mission Aborigines sought sanctuary at Swan Bay on the north side of Macquarie Harbour, while the Ninene were placed in the hospital at the penal settlement. When Robinson asked Dray why they cried, she retorted, 'Why black man's wife not to cry as well as white man's?' The next day they left the hospital and Robinson returned them to Grummet Island. He had no idea what to do. No ship arrived to take them to Flinders Island, and he could not countenance their returning to the bush to die. He considered that these sadnesses had been sent to try his patience and diligence. But he

Macquarie Harbour. Artist and date unknown, State Library of New South Wales, Sydney.

did not falter in his fervent belief that he had removed them for their own good.[19]

On 31 July, Wyne and another man died, and seven others became critically ill. Robinson blamed the doctor, the hospital and the penal settlement for the calamity. He could not see that confinement, the dramatic change in diet and the loss of their land were more responsible for Aboriginal deaths than the erratic behaviour of a doctor. When the Ninene pleaded with Robinson to take them away he refused, because he was afraid they would escape and all his work would be lost. It was not until 6 August, when twelve of the twenty-seven Ninene and Peternidic people had died, that Robinson removed them to the pilot station at Cape Sorell.[20]

Robinson was distraught by the deaths. He suffered bad dreams, became depressed and despaired of the ship *Tamar* ever returning to rescue them. When it finally arrived, in the middle of August, the master, Captain Bateman, told him that a further nineteen Aborigines had died at Flinders Island. Undeterred by this horrifying news, he set off on 12 August in search of the remaining Tarkininer and Peternidic, but by the time he reached Sundown Point on 4 September, they had retreated inland to the Hampshire Hills and the mission Aborigines, appeared determined not to find them.

Captured Aborigines at Macquarie Harbour. John Gould, State Library of New South Wales, Sydney.

On 23 September the entire party, comprising the mission and captured Aborigines, embarked with Robinson and his two eldest sons, George and Charles on the *Tamar* and arrived in Hobart Town on 18 October. After meeting the governor, the eleven surviving Ninene and Peternidic who had surrendered in July, including Dray, Towterrer and Wongerneep and their baby, Mathinna, were despatched to Flinders Island.[21]

Each mission was becoming more hazardous and unbearable for Robinson. Ready supplies and shipping were difficult to sustain, his servants were unruly and the mission Aborigines were becoming more rebellious. The spirit of adventure had long since died. His work was now largely a mopping-up operation which in other colonies at a later date were carried out by military and native police parties. No government agents spent so much time in the bush bringing in the last few.

On 20 February 1834, Robinson set out from Studland Bay with the mission Aborigines and his two sons in search of the remaining western Aborigines. Two days later they reached the Arthur River and on 28 February the mission Aborigines located eight Peternidic people, comprising two couples, a twelve-year-old boy, two little girls and an infant. They told Robinson they had fought the Tommeginer a short time before and that one of their own people had been killed as well as a Tommeginer. He hastily took them to Hunter Island and on 6 March set off to find the others. Once again he crossed the Arthur River and camped at Sundown Point. The next morning the mission Aborigines set off; on 14 March they found one family near the Arthur River, and three weeks later, on 7 April, they located the other family at Sandy Cape. There were three couples, including Heedeek and Narrucer, another man and two children. Heedeek told Robinson:

> They had declared their intention was never to be subdued, that as they had plenty of dogs they would retire to the mountains and live on Quoiber, i.e. badger. They had formed a plan to kill me and my aboriginal attendants by laying in ambush, and had stuck sharp pointed sticks in their pathways to wound the feet of my native attendants, some of which we discovered. My natives were averse to follow after or look for them from an apprehension that they could not be found and that if we did they would assuredly kill us.[22]

They all returned to Cape Grim on 12 April, and Robinson had the satisfaction of farewelling the last of the west coast people to Flinders Island on 24 April. He now turned towards Emu Bay to find the Tommeginer. For the next two months he followed the Aboriginal roads at the back of the Hampshire Hills and across the high country to the east of Mount Roland and Mount Vandyke to Den Plain without success. At the end of July he went to Launceston, leaving his two eldest sons in charge of the mission Aborigines at the Mersey River. They proceeded along the Aboriginal track across the Central Plateau in Big River country to the River Ouse, which they reached in October. On 28 December, while on the Black Bluff Range,

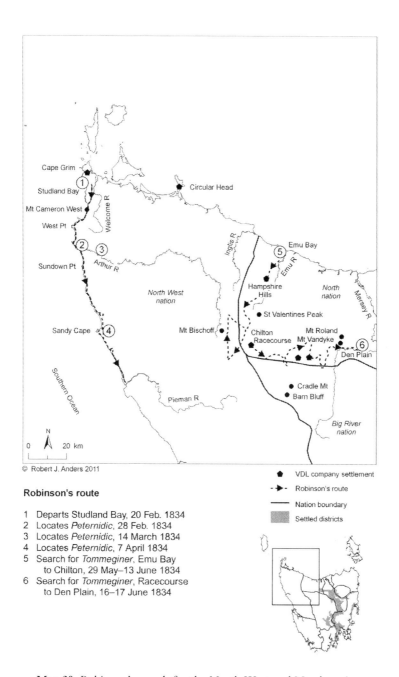

© Robert J. Anders 2011

Robinson's route

1 Departs Studland Bay, 20 Feb. 1834
2 Locates *Peternidic*, 28 Feb. 1834
3 Locates *Peternidic*, 14 March 1834
4 Locates *Peternidic*, 7 April 1834
5 Search for *Tommeginer*, Emu Bay
    to Chilton, 29 May–13 June 1834
6 Search for *Tommeginer*, Racecourse
    to Den Plain, 16–17 June 1834

♠ VDL company settlement
-▶- Robinson's route
······ Nation boundary
▨ Settled districts

Map 30 Robinson's search for the North West and North nations,
20 February – 17 June 1834

they saw the smoke of the Tommeginer and a day or so later succeeded in meeting them. There were eight of them—one man, four women and three boys. The eldest boy was eight years old. They were in 'a sickly state' and were anxious to join their compatriots on Flinders Island 'but had been afraid to give themselves up'.[23]

Robinson reported to the colonial secretary on 3 February 1835: 'The entire Aboriginal population [is] now removed.' But in February 1836 reports were received from the VDL Company that some Aborigines had visited their outlying huts. The following month Robinson, now at Flinders Island, despatched nine of the mission Aborigines and his two sons to search for them. On 20 November they met a family consisting of a couple and their four children near Cradle Mountain, but the family refused to surrender. They said they were frightened by some of their compatriots at Flinders Island who had previously been hostile to them. Neither Robinson's sons nor the mission Aborigines tried to change their minds, for they possibly envied their freedom. The family surrendered in 1842.

Robinson's experiences behind the frontier had subtly changed his view of conciliation. Convinced that he was capturing the Aborigines for their own good, he was able in all conscience to use the threat of firearms to achieve his objective. He interpreted their hostility not as resistance in defence of their land and their way of life but as a response to violent encounters with sealers, settlers, soldiers and convicts. He was also unable to attribute their rapid death rate in captivity at Macquarie Harbour to anything more than a temporary adjustment on the long road to Christianity or to incompetent care by the doctor.

Yet on the west coast Robinson had encountered several intact families with children. Until the attack by the Tarkinener on his party at the Arthur River in September 1832, he had been sympathetic to their determination to fight for their country and had suffered momentary pangs of conscience when he forced their surrender. But the incident at the Arthur River changed all that. He now believed that they had become too dangerous to remain in undisturbed possession of their country and that they should be 'removed for their own good'. Arthur agreed. Both men firmly believed that they were saving the western Aborigines from certain extermination and extinction and providing them with the benefits of British civilisation and Christianity. In taking this humanitarian view, they manifested a far more progressive stance towards the Aborigines than was shared by most of the settlers, who considered that they had no human propensities and thus had no reason to exist.

But if Arthur and Robinson truly believed that they had removed the North West and South West nations from their homelands for their own good, were they prepared for the consequences? In an ironic turn of events, the VDL Company ceased to graze sheep south of Cape Grim at the end of 1832, and in 1833 the penal station at Macquarie Harbour was relocated to Port Arthur. After that the west coast attracted very few colonists until the timber and mining boom of the 1870s. According to Vivienne Rae-Ellis, in 1922 the photographer J.W. Beattie recorded the story of a man known as Squeaker Smith, who, when engaged in sawing pine at Port Davey possibly in the 1880s, 'shot two male blacks who came around'. Rae-Ellis says that 'Beattie added that Smith's mother was still alive and the incident was well known to a large number of elderly people living in the Ida Bay area'.[24]

Would the South West and North West nations have survived had Robinson not captured and removed them? James Boyce considers that the forced removal of the western nations constituted an act of ethnic cleansing that was tantamount to genocide.[25] It is impossible not to agree. Of course they should have remained in their country. Even so, their numbers had dramatically fallen from about 600 in 1824 to fewer than 150 in 1832. In the two years following Robinson's first meeting with the South West clans in 1830 their number appears to have nearly halved from sixty to thirty-five. Some of the clans of the North West nation also seem to have been thinned by introduced disease when Robinson encountered them in 1832. It would appear then that by 1832 both nations were in grim decline. But the survival of one family in the north-west until 1842 when they surrendered to employees of the VDL Company, and the possible survival of another in the south-west until the 1880s, indicate that they were hardier and more resourceful than either Arthur or Robinson realised.

But both men faced a great moral dilemma. They had every reason to expect that the western nations would be exterminated, thus ensuring that the reputation of the British Empire would become even more 'indelibly stained'. Arthur may have authorised the policy of ethnic cleansing and Robinson may have carried it out, but paradoxically they did so as the humanitarian agents of British imperialism. They truly believed that by removing the western nations they were preventing rather than enhancing their extermination. They also believed that it was better the Aborigines should die in the arms of God than from the settlers' guns. The only other solution would have been to remove the settlers from Van Diemen's Land. But, at the time, such a suggestion was unthinkable.

The forced removal of the South West and North West nations remains one of the most shameful episodes in Australian history. It stands today as a stark reminder of the brutal consequences of British settler colonialism and the settlers' belief that Van Diemen's Land should become 'native free'.[26] The great tragedy is that it was completely unnecessary.

PART IV

INCARCERATION
1835-1905

14

Wybalenna, 1835–39

When G.A. Robinson arrived at the Aboriginal Establishment at Wybalenna, Flinders Island, on 16 October 1835, to take up the position of superintendent, he was accompanied by nine mission Aborigines and eight children from the Orphan School in Hobart. He expected that within a very short time he would remove all the Aborigines to South Australia. The British government had accepted in principle Arthur's suggestion made in January 1832 that the 'native inhabitants' of any new colony in Australia should be conciliated before settlement actually took place. But it had yet to act on it. In February 1835, Lieutenant-Governor Arthur had raised with Robinson the possibility of using the Tasmanian Aborigines to open 'a friendly communication' with the Aborigines at Portland Bay in the Port Phillip District, now Victoria, where the Henty brothers had established a settlement in 1834. Robinson had strongly endorsed the proposal. Nothing came of it, but Arthur was confident that the position of protector of the Aborigines would be created in the proposed new colony in South Australia and he intended to recommend Robinson to the post. So Robinson had every reason to believe that both he and the entire Aboriginal Establishment would soon be relocated to South Australia. Until then, Wybalenna would operate as a transit camp.[1]

The 112 Aborigines who formed the Establishment were the survivors of nearly 300 people who had surrendered to Robinson's mission over the previous five years. They included seven chiefs: Montpeliater and Tongerlongter from the Oyster Bay and Big River nations; Rolepa and Kalebunna from the Ben Lomond and North Midlands nations; Mannalargenna, also from the Oyster Bay nation; and Heedeek and Towterrer from the North West and South West nations. They led far more cohesive groups of compatriots than previously realised. Tongerlongter, chief of the Oyster Bay nation, and his wife, Drometeemetyer, were accompanied by several warriors from the Big River people and about twenty of their relatives. Rolepa, the chief of the Ben Lomond nation, his wife, Luggenemenener, his sons, Maulboyheenner and Walter George Arthur, had about twenty of his relatives. Kalebunna, the chief of the North Midlands nation, was Umarrah's brother and was responsible for his relatives. Mannalargenna was accompanied by his son Kartiteyer and about thirteen of their relatives. His daughter, Wapperty, lived with one of the sealers on a nearby Bass Strait island, and his wife, Tanlebonyer, had died a few months earlier. Wymurrick, chief of the Peerapper clan and Heedeek, the chief of the Tarkinener clan and his wife, Narrucer, led about thirty relatives; and Towterrer, chief of the Port Davey people and his wife, Wongerneep, and their child, Mathinna, had about fifteen relatives.

They formed three distinct groups, based on linguistic and cultural affiliation. The largest was the western group, which comprised forty-six people from the North West and South West nations including Woorraddy and Truganini from the South East nation. The Ben Lomond people formed the second largest group, thirty-six people from the Ben Lomond, North Midlands and North East nations. The smallest was the Big River group, comprising about twenty-three members of the Oyster Bay and Big River nations.

Robinson had promised the Aborigines that Wybalenna would offer 'uninterrupted tranquility in the society of their kindred and their friends, their wants and necessities were to be amply supplied in addition to which they were to enjoy their native amusements. Moreover their customs were to be respected, and not broken into by any rash or misguided interference.'[2] Arthur was also determined that they 'should not want for anything'.[3] He had appointed a catechist, Robert Clark; a surgeon, James Allen; a store-keeper, a coxswain and a gardener to assist in the Establishment's day-to-day running; a military detachment consisting of a corporal and four soldiers of the 50th Regiment to maintain law and order; and sixteen male convict

© Robert J. Anders 2011

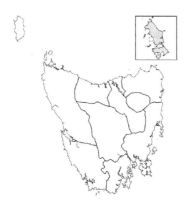

Map 31 Wybalenna, Flinders Island, 1835–47

labourers who were detailed to bake bread, make clothes, cut wood, dig the abundant vegetable gardens, build new huts, fetch and carry the water from the nearby lagoons, make roads and paths, tend the poultry, cattle, sheep, cows and pigs as well as the Aborigines' sheep on Prime Seal Island and carry the provisions to and from the store. In all, forty-six Britons including the families of the civil and military personnel serviced Wybalenna. Never again would a government-supported Aboriginal Station in Australia enjoy such a high level of financial support and employ such a large number of skilled people to look after a relatively small number of Aborigines. Even so, twenty-eight Aborigines had died in the previous two years, including the Big River chief Montpeliater. Many of the others were homesick and desperate to return to their own country, and most of them were delighted when Robinson told them that they would soon leave Wybalenna and relocate to the Australian mainland.[4]

They largely carried on their own lives independently in the bush, living in three separate groups in communal huts away from the main settlement. The men hunted bush foods like possums, kangaroos and wallabies and organised regular ceremonial gatherings. The women harvested Cape Barren geese and mutton-birds when in season and collected their eggs and dived for shellfish. They also conducted illicit sexual relations with the sealers and male convicts who regularly and illegally visited their campsites. The men in turn raided each other's camps for women and jostled for political dominance with Robinson by presenting him with hindquarters of wallaby and freshly caught mutton-birds.

On 7 November, Robinson celebrated his arrival at Wybalenna with a formal dinner held in the late afternoon. The civil officers served the Aborigines with wine, fresh mutton, rice and plum pudding. Afterwards, the Aborigines played cricket and in the evening were entertained by a fireworks display. A few days later, under the direction of the surgeon and Robinson's sons, some of the Aboriginal men cut a road from Robinson's house to the jetty, a distance of one and a half kilometres. A few weeks later they were reaping barley. Robinson was convinced that these activities were signs that the Aborigines wanted to become 'civilized' like the British.[5] He had already encouraged some of the men to cut their hair, prevented the women from cohabiting with the convicts, if not the sealers, and isolated the mission Aborigines from the communal atmosphere of the large huts in the hope that they would set a good example to the others by building fences and digging gardens for their own use.[6]

On 4 December the apparent idyll came to an abrupt end with the death of Mannalargenna. Aged about seventy, he had been the best known and most important of all the chiefs in Aboriginal Tasmania. He came from the Leetermairremener clan at St Patricks Head in the Oyster Bay nation and had developed important political and social relations with the sealers before 1820. During the Black War he had become a feared guerilla leader, and his surrender to Robinson in November 1830 had been

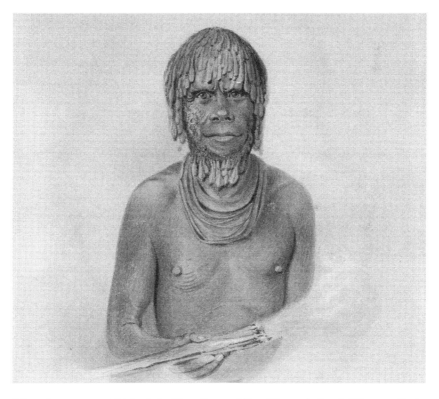

Mannalargenna, a Chief of the East Coast of Van Diemen's Land. Thomas Bock, National Library of Australia, Canberra.

considered by Arthur a major turning point in ending the hostilities. He had assisted Robinson in tracking down his rival chief Umarrah, from the North Midlands nation, and two others, Montpeliater and Tongerlongter, from the Big River and Oyster Bay nations. He had also assisted Robinson in organising the surrender of the North, North West and South West nations between 1832 and 1834. His wife, Tanlebonyer, who came from Little Swanport and had been with him in all the missions, had died in Hobart in May 1835. After that he had become depressed. On the voyage from Hobart to Flinders Island in October, as the ship sailed past St Patricks Head, he had carefully examined his country with the aid of a telescope and sighed with despair, knowing that he would never return home. A month before he died, he had attempted to forge a new relationship with another woman but he appeared to have lost his zest for life. He died with son Kartiteyer, at his side.[7]

Mannalargenna's death was a severe blow to Robinson. He had been one of his most important confidants, 'and though an aged person he never once drew back or threw obstacles in the way'. He had also forced Robinson to promise to guarantee the independence of his people at Wybalenna on the understanding that it was compensation for the loss of their country. In his eulogy Robinson described Mannalargenna as the last of the great chiefs, who had encouraged his people to learn the blessings of civilisation. In keeping with this belief he ordered that Mannalargenna should be buried rather than cremated in order to deprive the women of his bones to use as relics.[8] But they had already taken what they required.

A few weeks later, at the tyereelore's request, Robinson changed some of their names, given to them by the sealers, to more suitable English names. For example, Drummernerlooner, known as 'Jumbo' to the sealers, was renamed Louisa, and Tarenootairrer, who was known as 'Tib', became Sarah. Goneannah was renamed Patty, and Pierrapplener, who was known as 'Dinah', was renamed Anne. 'Bangum' was renamed Flora, and Woretermoteryenna, who was known as 'Bung' to the sealers, was renamed Margaret.

The name changes proved so popular that other Aborigines requested English names as well. Wooraddy was renamed Count Alpha because he was the first surviving Aboriginal man that Robinson encountered at

Bruny Island in 1829. Truganini became Lalla Rookh after the beautiful Indian princess in the popular poem by Thomas Moore and Dray, from the South West nation, was renamed Sophia. Tongerlongter, the chief of the Oyster Bay people, became King William after the reigning king of England, and his wife, Drometeemetyer, became Queen Adelaide; Rolepa, the chief of the Ben Lomond nation, was renamed King George after the long-lived George III, and his wife, Luggenemenener, became Queen Charlotte. Callerwarrermeer, one of the warriors from the Big River nation, was renamed Tippo Saib after the great Hindu warrior defeated by the British in India thirty years before; the fearless young warrior Pevay was renamed Napoleon; and Mannalargenna's son Kartiteyer was renamed Hector in honour of the ancient Greek warrior. Pyterrunner, aged sixteen, whose mother, Tingernoop, was from Port Davey, was renamed Matilda after the English warrior queen.

By renaming some of the chiefs as kings and the young warriors after heroes in recent as well as ancient history, Robinson wanted the Aborigines to believe that their own authority structure was similar to that of the British and thus more readily understand the nature of his program.[9] But he also knew that most of them were already known by at least two names, one which they used in their own country and another when visiting the country of other nations. Truganini, for example, used that name when in her own country in the D'Entrecasteaux Channel, but she used the name Lydgudgee when visiting other nations. In adopting a third name, Lalla Rookh, she was acknowledging her 'new' country at Wybalenna. Robinson was hopeful that the younger generation would retain their new names as part of the transition to their new lives in a British society. Many did so, but when they were ill they often reverted to the names from their own country in the hope that their 'home' spirits would help them to survive or guide them to their ancestors.

By March 1836 Robinson had put in place for the fourteen children a rigid daily routine designed to hasten their transition to British society. It became the basis for all other programs for the assimilation of Aborigines across Australia. First they were separated from their parents. The girls, like Mary Ann, were sent to live at the storekeeper's house, and the boys, like Walter George Arthur, lived with the catechist, Robert Clark. They rose at half-past six, washed and said their prayers, and at seven o'clock assembled with the catechist and his family to read the Bible. At half-past seven they had breakfast with Robinson and his family. Then they went to school until noon, when they had lunch, and returned to school at two o'clock, where they remained until tea at half-past three. At six o'clock they helped the adults at the evening school until eight, when they returned to the catechist's house for family worship, and at nine o'clock they went to bed.[10]

The eldest boy, Walter George Arthur, aged fifteen, had spent most of his childhood at the Orphan School in Hobart. He could read and write English, and Robinson expected that he would become the Aborigines' future leader and that the boys, like Thomas, and Peter and Davy Bruny, would become skilled tradesmen like himself. But Walter's father, Rolepa, who was the chief of the Ben Lomond nation and also living at Wybalenna, expected that as the son of a man of high degree Walter would in time become the chief of their own people and expected him to observe their customs and cultural requirements.[11] In time he fulfilled the expectations of both groups.

The girls were already serving as housemaids to the civil officers. Mary Ann, aged about sixteen, was the daughter of Tarenootairrer, or Sarah, and sealer James Parish, who had brought her to Flinders Island in about 1834. She seems to have had some schooling in Launceston. She was much smarter than either Robinson or the catechist, Robert Clark, would have liked, and she became a persistent critic of Robinson's regime. Another young girl was Bessy Clark, or Pangernowidedic, from Port Davey, whose mother, Tingernoop, was also at Wybalenna.

The fifty Aboriginal women, who had an average age of about thirty, were placed under the charge of Mrs Clark. At nine o'clock each morning she was expected to inspect their general appearance and then examine their huts and windbreaks to check whether their grass-filled mattresses had been aired or washed, the floors and tables swept, and the crockery and cutlery cleaned. Then she would send them to the store for rations of meat and vegetables. At midday they cooked damper and stew on open fires outside the huts and in the afternoon they attended sewing classes for two hours. On Fridays after dinner they were to wash everyone's clothes, and on Saturdays they cooked a second damper for Sunday. In the evenings between six and eight o'clock on Mondays, Wednesdays and Fridays and between seven and eight on Tuesdays and Thursdays they were expected to attend evening school to learn their letters and to hear stories from the Bible. Some of the women, such as Tarenootairrer, were tyereelore and had learned a variety of domestic skills, which Mrs Clark and Robinson believed could be useful in training the other Aboriginal women. Instead, they became active opponents of the regime.

Unlike the women and children, the fifty-six men had no specific routine devised for them. Apart from attending evening school, they were expected to cultivate the gardens, build roads, clear forest land, erect fences and shear sheep. But they resented the hard manual labour, which they considered as 'convicts work', and expected that they should be paid to do it. So they 'worked' when it suited them. For the senior men, maintaining their culture in song and dance, preparing the younger men for initiation, hunting game for fresh meat and keeping the women under control were the most important aspects of their daily lives.

Yet on Sunday mornings they sometimes acceded to Robinson's request to stand outside their huts with the women to await his inspection. On these occasions the women wore checked gingham petticoats and scarves about their necks and heads, and the men wore canvas trousers with tail coats buttoned to the waist. After breakfast they proceeded to chapel from eleven o'clock to one o'clock, where they had to put up with Robinson's exhortations to lead a good Christian life. After lunch they returned to the chapel for hymn singing, which they clearly enjoyed.

After five months Robinson was encouraged by their response to the routine. But in reality the adults continued their own lives and cultural practices. They hoarded ochre, performed ceremonies in secret and adorned their huts with drawings of their exploits in their own country. Conflict often broke out among the men from the three major national groupings—the western, the Ben Lomond, and the Big River—over women and dogs, and sometimes Robinson had to send a particular group out hunting for a few days to forestall violence.[12] The intermittent arrival of ration ships forced Robinson to rely increasingly upon Aboriginal food sources, but by 1837 these had largely been hunted out.

By then the staple rations of damper, tea and stews made from salt meat, cabbage and turnips dominated their diet. Many of the Ben Lomond, Oyster Bay and Big River people had adjusted to these foods in the Settled Districts long before, but for the western people these rations were often inadequate. The real problem was the contaminated water supply and irregular supplies of fresh meat. Major Thomas Ryan, the commandant at Launceston, who reported on conditions at Wybalenna in March 1836, was also aware of the problem. Experience in India had taught him that a salt meat diet not only produced disease but also reduced the ability of people to procreate. He warned Arthur:

> If it is the wish of the Government to propagate the species it is our bounden duty to provide all the means that are in our possession for the accomplishment of so desirable an end—if not, I tremble for the consequences, the race of Tasmania, like the last of the Mohicans will pine away and be extinct in a quarter of a century. [They live in] an artificial society where most of their traditional food resources have been hunted out, and living in damp, poorly ventilated huts with impure water and inadequate provisions.[13]

Major Ryan found it hard not to draw the conclusion that the Aborigines were being deliberately exterminated in a manner that involved considerable pain and suffering. He recommended that the Establishment at Wybalenna should be relocated to a new site on Flinders Island where fresh water was available along with vastly improved rations, including fresh meat. But Robinson was reluctant because he was expecting to relocate to South Australia. Until then he arranged for fresh water to be brought to the settlement in barrels, ordered regular supplies of fresh mutton from the flock of sheep on Prime Seal Island and encouraged the Aborigines to hunt for their own supplies of fresh meat.[14]

The long wait for a decision about the Aborigines' future came to an end in mid September when Robinson was summoned to Hobart to meet

with Arthur. He was unprepared for what followed. Arthur was authorised to offer Robinson the appointment as chief protector of the Aborigines
in South Australia but at only half the expected salary and on condition that
he took only ten Tasmanian Aborigines with him. The British government
had also refused his claim for greater recompense for his previous work
even though Arthur had made clear that his services were 'worth ten times
the amount he was paid'.[15] Robinson was so shocked by the government's
mean-spirited offer and its apparent indifference to the fate of the Tasmanian Aborigines that he immediately rejected the appointment. Everything
he had believed in and worked so hard to achieve now appeared in ruins.[16]

Arthur considered that Robinson had misunderstood the British government's intentions. Nevertheless, he urged Robinson to plan ahead for the
next position of protector of the Aborigines, which would soon be made at
Port Phillip. Robinson embraced the possibility and in late December he
visited Melbourne with six of the mission Aborigines as the official guest
of the Port Phillip Association. The Aborigines were 'highly delighted
with the country'.[17] But he was told that if the entire Establishment were
to relocate to Port Phillip he would have to disprove the settlers' belief that
the Tasmanian Aborigines possessed certain 'anti-civilizing properties' and
demonstrate that they could adapt to the British way of life, by converting
to Christianity, learning to read and perhaps write in English, adopting
British standards of personal cleanliness, dress and housing, knowing
how to farm the land and eat salt meat and how to accumulate money and
material possessions.[18]

Aware that it would be at least eighteen months before the appointment
at Port Phillip could be offered and still uncertain that all the Aborigines
would be permitted to relocate there, Robinson returned to Wybalenna
determined to show that they could meet the requirements. In undertaking the task, he would be better resourced financially than any other
mission superintendent in nineteenth-century Australia. He was also better
equipped emotionally to undertake the task, for he knew personally every
Aborigine at Wybalenna, and each of them placed great faith in his ability
to protect their interests. This enabled him to focus on several material
aspects that could bring ready results.

He began with a building program to provide British-style housing. He personally designed and supervised the construction of a single-level brick terrace of twenty separate one-room apartments and a store room around an L-shaped courtyard. Recent archaeological excavation of the site indicates that they were 'by no means inferior housing in late Georgian terms even for skilled labourers.' They were well designed and built of sound materials.[19]

Once building had commenced, in February 1837, he began to reorganise the social relations among the major Aboriginal groups. First, he appointed constables from among the most important male Elders, such as Wymurrick, to control the sexual promiscuity among the younger men and to offer them one shilling for every dog they killed. As Penny van Toorn points out, this 'may have translated in his own cultural terms into the senior men's traditional responsibility of controlling younger men's access to women'.[20] He also remunerated the chiefs if they attended evening school regularly, and it appears that Wymurrick readily adapted his own beliefs with an understanding of the Bible. In 1837 he was an eloquent and elegant speaker, who readily exhorted his people in a mixture of English, his own language and the *lingua franca* of Wybalenna.[21]

But in this initiative Robinson was hampered by a fresh outbreak of gastroenteritis and pneumonia, which could have been caused by *Escherichia coli* bacteria in contaminated water, lack of fresh vegetables and the Aborigines' enforced sedentary lifestyle in campsites which attracted fleas and rats.[22] One by one the Aborigines temporarily deserted Wybalenna for the bush to restore their health. Whereas in 1836 there had been comparatively few Aboriginal deaths and four children had been born, in 1837 Robinson faced the horrible reality of twenty-seven deaths, including Tongerlongter and Towterrer; Montpeliater's widow, Bet; Rolepa's wife, Luggenemenener; Wymurrick's wife, Larratong; Mannalargenna's son, Kartiteyer; and several children from the western nations. It was as if the heart of the Wybalenna community was being torn out.

Undeterred, Robinson made provision for two of the boys from the Orphan School, Walter George Arthur and Thomas Bruny, to produce a newspaper, the *Flinders Island Weekly Chronicle*, as evidence of their adaptation to British ways. As the first Aboriginal newspaper in Australia, its purpose was 'to promote christianity civilization and Learning amongst the Aboriginal Inhabitants |and| be a brief but accurate register of the events of the colony moral and religious'.[23] The *Chronicle* appeared in thirty-one issues between 28 September 1837 and January 1838.[24] Each issue seems to have consisted of one page and was handwritten and hand copied in English; most were likely prepared by Thomas Bruny. It is not known how many copies were made of each issue, but put together they reveal important insights into the Aborigines' lives at Wybalenna. Most of the articles were exhortations to promote God-fearing behaviour and to show gratitude to Robinson for 'bringing them in':

> Now my friends you see that the commandant is so kind to you
> he gives you everything that you want when you were in the bush
> the commandant had to leave his friends and go into the bush and
> he brought you out of the bush because he felt for you he knowed
> the white man was shooting you and now he has brought you to
> Flinders Island where you get every things and when you are ill tell
> the Doctor immediately and you get relief you have now fine houses.
> I expect that you will not vex one another.[25]

But other articles revealed the determination by the adults to live their own lives. The men went hunting with guns without permission and often were away for days at a time on the other side of the island. The women defied Christian practice and collected wood on a Sunday and often fed freshly baked bread to their beloved dogs.[26] Rather than speaking the formal English that Robinson encouraged Thomas Bruny and Walter Arthur to write in the *Chronicle*, the adults spoke a *lingua franca* or creole English they had picked up from the sealers, shepherds and stock-keepers. Arthur had earlier forbidden any translation of the Bible into any of the Tasmanian Aboriginal languages on the grounds that they were 'uncivilized'.[27] In making this decision he inadvertently ensured that the Word of God would only be available to English speakers in the Aboriginal community, that is, the children. A visitor described the *lingua franca* spoken at Wybalenna as a mixture of English, words from Tasmanian languages, and others from the Australian mainland and perhaps from New Zealand. The catechist, Robert Clark, also communicated with the Aborigines in the *lingua franca* along with most of the convicts and civil officers. So there were several languages in use at Wybalenna, the formal written English used by Robinson and the *Flinders Island Weekly Chronicle*, the *lingua franca* spoken by everyone else and the different languages of each of the major national groups.[28]

Robinson's next step was to establish a weekly market. Between ten o'clock and noon every Thursday the Aborigines sold shell necklaces, wallaby skins, feathers, waddies and spears, and some of their needlework to the British residents. In turn the British sold the Aborigines clay pipes, sugar plums, fishing lines, crockery, shirts, beads, belts, buckles, marbles and cricket bats. But there was no trading between the Aborigines. Robinson used old English coins as a medium of exchange with *FI* (Flinders Island) marked on one side and *AE* (Aboriginal Establishment) on the other. From time to time the Aborigines sent shell necklaces and salted mutton-birds to Launceston for sale, and the money earned went into an Aboriginal fund to purchase tobacco and other British luxury items. Market days appear to have continued until the end of 1838.[29]

Despite these innovations, most of the adults only paid lip service to the 'civilization' program. The clan leaders continued their 'old' ways of adjusting their kinship structure, raiding each other's clans for women, undertaking regular hunting trips and performing ceremonies with portrayals in dance of their wartime combat with the settlers. The women kept relics, exchanged dogs, searched for shells and developed reciprocal relations with the convicts and sealers. The remaining chiefs were anxious that their sons and other relatives were properly initiated, so they would assume responsibility for their people when they died. They also saw the dichotomy between Robinson's teaching of the gospel and its fruits—the flogging of soldiers and convicts, the wrangling between the storekeeper and the catechist, the insolence of Robinson's sons towards their father, and the secret liaison between Robinson's daughter and the medical officer.[30]

Robinson's one redeeming feature was his refusal to use physical force, but he used moral and coercive force with devastating results. He isolated groups, denied rations to others, prevented some from hunting and encouraged spying—all the usual forms of behaviour that the superintendent of any asylum or institution can use to keep control. He could not see that moral coercion was contrary to voluntarism.

In the winter of 1837, as sickness raged through the community, formal instruction for the boys was abandoned as fresh water could not be procured, supplies of fresh meat could not be found and building materials failed to arrive. Most of the Aborigines fled to the bush to fend for themselves. By the end of the year twenty-nine people had died. The *Flinders Island Weekly Chronicle* reported:

> The brig Tamar arrived this morning at green Island ... Let us hope it will be good news and that something may be done for us poor people they are dying away the Bible says some or all shall be saved but I am much afraid none of us will be alive by and by and then as nothing but sick men amongst us. Why don't the black-fellows pray to the king to get us away from this place.[31]

Robinson was desperate. His chances of obtaining the position at Port Phillip had brightened, but the Tasmanian Aborigines' future had not. He wrote to the colonial secretary in Hobart:

> Should ... His Majesty's Government still object to their removal, and continue the settlement where it now is, I have no hesitation in stating that the race in a very short period will be extinct; and although it might be urged that the same results would occur were the translation permitted, still it would be found that by the admixture of the Flinders' Island aborigines with the aborigines of the country, the declension would not be observed, consequently the excitement not felt.[32]

He was dismayed by the fears expressed by the colonial press in Melbourne and by the government in Sydney that the inmates at Wybalenna were 'desperadoes' who would 'excite' the Aborigines at Port Phillip into 'wanton acts of violence'. But he could not conceive that the British government would let them die.[33]

In the midst of this despair the ten mission Aborigines—four couples, Wooraddy and Truganini, Fanny Hardwicke and Pevay, Maulboyheenner and Jenny, and the four young warriors Richard, Probelattener (Isaac), Lacklay and Little Billy (Edward)—returned to Wybalenna.[34] Since March 1837 they had been with Robinson's eldest son in the northern part of Van Diemen's Land in search of a family from the North nation which had evaded capture in 1834. They had finally tracked the family down but could not persuade them to surrender. Perhaps the mission Aborigines envied their life in their own country in preference to the horrors of Wybalenna. Indeed, when they returned, they were critical of the deaths that had taken place and Truganini predicted 'there would be no blackfellows to live in the new houses'.[35] They openly defied Robinson's authority in wearing ochre, incising their bodies with bottle glass and performing ceremonial dances late into the night.[36]

Robinson had even worse problems with the fourteen tyereelore. Their better health, familiarity with British customs and way of life and readiness to dispense with some of the more 'distasteful' traditional ceremonial dances had led him to believe that they could form the vanguard of his new society. But he soon discovered that they performed the equally shocking dances they had developed in cohabitation with the sealers and that their knowledge of English was liberally strewn with blasphemies that deeply shocked him. As well, the *lingua franca* they introduced to Wybalenna was a powerful weapon of ridicule. In the second half of 1837 they emerged as a significant dissident group, critical of the Establishment and resisting both Robinson's authority and that of the Aboriginal men.

In August 1837 Robinson organised 'marriages' for four of them, Emma, Flora, Patty and Rebecca. He believed that in their new married state under the control of their Aboriginal husbands they would become more tractable and bear children. But within a week they left their husbands for the bush, warning that they would not return until they could live as they chose. Robinson refused them rations, so they robbed the camp at night. Then he sent the young journalists Walter George Arthur and Thomas Bruny from the *Flinders Island Weekly Chronicle* to visit them. They 'told the women if they did not clean the houses and clean themselves they would put them in the paper. [The women] said they may speak but not write—they seemed to have a great abhorrence of being put in newspapers.'[37]

In early November some of the Aborigines moved into their new homes, the twenty apartments that had been built in the form of an L-shaped terrace which faced east to keep out the cold westerly winds. Each apartment had one room with two beds sufficient for four persons. There were two cupboards on either side of the fireplace, one latticed window and a small yard partly enclosed with a picket fence. The roofs were thatched with grass. The terrace formed part of a square, with the newly constructed chapel, designed to hold 200 people, occupying the opposite corner. After living in couples for a few weeks, they adapted the dwellings to their preferred mode of communal living. They cooked outside and allowed their dogs to sleep with them inside. But the women would not conform:

> Women you are still continuing to do what is improper—when you go into the bush—God may take away your lives very soon for your wickedness. You go about the settlement some of you living like

Residence of the Aborigines, Flinders Island. J.S. Prout, National Library of Australia, Canberra.

dogs—God does not like that—bad people will be sent to Hell—bad
people are the Devil's people.

Every woman should mind her own house and not be going to
other people's houses—keep your blankets clean—carry plenty of
wood to your houses for your fires take care of your clothes and sew
them when they are old and torn—do not throw them away when
you go to the bush hunting as you used to do.[38]

By then Robinson had abandoned his demand for a British nuclear
family lifestyle. A month before, he had found his prize pupil, Walter
George Arthur, in bed with that smart young woman Mary Ann. He abandoned the plan to train Walter as a catechist, and, following the arrival of an
ordained Presbyterian clergyman at Wybalenna in January 1838, the couple
were prepared for a Christian marriage in March. In drinking the toast at
the ceremony, the Aborigines appeared to say 'Go to hell' instead of 'Good
health'. When Truganini found her tobacco pipe missing, she asked the
culprit, Dawunga (Leonidas), whether 'God tell him to steal lubra's pipes?'
When Kalebunna (Ajax) called a woman black, she was most offended and
wanted to know if he was a white man. Robinson was embittered by this
'careless indifference and ingratitude', but he never faltered in his belief
that the course of all human history was progress towards what he believed
himself to be, and that there was nothing unreasonable in persisting with
this barren harvest.[39]

Nor did he falter in his determination to remove the Aborigines from
Wybalenna. To this end he exhorted the new lieutenant-governor, Sir John
Franklin, to pay an official visit to Wybalenna and see how 'civilized' the
Aborigines had become. Sir John and Lady Franklin arrived on 26 January
1838 with a bevy of officials. They were enchanted by the Aborigines
and Franklin agreed to support Robinson's quest to relocate them to Port
Phillip. But it was too late. The despatch from Lord Glenelg, the secretary
of state for the colonies, leaving the decision for removal in the hands of
the governor of New South Wales, Sir George Gipps, in whose jurisdiction
Port Phillip lay, had already been sent.[40]

In August 1838, armed with Franklin's support and a promise that the Van Diemen's Land government would continue financial aid once the Aborigines were at Port Phillip, Robinson arrived in Sydney to present his case to Governor Gipps and the Legislative Council. But his efforts were clouded by the deep divisions in the Sydney press following the massacre of twenty-eight Aborigines at Myall Creek in northern New South Wales by twelve stockmen in June. Eleven of the twelve perpetrators had since been arrested and charged with murder and were now awaiting trial in Sydney. This was the first time since 1799 that colonists had been arrested and charged with murdering Aborigines.[41] The press was in uproar about the arrests and Robinson was horrified by the colonists' careless indifference to Aboriginal rights. He contacted the leading clergy of all Protestant denominations and generated sufficient interest to form the Sydney branch of the London-based Aborigines Protection Society and used its first public meeting on 19 October to present an impressive address on Aboriginal rights.[42]

But his endeavours failed to impress the Legislative Council. Its members were in no mood to permit the Aboriginal 'desperadoes' from Van Diemen's Land to relocate to Port Phillip and 'subvert' the Aborigines there. Governor Gipps agreed. He offered Robinson the position of chief protector of the Aborigines at Port Phillip at a salary of £500 a year and a pension, once again on the condition that he took only the mission Aborigines with him. This time Robinson accepted the appointment. Sir John Franklin had told him that once the mass hysteria arising from the Myall Creek trials had subsided he could probably transfer the other Aborgines.[43]

Robinson returned to Flinders Island in January 1839, selected fifteen Aborigines and departed for Port Phillip on 25 February. They were Truganini and Woorraddy, Pevay and Fanny Hardwicke, Walter George Arthur and Mary Ann, Lacklay and Pyterrunner (Matilda), Maulboy-heenner and Jenny, Woorraddy's sons Peter and Davy Bruny, the New Holland sealing woman Charlotte and her son Johnny Franklin, and the part-Aboriginal boy Thomas Thompson. Only six of them returned to Flinders Island in 1842. Robinson's last gift to Wybalenna was the Spanish influenza he had contracted in Sydney, from which eight of the Aborigines died. At the height of the epidemic, in March, Robinson's eldest son wrote to his father:

> It would be impossible to describe the gloom which prevails ... from the bereavement of so large a portion of their kindred and friends, and the anxiety they evince to leave a spot which occasions such painful reminiscences is hourly increasing ... the males [*sic*] ... attenuated forms ... proves them to be the greatest suffered, and that the island has been a charnel house for them.[44]

Robinson had taken the group of Aborigines who were educated and articulate and thus strong enough to voice outrage at their treatment. His efforts to take the rest to Port Phillip failed. Neither Lieutenant-Governor Charles La Trobe at Melbourne nor Governor Gipps in Sydney was prepared to countenance them on the Australian mainland.

Robinson's attempts to 'Christianize and civilize' the Aborigines at Wybalenna along with his earlier conciliation and removal policies sullied his reputation ever afterwards. But rather than considering his behaviour as that of a man on the make, as his biographer argues, it could more fruitfully be placed in the context of Aboriginal policy-making then taking shape in the Australian colonies. Robinson was the first government employee in Australia to argue for a coherent policy which recognised Aboriginal rights, and his ideas and beliefs were later taken forward by Aboriginal protectors such as Walter E. Roth in Queensland in the 1890s.[45] Robinson may have had many human failings, but he was thwarted and betrayed by the British government and the settler governments in the Australian colonies. His superb ethnographic work in recording the Tasmanian Aborigines and his policy-making on their behalf surely make him Australia's first government anthropologist. He was the first in a long and impressive line of government anthropologists who genuinely believed that the Aborigines had rights to their country and should be saved from the settlers' guns. Indeed, his forced removal of the western nations in the 1830s was replicated across Australia until the last group of Aborigines 'came in' in the 1950s. It was not the man who was at fault. Rather, it was the stubborn belief held by the settlers that they had sole right to Aboriginal land and their preparedness to go to any lengths to take ownership of it that should be questioned.

From the time of Robinson's arrival at Wybalenna in October 1835, when 123 Aborigines greeted him, to his departure three and a half years later, fifty-nine of them had died, eleven others were born or arrived separately, and fifteen accompanied him to Port Phillip. Only sixty Aborigines remained at Wybalenna. Of the forty-six western people who had greeted Robinson in October 1835, only twenty-two remained in 1839. The Big River, Oyster Bay and South East people had fared little better. Of the thirty-five recorded in October 1835 only fifteen remained in April 1839, although five accompanied Robinson to Port Phillip. The Ben Lomond people had fared best of all. Of the thirty people recorded in October 1835, twenty-one remained in April 1839. All of the chiefs apart from Heedeek from Sandy Cape had died, and political control of the three major Aboriginal groupings had passed to the next generation of men, aged in their late twenties and early thirties. Most of them were in relatively stable relationships and some of them were parents of children. So, even though only sixty Aborigines remained at Wybalenna, they appeared young enough and in sufficient numbers to produce more children to survive. Above all, they did not face an impossible future.

15

Wybalenna, 1839–47

With the departure of the fifteen Aborigines for Port Phillip, the lives of the sixty others who remained at Wybalenna entered a new phase. They were no longer considered the survivors of the unjust dispossession of their country, but rather as the expensive and ungrateful inmates of an asylum. Over the next five years, three government inquiries halved annual expenditure from £4,000 to £2,000, and by 1846 the sum was further reduced to £1,500. At that time the nexus between thrift and Aboriginal rights became apparent when Aboriginal leaders asserted their independence.

The report of the first board of inquiry, held in March 1839, set the tone for its successors. Wybalenna was expensive to run and the Aborigines were so ungrateful, lazy and indolent that they should be sent to the mainland of Van Diemen's Land to work as agricultural labourers. But the settlers' insistence on a 'native free' island and the British government's reluctance to scatter a people they had so zealously captured precluded this economically rational solution from taking place. Instead, the colonial government halved the annual expenditure and reduced the British staff from forty-six to sixteen: a commandant at a much reduced salary, a medical officer, a storekeeper, a chaplain, a coxswain, five convicts, and the military detachment of a sergeant and five soldiers. But each of the civilian officers had such large families that they formed a larger group than in Robinson's time.[1]

The new commandant, Captain Malcolm Laing Smith, formerly police magistrate at Norfolk Plains and a veteran of the Black War, arrived in April 1839. He settled his large family into the commandant's house and left the supervision of the Aborigines to his sons. So long as the Aborigines co-operated in basic tasks such as collecting wood, digging the gardens and attending the chapel, they were left to their own devices. But upon any sign of insubordination they were confined to gaol.

They now appeared more settled in the twenty apartments in the L-shaped terrace. The western people and their affiliates formed the largest group. They were originally led by Heedeek from Sandy Cape, who had lost his wife, Petuk, in early 1839. After his death, in April 1841, the warrior Drinene (Neptune), then aged twenty-five, became their leader. He was married to Amelia, a sealing woman, and had a son, Moriarty, and a daughter, Emily. Frederick, aged about thirty, was married to Ryinrope, but their daughter, Helen, had died in 1837. Dawunga (Leonidas) was married to Patty, but they had no children. Nicermenic (Eugene), from Robbins Island, was married to Tarenootairrer (Sarah), who originally came from the George River on the north-east coast; Tarenootairrer already had two children— Mary Ann, and Fanny Cochrane. Nicermenic and Tarenootairrer also had a son, Adam, at Wybalenna in June 1838. Wymurrick, aged about forty, was married to Narrucer, who had first met Robinson at Robbins Island in 1830 and had evaded capture until 1834. They had two daughters: Martha, born in 1835, and Catherine, born in 1839. The adult daughters of Wyne, the chief from the west coast, had married but died by the end of 1842. The future of the western people rested with the children of Nicermenic and Tarenootairrer, Wymurrick and Narrucer, and Drinene and Amelia.

The Ben Lomond people and their affiliates were led by Rolebunna, originally captured in the Black Line, and married to Maria. This group had few children, but the tyereelores' domestic skills gave the group considerable power in the community. The final group, the Big River, now had fourteen people. Their most active male warriors, Alexander, Augustus and Washington, who were all in their twenties, most assiduously performed ceremonies.[2] They would become future leaders of the community.

An archaeological excavation of the apartments indicates that each group readily accepted European manufactured items, like handkerchiefs, buttons, fish hooks, clay pipes, blue beads, knives and forks, marbles, gun flints, nails, china and bottle glass, tobacco, tea and sugar, that were advantageous to their own way of life. Some of these items were earned from day labour such as making roads and cutting grass and from the sale of wool and kangaroo skins in Launceston. Other items were acquired from trading kangaroo skins, shell necklaces, spears and mutton-birds with the convicts, soldiers and sealers. Still other items such as tobacco, sugar and tea were provided as part of their regular rations. They also managed the livestock that Arthur had presented to them in 1835 and regularly took them to pasture at Grass Tree Plains, Stoney Castle and Prime Seal Island, but they would perform no other labour unless they were paid. As they pointed out on more than one occasion, they believed that the whole of Flinders Island belonged to them and that the Aboriginal Establishment had been created to meet their needs. They should not be expected to work 'like prisoners' and they had no desire to live like 'white people'.[3]

The women evidently wore blanket dresses made of tough Maria Island cloth and Scotch caps, and the men wore coats but not trousers. Some of the women seem to have regularly swept their apartments while others let debris accumulate in middens. Some bought materials to make a wooden floor and others survived on the cold brick. It is likely that they consumed kangaroos and wallabies, possums and rabbits as well as fresh and salted mutton, beef and pork. They left their apartments when disease erupted and joined regular hunting parties, sometimes of several weeks' duration, to restore their health. The outside hearths remained their major place of socialising and talking. They organised their ceremonial lives around the seasons, in which mutton-birding and kangaroo hunting played critical parts. With their own *lingua franca* as the major form of verbal communication, the Aboriginal community at Wybalenna began to adjust to its new situation.[4]

The same could not be said of the 'carers'. In May 1841, in the midst of internecine squabbling among the civilian staff, a second inquiry recommended combining the positions of commandant and surgeon, halving again the civilian staff from sixteen to eight and reducing the military detachment to a sergeant and two soldiers. But this time the report impacted more directly on the Aborigines. As a cost-cutting measure, eight of the children, including Fanny, then aged seven, were removed to the Orphan School in Hobart.[5]

Commandant Smith was replaced first by Dr Peter Fisher, who had been medical superintendent of a convict ship, and then by Dr Henry Jeanneret, a Scottish medical officer who, according to Charles La Trobe, was 'not quite sane'.[6] When Jeanneret arrived at Wybalenna with his family in August 1842 he found fifty-two Aborigines in residence, consisting of twelve 'married couples', eleven single men, six single women and eleven children. He considered that their dogs, which were central to their social relationships, were a menace to tidiness, and they destroyed crops and stock with impunity. But the Aborigines were indifferent to his position. At night they still performed ceremonies and by day they went hunting for mutton-birds and shellfish without his permission.[7]

Jeanneret's position was immediately contested by the return of seven of the fifteen Aborigines that Robinson had taken to Port Phillip in 1839. They were Walter George Arthur, aged twenty-two, and his wife, Mary Ann, aged twenty-five; Truganini, aged thirty, and Woorraddy, aged about fifty, and his son Davy Bruny, aged seventeen; Fanny Hardwicke, aged about thirty; and Pyterrunner (Matilda), aged twenty-two. Davy Bruny's father, Woorraddy, aged about fifty, set out with them but sadly didn't make it to their destination. They were accompanied by Tillarbunner (Jack Allen), aged about twenty, who had been taken to Port Phillip by John Batman in 1835.

In Melbourne, Walter Arthur had tasted freedom and independence. He had worked first as a stockman, making at least two overland trips to Adelaide, and according to his biographer he seems to have quickly learned that paid work brought respect. He had later worked on the pastoral property purchased by Robinson's two older sons, George and Charles, maintaining a close relationship with their father, whom he called 'my dear old master'.[8] He had met some of the Victorian Aborigines at the nearby ration station, observed some of their ceremonies and noted that they were experiencing the horrors of dislocation and despair just as his own people had a decade earlier. His biographer suggests that these experiences led Walter Arthur to 'question whether white society had any place in which Aboriginal people could be accommodated on a basis of equality'.[9]

In the meantime Mary Ann had worked as a servant in Robinson's household in Melbourne, and after Robinson could not gain government funds to support them he sent five of the others, Truganini, Pevay, Maulboyheenner, Fanny Hardwicke and Pyterrunner, to Assistant Protector William Thomas's station at Narre Narre Warren near the Dandenongs. But they appear to have removed themselves from Thomas's care, and in August 1841, under Pevay's leadership, they began looting shepherds' huts in the Westernport district, and wounded four stock-keepers. On 6 October, after stealing some firearms, they shot dead two whalers and over the next six weeks eluded a large police pursuing party until they were captured in a gun battle towards the end of November.[10] At their trial, although they could make statements that could be presented in court, they were not permitted to give evidence in the witness box in their own defence. Robinson presented strong testimonies of their good character, but the two men, Pevay and Maulboyheenner, were found guilty, while the three women were acquitted. The jury recommended mercy for the two men in view of their 'general good behaviour', but the trial judge, John Walpole Willis, was not convinced. He sentenced them to hang on 20 January 1842, the first executions to take place in Melbourne.[11]

Walter Arthur and Robinson visited Maulboyheenner and Pevay in gaol two days after their sentencing. They found that Maulboyheenner was unable to sleep, had lost his appetite and wept constantly. But Pevay was unrepentant. On the morning of the execution, he ate a hearty breakfast, snapped his fingers and shouted that he 'did not care a fig for anything'. He declared that after his death 'he would join his father in Van Diemen's Land and hunt kangaroo. He also said that he had three heads, one for the scaffold, one for the grave and one for V.D. Land.' When the plank dropped Pevay died instantly, but Maulboyheenner was less fortunate: his noose was not tight enough and he died in the most dreadful agony.[12] Two days later, Walter Arthur was arrested for drunkenness. As his biographer notes, 'It would seem that Walter was trying to escape the outcome of events in which he was powerless to intervene.'[13] Truganini, Pyterrunner and Fanny Hardwicke were bundled back to Flinders Island.

Woorraddy, perhaps dreading the indignity of the return to Wybalenna, died as the ship docked at Green Island, within sight of Flinders Island. He was among the first Aborigines that Robinson had met at Bruny Island in 1829 and was then a proud warrior with a wife and three young sons. After his wife had died from influenza, he began an association with Truganini, and over the next five years they had assisted Robinson in all his missions in Van Diemen's Land, providing him with critical information about the customs, languages and religious beliefs of their compatriots. Woorraddy was a powerful reminder of Aboriginal life before the Black War. During the mission years, his two remaining sons, Peter and Davy Bruny, were sent to the Orphan School in Hobart, where they learned to read and write, before they rejoined him at Wybalenna in 1835. According to Penny van Toorn, Woorraddy practised reconciliation. At Wybalenna in April 1838 he spoke in his own Bruny Island language to address the weekly prayer meeting and constructed his own narrative of the Black War to relate to the entire community:

> The white men have killed us all; they shot a great many. We are now only a few people here and we ought to be fond of one another. We ought to love God. God made every thing, the salt water, the horse, the bullock, the opossum, the wallaby, the kangaroo and wombat. Love him and you will go to him by and bye.[14]

According to van Toorn, the speech is evidence of the 'birth of a new, pan-Tasmanian Indigenous social consciousness, possibly based on Jesus' commandment to "love one another" (John 15:12)'.[15] Woorraddy's son Peter appears to have been apprenticed as a bootmaker and Davy became a shepherd. In 1839 both boys accompanied their father to join Robinson's mission at Port Phillip. Peter subsequently disappears from the record, but Davy remained with his father and may have looked after him during his final days. The story of Woorraddy's family, fragmented by death and cultural dislocation, became typical of many dispossessed Aboriginal families across colonial Australia.[16]

Later that year, another group arrived at Wybalenna. They were the family that had remained in the hills behind Cape Grim after refusing to surrender to Woorraddy and other mission Aborigines in 1837. They finally 'gave themselves up' in 1842 near the Arthur River because, they said, they were lonely. The family included William Lanney, aged seven, his parents and four brothers. By the end of 1847 both parents and two of his brothers had died, leaving William, Charles and their brother known as Barnaby Rudge.[17]

The Aborigines from Port Phillip quickly contested Henry Jeanneret's authority. Walter Arthur, Mary Ann, Tillarbunner (Jack Allen) and Davy Bruny could read and write in English, had tasted freedom and had developed a sophisticated understanding of their legal rights. Even before their return to Wybalenna they had heard stories of Jeanneret's 'rigid and severe' regime and together with Walter and Mary Ann assumed leadership of the entire community. The three men refused to dig the gardens unless they were paid and refused to unload the stores unless they were given extra rations and Mary Ann refused to clean her house until she had better clothes.[18]

Their independent stance disturbed Jeanneret's 'improvement' program. He believed that all the Aborigines should be forced, by threats of violence, to perform considerable labour in return for normal rations and considered that Walter Arthur's refusal to co-operate was 'assiduous in endeavouring to excite disaffection'.[19] But Walter and Tillarbunner (Jack Allen) believed that basic food rations were bare compensation for the loss of their country. They told Jeanneret that Wybalenna had been created not for their benefit but for the benefit of the British who had taken their country. Jeanneret responded by removing three more children to the Orphan School at Hobart.[20]

Jeanneret's overbearing and capricious behaviour also irritated his superiors in Hobart, and in December 1844 he was suspended from office.[21] His successor, Dr Joseph Milligan, arrived at Wybalenna with the children from the Orphan School including Fanny, and the catechist Robert Clark, who had previously served at the Aboriginal Establishment between 1834 and 1839. The Aborigines were overjoyed to see their children and welcomed the catechist, who remained with them until his death in 1850. Milligan appears to have enjoyed a better relationship with Walter Arthur and there was no active resistance to his administration. The fifty-seven Aborigines at Wybalenna in 1845 still kept large numbers of dogs, lived communally in three groupings at the Aboriginal terrace, consumed Aboriginal and European food, and performed ceremonial activities and initiated their children into their traditions.[22]

On 30 December 1845 their apparent independence was disturbed by the awful news that Jeanneret's appeal against his suspension had been upheld in London and he would return to Flinders Island shortly. Walter Arthur now took matters into his own hands. He wrote to the influential Quaker in Hobart George Washington Walker and told him that his people did not want another commandant, for they could grow their own wheat and potatoes and use mutton-birds and their eggs for provisions, together with the mob of sheep that still remained from a bequest made by Arthur in 1832 and that the catechist, Robert Clark, could provide for their spiritual needs. But above all they wanted land so they could be entirely independent. He concluded:

> The remainder of my country people are desirous of doing all we can to support ourselves upon Flinders without our being any more expensive to the Government . . . the Blacks would all petition the governor to get land to earn for themselves but they are afraid and when they will not work for other people they are called Idle and Lazy, altho' we are paid but very little.[23]

Two months later, on 17 February 1846, Walter Arthur and seven of his compatriots who could read and write English drew up the first petition to a reigning monarch by an Aboriginal group in Australia. The petition requested Queen Victoria not to allow Jeanneret to return to his post and asserted that they were 'free Aborigines'. It read in part:

> The humble petition of the free Aborigines Inhabitants of Van Diemen's Land now living on Flinders Island . . . That we are your

free children that we were not taken prisoners but freely gave up our country to Colonel Arthur then the Governor after defending ourselves.

Your petitioners humbly state to your Majesty that Mr Robinson made for us and with Colonel Arthur an agreement which we have not lost from our minds since and we have made our part of it good.

Your petitioners humbly tell Your Majesty that when we left our own place we were plenty of people, we are now but a little one.

Your petitioners state they are a long time at Flinders Island and had plenty of superintendents and were always a quiet and free people and not put into gaol.

Your Majesty's petitioners pray that you will not allow Dr Jeanneret to come again among us as our superintendent as we hear he is to be sent another time for when Dr Jeanneret was with us many moons he used to carry pistols in his pockets and threatened very often to shoot us and make us run away in a fright. Dr Jeanneret kept plenty of pigs in our village which used to run into our houses and eat up our bread from the fires and take away our flour bags in their mouths also to break into our gardens and destroy our potatoes and cabbage.

Our houses were let fall down and they were never cleaned but were covered with vermin and not white-washed. We were often without clothes except a very little one and Dr Jeanneret did not care to mind us when we were sick until we were very bad. Eleven of us died when he was here. He put many of us into jail for talking to him because we would not be his slaves. He kept us from our rations when he pleased and sometimes gave us bad rations of tea and tobacco. He shot some of our dogs before our eyes and sent all the other dogs of ours to an island and when they told him that they would starve he told us they might eat each other. He put arms into our hands and made us assist his prisoners to go to fight the soldiers but he made us go to fight. We were never taught to read or write or to sing God by the doctor. He taught us a little upon the Sundays and his prisoner servant also taught us and his prisoner servant also took us plenty of times to jail by his orders.

The Lord Bishop seen us in this bad way and we told His Lordship plenty how Dr Jeanneret used us.

We humbly pray your Majesty the Queen will hear our prayer and not let Dr Jeanneret any more to come to Flinders Island.

Walter G. Arthur, chief of the Ben Lomond nation, aged 27

King Alexander (Druemerterpunna), Big River nation, aged 35

Jack Allen (Tillarbunner, Batman's Jack), Ben Lomond nation, aged 25

Augustus (Thermanope), North West nation, aged 26

Davy Bruny, Nuenonne clan, South East nation, aged 24

King Tippoo (Callerwarrermeer), Big River nation, aged 35

Neptune (Drinene), North West nation, aged 33

Washington (Maccamee), Big River nation, aged 40.[24]

Jeanneret returned to Flinders Island before the petition could be despatched. When he learned of their move against him he accused Davy Bruny and Tillarbunner (Jack Allen) of 'inciting the others to riot and to set the authorities at naught and that [Walter had] wantonly seized a musket, with intent to besiege my house at night.'[25]

But the petitioners fought back. This time they wrote directly to the lieutenant-governor, Sir William Denison, in Hobart. Jack Allen said: 'We want to tell you we do not like the man you sent down here for superintendent. We have to work for the clothes on our backs.' Washington (Maccamee) wrote: 'Dr. Jeanneret is a very bad man to me and my countrypeople— Please let me and my wife come to Hobart Town to see you. Dr. Jeanneret had put me in jail for speaking out for my rations which he stopped for two days.' Walter George Arthur wrote: 'We black people are threatened by Dr. Jeanneret to be hanged if we write any more about him we want a Protector, we are threatened to be put into Jail . . . we are threatened to have our rations stopped if we do not work.' Davy Bruny wrote: 'Dr. Jeanneret says we must work for our clothes—Governor, I like work very well for white man when he pay me, but Dr. Jeanneret want to make me and

my wife work at his own garden ... and then pay me out of the government stores with the clothes you send down to us. He growl at us too much
for we blackfellows no like work in his garden.' And Mary Ann wrote:
'Dr. Jeanneret wants to make out my husband and myself very bad wicked
people and talks plenty about putting us into Jail and that he will hang us
for helping to write this petition to the Queen from our countrypeople ...
Dr. Jeanneret does not like us for we do not like to be his slaves nor wish our
poor country people to be treated badly or made slaves.'[26]

Lieutenant-Governor Denison ordered an inquiry into the petition's
validity, including Jeanneret's complaint that Robert Clark and his family
had ill-treated the children, and into Jeanneret's seventeen-day imprisonment of Walter Arthur. It found that the Aborigines were well aware of the
purport of the petition, and that Clark had not intentionally ill-treated the
children but had on several occasions chained and flogged Fanny, aged ten,
for disobedience and in retaliation she had attempted to burn down Clark's
house. It also found that Jeanneret had had no legal right to imprison
Walter Arthur.[27]

In London, the petition was received by Queen Victoria. James Stephen,
the under-secretary of state for the colonies, interpreted the petitioners'
claim for independence as a request to return to their own country: 'Why
we should persevere in a policy at once so costly to the author, and so fatal
to the objects of it, I cannot imagine, particularly as the establishment had
been created not so much with a view to any benefit to [the Aborigines]
as from a regard to the interests of the Colonists.'[28] He recommended that
Wybalenna should be abandoned for a new site in Van Diemen's Land.

In Hobart, Denison agreed but for a different reason. He was perturbed
that the women's sexual liaisons with the sealers on the nearby islands
would contaminate the remaining 'full-bloods' and that their offspring, by
virtue of their Aboriginal descent, would demand financial support from
the government. For he was aware that the number of children born to
Aboriginal women living with the sealers was more than four times the
number born at Wybalenna over the previous fifteen years. Every visitor
to Wybalenna and the nearby sealing community could not help but notice
the vast discrepancy, but no one appeared willing to suggest that Aboriginal

survival could be ensured by the blending of both groups.[29] Rather, Denison appeared to believe that it was his responsibility to keep them quite separate. So he selected for their 'final home' a site that was far removed from Bass Strait—an abandoned penal station at Oyster Cove, on the western side of the D'Entrecasteaux Channel, between Snug and Kettering, about 30 kilometres south-east of Hobart. On 5 May 1847, he dismissed Jeanneret and in October he appointed Milligan to carry out the Establishment's relocation to Oyster Cove.[30] Denison acknowledged that he could not regard the closure of Wybalenna as an exercise in fiscal economy, but rather that 'it was due to the former owners of the soil that they should be carefully tended and kindly treated'.[31]

The prospect of the Aborigines returning to their own country created an outcry among the settlers. In Launceston the leaders of the anti-transportation movement called a public meeting on 30 September to protest the return of 'these savages to their primitive home'. Many respectable settlers, clouded with memories of the Black War twenty years earlier and of the 'depredations' committed by the five 'desperadoes' at Port Phillip in 1841, told the meeting that the Aborigines were still savage beasts, and that if they escaped from Oyster Cove, as they would try to do, they would again place the security of the island in jeopardy. The anti-transportationists also claimed that the Aborigines' return was a ploy by Denison to forestall their campaign for self-government, for the British government bore financial responsibility for both the convicts and the Aborigines. They argued that, unless transportation was abolished and the Aborigines placed in a cheap gaol beyond the fears of the settlers, the colony could not afford self-government. Further, they considered that the Aborigines had no proven potential as labourers and so it would be cheaper to leave them at Flinders Island rather than indulge in an expensive removal to Oyster Cove, which had the potential to become valuable farming land.[32]

For most of the Aborigines the removal was a release from the 'charnel house' that had incarcerated them since 1833. Only forty-nine of them made that journey to Oyster Cove—seventeen men, twenty-two women and ten children. They included ten couples, three with children, and three sole parents with children. Their average age was forty-two. Many of them suffered from chronic chest complaints, four of the women had become enormously fat, one was blind, another was senile and another suffered from acute arthritis. Between March 1839 and October 1847, thirty of their kin had died at Wybalenna. Of the eight children known to have been born there, only five had survived infancy. There was not one expression of sorrow or regret as they packed themselves, their dogs and their few possessions into the ship on a blustery day in early October. Yet as a community they could take pride in their extraordinary achievements. When their rights had been contested by an overbearing superintendent, their leaders had known how to use the colonial political system to remove him. They had also regained their children and the catechist, Robert Clark, who had long been their champion. And, against the odds, they had won the right to return to their own country. They now believed that they had a future.

16

Oyster Cove, 1847–1905

The Wybalenna Aborigines arrived at their new home at the Oyster Cove Aboriginal Station on 18 October 1847 and plunged into ceremony lasting several days.[1] It may have been hosted by Truganini and her stepson Davy Bruny, who were returning to their country after an absence of nearly twenty years. Six other women from Port Davey also had associations with the area. They included Tingernoop from the South West nation, who had first met Robinson in 1830, and her two grown-up daughters, Pyterrunner (Matilda), aged twenty-seven and now Davy Bruny's partner, and Pangernowidedic (Bessy Clark), aged twenty-two and partner of Thermanope (Augustus) from the North West nation. Pangernowidedic and Thermanope were the adoptive parents of the three orphaned brothers from the west coast, William and Charles Lanney and Barnaby Rudge. The fourth woman from Port Davey, Thielewanna (Henrietta) came from the sealers and had two daughters, Nancy and Hannah McSweeney. The fifth woman, Dray (Sophia), had first met Robinson at Bruny Island in 1829 and had shown him the route to Port Davey in 1830.[2] She had then rejoined her own people until their surrender in 1834. Finally there was Mathinna who was only thirteen years old and the orphaned daughter of the chief of the Port Davey clan, Towterrer, and his wife, Wongerneep. After her parents died at Wybalenna in 1837, Mathinna was taken to Government House in Hobart where she spent five years with Sir John and Lady Franklin as their surrogate daughter. On their departure for England in December 1843, they returned her to Wybalenna, where she struggled to adapt to a very different way of life.

At the new station, these women had surviving relatives from the North West nation. Kittewer (Amelia) and her partner, Drinene (Neptune), had two children: Emily, aged nine, and Moriarty, aged seven. Another woman, Toindeburer, had a grown-up son, Charley Clark, aged twenty-two, and the chief Wymurrick and his partner, Narrucer (Catherine), had two daughters, Catherine and Martha.

Others from the North West nation included Koonya (Patty), two younger men, Toeernac (Edmund) and Pallooruc (Frederick), who had recently lost their wives, and Fanny Hardwicke, who was Pevay's widow. Most important of all was Nicermenic (Eugene), about eighteen when Robinson first met him in June 1830. He had partnered Tarenootairrer (Sarah) from the North East nation and they had a son, Adam, who was a half brother to Sarah's older daughters, Mary Ann, who was married to Walter Arthur, and Fanny, born in 1834.

Walter Arthur was related to Ben Lomond people at the station. They included his mother, Dromedeenner, the couple Druerertattenananne (Cranky Dick) and Drummernerlooner (Louisa), Bangum (Flora), who had joined Robinson's mission in December 1830, and Koonerpunner. There were also the two men, Tillarbunner (Jack Allen) and George Robinson. This inter-connected group, comprising forty-one people in all, by virtue of their children and their extended kinship connections with Truganini and Davy Bruny, became the core of the new Oyster Cove community.[3]

Of the others, five came from the Big River nation. They included the couple Moomereriner (Alexander) and Gunneyanner (Caroline), who had no children, two widowers, Callerwarrermeer (Tippo Saib) and Maccamee (Washington), and Wild Mary, or Wilhemina. Two other women, Parthemeenna (Cuish) and Parateer (Daphne), were from Swanport. Finally, there was Wapperty, who was a daughter of Mannalargenna, and had grown-up children living on the Bass Strait islands. Like Parthemeenna, she had joined the community not long before it abandoned Wybalenna and regretted the move to Oyster Cove.[4]

Ironically, it seems the Port Davey people and others from the North West nation who had first met Robinson in 1830 had produced a sufficient number of children to ensure their survival. But Lieutenant-Governor

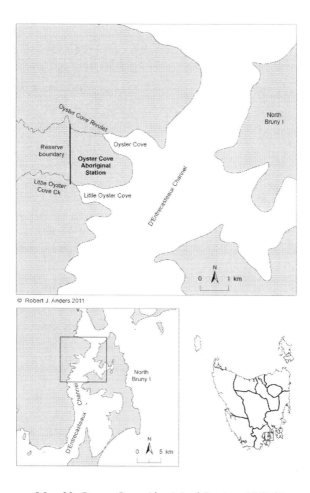

© Robert J. Anders 2011

Map 32 Oyster Cove Aboriginal Station, 1847–72

William Denison and Dr Joseph Milligan appear to have been determined to prevent the community's survival. They decided that the five boys, Moriarty, Adam, William Lanney, Barnaby Rudge and Charles, should be sent to the Orphan School in Hobart, where they would be 'educated and taught some means of obtaining subsistence for themselves'.[5] Charlie Clark, now aged twenty-two, was apprenticed to a settler for farm work. Four of the six girls, Hannah, Nancy, Martha and Mathinna, were also sent to the Orphan School, leaving Emily, aged nine, with her parents. Fanny Cochrane, aged thirteen and 'almost a woman', was allowed to live with her mother, Tarenootairrer, and stepfather, Nicermenic, and her half-sister Mary Ann and husband Walter Arthur.[6] Neither Milligan nor Denison appears to have considered either opening a school at Oyster Cove or sending the children to school nearby. The loss of the children had a deeply negative impact on their parents and on the well-being of the entire community.

The station was divided into two sections. The central part of about 40 hectares was situated at the mouths of the Oyster Cove Rivulet and Little Oyster Cove Creek and contained the original convict buildings, the superintendent's house and the school. The other section, of 688 hectares, about 1.5 kilometres west of the main settlement, was set aside for the Aborigines to hunt game to supplement their rations. In layout the central station differed little from the terrace at Wybalenna. The buildings formed a rectangle, with the chapel and schoolhouse at one end and the living quarters at the other. But, unlike the Establishment at Flinders Island, Oyster Cove station

Oyster Cove Aboriginal Station, Charles Edward Stanley, 1849. National Library of Australia, Canberra.

had no Aboriginal name. It was as if all signs of Aboriginality would now be erased.

Initially, the community leaders, Walter George and Mary Ann Arthur, were vastly pleased with their freshly painted apartments, furnished with chairs and tables, cupboards and beds, and glass windows. The ten couples lived on one side of the square and the fifteen single people occupied the other. When they found the earth floors too damp to sit on, they simply reverted to their practice at Wybalenna and cooked their food in large iron pots outside. Their rations were increased to 2 pounds (900 g) of meat a day, 2 ounces (57 g) of tea, a quarter of an ounce (7 g) of tobacco, and 2 ounces (57 g) of sugar. They also took advantage of the abundant shellfish in the D'Entrecasteaux Channel, hunted possums, wallabies and wombats in the Aboriginal reserve and rowed across to Bruny Island at the end of November for mutton-bird eggs and shell collecting. For a short time they maintained their health, but it was clear that they resented the removal of their children.[7]

By May 1848 they realised that the station had a major disadvantage. Built on mudflats with poor drainage and surrounded by hills that trapped the winter mists and fogs late into the afternoon, the main buildings were constructed of timber instead of brick and in winter offered no protection from the biting Antarctic gales that roared up the D'Entrecasteaux Channel. The entire station was subject to damp and vermin and for much of the year was a repository for the waste water from farms upstream. The original penal station, built in 1843, had been abandoned in 1845 when it failed to meet convict health standards. So the Wybalenna Aborigines had been removed to a place that had already proved unsanitary for convicts.[8]

Rather than live at Oyster Cove, Milligan carried out his duties in Hobart and left the Aborigines' day-to-day needs in the hands of their old friend the catechist Robert Clark, his wife and five children. Denison arranged for a magistrate to visit the station every week to inspect their clothes, houses, treatment and behaviour, and the quality and condition of the rations, and a medical officer was on call from Kingston. He rarely visited the station and no consistent record was kept of the Aborigines who died between 1847 and 1855.[9]

Anxious to demonstrate to the colonists that the new occupants at Oyster Cove were free, 'harmless and timid', Denison invited Walter and Mary Ann Arthur and twelve of their compatriots, including Truganini, to a Christmas party at Government House at New Norfolk. They were unused to this kind of white scrutiny, and Walter Arthur's biographer suggests that it was 'an occasion of cultural and social exclusion under a veneer of cordiality', but Denison appeared not to be aware of any difficulties. He considered that their infectious good humour and delight at everything they saw confirmed his view that they were no longer a threat to the colonists. The Hobart press disagreed. At least one prominent newspaper declared that they were a 'rough set' of 'savages' whose 'fickleness of disposition' would probably lead them to 'commit depredations against the settlers'.[10] But if Walter and Mary Ann Arthur felt they were under surveillance, the others took no notice.

Milligan appears to have taken some of the Aborigines on an excursion to South Cape in March 1848, enabling Truganini to visit her birthplace at Recherche Bay. After that many of them began a summer ritual of camping out for a month near present-day Huonville; some of the settlers in the region later recalled them whitening their faces and performing corroborees to frighten the rain away. In later years, they would leave the station every three months or so to camp in other places along the D'Entrecasteaux Channel. Indeed, many of the women like Truganini, Dray and Fanny Hardwicke as well as the women from the sealing community, Wapperty, Gunneyanner (Caroline), Bangum (Flora) and Coonia (Patty), were known to leave the station at regular intervals with some of the men, to conduct their own ceremonies and search for seasonal foods. They soon became a familiar sight in the district, often calling on the settlers with their dogs, and sometimes sharing a bottle and a yarn with them. Truganini in particular was later remembered with considerable affection. Some of the settlers recalled her marvellous eyesight, great good humour, extraordinary knowledge of the bush and the stars, and prowess as a swimmer.[11] Some of the men caught scale fish, using a rod and line from a boat, and hunted on Bruny Island; some of the women dived for shellfish, collected wood for the fires and kept a supply of relics and ochre. Sometimes, they were hired to dive for lost goods from wrecked ships. At other times, they were absent from the station for weeks at a time, hunting and conducting ceremonies further down the channel and at North Bruny Island.

Archaeological evidence suggests that the Aborigines used bottle glass to make scrapers and collected local stone to make stone artefacts. It would appear then that at least some of the women and men continued to make and use their own tools from the nearby Aboriginal tool-making site, while Walter and Mary Ann, Fanny and Pangernowidedic (Bessy Clark) lived a more British lifestyle.[12] But the station's main problem was that it exposed the Aborigines to alcohol, which was supplied by some of the local settlers or purchased at nearby public houses. They certainly drowned their sorrows when Robert Clark died in 1850, but they were also distraught at the steady loss of their own people. Each time one of them died, they would leave the station for a period of time so that Wrageowrapper did not take them too.[13]

Mary Ann and Bessy Clark complained to Denison about their damp, cold cottages and told him that they now regretted the move from Wybalenna.[14] In winter 1850 it seems that Milligan took some of them on a hunting excursion to Flinders Island, and the prospect of Wapperty and Flora returning to live with the emerging Islander community resurfaced on many occasions over the next two decades.[15] But it never happened.

In April 1851, G.A. Robinson paid a brief visit to the station. He had not seen most of the occupants since his departure for Port Phillip in 1839, but he noted that thirteen of them had died since their arrival at the station in 1847. Wapperty and Flora told him that they wanted to return to their families on Cape Barren Island, because Oyster Cove was 'unhealthy, too low, damp'. He was disappointed that they were no more elated at seeing him than any other old friend, although Mary Ann and her sister Fanny were particularly gracious in presenting him with strings of their very best shell necklaces. Perhaps even he could not confront the reality of settler colonialism on their lives, even though he had been its harshest critic.[16]

Denison departed Van Diemen's Land at the end of 1854, and the colony achieved self-government a year later, changing its name to Tasmania. By then only seventeen of the Oyster Cove community remained.

Denison never questioned the shocking death rate. Nor did he call
Milligan to account. Rather, like so many other colonists, Milligan believed
that the Aborigines themselves were responsible. He reported that the only
labour they performed was the 'procurement of their own firewood' and
that 'their natural indolence and love of ease [was] characteristic of the
Aboriginal races of these islands'. He also blamed the women's ill health on
huddling in their 'close overheated apartments' like 'hot house plants' and
the fact that they had stopped cultivating their gardens. This situation, he
said, was exacerbated by their 'immoral habits' of associating with white
men for sex and grog, little understanding that they were depressed and
frightened about their future. His obvious lack of compassion for them and
his unwillingness to take responsibility for the high death rate suggest that,
like most of the colonists, he believed that their fate was sealed and that he
had done his best to smooth the dying pillow. Yet some of the surrounding
settlers who had become friendly with the Aborigines later told scientist
Ernest Westlake that 'Dr Milligan used to give them something to shorten
their lives'.[17]

Like its predecessors the new government also cut costs. It replaced
Milligan with John Strange Dandridge and his wife, Matilda, who lived at
the station with their children. It seems they had known the Aborigines for
some time, and over the next twenty years they became their closest friends
and supporters. But, in keeping with other settler colonies on the Australian mainland, the new government decided that 'able-bodied' Aborigines
should be 'put to work' and that 'half-castes' should be expelled from
government care. Mary Ann Arthur was threatened with expulsion from
the station on the grounds that she was not a 'full-blood'. Walter Arthur
then wrote to the new governor, Sir Henry Fox Young, requesting that he
and Mary Ann, her sister, Fanny, and their mother, Tarenootairrer, should
be permitted to move from the station and live independently. They were
granted a 3-hectare block of land nearby and they constructed a three-room
bush hut. Walter was paid an allowance to support himself, Tarenootairrer and Fanny, and a small salary to help keep order at the station and
to look after the boats. He was later awarded an additional grant of just
over 1 hectare of land more suited to grow vegetables. With Dandridge's

strong support, he then applied to the comptroller-general 'to hire a Pass-holder Servant man'. But the application was refused; it was whispered that 'the spectacle of a blackfellow issuing orders to a white serf would not be altogether an edifying one'.[18]

The two boys, William Lanney and Adam, the only survivors of the five boys despatched to the Orphan School, along with Tillarbunner (Jack Allen), were apprenticed to whaling ships. Fanny Cochrane married a sawyer, John Smith, and the government gave her a dowry of £24 a year to reside at Nicholls Rivulet, not far from Oyster Cove. As her family increased and she became the centre of the community the dowry was increased to

Mrs Dandridge with Walter George Arthur and His Wife Mary Ann. Annie Benbow, c.1900, Crowther Library, Tasmanian Archive and Heritage Office, Hobart.

£50 per annum.[19] When her brother Adam died at their farm in 1857, aged nineteen, the entire Oyster Cove community arrived next morning, camped nearby and performed ceremonies to ensure that he 'properly' went to the next stage of his life. A year later when Fanny's mother, Tarenootairrer, died at Oyster Cove, her family arrived to take part in a similar farewell ceremony. Tarenootairrer was the only Aborigine at Oyster Cove to leave grandchildren, which she did by her daughter Fanny Cochrane Smith. Her descendants form part of the Aboriginal community today. Truganini now saw it as her responsibility to take Tarenootairrer's grandchildren on possum hunting expeditions and teach them songs and stories of her people.[20]

When James Bonwick visited the station in 1859, only fourteen Aborigines were still alive, comprising nine women and five men. They included the two couples Walter and Mary Ann Arthur, and Thermanope (Augustus) and Pangernowidedic (Bessy Clark); three men, William Lanney, Tippo Saib and Tillarbunner (Jack Allen); and six women, Caroline, Emma, Koonya (Patty) and Wapperty, Truganini and Dray. The women most admired William Lanney, aged twenty-four, as 'a fine young man, plenty beard, plenty laugh, very good, that fellow'.[21] Bonwick was deeply shocked that 'No means are adopted by Government to provide any religious instruction or emulation and no effort made to protect them from the vicious influence of the bad white man or to keep them from the destructive effects of strong drink. The remnant should at least be prepared for death and eternity.'[22] But like Milligan the government blamed their misery and squalor upon the 'inmates' and could not wait for them to die: 'There are five old men and nine old women living at the Oyster Cove Station—uncleanly, unsober, unvirtuous, unenergetic, and irreligious, with a past character for treachery, and no record of one *noble* action, the race is fast falling away and its utter extinction will be hardly regretted.'[23]

Their views were supported by the first scientific papers on the Tasmanian Aborigines, which spearheaded their transformation from a living people into scientific curiosities of 'extreme primitivism'.[24] One paper, prepared by Milligan, interrogated a limited range of data that he had collected about the Aborigines and concluded that their population in Tasmania in 1803 could never have exceeded 2,000.[25] The new estimate, which was far lower than Robinson's estimate of 6,000 to 8,000, effectively erased their humanity, and scientists from across the globe eagerly sought their skeletal remains as trophies of extinction. The hunt for Aboriginal remains began at this time, intensified over the following decades and continues, even today.[26] The impact of Milligan's estimate on the Oyster Cove community was immediate and terrifying. The realisation that many white people saw more value in them as skeletons than as a living people led them to fear for their lives. It is not surprising that more of them resorted to alcohol to drown the prospect of the impending horror.

In September 1859, Walter Arthur went to sea in a whaler for fourteen months, ostensibly to sober up after charges of alcoholism, but more likely to escape the increasing pressure from the settler government that he was never 'good enough' to be accepted by colonial society.[27] At Oyster Cove he was targeted by the settler government as a troublemaker, even though he and Mary Ann had built their three-roomed bush cottage complete with a portrait of Queen Victoria on the living room wall and were surrounded by the trappings of British evangelical respectability. It was Walter's particular regret that he and Mary Ann had no children. Like so many other Aboriginal men in his position, he appears to have developed a schizophrenic personality: sometimes he was a resistance leader demanding better conditions for his people; at other times he was a desperate conformist aching for the acceptance of white society. But he was never 'good enough'. As historian Cassandra Pybus cogently points out, 'There was simply no place in white society for this capable and obliging couple, except as a curiosity'. One blustery evening in May 1861, returning to the station by boat from a waterfront pub in Hobart, Walter Arthur fell overboard and was never seen again.[28] His death deprived the community of leadership essential to its survival.

At that point it seems the government gave up on the Oyster Cove community. Cassandra Pybus indicates that her ancestor, Henry Harrison Pybus, who lived in the region, offered to take responsibility for the remaining community at £500 a year. But she believes that his offer was made from financial necessity rather than philanthropic zeal.[29] By then Tippo Saib and Augustus, Bessy Clark's partner, had died, along with Flora,

Group portrait of nine Aborigines of Tasmania, 1860. Top row (left to right): Caroline, Patty, Emma; bottom row (left to right): Wapperty, Flora, Mary Ann, Jack Allen, Dray, Truganini. National Library of Australia, Canberra.

Caroline and Dray, the woman Robinson had first met at Bruny Island in 1829 and who had offered to guide him to Port Davey. Their deaths were followed by those of Tillabunner (Jack Allen) and Emma in 1866 and Patty, Wapperty, one of Mannalargenna's daughters, and Bessy Clark in 1867.[30] Shortly afterwards, in an attempt to make a name for himself in the scientific world, Hobart lawyer and collector Morton Allport disinterred the remains of Bessy Clark and sent them to the Hunterian Museum in London.[31] This act of barbarism must have terrified the only remaining people, William Lanney, Mary Ann and Truganini. As if to gain some protection, Mary Ann remarried, this time to a white man, Adam Booker, and they remained at the station.

As the last 'full-blood' male, William Lanney aroused feverish interest among bone collectors at home and abroad. He had arrived at Wybalenna in 1842 at the age of seven, one of five boys of the last family of Aborigines captured near the Arthur River. Between 1847 and 1851 he had attended the Orphan School in Hobart with two of his brothers, but they died, and when he turned fourteen he had gone to sea as a whaler. He appears to have found greater acceptance from his seafaring mates than any of his compatriots could expect from the colonists. He always visited his relatives at Oyster Cove when his ship was in Hobart, and it was a great disappointment to the women that he never married and produced children. But he took his responsibilities towards them very seriously. At the end of 1864 he lodged an official complaint with the colonial secretary that the women were receiving inadequate rations, noting that: 'I am the last man of my race and I must look after my people.' An official investigation revealed that when the supply vessel for the area failed to arrive from Hobart, the settlers bought or borrowed stores from the Oyster Cove station and so the women were sometimes starved. But it seems nothing was done to rectify the problem. Lanney's proudest moment came in 1868 when Prince Albert, the Duke of Edinburgh, visited Hobart and he was introduced to His Royal Highness as the 'king of the Tasmanians'. At least one observer considered that the prince 'looked like a larrikin while Lanne [*sic*] didn't'.[32]

On 2 March 1869, in Hobart on leave from his ship, Lanney became ill at the Dog and Partridge Hotel at the corner of Goulburn and Barrack streets. He died at one o'clock the following afternoon.[33] His friends, the banker George Whitcomb and the solicitor J.W. Graves, concerned to save Lanney from the clutches of body snatchers operating under the guise of science, immediately visited the premier, Sir Richard Dry, whose brother had been killed by Aborigines in 1827,

William Lanney, 1868. State Library of New South Wales, Sydney.

and persuaded him to agree that Lanney should be buried in consecrated ground. The premier then ordered the corpse to be removed to the morgue at the Colonial Hospital, where he believed that a guard could more readily keep watch over it. But this was not the case. The chief house surgeon, Dr George Stokell, was a leading member of the Royal Society of Tasmania, and the honorary medical officer, Dr William Crowther, was a member of the Royal College of Surgeons in London and each man was quick to support their interests.

After Lanney's body arrived at the morgue, the premier ordered Stokell not to allow entry to anyone. At six o'clock that afternoon, 3 March, Stokell received an urgent invitation to take tea with Mrs Crowther in Davey Street. He locked the morgue and set off, leaving the keys in the charge of the house steward. At half-past seven Dr Crowther and his son arrived and summoned the gatekeeper to find the hospital barber. Then, having obtained the keys from the house steward, Crowther, his son and the barber entered the morgue. The gatekeeper, suspecting treachery but fearing punishment, looked through the keyhole and saw three men standing over the bodies of William Lanney and the schoolmaster, Thomas Ross. At nine o'clock the gatekeeper saw Crowther and his son leave the hospital, the former carrying a parcel under his arm.

When Stokell returned a short time later he realised that 'something was up'. Upon entering the morgue he found that William Lanney's skull had been removed and the schoolmaster's skull inserted in its place. He alerted the Royal Society of Tasmania, and, with its agreement, at nine o'clock the next morning he cut off Lanney's hands and feet. Then a search was made for Lanney's skull.

At two o'clock that afternoon, 4 March, between fifty and sixty gentlemen led by Graves and Whitcomb presented themselves at the morgue to carry the coffin to the funeral service. But already rumours of mutilation had spread and they demanded an inspection of the corpse. The coffin was opened and Lanney's mutilated body was exposed to public view. After the cries of horror had subsided, it was decided that nothing could be done, for both Graves and Whitcomb realised that the premier, in placing the body in the hospital in the first place, was as much responsible for the violation as the mutilators. The coffin was sealed and draped with the Union Jack, some native flowers, spears and waddies and a possum skin. The procession then moved to St David's Church, where the service was read by the Reverend Mr Cox. On leaving the church the procession, numbering about 120 mourners, including many of Lanney's shipmates, retired to St David's Cemetery in Davey Street, where the second half of the service was read. Then the grave was closed over William Lanney, who had died on 3 March 1869, aged thirty-four years.

But science had yet to finish with William Lanney. That evening Dr Crowther arranged for a small group of men to assemble in Harrington Street, while in Salamanca Place another group awaited the arrival of Dr Stokell and members of the Royal Society. This time Stokell reached the cemetery first. About midnight his party dug up the body of William Lanney and took it to the rear of the hospital, where Stokell, Dr Judge and Messrs Burbury, Sheehy and Weir, all members of the Royal Society of Tasmania, examined it. Then they placed it in the morgue once again.

Having missed his opportunity the evening before, Dr Crowther hurried to the hospital the next morning, Sunday 5 March. Finding the morgue locked, he broke the door down with an axe, but all he found were a few particles of flesh. Stokell had removed what remained of Lanney's body early that morning into the house steward's garden. From there it was put in a cask on the Sunday night and later buried in the Campbell Street cemetery. There was not much left. Dr Stokell had a tobacco pouch made out of a portion of the skin, and other worthy scientists took possession of the ears, the nose, and a piece of Lanney's arm. The hands and feet were later found in the Royal Society's rooms in Argyle Street, and, over a century later, the head was located in the School of Anatomy at the University of Edinburgh.[34]

Now only two women resided at Oyster Cove—Mary Ann and Truganini. The government placed them in the direct care of the Dandridge family for £90 a year. In July 1871, Mary Ann had a seizure and was removed to the hospital in Hobart, where she died in August. It is not known what happened to her remains. Now there was only Truganini.[35]

By this time she was the best known Tasmanian Aborigine in the world. She was born at Recherche Bay in about 1812, the daughter of Mangerner, chief of the Lyluequonny clan of the South East nation. By the time she met Robinson at Bruny Island in 1829 at the age of seventeen, her mother had been stabbed by a party of sealers, her sister Moorinna had been abducted to Bass Strait by another sealer and there accidentally shot, and her fiancé, Paraweena, had been thrown out of a boat by sawyers who had then cut off his fingers while he clung to the side of the vessel. Following the death of her father in the winter of 1829, she had partnered Wooraddy, the recently widowed chief of the Nuenonne clan. Together, they accompanied Robinson on all his missions between 1830 and 1834. Truganini came to public notice when she saved Robinson from the Tarkinener clan at the Arthur River in 1832, by ferrying him across the water in a hastily constructed raft. Contrary to her biographer's claim, there is no evidence that she had a sexual relationship with Robinson.[36] There is no evidence in the colonial record that she bore children but there is some evidence in the Aboriginal record. Whatever her experiences, Truganini appears to have developed an independent spirit long before she arrived at Wybalenna in October 1835. She accompanied Robinson to Port Phillip in 1839, and in 1841 she was part of the group led by the two young warriors Maulboyheenner and Pevay that shot and killed two whalers, Yankee and Cook. Pevay and Maulboy-heenner were convicted and hanged, and Truganini and her two female companions, Fanny Hardwicke and Pyterunner (Matilda), were sent back to Wybalenna.

Then aged thirty, at Wybalenna she lived with the Big River man, Weernerpaterlargenna (Alphonso), but he died in 1847 just as the Establishment was relocating to her own country at Oyster Cove. Here, she came into her own. According to Cassandra Pybus, 'the actual site of the station was of great significance to the Nuenonne, as it held the stone quarry where they made their flaked stone implements. It would have been used by her father Mangerner and by Wooraddy.'[37] With Dray, she regularly took the other women on seasonal excursions to Bruny Island or visited Fanny Cochrane Smith's farm at Nicholls Rivulet, where she taught the children many aspects of their culture, including an understanding of the stars, how to catch possums, how to sing the corroboree songs of her childhood and how to find the right shells to make her luminous necklaces. She frequently expressed fears that upon her death she would be 'cut up' like William Lanney and placed in the museum and told the Reverend Henry Atkinson that she wanted to be buried 'in the deepest part of the D'Entrecasteaux Channel'.[38]

Following floods at Oyster Cove in the winter of 1874, Truganini was taken by the Dandridge family to live in Hobart, where she was often seen in Macquarie Street, an imposing if diminutive figure dressed in a serge dress, knitted cardigans and scarves with a red turban on her head, always accompanied by her dogs.

In early May 1876, she became ill. She died at Mrs Dandridge's

Portrait of Truganini, early 1870s. H.H. Baily, Hobart Town.

house in Macquarie Street, at two o'clock in the afternoon of 8 May attended by two doctors. She had told Mrs Dandridge, 'Missus, Rowra catch me, Rowra catch me' and died in her own way, on the floor 'with her dogs around her and a big fire in front'. She was aged about sixty-four.[39]

Mrs Dandridge wrote a note to Thomas Chapman, the colonial secretary, to inform him of the death, and the two doctors conveyed Truganini's body to the Hobart hospital. The *Mercury*, suspecting impending foul play, considered that the body would have been safer in Mrs Dandridge's house.[40] Chapman sent a memorandum to the surgeon superintendent of the hospital ordering him to allow no one to view the corpse. At this stage the government was undecided about its disposal. On 9 May the secretary of the Royal Society wrote to Chapman asking for possession of Truganini's 'corpse', since she was the last 'full-blood' and a valuable scientific specimen. Whatever the government originally had in mind, and from earlier correspondence with the Royal Society it had envisaged the body ending up in the museum, it felt unable to accede to the request. Instead, the government permitted the Royal Society to take a cast of Truganini's face and then ordered a 'decent interment' at the old Female Factory at the Cascades, in a vacant spot immediately in front of the chapel.[41]

The funeral took place at midday on 11 May with the premier, Alfred Kennerley, and twenty-five of Truganini's friends and sympathisers in attendance.[42] The remains had been wrapped in a white shroud and placed in a very plain coffin, and when the lid was removed to make sure that it was indeed Truganini, the *Mercury* reported that one of the ladies 'who assumes to herself a title as high as that of poor Truganini touched the face as if to make assurance doubly sure'.[43] The Reverend Canon Parsons then read the burial service of the Church of England. According to the *Mercury*, Truganini had been baptised at Oyster Cove by Bishop Nixon, but if that were the case then she would surely have been buried in consecrated ground like William Lanney. After the blessing, the coffin, covered with a bouquet of native flowers, was lowered into the grave. The *Mercury* suggested that the location was selected to make it easier for the body to be exhumed at a later date. This was indeed the case.[44]

Two years later, Truganini's remains were exhumed by the Royal Society of Tasmania and stored in a box.[45] In 1904 the society sent the box to Melbourne, where the professor of anatomy, R.J.A. Berry, articulated the remains into a skeleton for public display in the Tasmanian Museum as a trophy of white settler triumphalism. Here was incontrovertible evidence that Truganini was 'the last Tasmanian', symbol of 'the failure of an inferior race to thrive in the presence of a civilized people' and evidence of the closure of 'a remarkable epoch in Tasmania's history'.[46]

Truganini was not in fact the last 'full-blood', let alone the last of her people.[47] Despite the scientists' determined efforts they simply could not make the Tasmanian Aborigines become extinct. Too many of the women had left descendants in the Straitsmen communities on the Bass Strait islands. Another group, descendants of Dolly Dalrymple Johnson, was scattered across northern Tasmania, and Fanny Cochrane Smith had been recognised as Aboriginal by the Tasmanian government.[48] A photograph of her taken in 1888, at the age of fifty-four, reveals a handsome, assured black woman in late Victorian dress, adorned in possum skins and shell necklaces, and with wildflowers twisted in her hair. In 1899 and 1903, she made phonograph records of some songs that she had learned at Wybalenna and Oyster Cove. One of them, 'Dance Song' was in honour of a great chief.

> Lo! With might runs the man:
> My heel is swift like the fire
> My heel is indeed swift like the fire
> Come thou and run like a man;
> A very great man, a great man,
> A man who is a hero!
> Hurrah![49]

Fanny Cochrane Smith died aged seventy-four on 24 February 1905, a year after Truganini's remains had been articulated in the Tasmanian Museum. She had enjoyed excellent health all her life and had become widely known as a wise and deeply religious woman, who was desperately concerned for the future of her people. A fortnight before she died she contracted pleurisy and then pneumonia but she kept her strength until two hours before the end. She was buried the following day at Wattle Grove Cemetery at Port Cygnet.[50] Unlike Truganini, whose remains had already been exhumed, and most of her compatriots buried at the cemetery at Oyster Cove and at Wybalenna, whose remains were also exhumed for alleged scientific research, Fanny Cochrane Smith's remains were protected by her family

Fanny Cochrane Smith wearing a belt with wallaby pelts. Tasmanian Archives and Heritage Office, Hobart.

and left undisturbed. But her descendants never forgot her determination to see Truganini put to rest. Seventy years later, on the centenary of Truganini's death, one of her descendants, Roy Nicholls, led the successful campaign to retrieve Truganini's remains from the museum, cremate them and scatter her ashes in the deepest part of the D'Entrecasteaux Channel, as she had always wanted. By then Fanny's descendants had reconnected with the other Tasmanian Aboriginal community in Bass Strait and had joined with Dolly Dalrymple Johnson's descendants in the long campaign for rights and recognition.

PART V

SURVIVAL
1840-1973

17

The Islanders, 1840–1902

With the death of Truganini in 1876, many white Tasmanians firmly believed that the colony was now completely 'native free'. But this was far from the case. As pointed out in the previous chapter, Fanny Cochrane Smith and her family were settled at Nicholls Rivulet not far from Oyster Cove. Also, Dolly Dalrymple Johnson and her family were living in the village of Perth, south of Launceston; in western Bass Strait, a Tasmanian Aboriginal woman was part of the Thomas family on the eastern end of Kangaroo Island; and there may have been a descendant of Truganini in Victoria. But the largest group to retain its Tasmanian Aboriginal identity was the Islander community that had begun to take shape in the late 1830s on islands near to the Aboriginal Establishment at Wybalenna. When the Establishment relocated to Oyster Cove in 1847, the Islander community consisted of about twenty adults and twenty-eight children.

On Gun Carriage Island at the eastern end of Bass Strait there were four families. The first comprised Watanimarina, a daughter of Mannalargenna, her partner, the sealer Thomas Beeton, and their four children, one of whom was Lucy Beeton. The second comprised Thomas Tucker, who lived with an Indian woman, Maria Bengally; the third David Kelly and his Aboriginal son; and the fourth John Riddle and his children. On Woody Island there were three families. The first comprised Wottecowiddyer, another daughter of Mannalargenna, her partner, James Everett, and their four children. The second was Pollerwottelterkunne from Piper River, her partner, Richard Maynard, and their two children, and the third was a mainland Australian Aboriginal woman, Elizabeth, and her four children. Andrew Armstrong and his mainland Australian Aboriginal wife, Jane Foster, and two of their children had recently left the island for the west coast of Van Diemen's Land to catch seals and later returned to Clarke Island. On Long Island lived 'Black Judy', a woman whose Aboriginal name is unknown, from St Patricks Head, Edward Mansell and their child. They would later be joined by Richard Maynard's family. On Tin Kettle Island was Pleenperrenner from Cape Portland, her partner, John Smith, and their three children. On Cape Barren Island lived Nimerana (Teekoolterme), another daughter of Mannalargenna, her partner, John Thomas, and at least three of their children, along with Robert Rew and his part-Aboriginal wife, Frances Anderson. On Preservation Island lived the mainland Australian Aborigine Margery, who had survived James Munro, who had died in 1845, and two of their children. On Hunter Island, at the western end of the strait, lived Mary Ann Brown, daughter of Meeterlatteener from Piper River and sealer James Thompson. She was married to William Proctor and they had at least two children. There were other families on Kangaroo Island, but those associated with the Furneaux Group of islands in eastern Bass Strait became the backbone of a new community known as the Islanders. Three other white men entered this community in the succeeding twenty years— William Richard Brown, John Summers and George Burgess. After that the Islanders largely intermarried, forming the basis of the present-day community.[1]

The Islanders in the 1840s were seen by the outside world in sharply different ways. Some observers found the Elders 'hale, rubicund fellows, hearty and joyous', and the children 'sharp and intelligent', with 'ruddy dark complexion . . . fine eyes and teeth'. They resided in 'tolerably clean and comfortable' slab-and-plaster cottages and made their living from mutton-birding. Others found them 'barbarous', 'literally half-savage and half-civilised; half black and half white'.[2] British explorer John Lort Stokes noted that the collecting of eggs and mutton-birds was women's business. They used a stick with a hook which they put down the burrow to draw out the birds. But when large quantities of birds were sought, the men built

a hedge a little above the beach, sometimes half a mile in length. Towards daylight, when the birds are about to put to sea, the men

station themselves at the extremities, and their prey, not being able
to take flight off the ground, run down towards the water until
obstructed by the hedge, when they are driven towards the centre,
where a hole about five feet deep is prepared to receive them.

Stokes noted that 18,000 birds had been killed in one season. The feathers
were sold in Launceston and some of the birds were smoked and preserved
to provide meat to sustain the community during the winter along with
winter vegetables.[3]

Having survived eviction and harassment, the Islanders now began to
seek recognition as a new kind of Aboriginal community. In February
1848, Thomas Beeton applied to the Van Diemen's Land government for
the lease of Badger Island, but was refused on the grounds that it could be
required for a lighthouse. The government was not anxious to legitimise a
community that had long evaded regulation. The Bass Strait islands were
beginning to attract white settlers, so in the following year the government
sent the surveyor-general to the area, to make recommendations for its
future occupation. He found the Islander community scattered throughout
the Furneaux Group. Its members ran pigs and goats and grew wheat and
potatoes to supplement catches of kangaroos, seals and mutton-birds; they
visited each other's establishments, sometimes for months at a time, to exploit
seasonal food resources; and they pursued a lifestyle based on elements
from both Aboriginal and British societies. He reported that the Islanders
were 'kind and gentle', and upon the whole I consider them a primitive
and amiable people, and believe that the greatest harmony prevails amongst
them. The men are excellent boatmen and possess a capital description of
whaleboat . . . every encouragement should be given to a class of men most
invaluable as Pilots.' He recommended that a nominal rent of one shilling
a year be paid by the Islanders for occupation of their existing places, on
the understanding that the Crown possessed the right of resumption at
six months' notice. The government, too, recognised that 'the occupation
of the Islands by acknowledged Tenants is better by far than having them
occupied without leave or licence'.[4]

Two years later the Islanders, again led by Thomas Beeton, applied to
Lieutenant-Governor Denison for the appointment of a missionary-catechist

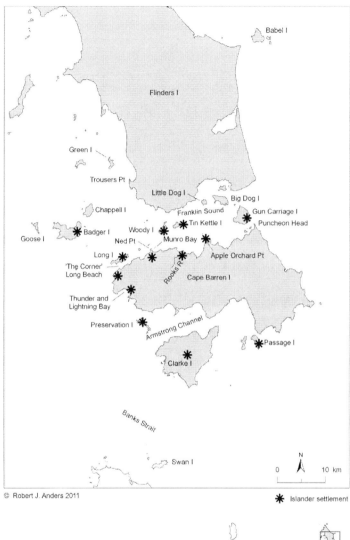

Map 33 Furneaux group of islands, eastern Bass Strait, 1840–80

to educate their children. They suggested that by virtue of their Aboriginality the salary should be paid from the Land Fund, which also maintained the Aboriginal Station at Oyster Cove. Denison refused their application on the grounds that they 'could not fairly be termed Aborigines', although there were at least seven Aboriginal women in the community. In his view there was only one official Aboriginal community in Van Diemen's Land—the Aboriginal Station at Oyster Cove. But he suggested that Bishop Francis Russell Nixon might take an interest in the Islanders' welfare.[5]

The geographical remoteness of the Islander community proved an attraction to the Anglican Church in Tasmania. In contrast to the Aborigines at Oyster Cove, who it was believed were dying out, the Islanders in their comparative isolation appeared thriving and industrious, sheltered from the 'pernicious influences' of the 'lower orders' of white society. 'The young men are prepossessing in their manners and address, and of athletic frame; the girls are modest in their demeanour and can make themselves useful in domestic affairs.'[6] The Anglican missionary society considered that these people should have some claim on any projected missionary enterprise.

In September 1854, Bishop Nixon paid his first visit to the Islanders. At Gun Carriage Island, still the centre of the community, he baptised some of the children and married Black Judy and Edward Mansell, who had lived together for twenty-five years. Lucy Beeton, then aged twenty-five, had become the Islanders' teacher. She had been educated privately in either George Town or Launceston and was already regarded as 'Queen of the Isles'. Her physical size enhanced her status. She weighed about 146 kilograms and had earned herself the nickname 'the commodore' from her practice of sailing to Launceston with a fleet of boats laden with produce, including mutton-birds, their eggs, feathers, fat and oil. Nixon was impressed with the Islanders' air of 'quiet domestic union' and apparent innocence of drunkenness and theft. But they had major economic and political issues to resolve. Thomas and Lucy Beeton took the opportunity to protest about the harassment they received from whites illegally occupying nearby islands, who interfered with their mutton-birding.[7]

Nixon's visit persuaded the government to lease other islands to the community. Between 1855 and 1860, Richard Maynard's son John and his family moved to Little Dog Island, James Everett's son George and his family moved to Cape Barren Island and the Beetons moved to Badger Island. By 1861 the Waste Lands Amendment Act had made available for lease islands or parts of islands for periods of up to fourteen years, and in 1865 the community received permission to lease up to 222 hectares. Its rapidly increasing numbers severely tested its established decision-making processes, which depended upon reciprocal arrangements. It was no longer possible for John Riddle to depasture his sheep on Thomas Beeton's lease on Gun Carriage Island in the dry season, in exchange for Beeton's 'birding' on Riddle's rookery. But the long-established seasonal visiting patterns continued, with a private season in family groups and a public season of mutton-birding in which everyone participated.[8]

The outside world was almost completely excluded from their proceedings. The Islanders operated their leases according to their needs, often incurring the wrath of the Lands Department, which found their lack of co-operation infuriating. One officer wrote in 1861: 'I . . . hardly think . . . any of the Straits inhabitants can be relied upon as I have most conflicting accounts given me by them of different matters. In fact they seem reluctant to give any informa-tion—they are evidently a most indolent, shiftless race of beings.'[9]

But they were determined that their children should be educated. When Thomas Beeton died, in 1862, Lucy found that her business responsibilities prevented her from continuing as their teacher so she invited Archdeacon Thomas Reibey at Launceston and the Reverend George Fereday, vicar at George Town, to visit the islands to discuss the appointment of a teacher for the sixty-six children, with the Islanders raising a portion of the salary. Reibey found the Islanders 'an intelligent and interesting people—simple and primitive in their habits, free from the vices of a more civilized life, and very anxious about the instruction of their children'. He failed to find a teacher so Lucy Beeton employed a young couple from Melbourne. In the meantime Reibey launched an appeal to raise £500 for a missionary boat to make regular visits to the islands, and Fereday acted as the Islanders' agent in Launceston.[10]

In 1866, following a misunderstanding about licence fees, some of the Islanders failed to renew their leases of the major mutton-bird islands. In the hiatus, a white settler leased four 16-hectare blocks on Chappell Island as grazing land for his sheep. The island contained the largest mutton-bird rookery in the Furneaux Group, and a distraught George Everett lodged a letter of protest on behalf of the Islanders about stock roaming freely on the island and the resultant impact on their livelihood: 'The rest of the halfcastes in Common with myself have been led to hope that the Government intend to reserve Chappell island for our use we there fore cannot help feeling the greatest alarm at seeing the only Rookery available to us being daily destroyed and ourselves and our children left to starve.'[11] But the surveyor-general dismissed the letter on the grounds that the sheep were removed during the mutton-bird season. In desperation the Islanders pursued the only avenue available to them as an Aboriginal community in the period following self-government in Tasmania. They petitioned Governor Du Cane for help.[12]

In August 1871, he held a meeting with them on Goose Island. They told him that they wanted exclusive rights to mutton-birding on Chappell Island and that, by virtue of their Aboriginality, Cape Barren Island should be granted to them to serve as the focal point of their life and identity. Du Cane sympathised with their grievances and pressed their claims upon the government. But it was unwilling to grant land on the Bass Strait islands and offered them instead (under the Waste Lands Act of 1870) 2- to 10-hectare leaseholds for homestead and agricultural pursuits on the western end of Cape Barren Island. It also agreed to appoint a schoolteacher and rewarded Lucy Beeton for her previous efforts to 'instruct and civilize' the Islander children with a lifetime lease to Badger Island at a yearly rent of £24. Secure in her new home with her two brothers and their families, Lucy then invited Truganini, who was then the only Aborigine still living at Oyster Cove, to join her. But it was too late. Truganini was too immersed in her own world to make the journey back to the islands.[13]

The government made one further concession in gazetting Chappell and Big Dog islands as mutton-bird rookeries. In taking these steps it appears to have accepted that the Islanders were a separate community whose special needs should be recognised and protected. But the concessions did not extend to land ownership and exclusive rights to the rookeries by virtue of their Aboriginal descent. By contrast, some white settlers were able to buy land parcels on other islands in the area.[14] It seemed that there was one law for white settlers and another for the Islanders.

Cape Barren Island is about 37 kilometres long and 27 kilometres wide. It is separated from its larger neighbour, Flinders Island, by Franklin Sound. Named for its barren appearance by Tobias Furneaux in 1774, it has granite peaks and low-lying scrub. The land, though 'quite unfit for cultivation', can graze sheep and cattle. With few trees to afford protection against the roaring forties on the island's western side, rocky coves provide some shelter, particularly at the area known as the Corner. In the 1870s the marine environment abounded with crayfish and seals. The area between Thunder and Lightning Bay and Ned Point had been inhabited at various times by the Islanders from about 1810. Apart from white families at Apple Orchard Point on the northern side and at Puncheon Head opposite Gun Carriage Island, it had attracted few 'outsiders', although by 1872 there were 143 white settlers living on various islands in the Furneaux Group.[15]

By then seven Islander families consisting of thirty-two adults and fifty-two children had settled on Cape Barren Island. George Everett and his family were at Thunder and Lightning Bay, John Smith and his family at Long Beach, the next generation of Mansells and Maynards and their families were at the Corner, along with Robert Rew's son, Thomas, at Rooks River and William Richard Brown at Munro Bay. With Richard Maynard on Long Island, the Beetons on Badger Island and old Edward Mansell on Passage Island, the community developed apace. The appointment of a schoolmaster, Henry Collis, who taught at Badger Island in the winter and at Long Beach on Cape Barren Island in the summer, conferred recognition and stability.[16]

The Islander community retained many traditions from its Aboriginal and British origins. Most families spent the summer on Cape Barren Island, which gave them ready access to the mutton-bird rookeries on nearby islands. Then, at the end of the mutton-bird season in May, they travelled to Badger Island for the winter. In July many of the women collected shells for stringing, and in November they met more of the community for 'egging'. At the same time it was still common for a number of families to visit each other until 'the neck of the flour bag became a little long'.[17] By the 1870s the pit method of catching mutton-birds had been superseded as the season's work was confined to chicks, with sufficient feathers being gathered for sale. The mutton-bird season extended over six weeks and was a family affair. Generally the men caught the birds, the children cut off wings and feet and the women plucked and scalded the birds and then helped the men to clean and pack them in brine. Mutton-birding was a very social occasion, an opportunity for families to renew friendships with other seldom-seen families.[18] The celebratory gatherings at the end of the mutton-bird season were as important as the season itself, for the Islanders drew no distinction between work and leisure. Singing and dancing was as important as mutton-birding; curing kangaroo and seal skin as important as sharing the flour bag.

By the 1880s the Islanders had what they called 'three harvests'. The season commenced with the harvesting of mutton-bird eggs, which were sold in Launceston. The second was the oil harvest, which occurred when the chicks had almost attained full size. The birds were heated over a fire and then submitted to pressure to force out the oil. The third was salting, which immediately followed oiling when the chicks were fully fledged. The products were bought by local merchants who then exported them from Launceston. The oil was used in Tasmania and Victoria for machinery, railway engines and carriages and for medicinal purposes, the fat was used for soap-making, but the market for feathers had diminished.[19]

The women continued other traditions of their mothers, such as stringing shell necklaces. At certain times of the year a range of shells the women had traditionally used for stringing were washed ashore. The young women combed the beaches, selecting with great care the types needed for the painstaking process of stringing. In the evenings they would string the shells into delicate, intricate patterns. One resident, Mrs Sarah Mansell, recalled in 1973 that as a child she was expected to string for several hours each evening, taking months to complete one necklace. For this woman, stringing was an important aspect of her existence.[20]

With the concentration of the community in one area, in 1872, Canon Brownrigg began regular missionary visits from Launceston to conduct baptisms and marriages and to inspect the schools. Although the Islanders looked forward to his annual visits, they knew from his first visit that he detested mutton-birding as an economic activity. Indeed, over the next decade he lobbied the government for the conversion of their leasehold land on Cape Barren Island to a reserve, so that the Islanders could be more rigorously controlled and receive 'guidance' to become small farmers and acquire 'civilized' habits. The Anglican bishop of Tasmania Charles Henry Bromby, who visited the Islanders in 1876, agreed. He considered that their Aboriginal ancestry had made them into a godless community addicted to drunkenness and sloth, and that their 'moral weakness' could be overcome only by relinquishing mutton-birding and becoming a 'settled' community, growing crops and receiving tuition in the 'sober virtues' of respectable white society.[21]

The Islanders wanted other things. Under the strong leadership of Lucy Beeton and George Everett they lobbied for protection from harassment in the mutton-bird industry and from the threatened loss of land for debt. Some of the Islanders also refused to pay leasehold rent because they considered the land theirs by occupation or by virtue of their Aboriginal ancestry. Indeed, in 1879 they petitioned the governor to reserve the whole of Flinders Island for them.[22] So, for opposing reasons, the Islanders and the Anglican Church worked together for the establishment of a reserve. Lucy Beeton was also concerned about the illegal removal of Aboriginal remains from the cemetery at Wybalenna.[23]

In February 1881 the government responded to the bishop's request and withdrew from lease 1,416 hectares of land on the western end of Cape Barren Island, from Thunder and Lightning Bay to Munro Bay, together with a further 202 hectares of Crown land. The government clearly intended the land to be for the exclusive use of the Islanders, but it did not wish to name them or officially extend to them any rights or privileges by virtue of their Aboriginality. The Islanders now had right of occupation but had no control over the land and no security of tenure. The proclamation represented a confused if well-intentioned attempt to protect them, but it fell far short of their needs.[24]

At first the Islanders believed that they had been granted land and set about planning a township. But when they found that they had no security of tenure and that their occupation could be revoked at any time some families departed for Flinders Island, which was then opening up to settlement. Only Brownrigg's assurances that revocation was unlikely brought some back. By 1884 some families at the Corner had built cottages and erected fencing, and Brownrigg was optimistic that the means had been established for their eventual transformation into small crop farmers.[25] He did not understand that the Islanders' relationship to the land rested on their Aboriginal heritage, including their pursuit of mutton-birding, and that their boat-building skills were the result of their descent from the sealers. Agriculture had never been a significant part of their existence and the land was unsuited to crop growing. For Lucy Beeton, who had fought so long for Islander recognition, the proclamation was a step forward. But it now appeared that to achieve lasting recognition they would have to place themselves under the 'protectionist-development' policies of the Anglican Church.

In 1889 the Right Reverend Henry Hutchinson Montgomery arrived in Hobart to take up his appointment as the fourth bishop of Tasmania. He was deeply committed to help the 'unfortunate sable people of the earth' in their struggle to receive the Christian faith and learn the rudiments of British civilisation. He attacked the 'problem of the half-castes', as the Islanders were known, with the enthusiasm of someone who was able to lose himself entirely in the joys of the unfamiliar. He noted that, unlike their counterparts at Wybalenna sixty years before, the Islanders were increasing in numbers. Since they already lived in an isolated environment and were seeking assistance for a new schoolteacher, having been without one for nearly a decade, he believed it possible to undertake a program of instruction in the principles of Christianity and agriculture.[26]

Montgomery persuaded the minister for Education to appoint a 'missionary schoolteacher' who would exemplify Christian standards of behaviour, instruct the sixty children and their parents in horticulture and agriculture, and combine the functions of postmaster and government representative. Cape Barren Island would take on the air of a training institution with the habits of the Islanders under constant scrutiny.

The man appointed was Edward Stephens, aged forty-seven. He arrived at the Corner with his family in August 1890 and found a community of 110 people, consisting of thirty adults and eighty children, who earned a livelihood from mutton-birding, piloting stores, sealing, whaling, fishing, itinerant labouring and snaring animals. For four months of the year, from February to May, the community was absent mutton-birding. In July some of the women went shell collecting at Thunder and Lightning Bay, and in November many of the men visited the rookeries to collect mutton-bird eggs. Most families contained about ten people and were housed in wooden cottages of two to four rooms surrounded by small gardens, with goats, pigs, poultry, some sheep and a few horses. With no shop, church, school, police station or post office, the jetty was the focal point for the community. Having been without a schoolteacher for some time, the Islanders hailed Stephens's arrival with enthusiasm.[27]

Stephens had worked with Aborigines since his childhood in South Australia and had turned to missionary work to control his alcoholism. During his eight-year reign on Cape Barren Island, he operated a repressive system of law and order in conformity with the reserve system then developing in other parts of Australia. The Islanders were at first impressed by his concern for their welfare, but as they became aware of his own failings and his determination to control their lives they withdrew their friendship and retreated into non-cooperation. Finally, they were forced to resist in more positive fashion to protect themselves from his worst excesses.

Six months after Stephens's arrival, Montgomery paid his first pastoral visit. He listened to the Islanders' requests for more favourable mutton-bird regulations and their pleas for land ownership. He then baptised a number of their children, inspected the new school, decided to build a church, which was completed two years later, and to consecrate a cemetery. He was impressed by the Islanders' boat-building and -handling skills and departed a week later, promising to present their grievances to the premier.[28]

Montgomery's visit led to the first regulations to govern the mutton-bird season.[29] He also had quite different ideas for Islander advancement. Rather than pressing their claim for communal ownership of land, he recommended to the premier that each Islander family be allocated a block of land near the school under the watchful eye of the schoolmaster and that if they did not farm their land then the lease should be withdrawn. Instead of pressing for the communal lease of mutton-bird rookeries, he recommended the introduction of a family licence system whereby the Islander families would compete with each other and with other settlers for the right to operate particular rookeries during the mutton-bird season. He was

Cape Barren Islanders, 1893. Taken on steps of the church at the Corner by Bishop Montgomery. From left to right: Henry Beeton, Philip Thomas, Jane Everett (Beeton), Nance Mansell (Thomas) and John Maynard. National Library of Australia, Canberra.

determined that the spirit of private ownership and individual achievement should replace what he called Aboriginal communalism, which he considered had been responsible for what he believed was their moral decline. He was now confident that if the Islanders were 'kept from drink, encouraged to become farmers by judicious grants, prevented from intermarrying too much, these islands would be a very happy region, famed for its salubrity and out of reach of the greater temptations'.[30]

On his second visit, in February 1892, Montgomery had no reason to doubt that the Islanders were moving in this direction. But Stephens was again wrestling with his craving for alcohol, and in June his difficulties were exacerbated with the arrival of a police constable to supervise the new mutton-bird regulations.[31] The two men could not get on either with each other or with the Islanders. For the next three years accusations of excessive use of alcohol and bad language by one or the other appeared to fracture the community. Some Islander families departed for Flinders Island and others kept their children from school.[32] Tensions climaxed in October 1895, when the ketch *G.V.H.* was wrecked off the west coast of Cape Barren Island with the loss of three lives. Stephens accused the Islanders of displaying false lights to cause the ship to founder, intending to loot its cargo. They in turn accused Stephens of adultery and attempted murder, of appearing before the children in a 'beastly state of intoxication' and of locking their children out of the school. Driven to the limits of endurance, Stephens fired shots at two Islanders who were entering the harbour in their boat and, it was reported, he threatened to 'shoot all the half-castes or any other caste be damned if he wouldn't'.[33]

Stephens was summoned to Hobart to explain himself. There, he told Montgomery how he had become the butt of the Islanders' mockery, a common pattern of Aboriginal defensive behaviour. For a moment Montgomery faltered, but then determined that Stephens's work must continue. He reprimanded Stephens for drunkenness and sent him back to his charges. But the Islanders had had enough. Unless Stephens was replaced, Thomas Mansell informed the director of education, all the children would be removed from the school. In September 1896, Mansell accused Stephens of threatening the Islanders with a pistol, and in turn Stephens accused

The Corner, Cape Barren Island, 1893. Bishop Montgomery, Tasmanian Archives and Heritage Office, Hobart.

them of incest and adultery. In Hobart, Montgomery told the minister for Education of his disillusionment: 'All that Stephens says about the Half-castes is just what I believe to be true. They are not improving except in some families. No one will ever keep their goodwill long. When they have tired of one man and they know he knows too much about them, they will try to get rid of him.'[34]

The director admonished the Islanders for their ingratitude, but by then Stephens had suffered a nervous collapse and surrendered his position to his son, Charles. During his convalescence, Stephens wrote of his difficulties with the Islanders:

> As liars I do think the men are peerless. I will give one instance at my own expense. It went the round of the islands, and was believed to be a fact, that Bishop Montgomery, on one of his visits, found me sitting on the roof of the water closet; and I had only my nightshirt

on, and was singing the national anthem! He asked me what I was doing and I told him 'I was showing my loyalty to the Queen'. He said, 'Oh, come down and come inside and we will make a night of it'. And we did so. They said they knew I was a drunkard but the Bishop was a 'bloody sight worse!'[35]

The Islanders considered Stephens's retirement as their victory. In 1897 they formed an Islander Association, which initiated petitions to government to secure control of mutton-birding and gain land tenure. They also tried to establish a newspaper and a health benefit organisation. But neither Montgomery nor Charles Stephens could tolerate any display of Islander independence and considered that the association was a threat to their authority. In 1898, Montgomery took the chief inspector of education to the island and in the following year the minister for Justice. A meeting called with the latter attracted only four Islanders. The presence of such authority figures drove many of them into the scrub, for they had been threatened with the loss of their leasehold land on the grounds that it had not been cultivated.[36]

To further undermine the Islander Association, on Montgomery's advice a government committee was established to investigate the condition of the 'reserve' and the mutton-bird industry. Montgomery now believed it had been a mistake to concentrate the '"half-castes" into a township which had brought its own special evils'. They had developed, he said, a 'settled hatred' for himself, the schoolmaster and the constable, and had expressed a wish not to become 'like white people'.[37] Charles Stephens believed that the second- and third-generation Islanders were of weaker character than the first and thus needed more rigid instruction. But the Islanders resisted with the only means open to them: 'They actually stand on the bank out of my sight, with a clock and check my time of going into school with theirs', Stephens wrote, 'then they lie in the sun until it is time for the children to go home, when they look at the clock to see if it is exactly to the minute. If a little before, they would bring a charge of neglect of duty, if a little over, they would get up a petition saying that the teacher was overtaxing the brains of the scholars.'[38]

In May 1900 the report of the committee of inquiry recommended an annual licensing fee for mutton-birding and proposed that the land originally withdrawn from lease in 1881 be thrown open to Islander selection with fourteen years to pay. Those Islanders not wishing to cultivate the land could lease a homestead block of 2 hectares at the rental of £1 a year; the remainder of the land could then be leased to outsiders.[39] However, only the mutton-bird licensing system was enacted. With the land ownership issue unresolved, the Islanders found their occupation of the 'reserve' was as insecure as at any time since 1881; this insecurity was exacerbated in 1902 when their major mutton-bird rookery, Chappell Island, was again leased to 'outsiders' for grazing in the 'off season'.

After a final visit to the Islanders in August 1901, Montgomery departed Tasmania no more aware of their need for recognition as an independent Aboriginal community than on his first visit twelve years before. His successor, Bishop Mercer, hardly bothered about their existence. In Hobart the view was taken that since Montgomery had failed to earn their gratitude, it was unlikely that anyone else would succeed. In 1902 a debate in the Tasmanian Parliament on the future of the Islanders lapsed for want of a quorum.[40]

The Islanders' sixty-year quest for land and recognition as an Aboriginal community had led them initially to make an alliance with the Anglican Church, but it rarely operated to their benefit. Yet without the church they would not have achieved the right to occupy the westen end of Cape Barren Island or to gain better regulation of the mutton-bird industry. They had also produced strong leaders in Lucy Beeton and George Everett, who successfully petitioned the governor for support in times of crisis. Above all the community had survived and increased and was prepared for the challenges which lay ahead.

18

Resisting protection and assimilation, 1908–73

In 1908 the 200 Islanders who lived on Cape Barren Island bore characteristics common to Aboriginal communities in other parts of south-eastern Australia. They were predominantly of British descent; they generally intermarried; they were not homogeneous in physical appearance; they had no wish to look as white as possible; the older people liked to return to their place of birth to die; those of lighter colour liked to retain their identity as Aboriginal; they spoke English but retained remnant elements of former Aboriginal languages; and they had 'covert' 'ideational differences' that set them apart culturally from white society.[1] Above all they believed that the land set aside for them in 1881 had been bequeathed to their ancestors as compensation for their forced removal from their homeland, Tasmania. Each time they were threatened with eviction they would remind the government of this salient fact. But the government was more interested in making them 'disappear'.

In January of that year the Islanders were very angry when they found that, without consulting them or offering them representation, the government had incorporated Cape Barren Island into the new Flinders Municipality. When they refused to pay rates and taxes to the council, the government appointed Police Commissioner J.E.C. Lord to investigate the conditions of the 'half-castes and to make recommendations about the muttonbird industry' with a view to preparing legislation to regularise their occupation of the reserve.[2]

The police commissioner considered that the Islanders should 'earn' legal security by taking out short-term homestead and agricultural leases,

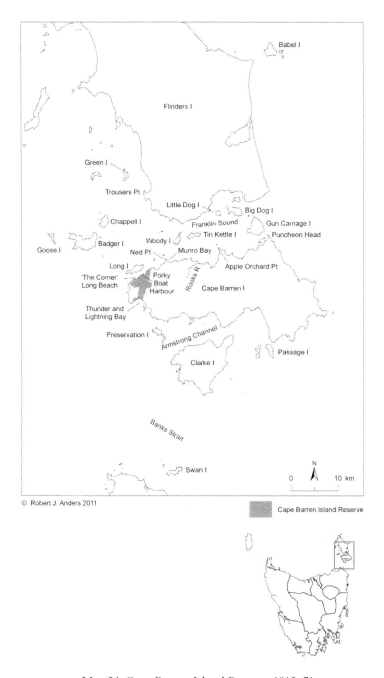

Map 34 Cape Barren Island Reserve, 1912–51

pursuing agriculture, improving the land and then, after a period of time, becoming eligible for long-term leases. He also considered that a manager or overseer should be appointed to 'strictly govern' them, thus replicating Bishop Montgomery's stance in the 1890s. But the Islanders believed, as they always had, that the reserve should be granted to them outright and that the mutton-bird industry should be reserved for their exclusive use. The government dismissed their claims in favour of Lord's recommendations. These included new regulations for the mutton-bird industry which set aside new islands as mutton-bird reserves and prohibited grazing in the off-season, but they failed to regulate the marketing of mutton-birds, thus opening the way for outsider operators.[3]

In January 1911 an official party consisting of Governor Sir Harry Barron, the premier, the minister for Lands and the chief health officer visited the reserve. They found 160 Islanders living in thirty-four cottages near the Corner. The Islanders told the official party that they wanted the reserve granted to them outright, and, if not, then they would prefer that each married man were leased 40 hectares of reserve land and each single man 10 hectares, in order to run cattle and sheep. They also wanted assistance to improve grasses and to develop suitable grazing cattle.[4]

The government decided otherwise. The draft reserve bill made the minister for Lands responsible for the Islanders, with the Lands Department secretary managing and regulating the use and enjoyment of the reserve and supervising the Islanders' interests and welfare. All land within the reserve was to revert to the Crown for resurvey and subdivision into homestead blocks of a quarter-acre (1,012 square metres) and agricultural blocks of 50 acres (20 hectares). All Islanders, male and female, over the age of eighteen were eligible to apply for these blocks, and after five years they would become rent-free on condition that a house had been erected after two years on the homestead block and the lessee resided in it for at least six months of the year and on condition that the agricultural block had been 'satisfactorily used'. If the licensed occupier defaulted, the minister could cancel the licence and the block would be forfeited, leaving other people to apply for it. The Islanders would be protected from seizure of land and goods, and the local schoolteacher could determine which non-Islander people could enter the reserve. After three years if anyone over twenty-one years of age was not a licensed occupier or lessee, he or she could be removed from the reserve, but could select a 50-acre (20-hectare) block elsewhere in Tasmania. No liquor was to be brought in or consumed on the reserve, and the act was to remain in force for twenty-five years.[5]

On the eve of the bill's introduction to parliament on 21 November, a letter signed by H.G. Everett on behalf of seventy Islanders appeared in the *Mercury*, stating serious objections. They considered the quarter-acre home-stead blocks too small, the restrictions and requirements on the agricultural blocks too severe, and the five-year period before the beginning of the rent-free lease too long. Instead, they suggested that the homestead blocks should consist of 5 acres (2 hectares) and that the rent-free lease should begin after one year. They also considered that unmarried eighteen-year-old women should not be eligible for blocks lest 'outsiders' be encouraged to marry into the community and thus threaten its identity. Above all they rejected the idea of a manager and the idea that the government knew what was best for them. Rather, they recommended that an Islander management committee should be empowered to make regulations for their own welfare and deter-mine who could enter the reserve.[6]

The bill was held over until a compromise was reached on some of the objections. The rent-free period on the blocks now began after three years instead of five and the homestead blocks were increased from a quarter-acre to 3 acres (1.2 hectares). But the government firmly rejected the idea of an Islander management committee. The bill was finally introduced to the Tasmanian House of Assembly on 12 September 1912. In the second reading, in defending his rejection of a management committee, the premier said the Islanders were an indolent people by virtue of their Aboriginal ancestry, and, although they had a 'moral' right to the reserve, they could have no 'legal' right until they had satisfied the conditions of the act. In other words, they could not manage their own affairs. The *Cape Barren Island Reserve Act 1912* became law on 6 December 1912.[7]

In failing to recognise the Islanders' right to self-determination, the act controlled their movements to and from the reserve. Like the legislation establishing Aboriginal reserves in other Australian states at the beginning of the twentieth century, the Cape Barren Island Reserve Act reflected the legal contradiction surrounding the recognition of Aboriginal rights. On the one hand it asserted that by virtue of their race the Islanders required special government regulation yet on the other hand it refused to recognise their race as Aboriginal. By insisting that they were a 'distinct' group of people with a 'separate' identity, the act placed the Islanders in legal limbo for the next forty years. On the one hand it denied the Islanders their Aboriginal identity, and on the other it performed nothing less than acrobatic legal contortions in insisting that they must be controlled by special legislation.

At first the Islanders were pleased with the main thrust of the act—recognition and security of land occupation. By 1914 the reserve had been resurveyed and twenty-seven families had been issued with licences of occupation. Many of them had erected new homes and laid out vegetable gardens, purchased sheep, cattle and horses, planted pine trees and built some roads. In the following year Phillip Thomas, the last of the second-generation Islanders, died. Born in 1831, he had become one of the community's best known sailors and mutton-birders and he left a large extended family which continues to this day.

At the outbreak of World War I twenty-one Islanders volunteered for service, six of whom gave their lives. The schoolmaster, J.W. Bladon, exhorted the Islanders to prove themselves equal to the white settlers by making great sacrifices of clothing and money, and by 1919 their contribution to the war was significantly greater than that of the surrounding settlers.[8]

But by 1922 only a few Islanders had qualified for a ninety-nine-year lease, few had repaid housing loans, and most had failed to fence their agricultural blocks. Poor mutton-bird seasons had placed the Islanders deeper in debt, and no assistance had been provided with cattle or grasses, in contrast to the help received by new settlers on Flinders Island.[9]

In December some of the Islanders petitioned the minister for Lands to amend the leasehold part of the act and give them outright ownership of the reserve. 'We are tired and disheartened', they wrote, 'not through owing big debts, but for having nothing to show of what we are improving the land for. You will notice this ground is only held as a lease and may be cancelled at any time and by granting us a deed you will give us the encouragement to make our land self-supporting.'[10] But the secretary for Lands, A.E. Counsel, saw no reason to accede to their request. 'The present ninety-nine year lease or vesting land is practically a grant deed', he wrote to the minister, 'but I suppose the name "lease" suggests an insecure title to those who don't understand its true value . . . If it should be decided to grant the fee simple of the land, that is the allotments, stringent conditions must be imposed as to their giving up all rights to the balance of the Reserve or else the trouble will continue as bad as ever.'[11]

The Islanders' view that the whole reserve should be granted to them as descendants of the original owners of Tasmania was beyond the government's understanding. Rather, the secretary for Lands wanted to remove the children to institutions on the Tasmanian mainland and appoint a manager to oversee the reserve. But he also realised that a manager would not necessarily produce guaranteed results, because the people did not want to work as agricultural labourers, and it was against the tenets of common law to remove children from their parents without their consent. However, with new child welfare legislation in place, he began an unofficial program of government harassment of Islander parents by education and health officers to remove their children on the grounds of neglect and ill health. At the same time he admitted that the Islanders were exploited by white residents in the area, who charged them high prices for food supplies and paid low prices for their stock and mutton-birds. He perused other reserve legislation on the Australian mainland and came to the conclusion that all Aboriginal reserves suffered an absence of agricultural pursuits and lack of government expenditure. Cape Barren Island Reserve, he concluded, required expenditure far beyond the coffers of the Tasmanian government.[12]

In October 1924 a parliamentary inquiry exposed the act's inherent contradiction. It refused to accept the Islanders' demand for self-determination but it did recommend that they should be allowed to elect a committee to advise the Crown lands bailiff about the act's supervisory powers. It further recommended that a short sealing season should be opened from December to February to allow the Islanders another supplementary industry and that they should have exclusive rights to additional mutton-bird licences.[13]

The Flinders Municipal Council vehemently opposed the recommendations. It considered that they would discriminate against the commercial
interests of the local white settlers. So the report lapsed, leaving the
Islanders in the clutches of the council, which took the view that unless
the Islanders paid their local taxes and dog licences it would not address
the unsanitary conditions on the reserve. Nor would it take responsibility for the Islanders who were classified as 'indigent', even though the
council's medical officer was paid a government subsidy to do so. In 1930
for example he refused to attend the confinement of Mrs Clara Mansell,
because of confusion over her indigent status. As a result her baby died.
Yet without the subsidy it is doubtful whether the council would have
been able to afford a medical officer at all.[14]

Truancy inspectors were often sent to Cape Barren Island to harass and
remove children who did not attend school, although the rate of attendance
was usually higher than at most schools on Flinders Island. The Islander
children whose parents had moved to Flinders Island were also harassed. In
February 1930 the head teacher at Lady Barron School on Flinders Island
denied that 'he had taken no action to check the white scholars calling the
half-caste scholars names', but later admitted that he caned the Islander
scholars more often than white children.[15]

In June 1929, A.W. Burbury, a lawyer from the attorney-general's
department, prepared another report. He had recently observed the
condition of the Pitcairn Islanders on Norfolk Island, and it is clear that
his experiences enabled him to listen to the Islanders' concerns with some
sympathy:

> They say that the whites 'took away their land and are now taking
> their kangaroos and mutton-birds' . . . the Act, too, has given them
> the belief that they have a claim on the State and that it was passed
> in recognition of their claim that their country had been taken from
> them by the whites. To an extent this view of theirs is justified, for,
> if the Act was not the result of a recognition that these people were
> entitled to something, why was it passed?[16]

He estimated that about £2,000 was the total annual income for the 200 Islanders on the reserve, with half coming from mutton-birding and the rest from invalid servicemen's and old age pensions and from miscellaneous minor work. He was shocked that they lived on salted mutton-birds for much of the year, and he considered that their living standards were dismal. Yet despite their poverty he found that they had a very strong attachment to the reserve and displayed exemplary conduct and manners. 'There is a warmth about them when speaking, the voices being soft and nicely lilted. They are fluent and convincing. In manner and courtesy they set an example which would put to shame many white folk.'[17]

He accepted their plea that the state government should acquire the whole of the island for the reserve, for the existing 2,428 hectares were inadequate for the community. But he also recommended that a missionary society should assume religious responsibility for the Islanders and that the federal government should assume financial responsibility, since it had more direct experience with Aboriginal reserves in the Northern Territory. Nor did he accept the Islanders' demand for their own self-management committee, preferring instead the appointment of a 'competent supervisor' to improve the land. Finally, he recommended that an inquiry be conducted into the mutton-bird industry and that the children should be encouraged to leave the reserve once they had finished school.[18]

Ignoring the recommendation about acquiring the entire island for the reserve, the state government instead approached both the Australian Board of Missions and the federal government to take over religious and financial responsibility for the Islanders. The board's chairman, the Reverend J.S. Needham, visited the reserve in December 1930 and was horrified when 'one man mentioned quite seriously, and he, to all appearances had no Tasmanian native blood in him—that if a case were brought in a Federal Court the Tasmanian Government would be forced to pay the half-castes rent for the island of Tasmania'.[19] Unwilling to grapple with the problem of Islander legal rights, he took the view that since they were not 'full-bloods' the board could not take responsibility for them. Rather, he recommended that they should be forced to leave the reserve and integrated into the general community. This view had already been put forward by

Dr Frank Gaha from the health department. But he had further recommended removing the children from their parents, as was happening
with Aboriginal families across Australia. Even so, he recognised that the
'solution is far from simple, if not altogether insoluble'.[20]

Yet Ida West, who was born in 1919, and Molly Mallett, who was born
in 1926, had different memories of the reserve.[21] They were raised in large,
God-fearing families with hardworking parents who imparted a strong
work ethic into their children. They were very shy, well-behaved children
and grew up surrounded by a vast network of relatives over several generations. Molly's father, James Maynard, had fought in World War I and on
his return had built the family a comfortable home at Porky Boat Harbour.
Her mother, Augusta, had been the island's midwife. Molly recalled that
her mother kept the house spotlessly clean and encouraged her children to
do well at school.[22] She excelled in her eight years at Cape Barren School.
The family raised their own poultry and grew their own vegetables, such
as potatoes, cabbages, tomatoes, onions, turnips and carrots, supplemented
by wallabies and fish. They consumed fresh mutton-birds in season and
relied on salted birds for the rest of the year. 'Sausages were just about the
only meat Mum ever bought. When a farmer killed sheep or cattle we'd get
to share it along with our neighbours. People on the Island always shared
whatever they had. That was part of our way of life.'[23]

When Ida West was about six, her family relocated to north Flinders Island,
where her father, Henry Armstrong, bought 4 hectares at Killiecrankie, and
for the next decade the family lived off the land, raising poultry, goats and
cattle, growing wheat and vegetables, catching wallabies, fishing and mutton-
birding. But Ida was haunted by the spectre of Wybalenna, which she saw
as the site of Aboriginal genocide. As she grew older she was determined
that it should be returned to Aboriginal ownership. At school she encountered racism from some of the pupils but she learned to stick up for herself.
But at the local dances it was a different story. 'You had to be white. At the
dances you had to put on all the powder and Pond's cream . . . If you were one
shade you had to put another on top of it . . . There wasn't many of our
people there to dance with and often we had to sit down all night.'[24]

Molly Mallett recalled

> We knew we were different but they—our parents—never told
> us we were Aborigines ... Important visitors to the Island would
> refer to us in their reports as 'half-castes'—only when there was a
> press release. There was nothing told to us, but we knew we were
> underdogs ... We were treated like imbeciles—'blasted animals'!
> I remember politicians that came over. They threw boiled lollies
> into the black dirt for us to scramble after, but our parents wouldn't
> let us do it. They would shake hands with our parents then would
> leave |$4| in their hand. Would it be to see the scramble show after
> the boiled sticky sweets that were thrown into the black dirt? We
> were a proud race of people and we still are today.[25]

At the end of 1931, as the full blast of the Depression was felt throughout Australia, dole money was made available to the Islanders through the
Flinders Council. The men were paid five shillings a week, half the whites'
dole rate, to mend roads, repaint and renovate their homes, buy seed, lay
out and plant their gardens, dig wells, install water tanks and repair fences.
One hundred Islanders were supported by the dole by 1936. Social and
sporting activities developed, and dances, horse races and football matches
were frequently held. The state government provided funds to appoint
a bush nurse at the reserve, with others serving at Babel and Chappell
islands during the mutton-bird season. The funds also covered the medical
officer on Flinders Island to call at the reserve every three months or when
required, for like other parts of Tasmania the Islanders were affected by the
polio epidemic of 1934 and Molly recalled that the 'women seemed to be
always making wreaths'.[26] A series of good mutton-bird seasons in the late
1930s improved the situation, and by the end of the decade the population
had increased to 300. The Islanders later recalled this period as the 'good
times'. A new hall was built, a memorial to the servicemen of World War I
was erected in the cemetery and in 1939 a new church was constructed.

Legislation in 1928 had begun to limit the mutton-bird season from
25 March to 30 April. Even so, it was still the year's most important
economic and social event, providing an opportunity for families to renew
kin relationships, with dances held on Saturday nights during the season on

Big Dog Island. The industry now attracted commercial operators like the Holloway brothers, and by the outbreak of World War II they owned the majority of sheds on Babel Island; the Islanders became employees as paid supervisors or operators. The entire community moved now to Babel Island for the season, and in the large extended families every person knew their elders as 'Auntie' or 'Uncle'. Some Islanders recalled the Boxing Day sports from this period, which were often followed by a ball for which the Brown family boys played their unique style of music. But there were restrictions on entry by non-Islanders to the reserve, even by those who had married into the community, and there was still a curfew on being allowed out after dark.[27]

The most traumatic event for the Islanders in this period was the visit by anthropologist Norman Tindale in 1939. As Molly Mallett recalled, 'he was looking for specimens for the testing of an Aboriginal-European community. I have learnt since that Tindale was looking for the scientific point of view.'[28] Indeed, Tindale was interested in the 'Tasmanian half-castes' in the context of scientific interests in 'hybridization'. For him Tasmania represented what he believed would eventually happen in the rest of Australia—the 'extinction of full-blooded Aborigines' and the emergence of increasing numbers of 'mixed bloods'. By measuring and analysing the Islanders' physical and mental characteristics, he believed he could show that they could be absorbed into the dominant white community without any 'throw backs', one of the white urban fears of the 1930s.[29] But, for the Islanders, Tindale broke every protocol. He not only failed to treat the Elders with respect; he also made the teenage girls and boys get undressed in front of each other in preparation for his examination. It was a humiliating experience. Molly Mallett recalled:

> I was very embarrassed, we were taught never to expose our bodies to the opposite sex. Even when we went swimming we had to keep our bodies covered with a top. I was well developed at 13 years old. I cried all the time, I wasn't the only one who had their head measured, looked up nose, in ears, structure of cheek bone, hair, fingers, toes recorded. Did we have four fingers and one thumb on hands, toes on our feet?[30]

Cape Barren Islanders, 1940. Tasmanian Archives and Heritage Office, Hobart.

It is not surprising that families began to leave the reserve at this time. Some relocated to Flinders Island, but an increasing number relocated to Launceston, Burnie and Devonport, and others found their way to Hobart. Some of the men found work on the railways, Hydro projects and in the mining industry, and some of the women worked in the woollen mill in Launceston. World War II opened further opportunities. Many Islanders volunteered for service, while others were drafted under the Manpower Authority and worked in factories in Launceston and in fruit-picking in the Derwent Valley. By 1944 only 106 people remained on Cape Barren Island from a pre-war level of 300.[31] At war's end many Islanders remained on the Tasmanian mainland, or in Melbourne, or on Flinders Island. The reserve population never recovered its prewar level.

These changes led the Tasmanian government in 1944 to inquire into the future of the reserve. The inquiry was conducted in the light of the agreement reached in 1937 by state and federal ministers to adopt an assimilation policy for Aborigines and was influenced by the decision by the Commonwealth statistician not to include in any future Aboriginal census any Aborigine who was less than 'octoroon'. The decision placed the status of the Islanders as an Aboriginal people in doubt. The government now took the view that if the Islanders were not Aboriginal according to the census then there was no need for a reserve. So in 1945 the Reserve Act was renewed for only a further five years.

The act's overall intention was to encourage the Islanders to decide whether to become agricultural farmers at Cape Barren Island or relocate to the Tasmanian mainland. It was anticipated that all reserve land not granted or selected by the Islanders would revert to the Crown and the reserve and laws relating to it would be abolished. The government expected that most of the Islanders would move to the Tasmanian mainland and become 'absorbed' into the white population.

But the Islanders were angry. Once again they had not been consulted. Once again they had been defined by others, this time as white people.[32] At the end of 1947, when complaints reached the press that the Islanders lived in squalor, another parliamentary select committee was sent to investigate reserve conditions. The members were surprised to learn that none of the 130 Islanders in residence had any desire to leave the reserve. As on so many previous occasions they told the committee that the reserve had been bestowed on their ancestors in 1881 by the government as compensation for the loss of their country, the island of Tasmania. But life had changed since the halcyon days of the 1930s. Apart from mutton-birding there was no regular work on the island, and no new houses had been built.

Rather than responding to the Islander demands for new development projects, the committee recommended that the projected closure of the reserve in 1951 should proceed, and that it should cease to exist by 1958. By that time the Islanders should have been 'gradually absorbed into the rest of the Tasmanian population'. Having adopted the assimilation policy the committee would not hear the Islanders' plea that the reserve had originally been established in recognition of their Aboriginal ancestry.[33]

Indeed, in denying this vital fact, the select committee considered that it had adopted a 'progressive' approach to the Islanders. It was based on the oppressive ethnocentric view of 'difference' that had taken hold in the Western world following World War II. Before then the Islanders had been discouraged from leaving the reserve for fear that they would racially 'pollute' the white population on the Tasmanian mainland. Now they were encouraged to abandon the reserve and relocate to the Tasmanian mainland, where their 'differentness' would disappear through assimilation into the dominant white population. But many Islanders disagreed. As the descendants of the original owners of Tasmania, they considered the report's recommendations were tantamount to cultural genocide.

Although the terminology of the 1948 report had changed from that in earlier reports, the government's belief that the Islanders were a people incapable of determining their own future had not. Every government report since 1908 had acknowledged that the Islanders firmly believed the reserve had been bequeathed to them by virtue of their Aboriginal ancestry in compensation for the loss of the island of Tasmania. Only Burbury's report of 1929 had acknowledged that 'if the Act was not the result of a recognition that these people were entitled to something, why was it passed?' Yet even he had considered that the act was a dangerous recognition of Islander rights.

Before the act expired in 1951 some Islanders took out thirty-five leases on the reserve. They also bought cattle and sheep and fenced their homestead and agricultural blocks. But the rest 'sat' on their land. They considered that they had already paid for their leases after the 1912 act and they were not going to pay for them again. Thus, by the time the act expired only one lessee was eligible for a land grant on his agricultural block. The government had a long-term objective of Islander removal, which it intensified with Aboriginal child removal. It took the view that with the legal termination of the reserve in 1958 the Islanders as a separate people would no longer legally exist.[34]

By then only 120 Islanders remained on the now defunct reserve. They preserved their existence by fleeing when state health and welfare authorities arrived in search of 'neglected' children, refusing to find employment off the island, and making strong expressions of attachment to the old reserve. Their dreadful predicament was inadvertently revealed in a report on their condition for the bishop of Tasmania made by the council clerk on Flinders Island, C.I.A. Booth, a former schoolteacher on the reserve. The Islanders told him that they belonged nowhere because the government did not recognise them as Aborigines and no one else recognised them as 'white people'. Even though he was critical of them he acknowledged that they showed a 'marked tendency towards courtesy when rightly approached, displayed a respect for elderly people and a great love for their children and expressed concern for the future of their own community'.[35] But, like so many of his contemporaries in authority, he could not countenance their right to exist as a community on their own terms.

By the mid 1960s half of the remaining Islanders had taken up social welfare department homes and jobs in Launceston, Burnie and Devonport. A series of poor mutton-bird seasons, unemployment and the fact that no money had been spent on the island since 1944 had induced them to leave. The fifty or so who remained refused to leave the reserve even for short periods because they were frightened the land might be taken from them in their absence, as had occurred at the Framlingham Reserve in Victoria. The Islanders' resistance to assimilation at this time was part of a general resistance by Aboriginal communities in settled Australia threatened by removal or closure of reserves.

In Launceston the Islanders congregated in Invermay, one of the city's poorer suburbs, where they were often refused service in hotels and suffered discrimination in employment. The older people missed 'the quiet and peacefulness' of the island and looked forward to the mutton-bird season, when they could meet up with their own people again. Some of the children, like Phyllis Pitchford, would spend one year on Cape Barren Island with her father and the next in Launceston with her mother until she attended high school, where she excelled. Others, like Val Tiffin, recalled reconnecting with older Aboriginal places in the Tamar Valley. Others would spend some months on Cape Barren, then Flinders, returning to Launceston at the end of the year. This migratory pattern had begun in the 1920s when the first families had relocated to Launceston and was a variation of an earlier pattern established in the 1870s when the Islander families visited each other 'until the neck of the flour bag became a little long'.[36]

At the beginning of 1968, in an attempt to prod the government into final removal of the Islanders, the Flinders Council lobbied the Tasmanian Parliament for a select committee to examine the future development of Cape Barren Island. The members estimated that 20,000 to 24,000 hectares on the island were suitable for pasture and 240 hectares were ploughable. Some of this land was on the old reserve.[37]

In July 1968 the Tasmanian government's chief secretary, Brian Miller, believing that were the Islanders presented with attractive alternative conditions they would leave, and realising that the recent acquisition of powers by the federal government from the referendum of May 1967 to assist Aboriginal people would be a useful means of gaining funds for their removal, decided to attend a meeting of federal and state ministers for Aboriginal Affairs. Once again the government's conundrum was exposed. On the one hand the chief secretary denied the Islanders their Aboriginal ancestry to lay claim to the old reserve, yet on the other he told the *Examiner* that 'the interests of the Bass Strait Islanders must be preserved' and used their Aboriginal ancestry to gain finance to re-house them on the Tasmanian mainland.[38]

In support of Miller's policy, in August the *Mercury* ran a series of pro-assimilation articles on the Islanders, written in a patronising manner to which Aborigines in settled Australia had become accustomed. On Cape Barren Island the reporter found a group of charming, eccentric and stubborn people living in squalor. They had no work, hated whites and refused to move to Launceston to join their happy relatives, one of whose children had become a successful footballer. The reporter was in no doubt that when they were relocated to Launceston they would not only lose their anti-social habits; they would also find that they would be readily accepted by the dominant white society.[39]

The Islanders lost no time in pressing their case in the local press. 'Instead of our having a hatred for white people, the boot is on the other foot. They have a set on us. Whose crime is it that we are of mixed blood? The government put us here. It is our home. We are happy, and all we ask is that work be made available for us. Then we shall have pleasure in inviting reporters to see for themselves whether we have to be stood over to be made to work.'[40]

The Islanders were fighting 'silent eviction', for it now seemed unlikely that they would 'ever be masters of their own small domain'. Those who stayed resented those who had departed, for in their view Launceston represented an invitation to 'drunkenness, loose living, the hell of urban

poverty'. Indeed, many of their relatives on mainland Tasmania wanted to
return, 'if some sort of future was allowed them at home'.[41]

The chief secretary returned from the meeting with $25,000 for Islander
housing on the Tasmanian mainland. At this point the schoolmaster at
Cape Barren, not known for his liberal views, spoke out: 'I believe that any
person who has made a place his home for many years should not be forced
to leave it, by a person or by a government.' A Launceston resident was
even more to the point: 'The Islanders have simply asked for an industry on
their own land. Why can't we supply it?'[42]

The Office of Aboriginal Affairs in Canberra was also concerned about
the allocation of funds. Charles Perkins, who was then employed by the
office, visited Tasmania late in 1968 and expressed his dissatisfaction about
the lack of consultation with the Islanders. The issue came to a head in
April 1970 when the Tasmanian government advertised for a 'resettlement
officer', located in Launceston, whose function would be 'to advise and

Cape Barren Island school children, 1972. Tasmanian Archives and Heritage
Office, Hobart.

encourage families on Cape Barren Island to re-settle on the Tasmanian mainland in housing provided by Commonwealth funds and to assist such families generally with their social welfare'.[43]

For a year a battle raged between state and Commonwealth officials over the dispersal of the Islanders and the appointment of the resettlement officer. By mid 1971 a compromise was reached. The resettlement officer's title was changed to 'community development officer', and would be located on Cape Barren Island to assist in its redevelopment.

The policy shift was accompanied by renewed activism by the Islanders. In August 1971, Abschol, a national student organisation with a strong base at the University of Tasmania, organised a conference of Islanders in Launceston. It was a turning point for the 200 Islanders who attended from all over Tasmania and the Bass Strait islands. They were surprised to find that nearly 2,000 of their people were scattered across Tasmania and Australia. Much of the first day was spent in recrimination about the past, but by the second day they had begun to pick up the threads of their kinship patterns. The conference agreed to press for Islander title to the old reserve and for the island as a whole.[44]

By the end of 1971, Cape Barren Island had seen an injection of Commonwealth funds, and for the first time since the Depression the Islanders had regular employment apart from mutton-birding. By the end of 1973 they had cleared the boxthorn, repaired the roads, installed concrete tanks, constructed a retaining wall and cleaned up the cemetery and war memorial. An Islander council had been formed under the control of the community development officer, a dam had been started and school facilities improved, and the population had increased to ninety people, half of whom were children.

In Hobart, the Commonwealth government, supported by Abschol, funded an Aboriginal Information Centre. With the Islanders on the Tasmanian mainland now calling themselves Aborigines and politically organised to lead their own campaigns for recognition, return of land and remains of their ancestors, it appeared that the assimilation era had ended.

PART VI

RESURGENCE
1973-2010

19

Reclaiming rights and identity, 1973–92

The Aboriginal Information Centre, with offices in Hobart and Launceston, soon became the focal point of Aboriginal activism in Tasmania. By 1977 it had been renamed the Tasmanian Aboriginal Centre (TAC) and had a clear agenda: to gain recognition and rights for the Aboriginal community as Tasmanian Aborigines, the return of the remains of their ancestors held in museums, the control of Aboriginal heritage and the return of land from which their ancestors had been unjustly dispossessed. This chapter explores some of the ways in which the TAC carried out its agenda between the critical years of 1973 and 1992. During this period, it became one of the most prominent and influential Aboriginal organisations in Australia, driven by a spirited group of Aboriginal activists. They included Karen Brown, Jim Everett, Cheryl Fulton, Rodney Gibbons, Rosalind Langford, Greg Lehman, Clyde Mansell, Denise Phillips (Gardner), Rocky Sainty, Heather Sculthorpe and Steve Stanton. But the best known was Michael Mansell, who gained international recognition. Much of their confidence, energy and purpose came from the regular TAC community meetings in Hobart, Launceston and Burnie, where their lively and humorous discussions were often reported in provocative articles in their newsletter *Pugganna News*. As political activists whose purpose was to overturn the course of history, they employed a sophisticated range of strategies to persuade the media, government and wider community of their case.

The first campaign, launched by the TAC's predecessor, the Aboriginal Information Centre, began in 1975 when its secretary, Roy Nicholls, a descendant of Fanny Cochrane Smith's, petitioned the Tasmanian Labor government to remove Truganini's remains from the vaults of the Tasmanian Museum and Art Gallery and cremate them on the centenary of her death, in May 1976. The proposal struck a deep chord with the government. Premier Doug Lowe was anxious to repair its tarnished reputation with the community following the decision made nearly 100 years earlier to permit the Royal Society of Tasmania to exhume her remains and place them on public display in the Tasmanian Museum and Art Gallery between 1904 and 1947. After a legal wrangle with the museum's trustees about ownership of the remains, the government finally took possession and a private cremation was held on 30 April. The ceremony was attended by Roy Nicholls, representatives of the Aboriginal community, the premier and the anatomist Dr Allan Wallace, who identified the skeleton by virtue of its missing parts. The ashes were then placed in a Huon pine casket. The next morning, the casket was taken on board the Islander-built launch the *Egeria*, which then sailed to the D'Entrecasteaux Channel, where the premier formally handed the ashes to Roy Nicholls, who scattered them over the channel with the words 'Truganini, you may now rest in peace.'[1]

The cremation generated international attention, and to many non-Aboriginal Tasmanians and the Tasmanian government it appeared that a terrible travesty from the past had finally been laid to rest. But Nicholls made the point clear that Tasmanian Aborigines were also looking ahead. Truganini, he said, may have represented 'the destruction of a way of life', but now the descendants of her people could 'look forward to the future with some cause, a reason for hope'.[2]

Nicholls lost no time in presenting the new premier, Bill Nielson, with the Aborigines' new agenda. In December 1976, he wrote to the premier demanding recognition of prior Aboriginal ownership of Tasmania and the return of land to Aboriginal people.[3] Nielson met with a delegation of Tasmanian Aborigines but rejected the claim outright. At that point the TAC changed tactics. In November 1977, about fifty Aborigines from the TAC set up an 'Aboriginal Parliament' outside Tasmania's Parliament House and then presented the speaker of the House of Assembly with a petition setting out their claims for land. The TAC's Secretary, Michael Mansell, told the media:

The Tasmanian Aboriginal Land Rights claim is for Cape Barren Island and for all sacred sites around Tasmania, particularly where rock carvings exist; it is for the Mutton Bird Islands surrounding Tasmania; it is for compensation for dispossession of land in Tasmania; and it is for the return of ownership to Aboriginal people of Crown land or otherwise compensation for this Crown land.[4]

Six months earlier, in May 1977, the TAC had demonstrated its ability to gain media attention when Queen Elizabeth II made an official visit to Hobart. After the Queen stepped from her car to attend a gala reception at the Wrest Point Casino, Michael Mansell, wearing a white tuxedo and sporting an afro hairstyle, dashed into the media spotlight and presented Her Majesty with some Tasmanian Aboriginal artefacts. In the glare of international publicity, the government was forced to respond.

Michael Mansell presenting petition to Queen Elizabeth II, Hobart, 1977.

Early the following year, the Tasmanian government established the Aboriginal Affairs Study Group, consisting of public servants, a consultant and representatives of the TAC, to investigate land rights, the mutton-bird industry and social development of the Tasmanian Aboriginal community.[5] At a key point in the deliberations, however, the TAC withdrew, claiming that the chair had tried to create divisions within the Aboriginal community in refusing to acknowledge its historical continuity from the past to the present.[6] The issue of historical continuity had already surfaced on the ABC TV program *Monday Conference* in September 1978 in which the film-maker Tom Haydon, director of the documentary film *The Last Tasmanian*, had told Michael Mansell that he was only a 'hybrid' Aborigine, and that he had no continuity with the 'traditional' extinct Tasmanian Aborigines. In a stunning riposte, Mansell had questioned why scientists wanted to believe that the Tasmanian Aborigines were extinct when in fact they had survived the horrors of colonial invasion. Scientists, he said, could not determine who was or was not a Tasmanian Aborigine. Aboriginal people themselves made that decision.[7]

When the study group recommended that sites of 'traditional' Aboriginal significance, such as Mount Cameron West and Rocky Cape, should be placed under the jurisdiction of the *Aboriginal Relics Act 1975*, and that 'sites of common and historical' or 'hybrid' significance, like the mutton-bird islands, should come under the jurisdiction of a newly created Aboriginal Lands Trust, the TAC argued again that the group had not understood the historical continuity of the Tasmanian Aborigines from the past to the present.[8] The bill that emerged from the report in 1981 granted a limited form of land rights, but in vesting control of the Aboriginal Lands Trust in the minister rather than in the Aboriginal community also failed to recognise historical continuity. As the first attempt at land rights legislation it showed that the Tasmanian government was prepared to consider the issue, but only on its terms. Even so, the upper house of the Tasmanian Parliament, the Legislative Council, opposed the bill and it was soundly defeated.

By then the decision by the Hydro Electric Commission to build a dam on the Franklin River that would flood south-west of Tasmania was dominating Tasmanian politics at the expense of other issues. The worldwide anger generated by the decision led to the collapse of the Labor government and the election of the Liberal government led by Premier Robin Gray in April 1982. Even though the new government was determined to proceed with the dam's construction, the issue was far from resolved. Several lobby groups had instituted legal challenges about the impact of the dam not only on the 'pristine wilderness' of south-west Tasmania but also on recently discovered Aboriginal cave sites which indicated Aboriginal occupation in Tasmania of at least 30,000 years. As the summer of 1982–83 approached, further protests were planned to blockade the dam site.

Until the 'rediscovery' of Kuti Kina and Deena Reena caves at the end of 1981, the TAC had refused to support the 'Save the Franklin' campaign because the environment movement's concept of 'wilderness' did not acknowledge prior Aboriginal occupation of Tasmania.[9] But the caves' rediscovery led the TAC to develop a new approach. It would not only oppose the flooding of the Franklin River on the grounds that it would destroy Aboriginal heritage, but it would also contest the scientific 'owner-ship' of Tasmanian Aboriginal heritage by the archaeology profession.

In April 1982 the TAC had written to the Tasmanian Liberal govern-ment requesting that the Aboriginal remains in the Crowther Collection in the Tasmanian Museum and Art Gallery be released to the Aboriginal community for cremation. The collection comprised three skeletons and thirty-four skulls of Tasmanian Aborigines who had died at Oyster Cove between 1847 and 1871 and which Sir William Crowther had dug up from the Oyster Cove cemetery as a young medical student early in the twentieth century. The museum's trustees were prepared to institute joint responsibility for the collection, but in a statement strongly supported by the archaeology profession, they refused to consider its disposal on the grounds that the destruction of Aboriginal remains was an irreversible action which would prevent any further scientific study of the material. Rosalind Langford, the TAC's secretary, saw the matter differently. She said that the 'collection was obtained illegally and is being kept illegally. The desecration of Aboriginal dead will not be tolerated for much longer.'[10]

The TAC then filed complaints in the Magistrates Court against the museum's director and the chair of the board of trustees, claiming that, under the Criminal Code and the Aboriginal Relics Act, they were in illegal possession of Aboriginal skeletal remains. Although the magistrate dismissed the case it attracted international attention, forcing the govern-ment to act. Late in December 1982 it agreed to legislation to return the Crowther Collection to the Tasmanian Aborigines.[11]

This decision coincided with the annual conference of the Australian Archaeological Association in Hobart, where Rosalind Langford deliv-ered a groundbreaking paper, 'Our heritage—your playground', outlining the conflicts over control of Aboriginal heritage that had arisen between archaeologists and Aborigines. The first was that 'the science of archaeology determined that Truganini was the last of our people'.

> The effect of this 'scientific fact' upon the 4000 Tasmanian Aboriginals who reside in this State has been incalculable. Science has proved that we don't exist. Science got what it wanted—some bones to parade through Europe enhancing the reputation of white colonials, leaving the Tasmanian Aborigines with a one hundred year struggle to defeat that view.[12]

Archaeologists, she pointed out, had openly opposed the return of the Crowther Collection to the Aboriginal community until one of its key figures had changed his mind. She acknowledged that some archaeologists had assisted many Aboriginal communities in preparing submissions for land rights, but the criteria of land eligibility had been set by the conquerors, not by Aborigines.

So who owned Aboriginal heritage? Langford said that there was the view, represented by the dominant white culture, that heritage was the property of mankind. This view encouraged the exploitation and invasion of the lands and cultures of 'other' societies. But, she pointed out, 'If we |as Aboriginal people| cannot control our own heritage, what can we control?' It was vital that Kuti Kina and Deena Reena caves and the remains in the Crowther Collection were recognised as Tasmanian Aboriginal heritage. She concluded: 'We are the custodians. You can either be our guests or our enemies. That decision can only rest with you.'[13]

The majority of the delegates took the point. The conference resolved to support the return of the Crowther Collection to the Tasmanian Aborigines on the grounds that the unethical manner in which it had been acquired far outweighed its potential scientific value.[14] The resolution marked a departure from the tenets of scientific racism to a new understanding about Aborigines' ownership of their ancestral remains. But, even today, in some parts of the profession relations between the two groups remain strained. While some archaeologists have requested to work on projects such as the Jordan

River levee without Aboriginal consent, others have preferred to observe the protocols by working on TAC projects.

Six months later, in May 1983, counsel for the Tasmanian government's High Court challenge to the federal government's use of its foreign affairs power to stop the flooding of the caves claimed that the Kuti Kina Cave could not be of special significance to Aborigines because the Tasmanian Aboriginal race was extinct.[15] In response the TAC presented to the High Court affidavits which argued that the Tasmanian Aborigines still existed and that the state government had explicitly recognised that fact through its acceptance of federal government funds for Aboriginal projects.[16] In his affidavit Michael Mansell said that Kuti Kina Cave was the first tangible link between him and the state's 40,000-year-old heritage:

> The fact that the Aborigines could survive physically and cultur-ally in adverse conditions and over such a long period of time ... helps me counteract the feeling of racial inferiority and enables me to demonstrate within the wider community that I and my people are the equal of other members of the community.[17]

When the High Court ruled in July that the federal government had acted within its legal powers, one of the judges noted the significance of Aborigi-nal heritage in reaching his decision.[18] It represented another important step in the TAC's campaign for Aboriginal rights and recognition. A few months later Kuti Kina and Deena Reena caves were listed as part of the World Heritage Area of South West Tasmania.

Eight months earlier, in December 1982, the Sydney *Daily Telegraph* had reported that the skull of William Lanney had been located in the School of Anatomy at the University of Edinburgh, where it was on public display. But the university's professor of anatomy refused to consider returning the remains to Tasmania on the grounds that 'research would suffer'.[19] The TAC lost no time in writing to the university asking for the return of all Tasmanian Aboriginal remains so that they could be 'appropriately disposed of'. The manager of the TAC, Denise Phillips, told the media, 'We think it's quite wrong for them to be on display' and warned that it was prepared to take the University of Edinburgh to court if it would not return the skulls voluntarily.[20] The TAC campaign for the return of Tasmanian Aboriginal remains in overseas museums had begun.

But the return of land proved more intractable. Following the collapse of national Aboriginal land rights legislation at the end of 1983, the Tasmanian Aboriginal Land Council (TALC), which the TAC had established to negotiate with federal and state governments on this issue, decided on a more activist approach. In January 1984 a group of Tasmanian Aborigines occupied Oyster Cove, one of the historic sites it had listed for return to Aboriginal ownership in 1979, and claimed land ownership. Oyster Cove comprised the 30.3 hectares proclaimed as an historic site by the Tasmanian government in 1981. The site included ruins of the Aboriginal Station where some of the TAC members' ancestors had lived, but not the cemetery from which their ancestors' remains had been illegally excavated by Sir William Crowther in the early twentieth century. The TALC claimed that the National Parks and Wildlife Service had not managed the site, which had been desecrated, and that it could better manage the site by declaring it an Aboriginal Keeping Place in preparation for the return of the Crowther Collection.[21]

At the entrance to Oyster Cove the TAC erected a sign which included a quote from the white Australian novelist Xavier Herbert:

> Until we give back to the black man just a bit of the land that was his, and give it back without provisos, without strings to snatch it back, without anything but complete generosity in concession for the evil we have done to him—until we do that, we shall remain what we have always been so far: a community of thieves.[22]

The bold move forced an immediate response from the federal and state governments. On 1 March the federal minister for Aboriginal Affairs, Clyde Holding, visited Oyster Cove and considered that the site would have come within the scope of national land rights legislation and thus should be returned to the Aboriginal community.[23] But when the Tasmanian attorney-general, Max Bingham, introduced legislation in the Tasmanian

Parliament to dispose of the Crowther Collection at Oyster Cove, it fell far short of the TAC's expectations. Bingham claimed that the disposal was not exclusively an Aboriginal affair, in that it 'would interest most thinking Tasmanians regardless of race or colour'. The TAC president, Rodney Gibbons, responded that although Truganini's cremation eight years earlier had been an achievement, the TAC now wanted complete control of the disposal of the Tasmanian Aboriginal remains in the Crowther Collection and that all relevant Aboriginal groups unanimously supported its stand.[24]

The *Mercury* agreed: 'The insensitive legislation introduced into State Parliament this week blatantly ignores the wishes of Tasmania's Aboriginal community. Whatever treatment [the skeletons] receive from the Tasmanian Aborigines, it can be no less dignified than the original actions of those who desecrated the Oyster Cove graves.'[25] Clyde Holding made the point that if the remains had belonged to non-Aboriginal people then the government would have handed them back immediately.[26] But the state cabinet decided to stick with its original legislation. When Michael Mansell pointed out that the cremation would take place in accordance with Tasmanian Aboriginal custom, whereby the remains would be wrapped in natural fibres and face east, the government pulled back. In an effort to save face it appointed Roy Nicholls, who had scattered Truganini's ashes over the D'Entrecasteaux Channel in 1976 when a TAC office bearer, to find out the views of the Tasmanian Aboriginal community. Nicholls reported in July that its members wanted the Crowther Collection returned to them through two Aboriginal Elders, Ida West and Ben Everett, and then cremated at Oyster Cove. At this point the government admitted defeat. In a complete about-face, it decided to return all Tasmanian Aboriginal skeletal remains that were held in the major museums in Hobart and Launceston.

Three hundred people attended the four-day cremation ceremony at Oyster Cove in May 1985. Alma Stackhouse, chair of the Tasmanian Council of Aboriginal Organisations, said that the cremation ceremony had made the site more sacred.[27] It was a stunning victory for the TAC and a further acknowledgement that the modern Tasmanian Aboriginal community was connected to its ancestral past.

Two months later the TAC sent Michael Mansell to Europe and America to locate and identify the remains of 220 Tasmanian Aborigines in museums. Most of them, he said, had originally been murdered. Although museums in Dublin, Edinburgh, Stockholm and Chicago were sympathetic to his quest, others were indifferent to the view that indigenous peoples had the right to the remains of their ancestors.[28] The visit transformed international perceptions of the Tasmanian Aborigines; once considered an extinct people, they were now seen as a modern indigenous people who wanted their ancestors removed from the clutches of science.

By then Michael Mansell had become a national political figure in his own right. In 1985 he was thirty-four years old. He was born in Launceston in 1951 to a third-generation Islander family descended from the original unions of Watanimarina and Thomas Beeton, and Black Judy and Edward Mansell. His childhood and adolescence were typical of many Aboriginal youths in south-eastern Australia during the assimilation period. His parents, Clyda and Clarence Mansell, had moved their family from the Cape Barren Island Reserve to Launceston at the end of World War II in search of work. They lived for a time in Lefroy and then George Town, where Michael attended high school. He was a poor student and had failed almost every exam by the time he left school at fifteen. He worked at the smelter at Bell Bay and then as a labourer on the railways but was sacked when he punched a workmate who taunted him about his Aboriginal origins. With only the occasional job, he wandered the streets of Launceston drinking and fighting, and watched as one by one his Aboriginal mates were carted off to Risdon prison. He was, however, an outstanding footballer and played senior Australian Rules football, first for the Launceston club at seventeen and then, after a serious car accident, for North Hobart. In 1973, at the age of twenty-two, he joined the TAC in Launceston as a volunteer, and by 1976 he had been appointed its state secretary, which saw him become its chief spokesperson and activist. He then completed a law degree at the University of Tasmania and was admitted to the Tasmanian Bar in October 1984.[29]

In some ways Mansell's experiences were similar to other urban Aborigines of his generation. But they differed in other important ways. He was not 'stolen' from his family as a child and thus had not 'lost' his Aboriginal identity. Rather, he had imbibed his Aboriginal heritage, including the seasonal practices of mutton-birding, from his parents and numerous relatives across northern Tasmania and the Bass Strait islands. His understanding of injustice was compounded while working at Bell Bay, and his prowess at football gave him a sense of purpose after his car accident. This was reinforced by Pierre Slicer from the Aboriginal Legal Service, who persuaded him to study law, because, as he said, the Aboriginal movement needed Aboriginal lawyers to fight for its rights. Mansell combined his Tasmanian Aboriginal identity, keen intelligence, considerable political skills and compelling media presence with a fearless and cheeky irreverence for authority and a strong commitment to justice for Tasmanian Aborigines. This remarkable combination of talents, ability and hard work, along with the painful reality that he often had to assert his Tasmanian Aboriginality in the media on a daily basis, made him a major spokesperson for Tasmanian Aborigines on the national political stage.

At the end of 1985, the issue of the return of Aboriginal land in Tasmania was still unresolved. The federal minister tried to negotiate directly with the Tasmanian government on the matter and invited the TALC to prepare a schedule of claims. The council claimed nineteen separate sites classified in three areas—historic, economic and sacred—and representing 'mere dots on the map of Tasmania'.[30] This marked a significant departure from the 1977 claims, which had listed not only the return of all Aboriginal sacred sites, the mutton-bird islands and unalienated Crown land but also financial compensation for all alienated Crown land. But the overriding political point remained: the Tasmanian government had to acknowledge that Tasmanian Aborigines were the prior owners and occupiers of Tasmania.

The four *historic* sites were Oyster Cove, Cape Barren Island, Wybalenna and Cape Grim. The first three were on Crown land leases, but Cape Grim was privately owned by the VDL Company. The TALC wanted Aboriginal management and control of Oyster Cove and Cape Barren Island as 'living Aboriginal sites', but it was willing to lease back management of Wybalenna and Cape Grim as sites of Aboriginal genocide to the National Parks and Wildlife Service.

The eleven *economic* sites were mutton-bird islands in the Furneaux and Hunter groups in Bass Strait (see Map 35). They were all on Crown land leases. In the Furneaux Group the islands were Big Dog and Babel, which were listed in the land bill in 1981, as well as Little Dog and Chappell. In the Hunter Group the islands were the Crown leases of Steep Head, Petrel, Stack, Albatross, Doughboys and Three Hummock as well as Robbins Island, which was in private ownership. These two clusters of islands, the TALC argued, would consolidate the Tasmanian Aboriginal economy in the mutton-bird industry.

The four *sacred* sites included the Kuti Kina and Deena Reena caves and the Maxwell River caves, later known as Ballawinne, which contain the most spectacular gallery of cave paintings known in Tasmania and had only been rediscovered in January 1986. The TALC supported World Heritage listing of this new find similar to that enjoyed by Kuti Kina and Deena Reena caves. The other two sites were Mount Cameron West on the west coast of Tasmania and Cave Bay Cave on Hunter Island. The TALC proposed the return of all four sites, which it would then lease back to the NPWS for management and conservation. In this way, the TALC argued, Aboriginal ownership would be recognised and Commonwealth funds would guarantee the sites' maintenance and protection, similar to the system that operated at Uluru in the Northern Territory.[31]

The list was favourably greeted by the *Mercury*, which declared on 20 May 1985: 'The plea for land rights . . . at last offers an opportunity for making what is, after all, little more than a token contribution towards redressing the balance.' The Tasmanian government disagreed and did everything possible to thwart the negotiations. Five months later, the *Mercury* revealed that the federal government, in trying to overcome state government intransigence, had plans to swap 134 hectares of Commonwealth land at the former Quarantine Station on Bruny Island for the 30.3-hectare site at Oyster Cove. Other possible land swaps included Commonwealth-owned Swan Island in Bass Strait in return for some of the mutton-bird islands. But the Tasmanian government refused to negotiate on the grounds that the plan was 'land rights by stealth'.[32] For its part the TAC also considered that the negotiations were being carried out in an underhand manner and with only minimal consultation with the Aboriginal community. The process placed it in the position of a supplicant being thrown scraps of land at the behest of the victors. Rather than continuing in this demeaning position, the TAC decided, on the eve of the bicentenary of white invasion of Australia, to promote the idea of a sovereign Aboriginal nation.[33] The new campaign for sovereignty placed Michael Mansell in open conflict with Clyde Holding and alerted the Australian nation to Aboriginal aspirations to sovereignty in the most direct way since the Aboriginal tent embassies in Canberra in the early 1970s.

On 18 April 1987, Michael Mansell set off on a twelve-day visit to Libya, funded by Aboriginal organisations on the Australian mainland, to attend the World Conference against Zionism, Racism and Imperialism. He spoke to the conference as a survivor of a sovereign people whose country had been taken from them and whose rights had been suppressed ever since. In response the conference recognised Australian Aborigines as a sovereign people. Mansell never asked the Libyans for money and they never offered any. Nor did he advocate violence.[34]

Clyde Holding demanded assurance from the TAC that no federal funds had been used to finance the trip and sent the auditors down to scour the books for any financial discrepancies. They found none. He then threatened to cut the TAC's funding if it chose to accept funds from the Libyan government.[35] Mansell saw nothing wrong with Aborigines seeking support and recognition from Libya. 'In one day they recognised that the Aboriginal people in Australia are a nation of people', he said. 'Australia was invaded by a bunch of terrorists from England, and the fruits of that terrorist activity are now vested in the Australian Government who refuse to give it up to Aboriginal people. So who is the terrorist?'[36]

In focusing 'the thoughts of white Australia on the lot of the Australian Aborigines', the Melbourne *Age* acknowledged that Mansell's excursion to Libya was a massive publicity coup.[37] He now used it to call on the federal government to begin immediate negotiations on Aboriginal sovereignty, putting forward a list of demands which included doubling the Aboriginal Affairs budget in 1987–88, transferring Crown rights to land held by the federal government back to the Aboriginal people, cancelling the bicentennial celebrations, sacking the minister for Aboriginal Affairs, Clyde Holding, and legislating a program to overcome the high unemployment and imprisonment rates among Aborigines.[38]

On 27 May 1987, the twentieth anniversary of the referendum which gave powers to the Commonwealth to take greater responsibility for Aboriginal affairs, Clyde Holding addressed the National Press Club in Canberra. Just as he began to outline his 'agenda of reconciliation', Mansell leaped to his feet and accused him of treating Aboriginal issues as a welfare problem. Before a stunned audience of reporters Mansell called not for reconciliation but the creation of a separate Aboriginal nation, in which Aboriginal people would own all unalienated Crown land.[39]

How was it possible for Mansell to grab the national media spotlight on Aboriginal affairs? The federal government had only itself to blame. It had dismissed the nation's peak Aboriginal body, the National Aboriginal Conference, in 1985 and had failed to introduce national land rights legislation. Since there was no national Aboriginal body left to negotiate with the federal government, Mansell filled the void and placed the minister into a reactive position. While the media did not support the concept of an Aboriginal state, they were certainly prepared to give it publicity.[40]

Six weeks later, Clyde Holding was relieved of his portfolio. When the new minister for Aboriginal Affairs, Gerry Hand, canvassed the idea of a treaty, Mansell said the suggested provisions were too limited and too late. The issue now, he said, was Aboriginal sovereignty. He had already announced that he planned to visit Fiji to talk with army coup leader Colonel Rabuka in the hope that he would recognise an Australian Aboriginal nation. In March 1988 he set off for New Zealand to canvass the sovereignty concept among Maori leaders and to invite them to join him in attending an indigenous people's liberation conference in Libya.[41]

Mansell told the Hobart *Mercury* on 9 April that the only way in which the federal government could restore confidence among the Aboriginal community in the bicentenary year would be to get rid of massive white bureaucracy in Aboriginal Affairs, introduce uniform land rights legislation, place top priority on Aboriginal health and commence serious negotiations with Aboriginal leaders about Aboriginal sovereignty.

The Melbourne *Age* was intrigued that at a time when most Australians believed the Tasmanian Aborigines were extinct a person like Michael Mansell could become the unofficial leader of the Aboriginal community in Australia. The TAC's legal adviser, Pierre Slicer, put it like this:

> It is not surprising that Australia's most extreme Aboriginal activist should have emerged from Tasmania, it is history on the rebound. Nowhere in Australia have people who feel themselves to be Aborigines been taken closer to the physical fact of extinction nor to the edge of the ultimate cultural abyss: being told that they do not exist. If Mansell's behaviour was outrageous, it is because he is outraged. Ten years ago they said that Mansell wasn't an Aborigine. Now they're saying he's bad for Tasmanian Aborigines.[42]

And there the matter rested for the remainder of the bicentenary year.

In May 1989, following the formation of the Labor–Green Accord government in Tasmania led by Premier Michael Field, Aboriginal land legislation was back on the agenda. In February 1990, John White, the minister assisting the premier on Aboriginal Affairs, released a discussion paper, 'Land rights for Tasmanian Aborigines', which went a considerable way towards meeting the concerns of the TAC. First, it declared that the Tasmanian government would recognise that Aboriginal people had occupied the land now known as Tasmania for over 30,000 years and had been displaced without either their agreement or compensation. The government now wished to grant inalienable freehold title to those areas of land of particular significance to the Aboriginal people. Second, it rationalised the land claims made by the TALC in 1986 to comprise 53,279 hectares of land. While it reinforced the concept of land claims being placed in three categories—sacred, economic and historic—it removed some sites from the original list of claims and added or expanded others. Michael Mansell considered the paper 'an enormously progressive step' but was disappointed that several 'key' sites like Rocky Cape and Cape Grim were absent from the list and the list of options.

There is no way the Aboriginal community will accept leaving things as they are or getting their land back under a white man's lease. What we want as a community is the right of permanent ownership, the control we had here before the white man came. We don't care how this is delivered. It is just what we want. Obviously from the options that have been provided, only the new legislation goes near doing what we want. I just wish the Government would stop talking about it and get on with it. They know what we want and it is up to them to deliver.[43]

Three days later the Liberal opposition leader, Ray Groom, reaffirmed his party's policy that 'traditional land rights' were not appropriate for Tasmania. He pointed out that although his party 'appreciated the sensitivity involved and believed Tasmanian Aboriginal people and their unique culture should be properly recognized' it also believed that 'all Tasmanians, regardless of their race, colour or religion, must have equal rights and equal opportunity to own land' and preferred the option of leaving things as they were, with the Aboriginal community continuing to occupy Oyster Cove.[44]

Michael Mansell was now fed up. On 16 July 1990, with the support of some Aboriginal activists on the Australian mainland, he established the Aboriginal Provisional Government (APG). It had a fourfold purpose: to change the situation in Australia 'so that instead of white people determining the rights of Aboriginal people, it will be the latter group who will do it'; to 'refute the assumption that Aborigines have always been regarded as a minority group in Australia'; to create an environment whereby Aboriginal people accepted responsibility for determining the long-term future, rather than acting as service delivery organisations for programs made for them; and to plan the long-term destiny of the Aboriginal people. Its ultimate objective was the establishment of a sovereign state for Aborigines.[45]

The APG was an expression of Mansell's own ideas about Aboriginal sovereignty. He intended that it should act as a ginger group in Aboriginal politics and prick the conscience of the wider Australian community. Some members of the TAC were unhappy about the association of the APG with their own organisation, so by the end of 1990 Mansell had distanced the APG from it. Rather, he used the APG as a platform from which to comment more freely about local and national Aboriginal politics without implicating the TAC. Indeed, the formation of the APG indicated how far Mansell had moved from the legislative concept of land rights that was on the Labor–Green Accord agenda.

Undeterred, on 3 April 1991, John White introduced an Aboriginal lands bill into the House of Assembly. It made provision for twenty-one areas of Crown land totalling 53,000 hectares to be handed back to the TALC. The opposition's spokesman on Aboriginal Affairs, John Barker, said that the Liberals would oppose the legislation because their policy was equal rights for all Tasmanians: 'We do not believe there should be special treatment for minority groups.' He also claimed that members of the Cape Barren Island Aboriginal community did not want land rights because they feared that Michael Mansell would gain power over them. They had been told this by members of the white-controlled Outer Islands Association, a lobby group specifically formed in the Bass Strait islands to oppose the bill.[46] But Greg Lehman, secretary of the TALC, saw the introduction of the legislation as a positive step:

> It's been a long wait. The Aboriginal community has been fighting for the return of land ever since the Europeans turned up and started taking land over. It's the culmination of a struggle of nearly 200 years, so that in itself is cause for some celebration. But it's not through yet and we've got the Legislative Council to contend with.[47]

The bill passed the House of Assembly on 11 April but was defeated in the Legislative Council on 12 July by twelve votes to eight.[48] The Tasmanian Parliament was not yet ready to concede the justice of the Aborigines' case.

A month before the bill had reached the Legislative Council, Aborigines had occupied Rocky Cape Aboriginal site and claimed it as a sacred site. Following the bill's defeat, Aboriginal community members on Flinders Island occupied the old farmhouse at Wybalenna and claimed it as an Aboriginal historic site.[49] Tasmanian Aborigines were continuing their strategy of land occupation to make their case for land rights.

By 1992 the TAC had achieved marked success in gaining recognition for modern Tasmanian Aborigines, as was shown in the dramatic increase in the number of people in Tasmania identifying as Aboriginal. Between 1976 and 1991 the identified Aboriginal population in Tasmania increased from 2,903 to 8,948, with an increasingly significant proportion living in the north-west of the state.[50] But the long-awaited breakthrough with government had proved elusive.

Breakthrough, 1992–95

The change of government in Tasmania in February 1992 appeared to signal a return to the negative policies of the previous Liberal government between 1982 and 1989. When the new Liberal premier, Ray Groom, announced that he would disband the Aboriginal Affairs Unit, the TAC responded by occupying the site of the first British settlement in Tasmania at Risdon Cove. Its members claimed that, as the site of the first massacre of Tasmanian Aborigines, in May 1804, it should be returned to them.[1]

These skirmishes, however, masked three remarkable shifts taking place in federal and state politics that made possible the return of some land to the Tasmanian Aborigines. First was the establishment of an elected statutory body, the Tasmanian Regional Aboriginal Council (TRAC), which was part of the Aboriginal and Torres Strait Islander Commission (ATSIC), created by federal legislation in 1989. The council consisted of eight members, one of whom was the chair, who were elected on a regional basis from Aboriginal constituencies in the south, north-west and north-east of Tasmania. ATSIC's brief was to give Aboriginal people more power to make decisions for themselves and their future through elected regional councils. From its annual budget ATSIC distributed funds to the regional councils for a range of programs under Aboriginal control.

The TAC boycotted the first election for the TRAC in 1990 on the grounds that its functions reduced the potential for Aboriginal self-determination from political initiatives to the level of welfare programs.[2] But individual Tasmanian Aborigines like Rodney Gibbons had no hesitation in standing for election. Before long Gibbons played a key role in identifying parcels of privately owned land for ATSIC purchase for the Aboriginal community.

The second shift in Aboriginal politics took place at the end of 1991, with the establishment of the National Council for Aboriginal Reconciliation following the recommendations of the report of the Royal Commission into Aboriginal Deaths in Custody. The council's charter was to promote greater understanding of Aboriginal people and their experiences in Australia. The members comprised Aboriginal and non-Aboriginal people, and the chair was Patrick Dodson, a well-known Aboriginal activist from the Kimberly region in northern Australia. The council's Tasmanian member was Elder Alma Stackhouse from Flinders Island and she promoted the charter of reconciliation with members of the Tasmanian Parliament, the media, the churches and a wide range of community groups. In due course the charter had a profound impact in changing the Tasmanian Liberal government's outlook on returning land to Aboriginal people.

The final shift was the Mabo judgment, handed down by the High Court of Australia on 3 June 1991, which held that the people of the Murray Islands, now known as the Meriam people, had retained native title to their land which was not extinguished by the annexation of the islands by the colony of Queensland in 1879 or by subsequent legislation. In reaching its historic decision the court abandoned the concept of *terra nullius*, which was offensive to Aborigines and Torres Strait Islanders, and established within common law principles a form of native title largely unrecognised before in Australia.[3]

At this stage neither the Tasmanian government nor the TAC made a formal response to the Mabo decision, for each considered that it could apply only to indigenous communities that had occupied their lands continuously since British invasion. Yet uncertainty about the implications of Mabo for Tasmania became another factor in the realignment of the debate about the return of land to Tasmanian Aborigines.

The Liberal government was not unsympathetic to Aboriginal claims to land in Tasmania but refused to discuss the issue in the language of 'land rights'. On 9 January 1993, Premier Ray Groom confirmed that discussions were taking place with the Tasmanian Aboriginal community whereby they could be given control over land but not title.[4] To that end the TAC and the TALC established a consultation process with the Aboriginal community, and towards the end of January organised a meeting on Cape Barren Island for Aboriginal people from all parts of Tasmania and prepared a document which outlined its current land claims. They included all the national parks and conservation areas, Cape Barren Island and parts of Flinders Island, most of the mutton-bird islands at the eastern end of Bass Strait, and Hunter and Three Hummock islands in western Bass Strait. The claims did not include privately owned land and so Cape Grim had been deleted.[5]

By the end of July the legislative limitations that the federal government intended to place on the Mabo decision in relation to Aboriginal land claims in Tasmania had become painfully clear. At a tense meeting in Hobart with the TAC, Frank Walker, the federal minister with responsibility for Mabo, stated that the federal cabinet had decided to give Commonwealth and state governments the right to veto native title claims over leases considered to be in the national interest. These could include residential, pastoral and tourist leases on Crown land. At this point, Michael Mansell said that the Aboriginal community had been fooled by Prime Minister Paul Keating's rhetoric: 'As soon as the opportunity was there to take on the vested interest groups and support Aborigines they abandoned ship and, like the rats in the State Government, the Federal Government has succumbed to the pressure.'[6]

Some months earlier, at the behest of the premier, the government's deputy leader in the Legislative Council, Tony Fletcher, had set out to interview as many Aboriginal people in Tasmania as possible, in order to find out their views about land and other issues. The journey led to a sea change in Fletcher's thinking about returning land to Tasmanian Aborigines, and he then persuaded the premier to reconsider the issue.

Fletcher's plan followed the protocols of reconciliation and involved, first, a forum of government, Tasmanian Aboriginal and other community groups at which a mechanism for dealing with common issues and, possibly, potential native title claims would be discussed. From this would follow formal recognition of Aboriginal groups in Tasmania and possibly their sacred areas and a formal statement of reconciliation that would have similarities with the Commonwealth model. Finally, it would involve possible increased funding. Groom said that he wanted to achieve an outcome that 'brought Tasmanians closer together'.[7]

On 16 December, at a special meeting with Tasmanian Aborigines in Launceston chaired by Grant Maynard from the TRAC, and attended by Elders Alma Stackhouse and Ida West as well as representatives from Cape Barren Island, the premier issued what he called his 'reconciliation document', titled 'Tasmanian Aboriginal people: a step towards full recognition and appreciation'. The premier said:

> Today's statement marks a first step towards achieving full and proper recognition of our Aboriginal people and their heritage and culture. It is not a matter of the Government telling Aboriginal people what they need or want, but beginning a process of genuine dialogue and discussion to determine, in the spirit of goodwill and co-operation, what steps have to be taken to achieve the goal of full recognition and appreciation.

He acknowledged that 'land is obviously a vital issue to Aboriginal people':

> In recognition of this the Government will discuss their interest in specific Crown land sites in various regions of the State with a view to transferring ownership or management of some significant sites to representatives of the Aboriginal community.
>
> The Government believes that there has to be a Tasmanian solution to this particular issue and that neither the land rights legislation which applies in a number of States nor Mabo provide appropriate solutions for Tasmania.[8]

He also announced initiatives to improve educational and cultural awareness of Tasmanian Aboriginal culture, the establishment of an Aboriginal Development Unit in the Department of Premier and Cabinet and the hosting of an Aboriginal forum in 1994 to be attended by representatives of the Aboriginal community and cabinet ministers. He believed the announcement was a 'turning point in Tasmania's history'. He then offered unconditional freehold ownership of up to seven Crown land sites, which could either be granted or sold for a nominal price and would thus avoid the need to get a bill through the Legislative Council.[9] The TAC cautiously welcomed the statement: 'It is a nice gesture which this Government has never done before. It is pleasing to know at last that Mr Groom recognises how our people were here first.'[10]

In April 1994, Tony Fletcher moved in the Legislative Council that it resolve

> to note that in 1991 the Parliament of the Commonwealth unani-
> mously enacted the Council for Aboriginal Reconciliation Act 1991
> to promote a process of reconciliation between the indigenous and
> wider Australian communities; to support the concept of constructive
> reconciliation between indigenous and wider Australian communi-
> ties; and in acknowledgement of this support, to adopt the vision
> of the Council for Aboriginal Reconciliation, namely—'A united
> Australia which respects this land of ours; values the Aboriginal and
> Torres Strait Islander heritage; and provides justice and equity for a
> vision shared by this House'.[11]

In encouraging all members to support the resolution he explained that, as a result of his involvement with the Aboriginal community over the previous twelve months, his understanding 'of the hopes, the aspirations, the goals and the needs of those Tasmanian Aboriginals with whom I have met in recent times' had been improved:

> [Their] greatest desire is the recognition of their heritage and recog-
> nition of their culture, the recognition of their roots—where they
> came from, that they were the first Tasmanians here and that they
> have contributed and have a capacity to continue to contribute in a
> very substantial way to the well-being of Tasmania.[12]

He reminded members that the Council for Aboriginal Reconciliation had stressed the importance of the reconciliation process when it said

|t|hat all political leaders and parties recognise that reconcilia-
tion between the Aboriginal and non-Aboriginal communities in
Australia must be achieved if community division, discord and
injustice to Aboriginal people are to be avoided. To this end, the
Commission recommends that political leaders use their best
endeavours to ensure bipartisan public support for the process of
Reconciliation and that the urgency and necessity of the process be
acknowledged.[13]

The Legislative Council passed the resolution unanimously and set the tone
for the Aboriginal forum hosted by the government on 21 May 1994. The
premier reaffirmed his commitment to meet with the wider Aboriginal
community as the next step and for that occasion would prepare a package
of proposals for the community to consider. It would involve matters of
land, education, heritage and culture, jobs and tourism, and the rewriting of the Aboriginal Relics Act of 1975, all in full consultation with the
Aboriginal community. To mark the occasion and following the request of
the Council for Aboriginal Reconciliation, the Aboriginal flag was flown
for the first time at Parliament House.[14]

   The representatives from twenty Aboriginal organisations who were
present said that they had been alienated from their traditions and that these
rights should be returned. They pointed out that members of the Aboriginal community needed to confer not only with one another but also with
the government in order to determine the process for the return of land.
They also recognised that land claims and compensation must be talked
about in a realistic way, so that the rest of the Tasmanian community would
not be alienated through fear that the whole of the state might be claimed.
The government responded by saying that, while everyone had an association with the land, it recognised that land had special significance to Aborigines and recommended that a working group could develop further the
wide-ranging consultation process. The Aboriginal representatives noted
that a community meeting organised by the Council of Aboriginal Organisations in Tasmania, a loose cluster of old and new Aboriginal groups,
was shortly to be held in Launceston and invited the premier to attend.

He agreed to have specific proposals ready for that meeting, at which it would be decided which Aboriginal people would then negotiate with the government.[15]

Michael Mansell welcomed the premier's plan. He said that a willingness on the part of government to work with rather than against the Aboriginal community was long overdue. 'While it may be too early to judge, positive action following the words could heal wounds which go back two centuries.'[16]

On 31 August the premier and Tony Fletcher met with members of the Aboriginal community in Launceston. Attended by about 300 Aboriginal people, once again the meeting was chaired by Grant Maynard from the TRAC. It elected a seven-member working party to represent the Aboriginal community in its negotiations with the premier about land and other economic issues and was briefed to report back to another Aboriginal community meeting in the following year. The premier told the meeting that the government was looking at transferring management and ownership of particular sites, but emphasised that it did not support land rights legislation as it applied in most other parts of Australia; nor would it grant large tracts of land to Aboriginal people in Tasmania. The particular area of land the government had considered was Oyster Cove, which the premier saw as a test case. There was also the question of to whom the land would be transferred.[17]

Agreement was reached on 17 October 1995 when the premier announced that he would introduce legislation to transfer 3,800 hectares of land to the Tasmanian Aborigines and would be managed by a statutory land council. The land comprised five mutton-bird islands—Babel, Badger, Big Dog, Steep and Chappell—and a small section of Cape Barren Island; three sacred sites—Kuti Kina, Deena Reena and Wargata Mina caves—in the Tasmanian World Heritage Area; and three historic sites at Oyster Cove, Risdon Cove and Mount Cameron West. The premier stressed that this was the government's first and final transfer of land to the Tasmanian Aborigines. 'This is not an open-ended process', he warned. 'We can't go beyond this. This is not land rights in the normal sense.' He did not consider that the transfer of land was a return of land for past appropriation; nor did he think it was appropriate for the government to apologise for the massacres and forced detention of the Tasmanian Aborigines in the nineteenth century.[18]

Michael Mansell knew better. 'The land areas fall short of the lands we had wrongfully taken from us. But this effort was never intended to address the continuing issue of dispossession. The government gesture is symbolic of a change beginning to take root in Tasmania.' Elder Ida West shook hands with the premier. 'I feel very happy', she said. 'Years have gone by to get this.'[19]

The Aboriginal Lands Bill passed both Houses of Parliament in November 1995. A couple of weeks later, on Sunday 10 December, Premier Ray Groom, at a moving ceremony at Risdon Cove, handed back one by one the titles to twelve sacred and cultural sites to Elders in the Aboriginal community. It seemed unimaginable that only three years earlier the TAC had locked horns with the government over the ownership of Risdon Cove. Now the premier was proud to say: 'This is a momentous occasion for Tasmania. It's been a long and difficult struggle . . . it's lasted almost 200 years. It's my view one of the blights of the history of our nation has been the treatment of Aboriginal people right around Australia. This is the step by the Tasmanian Government and the broader community to help rectify some of the hurt. Tasmania will be a better place as a result.'[20]

The land return was greeted with a standing ovation from the 300-strong crowd. Ida West said: 'I hope this is the start of getting back more of our land.' Michael Mansell said it was a great day for the Aboriginal community to reach a place where the rights to land were recognised. He saw it as the first step because he felt that the Aboriginal community would want to see more sites returned. 'As a starting point this is absolutely wonderful. There is a real feeling among the Aboriginal community as I travel around the State, of people wanting to get back to the land and I think there is going to be more and more land handed back.' He gave credit to Tasmania's politicians because they represented the only state in which 'every single party |in the parliament| voted in favour of a law handing land back to the Aboriginal community' and paid tribute to the premier for shepherding the legislation through the parliament.[21]

The legislation established a new elected statutory body, the Aboriginal Land Council of Tasmania, to manage the land that had been returned to the Aboriginal people. But rather than being the final transfer of land, as the premier had stipulated, the legislation opened the door to the next phase of Aboriginal politics in Tasmania. This included the now pressing issue of Aboriginal identity, the return of more land, an apology and compensation to the Stolen Generations and the return of Aboriginal cultural property from museums in Australia and overseas.

21

'Unfinished business', 1996–2010

The passage of the Aboriginal Lands Act of 1995 returned three other issues to the spotlight: Aboriginal identity; an apology and financial compensation to the Stolen Generations; and the repatriation of Aboriginal property from museums. They in turn informed the debate for the return of Wybalenna and Cape Barren Island to Aboriginal ownership. By 2010 the resolution of these issues had ramifications for the rest of Aboriginal Australia.

The vexed issue of Aboriginal identity had surfaced in Tasmania in 1990 when ATSIC held the first election for the TRAC. The TAC had questioned the Aboriginal identity of some who were elected to the TRAC, but so long as the applicant for inclusion on the ATSIC electoral roll appeared to meet the three criteria established by the ATSIC legislation—self-identification, community recognition and Aboriginal descent—there was no process for objection or exclusion prior to the election. This state of affairs led the TAC to persuade the Groom Liberal government in drafting the Aboriginal Lands Act in 1995 to impose a more rigorous test of evidence of Aboriginal identity for voters seeking inclusion on the roll to elect the Aboriginal Land Council of Tasmania (ALCT). The act stipulated that a person seeking to be included on the roll had to provide specific proof to the Aboriginal Advisory Committee whichwas established under the act, of his or her entitlement as an Aboriginal person according to the three-pronged definition accepted by the Commonwealth.[1]

To clarify the definition of Aboriginality in the ATSIC legislation, in August 1997 two members of the TAC, Edwina Shaw and Joanne James, who had stood for election to the TRAC in October 1996, questioned the

Aboriginal identity of eleven candidates who had stood for election, four of whom had been elected. They petitioned the Federal Court, and the case was heard in Hobart over nine days in August and September 1997, with Justice Ron Merkel presiding. The outcome of the case had Australia-wide ramifications.[2]

The hearing coincided with the report on the Stolen Generations based on the inquiry by the Human Rights and Equal Opportunity Commission, released in April 1997. It found that for most of the twentieth century state and federal government agencies had deliberately removed or 'stolen' Aboriginal children from their parents on a sustained basis and then placed them in institutions or adopted them out to white families. The purpose of 'removal' was to 'make Aboriginal children into white people'. It also found that churches and government agencies had failed to exercise their duty of care and many of the children had been cruelly treated and sexually abused. It recommended that the churches and state and federal parliaments should apologise to the 'stolen generation' and offer those affected financial compensation for the loss of their Aboriginal identity.[3]

The report shocked all Tasmanians, largely because most of the Aboriginal children in Tasmania had been 'stolen' within living memory; that is, between 1935 and 1980. Elder Ida West said that 'it is important to say sorry to them because what happened was so terrible'. Indeed it was. To the great credit of Tasmania's parliamentarians, they moved quickly to issue an apology, and on 13 August 1997 the Tasmanian Parliament was the first in Australia to make a public apology to the Stolen Generations.

To mark the occasion, the House of Assembly invited a survivor of the Stolen Generations, Annette Peardon, to address its members from the Bar of the House. She was the first member of the public to address the House in more than 100 years.

> The policy of removal of Aboriginal children from their people was born out of ignorance, ignorance for the basic human rights of Aboriginal children to be raised by their people. It was a policy of genocide, make no bones about it. The policy was deliberate and calculated to make Aborigines like white people. To make us ashamed of who we are. To deny our heritage and our families.

> That we stand before you today as the proudest of Aborigines you
> have ever seen or heard is evidence the genocide policy could not
> work. Today's response by this Parliament is a sign of community
> maturity of the State of Tasmania facing up to the responsibilities
> of harm caused to Aborigines by official policy instead of hiding
> behind notions of popular history . . . Surely some form of compen-
> sation is not too much to ask.[4]

In this optimistic environment the Federal Court case was heard in Hobart.[5]
The onus was on the petitioners to prove that the respondents did not fulfil
the three-pronged criteria of Aboriginality. Justice Merkel admitted that
the legislation which had established ATSIC had given 'little guidance as to
how to resolve the difficulties of proof' of Aboriginal identity or in 'tracing
descent and establishing identification'. In view of the gravity of the case
he decided to apply the Briginshaw standard of proof for the petitioners to
establish that a particular respondent was not an Aboriginal person. This
required that the court should not make a finding lightly on the balance
of probabilities but rather on more conclusive evidence produced by the
petitioners, such as deliberate false statements and/or the presentation of
falsified documents by the respondents.

The petitioners based their case on two arguments: descent and
communal recognition. In relation to the first, they argued that in view of
the small number of Aboriginal people and their families who had survived
the Black War in Tasmania it could readily be established who their
descendants were today. Therefore, in order to claim Aboriginal ancestry
in Tasmania, a person had to prove their descent from this defined group of
people. In the second case they argued that, since the TAC was the longest
standing Aboriginal organisation in Tasmania and had occupied a central
role in Tasmanian Aboriginal affairs, 'recognition of an individual as an
Aboriginal person by the TAC and those associated with it, was an important element of communal identification'.[6]

The respondents disputed the argument about Aboriginal descent on
two grounds. Some believed they were descended from Aboriginal people
from the Australian mainland; and others believed that they were descended

from Tasmanian Aboriginal women who bore children on the Tasmanian mainland in the nineteenth century and who had never appeared in the historical record. In this case absence of evidence was not evidence of absence. In relation to communal recognition, the respondents argued that there was more than one Aboriginal 'community' in Tasmania, not just the TAC.

Justice Merkel agreed that in relation to descent the respondents lacked substantive evidence but said that, since this case was an adversarial civil proceeding, the burden of proof lay with the petitioners to prove, according to the Briginshaw test, that the respondents' evidence was either false or clearly did not lead to Aboriginal ancestry. He determined that if a person did not have some Aboriginal descent then the person could not be an Aboriginal person but that evidence of self-identification and communal recognition could be probative of descent if no other record were available. This meant that Justice Merkel also accepted the respondents' argument that there was more than one Aboriginal 'community' in Tasmania and that the opinions of an individual person about another's Aboriginal identity were often based on subjective personal, social and political views and consequently varied from person to person. He preferred to rely on 'general community recognition, or recognition by a section of the community, rather than to a defined community'.[7]

In his judgment, delivered in April 1998, Justice Merkel determined that in all but two instances he was not persuaded that the petitioners had established that the respondents were not of Aboriginal descent. More importantly he considered that Aboriginal identity should be determined by 'independently constituted bodies or tribunals which are representative of Aboriginal people'.[8]

The fact that Justice Merkel had found that two of the respondents had no Aboriginal descent was vindication of the TAC's view that ATSIC had encouraged individuals with no historical connections to or experiences as Aboriginal people to claim Aboriginal identity in order to qualify for benefits to which the TAC believed they were not entitled. Michael Mansell predicted a jump in the number of people claiming Aboriginality.[9] A year later the *Sunday Tasmanian* noted the dramatic increase of more than 50 per cent in the number of people in Tasmania who identified as Aboriginal. In the 1991 census 8,948 had identified as Aboriginal, and in the 1996 census 13,873 had done so. The TAC said that it acknowledged only about 6,000 of them.[10] And there the matter rested until 2001.

In October 1997 a delegation of Tasmanian Aborigines comprising Laurie Lowery, Jeanette James and Caroline Spotswood had travelled to Europe to lobby museums and government officials for the repatriation of Aboriginal remains and property. At a seminar in London in early November, Spotswood named eleven European museums that had 'refused point-blank' to return Aboriginal remains and artefacts. She warned the UK museums that it was immoral for them to cling to artefacts plundered from the world's indigenous peoples:

> British museums can stand their ground as the last stronghold of imperialism or take account of a changed world and the place in it of indigenous peoples. Has cutting up people after they're dead and putting their body parts on display to strangers really enlightened and brought enjoyment to your people? And yet the reason our people were so treated was to enable 'accredited scholars' to study them, because we were 'ignorant savages'.[11]

At this stage, however, none of the UK museums was prepared to return the Tasmanian Aboriginal material to Tasmania.

The election of the Bacon Labor government early in October 1998 signalled another stage in the TAC's longstanding campaign for the return of more land.[12] The new premier decided immediately to advance what he called the 'unfinished business' of the Aboriginal Land Act of 1995, the return of Wybalenna Historic Site to the Aboriginal community. On 28 February 1999, in a brief ceremony at Wybalenna attended by about sixty Elders and members of the Flinders Island Aboriginal community, he announced his intention to transfer ownership of the site to the ALCT so that it could be managed by the Flinders Island Aboriginal Association. Elder Ida West drew attention to the many Aboriginal people who had died there between 1832 and 1847 and said that it had been a 'concentration camp'. 'This has put to rest the ghosts', she said. 'I never thought it would happen. It was like waiting for ships to come home that never came, but now they have. It is good for black and white people. No one is blaming anyone. All this was done many years ago. We have to go to bad places to try to heal, and you must do the healing, and it takes all colours to do it.'[13]

Premier Bacon went further: 'What happened at Wybalenna should never have occurred. It was the site of attempted genocide. You can't change history but you can address past injustices and our governments are direct descendants of the colonial governments of the 1830s.' It was fitting, he said, that Wybalenna was returned to the Aboriginal community because the first petition calling for recognition of Aboriginal land rights, sent to Queen Victoria in 1846, was from Wybalenna. He also acknowledged that his government had a responsibility to do what it could to rectify past injustices.[14] In March the legislation to transfer ownership of the Wybalenna site was passed unanimously by both Houses of the Tasmanian Parliament.

Encouraged by the strong cross-party support, the premier established a Working Party on Aboriginal Land and Cultural Issues, to negotiate with the Aboriginal community for the return of further parcels of land to Aboriginal people.[15] By October it had prepared a package for the 'Tasmanian Aboriginal community ... to regain control of eight culturally significant parcels of land'. The package comprised 52,800 hectares of land including the transfer of Crown land on Cape Barren, Clarke, Vansittart, Goose and Little Dog islands, and Aboriginal sites on the west coast at West Point, Sundown Point and Trial Harbour.[16] The opposition leader, Sue Napier, said that, while it was pleasing that there had been proper consultation with the Aboriginal community, there had been no consultation with the rest of the Tasmanian community. She had considered that the land transfers of 1995 would be all the land transferred to the Aboriginal community and that the transfer of Wybalenna earlier in the year had been the end point.[17]

By the end of 1999 the legislation had stalled in the Legislative Council. In the hiatus the premier was forced to agree to a committee of inquiry into the land package. It received more than 100 submissions, most of which opposed the legislation, and its report, handed down in early July 2000, rejected the land package. It agreed that the return of land was fundamental to a successful reconciliation process, supported the issue of Aboriginality to be determined by the Aboriginal community, supported Aboriginal control of Aboriginal burials and cremations, supported funding to assist environmental management of land previously transferred to the ALCT and supported indigenous centres of cultural excellence to assist wider community education. But it rejected the Bacon government's proposal for the return of land and wanted new criteria for land claims to be developed so that all future land claims could be addressed outside the political arena. The Labor leader in the Legislative Council, Michael Aird, said that the committee had attempted to develop a 'white model' of land transfer and had rejected the clear criteria which had been used to identify the eight parcels of land for transfer. At that stage the premier looked as if he was about to concede defeat.[18]

But he reintroduced the legislation into the House of Assembly and it was passed on 29 August. Then, in an attempt to generate wider community support, he adjourned the debate in the Legislative Council until later in the year. Support came from the leading newspapers in Hobart and Launceston, the Catholic and Anglican bishops, the Uniting Church and the lord mayor of Hobart. But it was not enough to convince the Legislative Council, which rejected the bill on 15 March 2001 by eight votes to six. Elder Ida West said the actions of the eight legislative councillors who voted against the hand-back of land had hurt her and her people. 'I will be going to Risdon Cove to bow my head in prayer and light a candle.'[19]

Debate now returned to the unresolved issue of Aboriginal identity. In August 2001, Marianne Watson appealed to the Supreme Court of Tasmania over the decision made by the chief electoral officer of Tasmania to exclude her from the electors roll for the ALCT. She had been originally excluded on the grounds that she did not produce sufficient evidence of Aboriginal descent, and when she lodged an objection to the decision the officer had referred it to the Aboriginal Advisory Committee for consideration. The committee had advised unanimously that the appellant did not meet the three criteria for inclusion in the electors roll.

In this case, heard before Chief Justice William Cox, Watson had to prove to the court that she was of Aboriginal descent. To this end she tendered photographic evidence of her ancestry which had been accepted by some Aboriginal Elders in Tasmania. The chief justice was satisfied that the appellant 'genuinely believes in her Aboriginality and in her frustration at being unable to establish it from records, many of which are incomplete and inconsistent, has followed a number of trails which have proved unproductive. I do not consider any criticism of her is warranted by the pursuit of different lines of research.' But he concluded that she had not established that she was entitled to be enrolled on the ALCT electors roll and dismissed the appeal.[20]

The decision opened the door for ATSIC to employ a more rigorous process for its regional council elections. At the end of 2001, under a review of the system for electing representatives to the TRAC, ATSIC decided to establish a trial electoral roll for the next round of elections, in November 2002. Where objections were raised to applicants for inclusion on the roll, an Independent Indigenous Advisory Committee would determine the question of eligibility based upon the Commonwealth criteria set out in the Federal Court case in 1998. ATSIC officers were hopeful that if the process succeeded it could become the blueprint for the compilation of indigenous electoral rolls for ATSIC regional councils in other parts of Australia.

Early in 2002, ATSIC advertised across Tasmania for applications from Aboriginal people to be included in a provisional roll. The list of applicants, 1,298 in all, was then published by the Australian Electoral Commission. ATSIC invited the Aboriginal community to lodge objections to individual names on the provisional roll. Objections were made to 1,158 names. The Independent Indigenous Advisory Committee, chaired by Clyde Mansell and comprising eight other members, Sharon Dennis, Leonie Dickson, Graeme Gardner, Ted Gower, Greg Lehman, Lennah Newsome, Rachel Quillerat and Ila Purdon, met in August 2002 and concluded that 480 persons whose applications had been objected to were Aboriginal persons, and they were enrolled. The committee then notified the other 678 applicants against whom objections had been lodged and invited them to make a submission in relation to the objection. Only 444 applicants, largely comprising members of six family groups, did submit evidence. But after consideration the committee accepted the original objections and so they were not recommended for inclusion on the final roll. In response 130 of them applied to the Administrative Appeals Tribunal for a review of the advisory committee's decision. The appeal was heard in Hobart on 20 September 2002, and the tribunal handed down its decision on 18 October, in time for the ATSIC Regional Council election in November.[21]

After hearing evidence from sixty-six witnesses the tribunal concluded that the 'really probative evidence of Aboriginal descent was the oral histories and traditions and not the archival material ... The credible family evidence we listened to day after day could not all be wrong. Indeed, it could not even mostly be wrong. In the end we decided that very little of it was wrong.'[22] In this regard the tribunal found that there was 'no requirement to find any actual line of descent nor to identify any full blood aborigine from whom the descent is traced'.[23]

Yet, as Michael Mansell later pointed out, four families of the applicants before the tribunal were clearly descended from convicts and at least two others were descended from free settlers in other Australian states.[24] At least two other families claimed descent from 'lost' Tasmanian Aboriginal tribes which the tribunal readily conceded had never existed.[25] Further, the tribunal's ruling indicated that it did not support Justice Merkel's suggestion that a body like the Independent Indigenous Advisory Committee should determine Aboriginal identity and so left unresolved ATSIC's problem of putting a process in place whereby Aboriginal people could determine who was an Aboriginal person.

At the ATSIC Regional Council elections held a month later, only 416 of the 750 people who were included on the trial electoral roll turned out to vote, about half the number who had voted in the 1999 elections. Even so, at least two people whose Aboriginality had been contested and who had successfully appealed to the tribunal were elected to the TRAC.[26] And there the matter rested until 2005. By then ATSIC had been abolished along with the TRAC. The issue of Aboriginal identity in relation to eligibility to vote for a statutory body was now an issue for the states, and Tasmania once again became the venue to resolve it.

On 8 September 2003, Elder Ida West died at the age of eighty-three. At a virtual state funeral held three days later at St David's Cathedral in Hobart she was farewelled by a congregation of more than 800 people. In an outpouring of public grief, the premier, the leader of the opposition and the Greens, the media, the TAC and the Anglican and Catholic bishops acknowledged her pivotal role in promoting reconciliation.[27] Indeed, Ida had personified Aboriginal reconciliation in Tasmania and her particular campaign to 'heal the wounds of the past'. Born in 1919 and raised on Flinders Island, she had led what Michael Mansell called a 'traditional life' of an Islander until she married at the outbreak of World War II and moved to Launceston, where she confronted racism from the white community. Later, in Hobart, she raised her family as a sole parent and gradually became more active in Aboriginal affairs. She was widely respected by all sides of politics and the wider community. In her last years she had become a Member of the Order of Australia and in 2002 was appointed ATSIC Aboriginal woman of the year. She had worked tirelessly for the return of Wybalenna to Aboriginal ownership and had regretted that Prime Minister John Howard had not apologised to the Stolen Generations. At her death she was probably the best known Aboriginal woman in Tasmania. Seven months later, in April 2004, her ashes were scattered at an Aboriginal site on Flinders Island, where a 'Healing Garden' was dedicated to her memory. It was a fitting memorial to a remarkable woman.[28]

A month later, on 3 May 2004, hundreds of Tasmanian Aborigines, politicians from all sides of politics, other dignitaries and supporters gathered at Risdon Cove on a cold and windy autumn day to honour the victims of the massacre 200 years earlier. Michael Mansell told the gathering:

> When the white invaders started killing us off on this day two hundred years ago, they also started killing our culture, our languages, our intimate knowledge of our lands, our child raising practices, our family connections, our trade routes, our economy, and every other aspect of our traditional way of living in this land for thousands of generations . . . But our presence here today shows that they have not succeeded in their attempts to destroy us as a people . . . [and] the presence here today of white supporters and friends also shows that we are now not alone in our right to keep us strong as a distinct people with our special rights as the original owners of

this land. More needs to be done though. We cannot go on with the piecemeal approach to the effects of our dispossession. They give us back a few parcels of land; they fund a cultural program here and there; they give us some money to provide a few services that they can't provide themselves. Then, as we've seen very recently, they take it all back again. That's not good enough any more.[29]

It was clear that the major issue remained the return of land. Following the re-election of the Bacon Labor government in July 2002 the TAC and the ALCT believed that the premier now had a mandate to proceed with the legislation.[30] But, in February 2004, Premier Bacon was diagnosed with lung cancer and he died in June of the same year. At his funeral the TAC acknowledged his commitment to the return of Aboriginal land. In October the new premier Paul Lennon tabled a bill to return more than 50,000 hectares of Crown land on Cape Barren, Clarke and Goose islands to the Aboriginal community. As in 2000 the bill faced a hostile Legislative Council. But this time the premier was prepared to flex his financial muscle to ensure its successful passage.[31]

When the bill reached the Legislative Council in March 2005 the premier had removed Goose Island from the land package and had guaranteed the Flinders Council up to $2 million for infrastructure to ensure any land changeover was cost neutral. These measures effectively undermined earlier opposition to the bill.[32] Nevertheless, support for the measure remained on a knife edge until one of the members of the Legislative Council, Paul Harriss, who had openly acknowledged his Aboriginal heritage but had opposed the bill because he saw it as a TAC plot, had a last-minute change of heart. The bill was passed in the Legislative Council late in the evening of 23 March 2005 amid scenes of jubilation. It was the first time in Tasmania that land currently occupied by Aboriginal people had been returned to them.[33]

Clyde Mansell, chair of the ALCT, said that the legislation had 'moved Aboriginal affairs 20 years in advance of the rest of Australia'. Premier Paul Lennon recognised that it was a defining moment in Tasmania's history, and the *Mercury* acknowledged that the Legislative Council's decision to pass the bill 'recognises that for at least 40,000 years the Aboriginal people

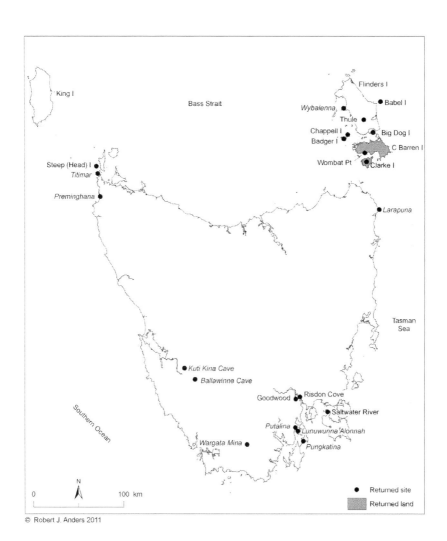

Map 35 Land returned to Tasmanian Aborigines, 2010

were owners of Tasmania. And that over the past two centuries their land was taken from them and their way of life placed under constant threat.'[34]

Six weeks later, on 10 May 2005, a grey, windswept day with rain squalls hurling across Cape Barren Island, an elated and excited crowd of about 200 people gathered at the Corner to watch the government officially return the land to the Cape Barren Island Aboriginal community. Proceedings began with a cleansing ceremony. Then the governor of Tasmania, William Cox, handed over the land titles to Denise Gardner, president of the Cape Barren Island Aboriginal Association.[35]

Once again, Premier Paul Lennon captured the moment: 'I've waited a long time to say I acknowledge the Aboriginal land on which I am standing and thank the Aboriginal people for asking me to speak today. This day is beyond any other in my life to date. It makes me proud to be Tasmanian.' Denise Gardner responded: 'We really do walk on our land now.'[36] Michael Mansell underlined the significance of the occasion:

> It isn't just the culmination of 30 years' struggle which started when we were just kids and walked in the streets and marched for land rights. Our tribal elders were rounded up in Tasmania and either imprisoned on Flinders Island and then taken to Oyster Cove and imprisoned until they were dead. The only way that our ancestors could preserve the future was to come to places like Cape Barren Island to survive.[37]

He reminded the crowd that the 1950s government policy of removal had decimated the island community. 'They took the kids to Launceston, Hobart and Burnie, but we took Cape Barren with us.' The Aboriginal people's struggle to own their own land, he said, had finally succeeded when Tasmania had a government with compassion and understanding which stood 'not against us but alongside us'.[38]

Three other items of unfinished business now remained: the issue of Aboriginal identity; the return of Aboriginal remains from overseas museums; and compensation for survivors of the Stolen Generations. Following the abolition of ATSIC in 2004, concerns had been raised about

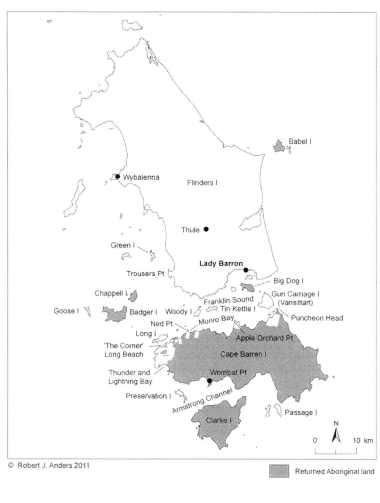

© Robert J. Anders 2011

Returned Aboriginal land

Map 36 Land returned to Tasmanian Aborigines, eastern Bass Strait, 1984–2005

the legal status of the Administrative Appeals Tribunal's decision of 2002 about how to determine the eligibility of people who claimed Aboriginal descent for inclusion on the electoral roll for the ALCT. In the legal hiatus elections to the council, which was a state body, had been deferred until amendments were made to the Aboriginal Lands Act. In June 2005 the Tasmanian House of Assembly passed the amendments, but, as predicted, they struck trouble in the Legislative Council. There, the leader of the government, Michael Aird, explained to the members that the proposed amendments had three purposes: to eliminate the need for reliance on the definition of Aboriginality arising from the uncertain status of the now defunct ATSIC act, to clarify and strengthen the process of onus of proof in relation to the three-part test of Aboriginality and to create a permanent electoral roll for the ALCT which would be maintained by Tasmania's chief electoral officer.

The Legislative Council members quickly realised that the chief electoral officer, rather than the Aboriginal communities, had been given extraordinary powers to determine Aboriginality for election to the ALCT. While this did not please the TAC or any other Aboriginal group in Tasmania, it was widely seen by the Legislative Council and the press as the best way to resolve the issue. The bill was passed on 16 June 2005.[39]

The chief electoral officer now called for nominations for inclusion on the electoral roll for the ALCT election projected for October 2005. But the disputed claimants had one last card to play. In 2007 they lodged an appeal in the Supreme Court arguing that the chief electoral officer had ignored the guidelines under the act in not properly implementing the process of determining Aboriginality for inclusion on the roll. The case was heard in the Tasmanian Supreme Court before Mr Justice Blow. He ruled on 8 November that every applicant for inclusion on the roll had to provide proof that they were an Aboriginal person as defined under the Aboriginal Lands Act.[40] The chief electoral officer completed the permanent electoral roll early in 2009, and the ALCT election was completed in June.[41] Today, the Tasmanian government imposes strict criteria for eligibility as an Aboriginal person for its programs and services and for membership and representation on Tasmanian government committees and boards.[42]

In the midst of the legal battle over Aboriginality, the TAC pursued the repatriation of Aboriginal cultural property from Australian and overseas museums. In 2001, UK Prime Minister Tony Blair had established a twelve-member Working Group on Indigenous Remains to identify collections in UK museums, address issues of their repatriation and recommend whether legislation was needed to allow museums that were constrained by laws to return indigenous remains to communities in Australia, New Zealand, North America and Africa.[43] The TAC sent a submission to the working group outlining its belief that three public museums in the UK held Tasmanian remains in their collections which should be repatriated unconditionally and that future UK legislation should mandate the compulsory repatriation of other indigenous human remains. In December 2001, Rodney Dillon, ATSIC commissioner for Tasmania, went to London to address the working group and nearly fell on the floor when he found that, contrary to widespread public belief, the Royal College of Surgeons still held the skulls of three Tasmanian Aborigines and the hair, jawbones, arm and leg bones of seven others wrapped in sinew and thread. The college also revealed that it held a slide with samples of the skin and hair of Truganini. Dillon later said, 'I couldn't speak. My tongue swelled up. We felt very close to Truganini because we have talked about her all our lives. We've grown up with her.'[44] The rumours of body mutilation following Truganini's death in 1876 had finally been confirmed.

Having admitted that the college held such items, its president, Sir Peter Morris, agreed to negotiate with the TAC for the repatriation of the Tasmanian remains in the coming year.[45] Dillon had already invited the working group chair, Professor Norman Palmer, to visit Tasmania to see for himself the places from which the remains had been stolen and to understand the grief that the Tasmanian Aboriginal community felt about the theft of their ancestors' body parts and why they wanted them returned for proper burial. Palmer arrived in Hobart in mid February 2002, and Dillon and TAC members took him to burial sites on Bruny Island, Oyster Cove and Risdon Cove. Although Palmer appeared to be sympathetic to their case, he said there were differences of opinion within the working group. He then invited a delegation from the TAC, which was planning a repatriation trip to London in May to collect the Tasmanian material from the Royal College of Surgeons, to make a personal presentation to the working group about the return of Tasmanian remains from public museums.[46] When Tony Brown and Jeanette James appeared before the working group in May 2002, they were told that the British public needed a lot more education to better understand Aboriginal issues and that the group would like to see cultural exchanges between museums and Aboriginal communities.[47]

Brown and James returned to Hobart on 14 June with the Tasmanian Aboriginal remains from the Royal College of Surgeons and were joined by Jay McDonald, Rose Smith and Caroline Spotswood, who had flown in from Melbourne with seven Tasmanian Aboriginal skulls and the top half of an eighth skull from Museum Victoria. Most of this latter collection had come to the museum from Dr Story, who had lived at Kelvedon near Swansea on Tasmania's east coast; the items had possibly originally been taken from a massacre site nearby.[48] The remains were taken with a police escort to Oyster Cove for a traditional ceremony to settle the spirits of the dead. Michael Mansell acknowledged that the campaign to return Aboriginal remains to Tasmania had received widespread support from the white community and from politicians of all parties, in particular the prime minister of Australia, John Howard, and his counterpart in the UK, Tony Blair, which was much appreciated by the Aboriginal community. 'I sincerely believe', he said, 'that the tide of attitudes in Tasmania is changing'.[49]

The working group's report of September 2002 recommended the repatriation of Tasmanian Aboriginal remains after DNA sampling. But some of the museums were still not ready to acknowledge the new political environment. A year later, Rodney Dillon led a delegation of Aboriginal people from across Australia to London to receive Aboriginal remains from two museums and to speak to other institutions about repatriating their collections of Aboriginal remains. But they got nowhere. Dillon found that the Museum of Natural History held the skin, organs and bones from 450 Aboriginal people 'harvested' in Australia between 1860 and 1930. Some had been excavated from graves that pre-dated British invasion; others were the remains of individuals who had been hunted down and murdered during a period when Aborigines had been regarded as less than human;

and still other remains had been dug up in the colonial period in order to conduct experiments, such as filling Truganini's skull with lead to 'prove' her lesser brain capacity. Dillon told the media that it was 'important for the spirits of our people to pass into the spirit world and they can't do that in the UK'.[50]

Following UK legislation in 2004 which forced public museums to repatriate human remains after DNA sampling, TAC delegates Leah Brown and Adam Thompson went to London in September 2006 to collect two burial bundles from the British Museum. While many UK museums have since repatriated more Aboriginal property, the campaign to repatriate Tasmanian Aboriginal property from museums in other parts of Europe continues. In July 2009 the Australian prime minister, Kevin Rudd, signed a memorandum of understanding with his Italian counterpart, Silvio Berlusconi, to repatriate Aboriginal remains from Italian museums and medical colleges.[51]

Since 1985 several hundred items of Tasmanian Aboriginal material have been located in museums in Australia and overseas, although not all have been repatriated to the Aboriginal community in Tasmania. As trophies of scientific racism these items remain highly prized in public and private collections worldwide. Sadly, the practice of cultural 'harvesting' continues. In March 2008 a petroglyph was illegally excised from an Aboriginal site in western Tasmania and probably sold to an international collector.[52]

The final item of unfinished business was financial compensation for the Stolen Generations. On 22 November 2006, Premier Paul Lennon introduced the Stolen Generations of Aboriginal Children Bill to the Tasmanian House of Assembly. It set aside $5 million for the compensation of 150 surviving members of the Tasmanian Stolen Generations from the period 1935 to 1975 with sums of between $25,000 and $40,000 each. About eighty children of the Stolen Generations victims were eligible for a payment of $5,000 each, or a maximum family package of $20,000.[53] Like the apology made by the Tasmanian Parliament to the Stolen Generations nearly a decade before, the Stolen Generations of Aboriginal Children Bill broke new ground. It was the first legislation in Australia to offer Stolen Generations victims and their families some form of financial recompense. A week later it was passed unanimously by both Houses of the Tasmanian Parliament.[54]

The Tasmanian Parliament also broke new ground in another important gesture of reconciliation. Annette Peardon, who had addressed the House of Assembly from the Bar of the House during the debate on the apology in August 1996, and her brother, Eddie Thomas, were invited to be the first citizens in Tasmania to address members of parliament from the Floor of the House. The significance was acknowledged by Annette Peardon.

> Ya pulingina palawa ... The stolen generation has been a national tragedy that has stained this country. I appreciate the work of the Tasmanian Government in taking a step forward to acknowledge the wrongs of the past. The time has come for ... other government leaders around Australia to follow the footsteps of the Tasmanian Government. We thank the Tasmanian Parliament for the first return of our lands in 1995; the apology for the stolen generation in 1997; the return of land in our home country, Cape Barren Island in 2005; and now the Stolen Generations of Aboriginal Children Bill.[55]

Michael Mansell had the last word: 'The payment of compensation', he said, 'closes the chapter on this sad part of Tasmanian history.'

In a significant gesture of bipartisanship, Premier Paul Lennon appointed Ray Groom, the former Liberal premier, who had initiated the Aboriginal Lands Act in 1995, as the Stolen Generations assessor. In his report, published in February 2008, Groom noted that a total of 151 claims were received, from which 106 were determined eligible to receive an ex gratia payment.[56]

In 2009, the TAC celebrated thirty-five years of operation, making it one of the longest serving and certainly one of the most prominent and influential Aboriginal organisations in Australia. In little more than a generation it has overturned the way all Tasmanians understand their history and their relationship to it. Michael Mansell was there at the TAC's beginning and is still there today. He has survived many changes of federal and state governments and is now considered one of Tasmania's elder statesmen. He is joined by a distinguished group of Aboriginal activists who have firmly embedded the Tasmanian Aborigines into wider Tasmanian cultural and political life.

Epilogue

In 2009, an archaeological survey of the Brighton region, on the north-western outskirts of Hobart, rediscovered an Aboriginal occupation site which preliminary dating indicated was 40,000 years old.[1] If the dating is verified then the site will become the oldest of known Aboriginal occupation of Tasmania. However, the site, now known as the Jordan River Levee, lies in the path of a proposed highway bypass. The TAC quickly realised the site's immense significance and, in order to preserve it, lobbied the Tasmanian government to re-route the bypass.[2] Following the government's delay in considering the request, the TAC then occupied the site to draw international attention to its significance. Two of their best known activists, Jim Everett and Michael Mansell, were arrested and charged with trespass.[3] Another TAC member, Aaron Everett, has since pointed out that the entire bypass route, which traverses the Jordan River valley, the heartland of the Black War in the 1820s, crosses massacre sites and other sites of major Aboriginal significance.[4]

Archaeologist Sandra Bowdler, who carried out important fieldwork on Aboriginal sites in Tasmania in the 1970s and 1980s, also considers that the site is of extraordinary significance to Tasmanian Aborigines. She argues that it not only provides unique insights about Aboriginal occupation of the region and 'represents evidence for human occupation during the Pleistocene ("Ice Age") in an area that previously lacked such evidence'; it also 'adds considerably to our understanding of the earliest occupation of

Tasmania and the range of adaptations made by human communities in colonising Tasmania'.[5]

Further, the site 'indicates an archaeologically instantaneous colonisation of Australia' by Aboriginal people. It not only matches the dates of c.41,000 BP for 'the oldest evidence of human occupation' in the north-west Kimberley area and the south-west of Western Australia, the Cape York area of Queensland and Lake Mungo in western New South Wales, but it also 'represents the southernmost extension of the early Aboriginal colonists of Australia, and demonstrates their ability to adapt with rapidity to a wide range of environmental situations'.[6]

Finally, Bowdler considers that in global terms the site is significant in adding to our current understanding of human evolution, which indicates that modern humans appeared in Africa between 200,000 and 100,000 years ago. If we accept that their major dispersal to other parts of the world, including East Asia, Southeast Asia and Australia, took place between 50,000 and 40,000 years ago, then the Jordan River Levee site is critically 'important in documenting the spread of modern humans to their maximum extent in the early phase of dispersal, and highlighting again the range of environments to which modern humans were able to adapt'.[7]

But the site could have even further significance to the Tasmanian Aborigines. If the final report, which the government appears reluctant to release, indicates relatively continuous occupation of the site, then it will be among the areas of longest continuous Aboriginal occupation in Australia. If this is the case, new understandings will emerge of how the Tasmanian Aborigines occupied the Jordan River region from the Pleistocene to the colonial era and how the Big River and Oyster Bay nations, whose countries lie in the region, managed over a long period of time one of the most resource-rich regions in Tasmania. This in turn could lead to a significant upward revision of the estimated population of the Big River and Oyster Bay nations at the moment of British invasion and to a further upward revision of the estimated number that were killed during the Black War in the 1820s.

In view of the site's immense significance, it seems extraordinary that it falls outside the protection of federal and state heritage legislation. The confrontations between the TAC and the Tasmanian government on this important issue indicate that there is still far to go in recognising the Tasmanian Aborigines' right to know about their past and to own the sites which contain information about how their ancestors lived and what happened to them.

Notes

ABBREVIATIONS

ALCT	Aboriginal Land Council of Tasmania
APG	Aboriginal Provisional Government
ATSIC	Aboriginal and Torres Strait Islander Commission
BPP	British Parliamentary Papers
CBS	Cape Barren School
Col. Sec.	Colonial Secretary, Hobart
CSD	Chief Secretary's Department
CSO	Colonial Secretary's Office
CT	*Colonial Times*
ED	Education Department
FM	Flinders Municipality
GI	General Index
GO	Governor's Office
HRA	*Historical Records of Australia*
HTC	*Hobart Town Courier*
HTG	*Hobart Town Gazette*
LSD	Lands and Survey Department
PD	Premier's Department
PRO	Public Record Office, London
ML	Mitchell Library
SLNSW ML	Mitchell Library, State Library of New South Wales
SMH	*Sydney Morning Herald*
TAC	Tasmanian Aboriginal Centre
TAHO	Tasmanian Archive and Heritage Office
TALC	Tasmanian Aboriginal Land Council
Tas	*The Tasmanian*
TPP	Tasmanian Parliamentary Papers
TRAC	Tasmanian Regional Aboriginal Council
U. Tas.	University of Tasmania

PREFACE

1 Ryan, *The Aboriginal Tasmanians*, 1981, 1982.
2 Ryan, *The Aboriginal Tasmanians*, 2nd edn.
3 Wolfe, 'Land, labor and difference', 867.
4 Anderson, 'Re-claiming TRU-GER-NAN-NER'.
5 Penn, *The Forgotten Frontier*; Mann, *George Washington's War on Native America*; Ford, *Settler Sovereignty*.

6   See Brantlinger, *Dark Vanishings*.

7   Brantlinger, *Dark Vanishings*, 18; West, *The History of Tasmania*, 315.

8   Cove, *What the Bones Say*, 44–5.

9   Milligan, 'On the dialects and languages of the Aboriginal tribes of Tasmania', 1859.

10 The term 'scientific racism' was first used by Dennis, 'Social Darwinism'.

11 Bonwick, *The Last of the Tasmanians*; Fenton, *A History of Tasmania*; Turnbull, *Black War*; Robson, *A History of Tasmania*, vol. 1.

12 Davis, 'On the osteology and peculiarities of the Tasmanians'; Calder, *Some Account of the Wars, Extirpation, Habits etc.*; Tyler, 'On the Tasmanian Aborigines as representatives of Paleolithic man'; Walker, *Early Tasmania*; Giblin, *The Early History of Tasmania*, vol. 2; Bryden, *The Story of Tasmanian Aboriginals*; Jones, 'The Tasmanian paradox'; Plomley, *The Tasmanian Aborigines*.

13 In Plomley's *Annotated Bibliography of the Tasmanian Aborigines*, more than 500 scientific papers, published between 1859 and 1965, invoke the scientific racism doctrine to explain the near demise of the Tasmanian Aborigines.

14 Ryan, *The Aboriginal Tasmanians*, 2nd edn, ixx–xx.

15 Windschuttle, *The Fabrication of Aboriginal History*, vol. 1, 386.

16 ibid., 160–2, 364.

17 Coleman, 'The Windschuttle thesis'.

18 Windschuttle, *The Fabrication of Aboriginal History*, vol. 1, 3.

19 See Bernard Lane, 'Orthodox history under the gun', *The Weekend Australian*, 28–29 Dec. 2002; *The Australian*, 11 Jan. 2003; see also editorials in *The Australian*, 14, 28 Dec. 2002.

20 They included Miranda Devine, *SMH*, 19 Dec. 2002; Michael Duffy, *Daily Telegraph* (Sydney), 21 Dec. 2002; Andrew Bolt, *Herald-Sun*, 23 Dec. 2002; P.P. McGuinness and Gerard Henderson, *SMH*, 24 Dec. 2002; Peter Ryan, *The Australian*, 10 Jan. 2003; Janet Albrechtsen, *The Australian*, 7 May 2003; see also 'History wars', *Sunday*, television program, Channel Nine, 24 May 2003.

21 Ryan, 'Who is the fabricator?'.

22 ibid., 254.

23 Inga Clendinnen, 'Dispatches from the history wars', *Australian Financial Review*, 31 Oct. 2003.

24 See report on the High Court decision in *SMH*, 2 July 1983.

25 *Mabo v Queensland (no. 2) ('Mabo Case')* HCA 23; (1992) 175 CLR 1 (3 June 1992).

26 Australian Human Rights and Equal Opportunity Commission, *Bringing Them Home*.

27 John Herron, 'No apology needed', *The Australian*, 27 May 1997.

28 Ron Brunton, 'Time to bury the genocide corpse', *Courier Mail*, 18 Aug. 2001; Paul Sheehan, 'Saved, not stolen: laying the genocide myth to rest', *SMH*, 4 July 2001.

29 *Aboriginal Lands Act 1995*; Parliament of Tasmania, *Hansard*, House of Assembly, 13 Aug. 1997.

30 Reynolds, *Fate of a Free People*, 121–57.

31 See Chapter 21.

32 Boyce, 'Fantasy island'; Breen 'Re-inventing social evolution'.

33 Tardif, 'Risdon Cove'; McFarlane, 'Cape Grim'.

34 Kiernan, *Blood and Soil*, 265–80; Madley, 'From terror to genocide'; McFarlane, *Beyond Awakening*.

35 This includes Boyce, 'Fantasy island'; Tardif, 'Risdon Cove'; McFarlane, 'NJB Plomley's contribution to north-west Tasmanian regional history'; see also Attwood, *Telling the Truth about Aboriginal History*, 106–16.

36 Semelin, 'In consideration of massacres'; Semelin, 'From massacre to the genocidal process'; Semelin, 'Towards a vocabulary of massacre and genocide'.

37 Semelin, 'In consideration of massacres', 383–4.

38   Windschuttle, *The Fabrication of Aboriginal History*, vol. 1, 146–9.

39   Ryan, 'Massacre in Tasmania'.

40   Ryan, 'List of multiple killings of Aborigines in Tasmania'.

41   Ryan, 'Massacre in the Black War in Tasmania', 483; see also Breen, 'Human agency, historical inevitability and moral culpability'.

CHAPTER 1

1   'Report of the Aboriginal Affairs Study Group', 19–20; Plomley, *Friendly Mission*, 514.

2   Lourandos, *Continent of Hunter Gatherers*, 244.

3   ibid., 244–54; Sagona, 'The quest for red gold'.

4   Lourandos, *Continent of Hunter Gatherers*, 255.

5   ibid., 277–80; McFarlane, *Beyond Awakening*, 13–16; Murray and Williamson, 'Archaeology and history', 315–19; Taylor, 'The polemics of eating fish in Tasmania'.

6   Cameron, pers. comm., 17 Dec. 2010.

7   Davies, *Atlas of Tasmania*, 1–5.

8   Pardoe, 'Isolation and evolution in Tasmania', 1.

9   'Report of the Aboriginal Affairs Study Group', 19–20.

10   McFarlane, *Beyond Awakening*, 2.

11   'Report of the Aboriginal Affairs Study Group', 19–20.

12   Taylor, *A Study of the Palawa*, 12–22.

13   ibid.; Pardoe, 'Population genetics and population size in prehistoric Tasmania'.

14   McFarlane, *Beyond Awakening*, 23–4; Taylor, 'The polemics of making fire in Tasmania'; see also Plomley, *Jorgen Jorgenson*, 56.

15   Most of the information in this paragraph and the next, but not the interpretation, has been taken from Plomley, *The Tasmanian Aborigines*, 29–55.

16   ibid.

17   ibid., 29–31.

18   ibid., 32–5; for a description of a large hut in the north-east, see Plomley, *Friendly Mission*, 442; see also McFarlane, *Beyond Awakening*, 24–5; Jeffreys, *Van Diemen's Land*, 129.

19   Jones, 'Tasmanian tribes', 324.

20   Cameron, pers. comm., 8 July 2010.

21   See Plomley, *Jorgen Jorgenson*, 60.

22   Jones, 'Tasmanian tribes', 324–7; Plomley, *Friendly Mission*, 1006–13.

23   Jones, 'Tasmanian tribes', 325.

24   ibid., 325–7; Plomley, *Friendly Mission*, 1006–13.

25   Plomley, *Friendly Mission*, 1006–13; see also Plomley, *Weep in Silence*.

26   Jones, 'Tasmanian tribes', 325, 330.

27   Plomley, *The Tasmanian Aborigines*, 27.

28   Robinson's estimate was first published in 1875 by Calder, *Some Account of the Wars, Extirpations, Habits, etc.*, 17. The estimate of 7,000 in 1815 was made by James Kelly to the Aborigines Committee in 1830; see BPP, 'Van Diemen's Land', 51. The estimate of 10,000 was made by settler William Williamson in 1820; see Boyce, *Van Diemen's Land*, 99.

29   Jones, 'Tasmanian tribes', 329; Pardoe, 'Isolation and evolution in Tasmania', 1; Lourandos, *Continent of Hunter Gatherers*, 280; see also Murray and Williamson, 'Archaeology and history', 314–15.

30   Plomley, *Friendly Mission*, 1003; for a discussion of 'nation' and 'tribe' in the colonial period, see

Napier, *Colonization Particularly in Southern Australia*, 146; for a recent discussion of the use of the terms 'band', 'tribe' and 'nation' in Aboriginal Tasmania, see McFarlane, *Beyond Awakening*, 8; Blackburn, 'Imagining Aboriginal nations'.

31   Jones, 'Tasmanian tribes', 328.

32   ibid., 328–9.

33   ibid., 331–52; Plomley, *Friendly Mission*, 1006–13; Taylor, *A Study of the Palawa*.

34   Jones, 'Tasmanian tribes', 338–9; Brown, *Aboriginal Archaeological Sites in Eastern Tasmania*, 75–80; Duyker, *An Officer of the Blue*, 133–4; Plomley, *Friendly Mission*, 1006–13; Taylor, *A Study of the Palawa*, 347–53.

35   Jones, 'Tasmanian tribes', 339–40; Brown, *Aboriginal Archaeological Sites in Eastern Tasmania*, 75–80; Duyker, *An Officer of the Blue*, 133–4.

36   Jones, 'Tasmanian tribes', 340.

37   ibid., 351; Kee, *Aboriginal Archaeological Sites in North East Tasmania*; Plomley, *Friendly Mission*, 1006–13; Taylor, *A Study of the Palawa*, 139–46; Cameron, *Grease and Ochre*, 17, 130.

38   Jones, 'Tasmanian tribes', 351–2.

39   ibid., 352.

40   ibid., 343–4; Plomley, *Friendly Mission*, 1006–13; Taylor, *A Study of the Palawa*, 111–37, 156–9; Dunnett, *A Survey and Assessment of Aboriginal Archaeological Sites*, 1–6; Breen, *Contested Places*, 22–31.

41   Jones, 'Tasmanian tribes', 344–6; Breen, *Contested Places*, 22–31.

42   ibid., 341; Plomley, *Friendly Mission*, 1006–13; Taylor, *A Study of the Palawa*, 156–9; Cosgrove, *Aboriginal Economy and Settlement*, 43–4.

43   Jones, 'Tasmanian tribes', 342–3.

44   ibid., 348; Plomley, *Friendly Mission*, 1006–13; Taylor, *A Study of the Palawa*, 159; Ryan, 'List of multiple killings of Aborigines in Tasmania'; Kee, *Midlands Aboriginal Archaeological Site Survey*, 37.

45   Jones, 'Tasmanian tribes', 348–9.

46   ibid., 349.

47   ibid., 350; Plomley, *Friendly Mission*, 1006–13; Taylor, *A Study of the Palawa*, 39.

48   Jones, 'Tasmanian tribes', 332; Plomley, *Friendly Mission*, 1006–13; Taylor, *A Study of the Palawa*, 111; Stockton, 'The prehistoric population of northwest Tasmania'; Macfarlane, *A Regional Survey of Archaeological Sites*, 2–5.

49   Jones, 'Tasmanian tribes', 334–5.

50   ibid., 335; Plomley, *Friendly Mission*, 1006–13; Taylor, *A Study of the Palawa*, 111; Vanderwal and Horton, *Coastal Southwest Tasmania*, 43–50.

51   Jones, 'Tasmanian tribes', 335–6.

52   ibid., 336–7; Plomley, *Friendly Mission*, 1006–13; Taylor, *A Study of the Palawa*, 107–10.

53   Jones, 'Tasmanian tribes', 336–7.

54   Murray and Williamson, 'Archaeology and history', 319; Windschuttle, *The Fabrication of Aboriginal History*, vol. 1, 386; Taylor, 'The polemics of making fire in Tasmania'; Taylor, 'The polemics of eating fish in Tasmania'; Lourandos, *Continent of Hunter Gatherers*, 280.

CHAPTER 2

1   For Tasmanian Aboriginal perceptions of ships as large white birds and the British invaders as Wrageowrapper, see Plomley, *Friendly Mission*, 408.

2   *HRA*, series I, vol. iv, 152–4.

3   *HRA*, series III, vol. i, 198, 221.

4   *HRA*, series I, vol. iv, 61.

5   *HRA*, series III, vol. i, 664.

6   Vattel, *Law of Nations*, 88–9; Benton, *Law and Colonial Cultures*, 168; Banner, *Possessing the Pacific*, 15.

7   Ford, *Settler Sovereignty*, 97–102; King, 'In the Beginning . . .', 55–61.

8   Standfield, '"These unoffending people"'.

9   *HRA*, series I, vol. v, 502–4.

10 Kercher, *An Unruly Child*, 16–17.

11 PRO CO 201/35.

12 *HRA*, series III, vol. i, 198.

13 West, *The History of Tasmania*, 262.

14 McGowan, *Archaeological Investigations*, 84; Tardif, *John Bowen's Hobart*, 69–70.

15 TAHO LSD no. 11; Delano, *A Narrative of Voyages and Travels*, 440; Tardif, *John Bowen's Hobart*, 142–3; *HRA*, series III, vol. i, 237–8; Vallance, Moore and Groves, *Nature's Investigator*, 480–3.

16 *Historical Records of New South Wales*, vol. 5, 18.

17 BPP, 'Van Diemen's Land', 51–4.

18 *HRA*, series III, vol. i, 242–3; Fawkner, *Reminiscences*, 24.

19 Tardif, *John Bowen's Hobart*, 145; McGowan, *Archaeological Investigations*, 135.

20 Fawkner, *Reminiscences*, 24; BPP, 'Van Diemen's Land', 53; Bonwick, *The Last of the Tasmanians*, 35; McGowan, pers. comm.

21 Nicholls, *The Diary of the Reverend Robert Knopwood*, 51.

22 *HRA*, series III, vol. i, 242–3.

23 ibid., 237–8.

24 *Sydney Gazette*, 2 Sept. 1804.

25 BPP, 'Van Diemen's Land', 53–4; Fawkner, *Reminiscences*, 24; Nicholls, *The Diary of the Reverend Robert Knopwood*, 52.

26 BPP, 'Van Diemen's Land', 47–55; Fawkner, *Reminiscences*, 24.

27 *HTC*, 25 Sept. 1830; *CT*, 24 Sept. 1830; Bonwick, *The Last of the Tasmanians*, 35.

28 Tardif, *John Bowen's Hobart*, 148; Nicholls, *The Diary of the Reverend Robert Knopwood*, 128, 140, 146.

29 *HRA*, series III, vol. i, 281.

30 Nicholls, *The Diary of the Reverend Robert Knopwood*, 43, 45, 47.

31 Plomley, *Friendly Mission*, 408.

32 *Sydney Gazette*, 18 March 1804.

33 Nicholls, *The Diary of the Reverend Robert Knopwood*, 65; Plomley, *Friendly Mission*, 408.

34 *Sydney Gazette*, 18 March 1804; Backhouse, *A Narrative of a Visit*, 21; Nicholls, *The Diary of the Reverend Robert Knopwood*, 74–5.

35 *HRA*, series III, vol. i, 281, 371, 529.

36 Fawkner, *Reminiscences*, 90–1.

37 West, *The History of Tasmania*, 264.

38 Backhouse, *Narrative of a Visit*, 38–9.

39 Nicholls, *The Diary of the Reverend Robert Knopwood*, 104; BPP, 'Van Diemen's Land', 51.

40 *HRA*, series III, vol. i, 605–7.

41 ibid., 607, 629.

42 ibid., 658–9.

43 Collins, *An Account of the English Colony*.

44 Jones, 'Tasmanian Aborigines and dogs', 267.

45   ibid., 257–70.

46   Nicholls, *The Diary of the Reverend Robert Knopwood*, 132.

47   ibid., 126; John Oxley, 'Remarks on the country and settlements formed in Van Diemen's Land 1809', Archives Office of New South Wales, 2/8130.

48   Boyce, *Van Diemen's Land*, 48.

49   Nicholls, *The Diary of the Reverend Robert Knopwood*, 85; Paterson to Banks, 27 Nov. 1804, SLNSW ML A78–3, 177–9.

50   Fels, 'Culture contact'; Boyce, *Van Diemen's Land*, 58.

51   Plomley, *Jorgen Jorgenson*, 69.

52   Fels, 'Culture contact'.

CHAPTER 3

1   *HRA*, series III, vol. i, 421; BPP, 'Papers relating to His Majesty's settlements', 13.

2   Hainsworth, 'Iron men in wooden ships'; Cumpston, *The Furneaux Group*; Plomley, *Friendly Mission*, 1046; Cameron, *Grease and Ochre*, 50–2.

3   Cameron, *Grease and Ochre*, 72–3; McFarlane, *Beyond Awakening*, 41–63.

4   Belich, *Making Peoples*, 131; Plomley and Henley, *The Sealers*, 79, 80.

5   Plomley and Henley, *The Sealers*, 26; Cameron, *Grease and Ochre*, 75.

6   Cameron, *Grease and Ochre*, 76.

7   Stokes, *Discoveries in Australia*, vol. 2, 448.

8   Cameron, *Grease and Ochre*, 89, 99.

9   BPP, 'Van Diemen's Land', 36.

10   *Derwent Star*, 29 Jan. 1810, in West, *The History of Tasmania*, 264.

11   BPP, 'Van Diemen's Land', 36.

12   Schaffer and McKay, *Profiles of Norfolk Islanders*, vol. 2, part 2, 40–1; Plomley, *Friendly Mission*, 126.

13   Plomley, *Friendly Mission*, 510.

14   ibid., 508–10; Plomley and Henley, *The Sealers*, 25–6; Boyce, *Van Diemen's Land*, 84–6.

15   Cox, *Steps to the Scaffold*, 67–99.

16   Plomley and Henley, *The Sealers*, 25.

17   Parry, '"Hanging no good for black fellow"', 156–7.

18   Bowden, *Captain James Kelly of Hobart Town*, 35–44.

19   Plomley, *Friendly Mission*, 508–10.

20   Crawford, Ellis and Stancombe, *The Diaries of John Helder Wedge*, xliii.

21   Plomley and Henley, *The Sealers*, 25–6.

22   Plomley and Henley, *The Sealers*, 36; Plomley, *Friendly Mission*, 91–3, 123.

23   *HTG*, 25 April 1818.

24   Nicholls, *The Diary of the Reverend Robert Knopwood*, 273, 277, 294.

25   *HTG*, 24 May 1817.

26   W. Horton to Wesleyan Missionary Society, 3 June 1823, SLNSW ML BT.

27   SLNSW ML A860, 17 March 1819.

28   *HTG*, 25 April 1818.

29   ibid., 28 Nov. 1818; BPP, 'Van Diemen's Land', 50.

30   *HTG*, 10, 17, 24 April 1819; see Thomas Scott's drawing of the hut in 'Drawing and sketches of Van Diemen's Land 1820', SLNSW ML A1055/3, no. 39; Plomley, *Jorgen Jorgenson*, 93–4.

31   *HTG*, 27 March 1819; see also Nicholls, *The Diary of the Reverend Robert Knopwood*, 216.

32   *HTG*, 13, 27 March, 18 Dec. 1819; *HRA*, series III, vol. iii, 245–55.

33   'Proclamation', 13 March 1819, SLNSW ML A1352; *HRA*, series III, vol. iii, 510.

34   It was reproduced in Roth, *The Aborigines of Tasmania*, 40.

35   Cameron, *Grease and Ochre*, 89–90; for an account of the historical experiences of Tasmanian Aboriginal women on Kangaroo Island, see Taylor, *Unearthed*.

36   Serventy, 'Mutton-birding'; for an opposing account of Aboriginal involvement with mutton-birding, see Skira, 'Tasmanian Aborigines and muttonbirding', 38–41.

37   Plomley and Henley, *The Sealers*, 56.

38   Vamplew, *Australians*, 25.

39   SLNSW ML C 190; Boyce, *Van Diemen's Land*, 64–5.

40   *HTG*, 28 Nov. 1819.

41   'Sketchbook of Thomas Scott', SLNSW ML A1055/3, no. 58; Plomley and Henley, *The Sealers*, 36.

42   *HTG*, 17, 24 April 1819.

43   Boyce, *Van Diemen's Land*, 121.

44   Ritchie, *Punishment and Profit*, 238; BBP, 'Report of the commissioner of inquiry', 83.

CHAPTER 4

1   Scott, 'Land settlement'; Hartwell, *The Economic Development of Van Diemen's Land*, 108–30; Morgan, *Land Settlement*, 19, 22.

2   Giblin, *The Early History of Tasmania*, vol. 2, 297.

3   Morgan, *Land Settlement*, 19, 27; Breen, *Contested Places*, 13–33; Boyce, *Van Diemen's Land*, 145–50; Ryan, 'Massacre in the Black War in Tasmania', 487–90.

4   Morgan, *Land Settlement*, 143.

5   *HTG*, 25 April 1818; Wentworth, *Statistical, Historical and Political Description*, 4, 115; Dixon, *Narrative of a Voyage*, 47; Betts, *An Account of the Colony*, 95.

6   *HTG*, 3 Dec. 1823, 26 March, 2 April, 23 July 1824; for a detailed account of the incident at Grindstone Bay, see Calder, *Some Account of the Wars, Extirpation, Habits, etc*, 48–51; for an account of the reprisal settler massacre, see TAHO NS 323/1, 16–20 Nov. 1823.

7   *HTG*, 29 Oct. 1824; Melville, *The History of Van Diemen's Land*, 38–40.

8   Shaw, 'Sir George Arthur', 35–6; Rowley, *The Destruction of Aboriginal Society*, 87; see also Shaw, *Sir George Arthur*, 39–60.

9   Levy, *Governor George Arthur*, 104.

10   Melville, *The History of Van Diemen's Land*, 32–8.

11   *HTG*, 5 Nov., 15 April, 4 Nov. 1824, 12, 19 Jan. 1825; West, *The History of Tasmania*, 269; Mansfield to Arthur, 3 Nov. 1824, TAHO GO 52/2; 'Resolutions carried at public meeting', 15 Nov. 1824, TAHO GO 52/2; Richardson to Arthur, 25 April 1825, TAHO GO 52/2; Plomley, *Friendly Mission*, 49; BPP, 'Van Diemen's Land', 39; Shelton, *The Parramore Letters*, 61.

12   BPP, 'Van Diemen's Land', 20–1; Melville, *The History of Van Diemen's Land*, 56–9; *HTG*, 20 Sept. 1826.

13   *CT*, 18 Nov. 1826.

14   Morgan, *Land Settlement*, 148.

15   BPP, 'Van Diemen's Land', 20–1; *HRA*, series I, vol. xii, 21.

16   BPP, 'Van Diemen's Land', 20–1.

17   *HRA*, series I, vol. xii, 21; *HRA*, series III, vol. vii, 608–12, 693; BPP, 'Van Diemen's Land', 20–1.

18   *CT*, 15 Dec. 1826.

19   BPP, 'Van Diemen's Land', 6.

CHAPTER 5

1   Gordon to Col. Sec., 9 Dec. 1826, TAHO CSO 1/331, 194–5; *CT*, 15 Dec. 1826; *HTG*, 16 Dec. 1826.

2   *CT*, 15 Dec. 1826.

3   See *HTG*, 5 May 1827.

4   See *CT*, 4 May 1827; *HTC*, 24 Nov. 1827.

5   See Ryan, 'Massacre in Tasmania'.

6   Ryan, 'Massacre in the Black War in Tasmania'.

7   McMahon touches on this issue in 'The British Army', 60.

8   Cox, *Steps to the Scaffold*, 86. When Kickerterpoller died, at Emu Bay in May 1832, G.A. Robinson acknowledged that he was baptised; see Plomley, *Friendly Mission*, 641.

9   *CT*, 19 Jan. 1827.

10   ibid., 26 Jan. 1827.

11   ibid., 9, 23 Feb. 1827.

12   *HTG*, 24 Feb. 1827.

13   Dow and Dow, *Landfall in Van Diemen's Land*, 45.

14   TAHO CSO 1/316, 840; Bonwick, *The Last of the Tasmanians*, 117.

15   George, 'Extracts from a diary belonging to James George', 13: *CT*, 4 May 1827.

16   *HTG*, 20 April 1827.

17   TAHO CSO 1/316, 840; Bonwick, *The Last of the Tasmanians*, 99.

18   *CT*, 23 Feb., 17 March, 11 May 1827.

19   Vamplew, *Australians*, 25–6; for population increase, see *CT*, 15 June 1827; for hawthorn trees, see *HTG*, 17 March 1827; for a list of land grants in the region, see *HTG*, 26 Aug. 1826; for catarrh epidemic, see *CT*, 15 April, 8 June 1827.

20   See Ryan, 'Massacre in the Black War in Tasmania', 488–90.

21   *HTG*, 6 Jan. 1826; TAHO VDL 341, 6 June 1826; see also TAHO CSO 1/316, 15–37.

22   Plomley, *Friendly Mission*, 254; TAHO CSO 1/316, 15–37.

23   TAHO CSO 1/316, 15–37.

24   *CT*, 6 July 1827.

25   TAHO CSO 1/316, 15–40; *CT*, 6 July 1827.

26   *CT*, 6 July 1827; TAHO CSO 1/316, 15–30; Plomley, *Friendly Mission*, 253–4.

27   *CT*, 29 June 1827; *HTC*, 27 Oct. 1827.

28   *CT*, 27 July 1827.

29   Plomley, *The Aboriginal/Settler Clash*, 63–4.

30   TAHO CSO 1/316, 46.

31   *HTC*, 24 Nov. 1827.

32   Bridges, *That Yesterday Was Home*, 69.

33   TAHO CSO 1/316, 67–78, 84–5; *Tas*, 16 Nov., 1827; McKay, *Journals of the Land Commissioners*, 74.

34   Lennox, 'The Van Diemen's Land Company and the Tasmanian Aborigines', 170.

35   Thomas Archer to Col. Sec., 24 Nov. 1827, TAHO CSO 1/316, 70–5.

36   Arthur to Burnett, 26 Nov. 1827, TAHO CSO 1/316, 77; BPP, 'Van Diemen's Land', 21–2.

37   Hobler, *The Diaries of Pioneer George Hobler*, 40; Anstey to Arthur, 4 Dec. 1827, TAHO CSO 1/320.

38   Plomley, *The Aboriginal/Settler Clash*, 64–8.

39   ibid., 66–9; see also Abbott to Burnett, 12 Nov. 1827, TAHO CSO 1/316, 64.

40   *Tas*, 16 Nov. 1827; *HTC*, 17 Nov. 1827, 5 Jan. 1828.

41   TAHO CSO 1/323, 113; *HTC*, 15, 22 March 1828; Plomley, *Friendly Mission*, 537.

42   *HTC*, 22 March 1828.

43   ibid.

44   *HTC*, 5 April 1828; TAHO CSO 1/321; *Tas*, 11 April 1828.

45   BPP, 'Van Diemen's Land', 8, 10–11; *HTC*, 12 April 1828.

46   See Connor, 'The frontier war that never was', 21–3.

47   *HRA*, series III, vol. vii, 28.

48   Plomley, *Jorgen Jorgenson*, 35.

49   *HRA*, series III, vol. vii, 29.

50   ibid., 180–4.

51   TAHO CSO 1/316, 86–8.

52   Cox, *Steps to the Scaffold*, 87–8.

53   Melville, *The History of Van Diemen's Land*, 75–6.

54   BPP, 'Van Diemen's Land', 24–6; Arthur to Darling, 24 May 1828, *HRA* series III, vol. vii, 412–13.

55   See Pedder to Arthur, 3 April 1828, SLNSW ML A2170, vol. 9.

56   *HTC*, 5 April 1828; *CT*, 8 April 1828; *Colonial Advocate & VDL Intelligencer*, 1 May 1828.

57   *HRA*, series III, vol. vii, 26–9, 311–12; BPP, 'Van Diemen's Land', 4.

58   *HRA*, series III, vol. vii, 410–11.

59   Robert Ayton to Col. Sec., 1 March 1830, TAHO CSO 1/320, 152–4; 'Deposition at Launceston Police Office', 15 March 1830, TAHO CSO 1/330, 109.

60   *HRA*, series III, vol. vii, 412–13.

61   Plomley, *The Aboriginal/Settler Clash*, 70–3; Simpson to Col. Sec., 26 Aug. 1828, TAHO CSO 1/316, 104; Batman to Col. Sec., 18 Sept. 1828, TAHO CSO 1/320, 1/330.

62   *HTC*, 18, 25 Oct., 1, 8 Nov. 1828; *Tas*, Oct, 1828.

63   Visit to site by the author and interview with local residents, 15 June 2007.

64   *HTC*, 1, 8 Nov. 1828; *Tas*, 31 Oct. 1828; Anstey to Arthur, 13 Oct. 1828, TAHO CSO 1/316, 762.

65   BPP, 'Van Diemen's Land', 26.

66   *HRA*, series III, vol. vii, 626–30.

67   TAHO GO 33/7, 901.

68   *HRA*, series III, vol. vii, 626, 632–3.

69   McMahon, 'The British Army', 60; see also Finlason, *Commentaries upon Martial Law*, 6–10.

CHAPTER 6

1   Sherwin to Arthur, 23 Feb. 1830, TAHO CSO 1/316.

2   *HTC*, 25 Oct., 1 Nov. 1828; *Tas*, 31 Oct. 1828; TAHO CSO 1/316, 181, 186, 762, 799, 803; *CT*, 11 Feb. 1826.

3   Col. Sec. to Robertson, 17 Nov. 1828, TAHO CSO 1/331; *HTC*, 22 Nov. 1828.

4   BPP, 'Van Diemen's Land', 31; *HRA*, series III, vol. viii, 335; Plomley, *Friendly Mission*, 30.

5   BPP, 'Van Diemen's Land', 26–33.

6   Danvers to Anstey, 9 Dec. 1828, TAHO CSO 1/320, 22; *HTC*, 13 Dec. 1828.

7   *HTC*, 6, 13, 20 Dec. 1828, 17, 24, 31 Jan. 1829.

8   *CT*, 30 Jan., 27 Feb., 26 March 1829; *HTC*, 28 Feb., 7 March, 18 April 1829; *Launceston Advertiser*, 9 Feb., 16, 23 March 1829; Simpson to Col. Sec., 17 Feb. 1829, TAHO CSO 1/316.

9   Plomley, *Jorgen Jorgenson*, 81.

10   ibid., 81–2.

11   ibid., 68, 83; Calder, *Levee, Line and Martial Law*, 207.

12   Arthur to Col. Sec., 27 May 1829, TAHO CSO 1/317; Plomley, *Friendly Mission*, 30–1.

13   Anstey to Col. Sec., 10 March 1830, TAHO CSO 1/316, 189.

14   *Tas*, 28 Nov. 1828.

15   ibid., 19 Dec. 1828; *CT*, 16 April, 11 June 1830.

16   Plomley, *Friendly Mission*, 515–618; Reynolds, *Fate of a Free People*, 53.

17   *HTC*, 13, 20 June 1829; TAHO CSO 1/321, 284.

18   Robertson to Col. Sec., 17 Nov. 1828, TAHO CSO 1/331.

19   ibid.

20   Welsh to Arthur, 11 April 1828, TAHO CSO 1/327; Arthur to Col. Sec., 23 April 1828, TAHO CSO 1/316, 5 May 1828, TAHO CSO 1/740; BPP, 'Van Diemen's Land', 31–2; *HTC*, 17 March 1829.

21   Plomley, *Friendly Mission*, 11–14.

22   Frankland to Arthur, 4 Feb. 1829, TAHO LSD 17/1.

23   Manderson, 'Not yet', 228.

24   *HRA*, series III, vol. viii, 334.

25   *HTC*, 15, 29 Aug., 9 Sept. 1829.

26   *HRA*, series III, vol. viii, 454, 924–6 n. 472; BPP, 'Van Diemen's Land', 48, 49, 50, 52; Plomley, *Jorgen Jorgenson*, 70; Robinson to Col. Sec., 6 Aug. 1831, TAHO CSO 1/323, 49.

27   Arthur to Burnett, 13 July 1829, TAHO CSO 1/316, 291.

28   *HTC*, 15, 29 Aug., 9 Sept. 1892; Batman to Anstey, 7 Sept. 1829, TAHO CSO 320; *Launceston Advertiser*, 7 Sept. 1829.

29   *HTC*, 26 Sept., 17 Oct. 1829; Bonwick, *The Last of the Tasmanians*, 66.

30   *HTC*, 7, 14 Nov. 1829; Plomley, *Friendly Mission*, 99, 106.

31   *CT*, 23, 25 Sept. 1829; TAHO CSO 1/316, 311; see also *HRA*, series III, vol. viii, 958.

32   See Maps 17 and 18, in Plomley, *The Aboriginal/Settler Clash*, 48–9.

33   BPP, 'Van Diemen's Land', 32–3; Arthur to Darling, 18 Nov. 1829, SLNSW ML A1205; Williams to Arthur, 2 Nov. 1829, TAHO CSO 1/316, 361.

34   *HRA*, series III, vol. viii, 607.

35   Plomley, *The Aboriginal/Settler Clash*, 82–6; *Tas*, 26 Feb. 1830; *HTC*, 20, 27 Feb. 1830.

36   Plomley, *Friendly Mission*, 539.

37   *CT*, 19 Feb. 1830; the fortification can be seen in the painting *Montacute* in Hansen, *John Glover*, 117.

38   Torlesse to Arthur, 16 Feb. 1830, TAHO CSO 1/316, 425.

39   Sherwin to Arthur, 23 Feb. 1830, TAHO CSO 1/316, 430–4.

40   'Address of the inhabitants of the Clyde police district', 27 Feb. 1830, TAHO CSO 1/316, 440; *CT*, 19 Feb. 1830.

41   BPP, 'Van Diemen's Land', 34–5; see also *HRA*, series III, vol. ix, 764–5 n. 140.

42   Plomley, *The Aboriginal/Settler Clash*, 82–6.

CHAPTER 7

1   BPP, 'Van Diemen's Land', 47.

2   ibid.

3   TAHO CSO 1/332, 3, 9 March 1830.

4   Ayton to Aborigines Committee, 1 March 1830, TAHO CSO 1/320, 152–4; 'Deposition to Launceston Police Office', 15 March 1830, TAHO CSO 1/330, 109.

5   Robert Morley to Aborigines Committee, 15 March 1830, TAHO CSO 1/320, 103; for Dugdale's assignment to William Talbot, see TAHO NS 323/1, 5 June 1822; for Dugdale's application for conditional pardon, see *HRA*, series III, vol. ix, 666.

6 BPP, 'Van Diemen's Land', 49.

7 Horace Rowcroft to Aborigines Committee, 22 Feb. 1830, TAHO CSO 1/323, 104–6; F.D.G. Browne to P.A. Mulgrave, 28 Feb. 1830 TAHO CSO 1/323, 124–32; William Barnes to Aborigines Committee, 16 March 1830, TAHO CSO 1/323, 299–302.

8 BPP, 'Van Diemen's Land', 41.

9 ibid., 43–6.

10 *HRA*, series III, vol. ix, 166.

11 ibid., 167–8, 217.

12 Connor, *The Australian Frontier Wars*, 100–1.

13 *CT*, 19 Feb. 1830.

14 *Colonial Advocate*, 1 April 1830, 94.

15 Plomley, *Weep in Silence*, 325; *HRA*, series III, vol. ix, 195; Anstey to Col. Sec., 10 April 1830, TAHO CSO 1/316, 189; Moriarty to Col. Sec., 18 April 1830, TAHO CSO 1/316, 489.

16 *CT*, 30 July 1830.

17 *HRA*, series III, vol. viii, 587–8; *HRA*, series III, vol. ix, 311–12.

18 *HRA*, series III, vol. ix, 311–12.

19 ibid., 572–6.

20 Plomley, *The Aboriginal/Settler Clash*, 88–91.

21 Anstey to Arthur, 22 Aug. 1830, TAHO CSO 1/316.

22 *CT*, 30 July 1830.

23 BPP, 'Van Diemen's Land', 61.

24 ibid., 61–2.

25 'Address to His Excellency the Governor by the settlers of Jericho', 24 Aug. 1830, TAHO CSO 1/316, 596.

26 Anstey to Arthur, 22 Aug. 1830, TAHO CSO 1/316, 594; 'Report of the Aborigines Committee', 26 Aug. 1830, TAHO CSO 1/319; *CT*, 3 Sept. 1830; *HTC*, 4 Sept., 16 Oct. 1830.

27 BPP, 'Van Diemen's Land', 62–4.

28 ibid., 64–5; Henry Melville coined the terms Black Line and Black War in 1835; see Melville, *The History of Van Diemen's Land*, 89, 90.

CHAPTER 8

1 BPP, 'Van Diemen's Land', 65–6; *Tas*, 19 Nov. 1830; TAHO CSO 1/316, 726, 733, 799.

2 Connor, 'British frontier warfare logistics', 149.

3 Jorgenson to Anstey, 8 June 1829, TAHO CSO 1/320; for a discussion of events leading to Cherokee removal, see Wolfe, 'Settler colonialism and the elimination of the native', 391–2; Curthoys, 'Genocide in Tasmania: the history of an idea', 229.

4 Fenton, *A History of Tasmania*, 106; Reynolds, *Fate of a Free People*, 117.

5 Connor, 'British frontier warfare', 152.

6 Fenton, *A History of Tasmania*, 107–8; McMahon, 'The British Army', 60.

7 McMahon, 'The British Army', 60.

8 Esdaile, pers. comm.

9 Darwin, *Narrative of the Surveying Voyages*, 533.

10 See Thorpe, 'Aborigines, settlers and the fauna war'.

11 Plomley, *Friendly Mission*, 521–3, 565.

12 *Launceston Advetiser*, 13, 20 Sept. 1830.

13 *HTC*, 2, 9, 16 Oct. 1830; TAHO CSO 1/316, 737, 742.

14   Connor, 'British frontier warfare', 151–2.

15   ibid., 150; for a list of settlers who participated in the Line, see Fenton, *A History of Tasmania*, 108–9.

16   BPP, 'Van Diemen's Land', 71.

17   Connor, 'British frontier warfare', 154.

18   *HTC*, 18, 30 Oct. 1830.

19   *CT*, 22 Oct. 1830; *HTC*, 20 Nov. 1830; *Tas*, 29 Oct. 1830; TAHO CSO 1/316, 663, 667, 674.

20   Plomley, *Jorgen Jorgenson*, 107.

21   *HTC*, 30 Oct. 1830; Connor, 'British frontier warfare', 154–5.

22   *HTC*, 30 Oct. 1830.

23   ibid.

24   Walpole to Col. Sec., 27 Oct. 1830, TAHO CSO 1/332.

25   Plomley, *Friendly Mission*, 311.

26   ibid., 523.

27   *HTC*, 13, 20 Nov. 1830.

28   *HRA*, series III, vol. ix, 659.

29   *CT*, 19 Nov. 1830; see also Plomley, *Friendly Mission*, 527; Calder, *Some Account of the Wars, Extirpation, Habits, etc.*, 56.

30   *CT*, 10, 24 Dec. 1830.

31   ibid., 12, 19, 26 Nov., 3 Dec. 1830, *Tas*, 19 Nov. 1830; *HTC*, 27 Nov. 1830; TAHO CSO 1/317, 490; Plomley, *Friendly Mission*, 555.

32   TAHO CSO 1/316, 920–37; *HTC*, 20 Aug. 1831.

33   *HTC*, 19 Sept., 1 Oct. 1831.

34   ibid., 24 Sept. 1831; *Tas*, 29 Oct. 1831.

35   *HTC*, 5, 26 Nov. 1831; *CT*, 23 Nov. 1831; see Emily Stoddart, *The Freycinet Line*, 11–13; Bonwick, *The Last of the Tasmanians*, 179.

36   Robinson, *Friendly Mission*, 555.

37   ibid., 602–3.

38   Torlesse to Col. Sec., 10 Feb. 1832, TAHO CSO 1/317; *The Courier*, 24 March, 28 April 1837.

39   Calder, 'Some account of the country'.

40   Plomley, *The Aboriginal/Settler Clash*, 73–100.

CHAPTER 9

1   See Map 18 in Chapter 6.

2   Reynolds, *An Indelible Stain?*, 61–5; see also Reynolds, *Fate of a Free People*, 81–2, 87–119.

3   Windschuttle, *The Fabrication of Aboriginal History*, vol. 1, 389–90.

4   Boyce, *Van Diemen's Land*, 197–8.

5   Windschuttle, *The Fabrication of Aboriginal History*, vol. 1, 372–6.

6   Boyce, *Van Diemen's Land*, 201–2.

7   Broome, *Aboriginal Victorians*, 81.

8   Ryan, 'Settler massacres on the Port Phillip frontier'.

9   Evans, 'The country has another past', 31.

10   Reynolds, *Fate of a Free People*, 51–2.

11   Evans, 'The country has another past', 31.

12   Reynolds, *The Other Side of the Frontier*, 121–5; Reynolds, *Frontier*, 53; Broome, 'The struggle for Australia', 116–20; Broome, 'The statistics of frontier conflict', 88–90.

CHAPTER 10

1   Plomley, *Friendly Mission*, 51.
2   SLNSW ML A7061, 40.
3   Robinson noted on 27 Nov. 1829 that he was reading James Adair's *History of the American Indians* (1775) and William Robertson's *History of America* (1777); Plomley, *Friendly Mission*, 102.
4   Plomley, *Friendly Mission*, 141.
5   Rae-Ellis, *Black Robinson*, 99–104.
6   Plomley, *Friendly Mission*, 57–115.
7   ibid., 281, 369.
8   ibid., 83.
9   ibid., 59.
10 ibid., 60, 63.
11 ibid., 62–9.
12 ibid., 63, 89, 108–9.
13 ibid., 143.
14 ibid., 80.
15 ibid., 102.
16 ibid., 102.
17 ibid., 102.
18 ibid., 107, 276.

CHAPTER 11

1   McRae, 'Port Davey and the South West', 48; Plomley, *Friendly Mission*, 160; Maxwell-Stewart, 'Competition and conflict', 1–20.
2   Plomley, *Friendly Mission*, 143–50.
3   ibid., 162–5.
4   ibid., 167–8.
5   ibid., 171–6.
6   ibid., 177–88.
7   ibid., 189–91.
8   McFarlane, *Beyond Awakening*, 53.
9   Maxwell-Stewart, 'Competition and conflict', 12.
10 McFarlane, *Beyond Awakening*, 65–88.
11 McFarlane, 'NJB Plomley's contribution'; Plomley, *Friendly Mission*, 206–7, 215–17, 266–7 n. 103.
12 Plomley, *Friendly Mission*, 212.
13 ibid., 212–14.
14 ibid., 217.
15 ibid., 218.
16 ibid., 224–5.
17 Breen, *Contested Places*, 23–31.
18 Ryan, 'Massacre in the Black War in Tasmania', 489–90.
19 *HTG*, 6 Jan. 1826.
20 TAHO VDL 341, 6 June 1826; TAHO CSO 1/316, 15–37.
21 Ryan, 'Massacre in the Black War in Tasmania', 492–3.
22 'Quamby', TAHO GI; Residents at Deloraine, interview by author; Plomley, *Friendly Mission*, 231.
23 Plomley, *Friendly Mission*, 326, 872.

24 ibid., 636.

25 ibid., 237.

26 ibid., 248–51.

27 ibid., 251.

28 ibid., 251.

29 ibid., 258–9.

CHAPTER 12

1 Plomley, *Friendly Mission*, 279, 466–8 n. 6.

2 Plomley and Henley, *The Sealers*, 76, 84.

3 Plomley, *Friendly Mission*, 296, 470 n. 43.

4 ibid., 470 n. 44.

5 ibid., 296, 298–9.

6 ibid., 297; see also Gray to Col. Sec., 19, 24 Oct. 1830, TAHO CSO 1/316.

7 Plomley *Friendly Mission*, 300; see 471 n. 51.

8 ibid., 302–9.

9 ibid., 309–11.

10 ibid., 312–15.

11 ibid., 329–30, 332, 337–8.

12 ibid., 350.

13 BPP, 'Van Diemen's Land', 80–2.

14 ibid., 82.

15 ibid., 81.

16 ibid., 79.

17 ibid., 79.

18 Plomley, *Friendly Mission*, 480–3 nn. 111–21.

19 ibid., 351–2.

20 ibid., 380.

21 ibid.

22 ibid., 488 n. 159.

23 ibid., 489–93 n. 166; Plomley and Henley, *The Sealers*, 86.

24 Plomley, *Friendly Mission*, 427.

25 ibid., 500 n. 232.

26 ibid., 427–47.

27 Robertson to Col. Sec., 17 Nov. 1828, TAHO CSO 1/331; Plomley, *Friendly Mission*, 193, 265 n. 82; Stuart, 31 Jan. 1831, TAHO CSO 1/321; Lyttleton, 3 Jan.1831, TAHO CSO 1/316; Stuart, 7 Feb. 1831, TAHO CSO 1/316; Clark, 12 March 1831, TAHO CSO 1/316; Laing-Smith, 21 March 1831, TAHO CSO 1/316; Lyttleton, 18 April 1831, TAHO CSO 1/329.

28 Robertson to Col. Sec., 17 Nov. 1828, TAHO CSO 1/331.

29 Plomley, *Friendly Mission*, 447–8.

30 ibid., 454–60.

31 ibid., 606–7.

32 ibid., 519.

33 ibid., 535–6.

34 ibid., 522–8.

35 ibid., 529.

36   ibid., 540.

37   ibid., 556.

38   ibid., 506–7.

CHAPTER 13

1   Plomley, *Friendly Mission*, 619–21.

2   'Statement of Capt. Bateman to Aborigines Committee', Feb. 1832, TAHO CSO 1/319; Bonwick, *The Last of the Tasmanians*, 248; Plomley, *Friendly Mission*, 681–2 n. 8; 'Statement by Maclachlan', 27 Feb. 1832, TAHO CSO 1/318; Arthur to Darling, draft letter, Feb. 1832, TAHO CSO 1/316.

3   Plomley, *Friendly Mission*, 622–5.

4   For details of Kickerterpoller, see Chapters 3–7; for Robinson's regret, see Plomley, *Friendly Mission*, 641.

5   Plomley, *Friendly Mission*, 626, 642, 738.

6   ibid., 648–68.

7   ibid., 669–73.

8   Robinson to Whitcomb, 10 Aug. 1832, SLNSW ML A612, 155–6; Robertson to Bedford, 30 Jul. 1832, TAHO Bedford Papers, NS 65.

9   Plomley, *Friendly Mission*, 682.

10   ibid., 684–9.

11   ibid., 689–91.

12   ibid., 697–717.

13   ibid., 837–9 n. 6.

14   ibid., 839–41 n. 7, 750, 753–4.

15   ibid., 757–62.

16   ibid., 762–3.

17   ibid., 764–93.

18   ibid., 805.

19   ibid., 807.

20   ibid., 808–13.

21   ibid., 813–56.

22   ibid., 909.

23   ibid., 959–60.

24   Rae-Ellis, *Trucanini*, 149.

25   Boyce, *Van Diemen's Land*, 295–6.

26   Darwin, *Narrative of the Surveying Voyages*, 539.

CHAPTER 14

1   Plomley, *Friendly Mission*, 963–4.

2   ibid., 975 n. 28.

3   Plomley, *Weep in Silence*, 353.

4   ibid., 299, 328, 1028–39; SLNSW ML A573, 30 April 1836.

5   Plomley, *Weep in Silence*, 306–12.

6   ibid., 306–13.

7   ibid., 312–13.

8   ibid.

9   Robinson to Col. Sec., 4 July 1836, SLNSW ML A2170, vol. 28; for list of names, see Plomley, *Weep in Silence*, 836–71.

10   The information in this and the following three paragraphs is from Clark to Robinson, Dec. 1835, SLNSW ML A7063, vol. 24.

11   See van Toorn, *Writing Never Arrives Naked*, 105.

12   Plomley, *Weep in Silence*, 323–34.

13   'Report of Major Thomas Ryan', March 1836, SLNSW ML A7063, vol. 24.

14   Plomley, *Weep in Silence*, 353.

15   Shaw, *Sir George Arthur*, 132.

16   Plomley, *Weep in Silence*, 379–97.

17   ibid., 405–13.

18   ibid., 412–13.

19   Birmingham, *Wybalenna*, 179.

20   Van Toorn, *Writing Never Arrives Naked*, 116.

21   ibid., 116–17.

22   Dammery, 'Walter George Arthur', 83.

23   Rose, *For the Record*, 3.

24   Van Toorn, *Writing Never Arrives Naked*, 104.

25   *Flinders Island Weekly Chronicle*, 17 Nov. 1837, cited in Rose, *For the Record*, 17.

26   *Flinders Island Weekly Chronicle*, 28 Oct., 6 Nov., 21 Dec. 1837, cited in Rose, *For the Record*, 12, 13, 19.

27   Van Toorn, *Writing Never Arrives Naked*, 100 .

28   Davies, 'On the Aborigines of Van Diemen's Land', 411; Plomley, *Weep in Silence*, 328.

29   BPP, 'Australian Aborigines', 7; see also SLNSW ML A7044, vol. 23, 218–327.

30   Plomley, *Weep in Silence*, 5–81, 43.

31   *Flinders Island Weekly Chronicle*, 17 Nov. 1837, cited in Rose, *For the Record*, 17.

32   BPP, 'Australian Aborigines', 7.

33   ibid., 7.

34   Plomley, *Weep in Silence*, 463.

35   ibid., 485.

36   ibid., 468.

37   ibid., 489.

38   Encl. in Robinson to Col. Sec., 4 July 1838, SLNSW ML A7045, vol. 24.

39   Plomley, *Weep in Silence*, 511, 543.

40   Robinson to Col. Sec., 4 July 1838, SLNSW ML A7045, vol. 24; Plomley, *Weep in Silence*, 523–30; Franklin to Glenelg, 12 Feb. 1838, PRO CO 280/93, 171–2; Glenelg to Gipps, 31 Jan. 1838, BPP, 'Aborigines (Australian colonies)', 4.

41   Reece, *Aborigines and Colonists*, 4–61.

42   Plomley, *Weep in Silence*, 582–98.

43   ibid., 598–604; Gipps to Glenelg, 10 Oct. 1838, SLNSW ML A1219, 450–1, Gipps to Glenelg, 10 Nov. 1838, SLNSW ML A1219, 611–20.

44   George Robinson Jnr to G.A. Robinson, 28 March 1839, SLNSW ML A7071, vol. 50.

45   Reynolds, 'Walter Edmund Roth'.

CHAPTER 15

1   'Report of the Board of Inquiry', 25 March 1839, SLNSW ML A7071, vol. 50; SLNSW ML A573.

2   Information in the preceding three paragraphs has been compiled from Ryan, *The Aboriginal Tasmanians*, 2nd edn, Appendix 3.

3 'Report of the Board of Inquiry', 10 June 1841, encl. no. 7, in Franklin to Russell, 6 Aug. 1841, PRO CO 280/133, 165–7.

4 Birmingham, *Wybalenna*, 175–96.

5 'Report of the Board of Inquiry', 10 June 1841, encl. no. 7, Franklin to Russell, 6 Aug. 1841, PRO CO 280/133, 165–7.

6 See La Trobe's remarks on Jeanneret to Administrator [La Trobe], 5 Nov. 1846, TAHO CSO 11/27/658, 202–4.

7 Jeanneret, *Vindication of a Colonial Magistrate*, 38; Rutledge, 'Charles Edward Jeanneret'; Plomley, *Weep in Silence*, 134–9.

8 Dammery, *Walter George Arthur*, 20.

9 ibid.

10 McFarlane, *Beyond Awakening*, 199–203.

11 Davies, 'Aborigines, murder and the criminal law', 315–19.

12 Dammery, *Walter George Arthur*, 22; McFarlane, *Beyond Awakening*, 208–11.

13 Dammery, *Walter George Arthur*, 23.

14 Cited in van Toorn, *Writing Never Arrives Naked*, 117.

15 Van Toorn, *Writing Never Arrives Naked*, 117.

16 Jeanneret to Col. Sec., 16 July, 15 Sept. 1842, TAHO CSO 8/157/1166.

17 Plomley, *Weep in Silence*, 140.

18 G.W. Walker to Harriet Jeanneret, 16 Sept. 1842, TAHO CSO 8/157/1166; Jeanneret to Col. Sec., 20 Dec. 1842, TAHO CSO 8/157/1166; Dammery, *Walter George Arthur*, 26; Stokes, *Discoveries in Australia*, vol. 2, 468.

19 Jeanneret to Col. Sec., 6 June 1843, cited in Plomley, *Weep in Silence*, 142.

20 Jeanneret to Col. Sec., 16 Nov. 1842, 31 March 1843, TAHO CSO 8/157/1166; Jeanneret, *Vindication of a Colonial Magistrate*, 54.

21 Rutledge, 'Charles Edward Jeanneret', 472.

22 Broadfoot, 'An unexpected visit'.

23 Walter George Arthur to G.W. Walker, 31 Dec. 1845, SLNSW ML A612, 221–3.

24 Cited in Plomley, *Weep in Silence*, 148–9.

25 Jeanneret to Milligan, 17 March 1846, PRO CO 280/195, 337; Jeanneret to Col. Sec., 12 June 1846, PRO CO 280/195, 352.

26 John Allen, Washington, Walter George Arthur and Davy Bruny to Governor, 16 June 1846; Mary Ann Arthur to Governor, 10 June 1846, PRO CO 280/195, 319–28.

27 TAHO CSO 11/27/658.

28 Remarks by James Stephen, 30 Jan. 1847, on Wilmot to Gladstone, 13 Aug. 1846, PRO CO 280/195, 302.

29 Stokes, *Discoveries in Australia*, vol. 2, 451, 469.

30 Denison to Grey, 7 Dec. 1847, PRO CO 280/215, 3–4.

31 ibid. 5.

32 *Examiner*, 2 Oct. 1847.

CHAPTER 16

1 Denison to Grey, 7 Dec. 1847, PRO CO 280/215, 5.

2 Ryan, *The Aboriginal Tasmanians*, 2nd edn, Appendix 3, 315–26.

3 ibid.; see also Plomley and Henley, *The Sealers*, 84.

4 Plomley and Henley, *The Sealers*, 75–88.

5   Denison to Grey, 7 Dec. 1847, PRO CO 280/215, 6.

6   Plomley, *Weep in Silence*, 173.

7   Denison to Grey, 7 Dec. 1847, PRO CO 280/215, 3–4.

8   Calder, *Some Account of the Wars, Extirpation, Habits, etc.*, 112.

9   Plomley, *Weep in Silence*, 172, 945.

10 Dammery, *Walter George Arthur*, 37–8; Denison, *Varieties of Vice-Regal Life*, vol. 1, 69–70; *Hobart Town Advertiser*, 21, 24 Dec. 1847.

11 Plomley, *Weep in Silence*, 188; Plomley, *The Westlake Papers*, 13, 19, 28, 30, 31.

12 Allen and Jones, 'Oyster Cove', 229.

13 Plomley, *Weep in Silence*, 176–7; Bonwick, *The Last of the Tasmanians*, 278–9.

14 Denison, *Varieties of Vice-Regal Life*, vol. 1, 104.

15 Plomley, *Weep in Silence*, 188.

16 Robinson, 26–28 April 1851, SLNSW ML A7088, vol. 67, part 2; Milligan to Col. Sec., 31 July 1851, TAHO CSO 24/284/6314.

17 Crowther, 'The final phase of the extinct Tasmanian race', 29; Plomley, *The Westlake Papers*, 12, 18, 19, 25, 57.

18 Plomley, *Weep in Silence*, 182–3; Dammery, *Walter George Arthur*, 39–41.

19 Plomley, *Weep in Silence*, 189; *Mercury*, 27 Feb. 1905.

20 Plomley, *The Westlake Papers*, 60.

21 Bonwick, *The Last of the Tasmanians*, 282–3.

22 Oyster Cove Visitors Book, 21 May 1859.

23 Hull, *Royal Kalendar*, 20.

24 Milligan, 'On the dialects', 1856, 410–14.

25 ibid., 412.

26 MacDonald, *Human Remains*, 87.

27 Dammery, *Walter George Arthur*, 45.

28 Bonwick, *The Last of the Tasmanians*, 284; Pybus, *Community of Thieves*, 163–5.

29 Pybus, *Community of Thieves*, 166–7.

30 Dandridge to Col. Sec., 20 Dec. 1865, 14 Feb. 1867, TAHO CSD 4/77/231.

31 MacDonald, *Human Remains*, 120.

32 Bonwick, *The Last of the Tasmanians*, 395; 'Complaint by Aboriginal "Billy"', 5 Dec. 1864, TAHO CSD 4/77/231; Plomley, *The Westlake Papers*, 52.

33 The following account of the disposal of William Lanney's body is taken from 'Statement made by Charles Williams, gatekeeper at the General Hospital, Hobart, Tasmania, giving an account of the death of "King Billy" or "William Laney"—1869', Alex Morton MSS, SLNSW ML A612; see also *Mercury*, 3, 4, 18, 20, 27 March, 21 May 1869.

34 MacDonald, *Human Remains*, 182; *Daily Telegraph* (Sydney), 23 Dec. 1982.

35 Dandridge to Col. Sec., 29 Sept. 1869, TAHO CSD 7/33/450; Dandridge to Col. Sec., 12 Oct. 1871, TAHO CSD 7/26/215.

36 Pybus, 'Robinson and Robertson', 260–2; West, 'Truganini', 1104–5.

37 Pybus, *Community of Thieves*, 171–2.

38 Brownrigg, *The Cruise of the Freak*, p. 8; Col. Sec. to Dandridge, 11 March 1872, TAHO CSD 7/33/450; Dandridge to Col. Sec., 31 July, 21 Aug. 1873, TAHO CSD 10/31/488; *Mercury*, 9 May 1876; Plomley, *The Westlake Papers*, 50.

39 *Mercury*, 9 May 1876; Plomley, *The Westlake Papers*, 46; Rae-Ellis, *Trucanini*, 147–8.

40 Mrs Dandridge to Col. Sec., 8 May 1876, TAHO CSD 10/31/488; *Mercury*, 9 May 1876.

41   Secretary of the Royal Society of Tasmania to Col. Sec., 9 May 1876, TAHO CSD 10/31/488; Col.
      Sec. to the Royal Society of Tasmania, 19 July 1864, TAHO CSD 4/77/231; Col. Sec. to the Royal
      Society of Tasmania, 10 May 1876, TAHO CSD 10/31/488; memo to Col. Sec., 10, 11 May 1876,
      TAHO CSD 10/31/488; Rae-Ellis, *Trucanini*, 148.
42   For a full account of the funeral, see Rae-Ellis, *Trucanini*, 149–52.
43   *Mercury*, 12 May 1876.
44   ibid.
45   *The Weekly Examiner*, 14 Dec. 1878.
46   See Anderson, 'Re-claiming Tru-ger-nan-ner'; MacDonald, *Human Remains*, 88, 123.
47   Tindale, 'Tasmanian Aborigines on Kangaroo Island'; Basedow, 'Relic of the lost Tasmanian
      race'; see also Taylor, *Unearthed*.
48   Pybus, *Community of Thieves*, 183.
49   Clark, *The Aboriginal People in Tasmania*, 38.
50   Plomley, *The Westlake Papers*, 63; *Mercury*, 27 Feb. 1905.

CHAPTER 17

1   See Bladon to Premier, notes, 30 Nov. 1911, U. Tas., Bladon Papers; TAHO CSO 24/66; Plomley,
     Friendly Mission, 1015; Mollison, *The Tasmanian Aborigines*, vol. 3, part 1, notes on Armstrong
     and Proctor families; Tindale, 'Results of the Harvard–Adelaide Universities Anthropological
     Expedition', 10–15; Plomley and Henley, *The Sealers*, 34–88; for the community on Kangaroo
     Island, see Taylor, *Unearthed*.
2   J. Milligan to R.C. Gunn, 17 Nov. 1844, SLNSW ML A316; Broadfoot, 'An unexpected visit';
     Stokes, *Discoveries in Australia*, vol. 2, 451.
3   Stokes, *Discoveries in Australia*, vol. 2, 452–3.
4   TAHO CSO 24/66; Col. Sec. to Denison, 7 Jan. 1850, TAHO CSO 24/93/3033.
5   *Tasmanian Church Chronicle*, 6 March 1852.
6   ibid.
7   Nixon, *The Cruise of the Beacon*, 42; Breen, 'Lucy Beeton'.
8   TAHO LSD 1/51/33; *Church News*, 21 Nov. 1864, 389.
9   TAHO LSD 1/51/52.
10   TPP, 'Letter from the Venerable Archdeacon Reibey', 3; TPP, 'Half-caste Islanders in Bass
     Straits'; Breen, 'Lucy Beeton'.
11   George Everett to Minister for Lands, Dec. 1871, TAHO LSD 1/51/459.
12   Surveyor-General to Col. Sec., 17 Feb. 1868, TAHO LSD 1/51/32; George Everett to Surveyor-
     General, 30 Nov. 1869, TAHO LSD 1/51/32; TPP, 'Report on the state of the Islands'; *Church
     News*, April 1871.
13   TAHO CSD 7/45/833; *Tasmanian Government Gazette*, 30 April 1872; TAHO CSD 22/336/104/37;
     Breen, 'Lucy Beeton', 24; Brownrigg, *The Cruise of the Freak*, 8; Col. Sec. to Dandridge, 11 March
     1872, TAHO CSD 10/31/488.
14   *Tasmanian Government Gazette*, 30 April 1872; TAHO CSD 22/336/104/37; see Skira, 'Tasmanian
     Aborigines and muttonbirding', 97.
15   Brownrigg, *The Cruise of the Freak*, 79; Murray-Smith, 'Beyond the pale', 184.
16   Brownrigg, *The Cruise of the Freak*, 6; TAHO CSD 7/45/833.
17   *Examiner*, 8 March 1884.
18   Skira, 'Tasmanian Aborigines and muttonbirding', 156.
19   ibid., 158.
20   Mansell, pers. comm.

21 *Examiner*, 6 Feb. 1876; Murray-Smith, 'Beyond the pale', 184–5; Rowley, *The Destruction of Aboriginal Society*, 100.

22 TAHO LSD 2/4/54 (6158/1-) [7].

23 Skira, 'Tasmanian Aborigines and muttonbirding', 143.

24 *Tasmanian Government Gazette*, 15 March 1881; TAHO CSD 13/6/168.

25 *Examiner*, 8 March 1884.

26 Hart, 'The Church of England in Tasmania', 49.

27 *Church News*, Dec. 1891, 563.

28 TAHO GI NS 373/11, 9 July 1899; *Church News*, Aug. 1891, 444–5.

29 *Tasmanian Government Gazette*, 15 Dec. 1891, 2449.

30 *Church News*, Dec. 1891, 563.

31 The inhabitants of Cape Barren Island to Montgomery, 5 Feb. 1892, U. Tas., Montgomery Papers; Diary, Nov. 1891, SLNSW ML A1248/2.

32 Diary, Sept. 1892, SLNSW ML A1248/2.

33 *Church News*, Aug. 1894, 123–5; 'Report of J. Masters', 7 Aug. 1893, TAHO ED 3713/1077 110/732; annual examination, Cape Barren School, 19 Nov. 1894, TAHO ED 3713/1077 110/733; E.W. Stephens to Montgomery, Nov. 1895, U. Tas., Montgomery Papers; anon. to Minister for Education, 12 Feb. 1896, TAHO ED 3713/1077.

34 Montgomery to Rule, 9 March, 7 April 1896, TAHO ED 3713/1077; T.E. Mansell to Rule, 12 May 1896, TAHO ED 3713/1077; Rowley, *The Destruction of Aboriginal Society*, 96; Montgomery to Minister for Education, 4 Oct. 1896, TAHO ED 3713/1077 110/335.

35 'The Furneaux Islands', n.d., U. Tas., Stephens Papers.

36 C.E. Stephens to Montgomery, 28 Nov. 1899, U. Tas., Montgomery Papers; TAHO GI NS 373/11, 12 Aug. 1899; Hart, 'Church of England in Tasmania', 62–3.

37 Montgomery to Police Commissioner, 26 Aug. 1899, U. Tas., Montgomery Papers.

38 C.E. Stephens to Montgomery, 28 Nov. 1899, U. Tas., Montgomery Papers.

39 C.E. Stephens to Montgomery, 29 May 1900, U. Tas., Montgomery Papers.

40 *Examiner*, 27 Aug. 1902.

CHAPTER 18

1 Bell, 'Some demographic and cultural characteristics', 431–7.

2 FM, Flinders Council Minute Book, 26 Feb. 1908; Rowley, *The Destruction of Aboriginal Society*, 182; TPP, 'Report upon the state of the islands'.

3 FM, Flinders Council Minute Book, 2 June 1910; TPP, 'Report upon the state of the islands'.

4 Premier of Tasmania to Warden of Flinders Council, 3 March 1910, TAHO PD 1/224/225; *Examiner*, 12 Jan. 1911; Premier to Bladon, 20 Oct. 1911, U. Tas., Bladon Papers.

5 Premier to Bladon, 20 Oct. 1911, U. Tas., Bladon Papers.

6 *Mercury*, 21 Nov. 1911.

7 Bladon to Premier, 20 Dec. 1911, U. Tas., Bladon Papers; *Mercury*, 13 Sept. 1912.

8 Skira, 'Tasmanian Aborigines and muttonbirding', 81a; Skira, 'Aboriginals in Tasmania', 189; CBS, Cape Barren Island School and Punishment Book, 19 June 1916, 3 Nov. 1918.

9 E.A. Counsel, 'Report on the management of the half castes at Cape Barren Island', 4 Dec. 1922, TAHO LSD 643/30 1646/22.

10 'Petition from residents of Cape Barren Island Reserve to the minister for Lands', 8 Dec. 1922, TAHO LSD 643/30 1646/22.

11 'Remarks by Counsel to minister for Lands on back of petition', 12 Dec. 1922, TAHO LSD 643/30 1646/22.

12 W.J. Mansfield to Secretary for Lands, 18 Sept. 1922, TAHO LSD 643/30 1646/22; Rev.
    F.H. Gilles to Premier, 14 Feb. 1923, TAHO LSD 643/30 1646/22; Counsel, 'Report on the
    management of the half castes at Cape Barren Island', 4 Dec. 1922, TAHO LSD 643/30 1646/22.
13 TPP, 'Report of the Select Committee'.
14 TAHO CSD 22/336/104/37; FM, Flinders Council Minute Book, 5 July 1930.
15 FM, Flinders Council Minute Book, 8 Feb., 7 June 1930.
16 TAHO CSD 22/336/104/37.
17 ibid.
18 ibid.
19 Needham, 'Cape Barren Island'.
20 J.S. Needham, 'Report to minister for Lands', 24 Dec. 1930, TAHO LSD 643/30; TAHO LSD 51 [1].
21 West, *Pride against Prejudice*; Mallett, *My Past—Their Future*.
22 Mallett, *My Past—Their Future*, 1–5.
23 ibid., 17.
24 West, *Pride against Prejudice*, 23.
25 Mallett, *My Past—Their Future*, 41.
26 ibid., 22.
27 FM, Flinders Council Minute Book, 11 Oct. 1930, 17 Jan. 1931; King, 'Barren future'; *Examiner*,
    3 Oct. 1936; TAHO CSD 22/416/104/10; TPP, 'Report of the secretary for Lands'; Skira,
    'Tasmanian Aborigines and muttonbirding', 196–7.
28 Mallett, *My Past—Their Future*, 43.
29 Cove, *What the Bones Say*, 91.
30 Mallett, *My Past—Their Future*, 43.
31 TPP, 'Report of the secretary for Lands and surveyor-general's department 1944'.
32 TAHO CSD 22/531/104/7; *Cape Barren Island Reserve Act 1945*.
33 *Examiner*, 17, 21, 25, 27, 28 Nov., 4, 5 Dec. 1947; TPP, 'Report of Joint Committee'.
34 *Expiration of Cape Barren Island Reserve Act 1945*, 1951.
35 Victorian Aboriginal Group, *29th Annual Report* (1958); TAHO GI CBI file.
36 Breen and Summers, *Aboriginal Connections with Launceston Places*, 37–41; Wagstaff, Gibson and
    Manning, 'Cape Barren Island'; King, 'Barren future'.
37 TPP, 'Report of the Committee'.
38 *Mercury*, 12 July 1968; *Examiner*, 29 Aug. 1968.
39 *Mercury*, 17, 19, 21, 22, 23, 26 Aug. 1968.
40 ibid., 29 Aug. 1968.
41 Chobanian, 'Cape Barren', 20; King, 'Barren future'.
42 *Examiner*, 23 Aug., 3, 11 Sept. 1968; *Mercury*, 30 Oct. 1968.
43 *Mercury*, 12 July 1969; *Togatus*, vol. 41, no. 6, May 1970; Newcombe, 'Their barren existence';
    Tasmanian Government Gazette, 8 April 1970; *The Age*, 11 April 1970.
44 Minutes of the Conference of Cape Barren Islanders, U. Tas., Abschol Archives.

CHAPTER 19

1 West, *Pride against Prejudice*, 87–9; *Mercury*, 1 May 1976.
2 West, *Pride against Prejudice*, 90.
3 Ryan, 'The Survivors', 55.
4 Mansell, 'Land rights for Tasmania's Aborigines', 92.
5 TPP, 'Report of the Aboriginal Affairs Study Group'.
6 'Comments on recommendations of the Aboriginal Affairs Study Group'.
7 'The last Tasmanian'.

8   TPP, 'Report of the Aboriginal Affairs Study Group'; 'Comments on recommendations of the Aboriginal Affairs Study Group'.

9   *Aboriginal Treaty Newsletter*, Sept. 1982.

10 *Mercury*, 11 Aug. 1982.

11 *Adelaide Advertiser*, 20 Nov., 18 Dec. 1982.

12 Langford, 'Our heritage—your playground', 2.

13 ibid., 6.

14 *Mercury*, 11 Dec. 1982; Allen, 'Aborigines and archaeologists'.

15 *SMH*, 9 June 1983.

16 *Mercury*, 6 June 1983.

17 *The Age*, 8 June 1983.

18 *SMH*, 2 July 1983.

19 *Daily Telegraph* (Sydney), 23 Dec. 1982.

20 *SMH*, 29 Dec. 1982.

21 *Advocate*, 17 Jan. 1984; *Mercury*, 24 Jan. 1984.

22 TAC, *Oyster Cove*.

23 *The Australian*, 2 March 1984.

24 *Examiner*, 5 April 1984, *The Australian*, 6 April 1984.

25 *Mercury*, 6 April 1984.

26 *Canberra Times*, 12 April 1984.

27 *Mercury*, 17 April, 18 July, 10 Aug. 1984, 6 May 1985.

28 ibid., 9 July 1985; *The Australian*, 5 Oct. 1985.

29 *The Age*, 25 April 1987; *Advocate*, 2 Sept. 1987; *Pugganna News*, Sept. 1987.

30 TAC, *Land Rights in Tasmania*.

31 ibid.

32 *Mercury*, 22 Oct. 1986.

33 See Jim Everett, 'Aboriginal sovereignty', *Pugganna News*, Sept. 1987; see also *Tribune*, 20 May 1987; David Barnett, *The Bulletin*, 19 May 1987.

34 *Pugganna News*, June 1987.

35 *The Age*, 22 April 1987; *Examiner*, 23 April 1987.

36 *The Age*, 25 April 1987.

37 ibid.

38 *Daily Telegraph* (Sydney), 28 April 1987, *Mercury*, 28 April 1987.

39 *The Age*, 28 May 1987.

40 *Canberra Times*, 31 May 1987.

41 *Border Morning Mail*, 3 Sept. 1987; *Pugganna News*, Sept. 1987; *Sunday Examiner*, 15 Nov. 1987; *Examiner*, 9 Oct. 1987.

42 *The Age*, 30 April 1988.

43 *Mercury*, 11 Feb. 1990.

44 ibid., 14 Feb. 1990.

45 Mansell, 'Aboriginal Provisional Government'.

46 *Mercury*, 4, 5 April 1991.

47 ibid., 5 April 1991.

48 TPP, *Hansard*, Legislative Council, 12 July 1991, 1812.

49 *Advocate*, 18 June 1991; *Examiner*, 20 July 1991.

50 Australian Bureau of Statistics, *Census 1991*.

CHAPTER 20

1 *Examiner*, 22 May 1992.
2 *Mercury*, 8 Nov. 1993.
3 Phillips, 'Reconstructing the rules', 3.
4 *Examiner*, 9 Jan. 1993.
5 ibid., 19 Jan. 1993.
6 *Mercury*, 29 July 1993.
7 *Examiner*, 26 Nov. 1993; *Advocate*, 26 Nov. 1993.
8 Groom, 'Tasmanian Aboriginal people'.
9 ibid.; *Examiner*, 17 Dec., 1993.
10 *Examiner*, 22 Dec. 1993.
11 TPP, *Hansard*, Legislative Council, 27 April 1994, 521.
12 ibid., 525.
13 ibid., 526.
14 Groom, media release, 21 May 1994; *Advocate*, 21 May 1994.
15 The information in this and the previous three paragraphs has been summarised from the Department of Premier and Cabinet, 'Report of the Aboriginal forum'.
16 *Advocate*, 23 May 1994.
17 TPP, *Hansard*, House of Assembly, 15 Sept. 1994, 2117–18.
18 *The Australian*, 18 Oct. 1995.
19 ibid.
20 *Mercury*, 11 Dec. 1995.
21 ibid.

CHAPTER 21

1 *In the Matter of The Aboriginal Land Act*, 10.
2 *Edwina Shaw & Anor v Charles Wolf & Ors*; *Mercury*, 13 Aug. 1997; Curthoys, Genovese and Reilly, *Rights and Redemption*, 191–218; Sanders, *The Tasmanian Electoral Roll Trial*, 1–4.
3 Australian Human Rights and Equal Opportunity Commission, *Bringing Them Home*, Chapter 13.
4 TPP, *Hansard*, House of Assembly, 13 Aug. 1997, 18.
5 *Edwina Shaw & Anor v Charles Wolf & Ors*, 15.
6 ibid.
7 ibid.
8 ibid., 268.
9 *Mercury*, 21 April 1998.
10 *Sunday Tasmanian*, 11 April 1999.
11 *Mercury*, 6 Nov. 1997.
12 ibid., 21 Oct. 1998.
13 *Examiner*, 1 March 1999.
14 ibid.; *Mercury*, 1 March 1999; Bacon, press release, 28 Feb. 1999.
15 *Examiner*, 4 Aug. 1999.
16 Bacon, press release, 12 Oct. 1999; *Examiner*, 13, 14 Oct. 1999; *Mercury*, 13 Oct. 1999.
17 Napier, press releases, 12, 13 Oct. 1999.
18 *Mercury*, 5 July 2000.
19 Bacon, press release, 13 Sept. 2000; *Examiner*, 3, 13 Sept. 2000, *Mercury*, 17, 22, 24 March 2001.

20 *In the Matter of The Aboriginal Lands Act*.

21 *Patmore & Ors v Independent Indigenous Advisory Committee*.

22 ibid., 9.

23 ibid.; see also Sanders, *The Tasmanian Electoral Roll Trial*, 10–17.

24 *Pakana News*, 2003, 17–18.

25 *Patmore & Ors v Independent Indigenous Advisory Committee*, 7.

26 *Mercury*, 16 Nov. 2002.

27 ibid., 12 Sept. 2003.

28 ibid., 10, 11, 12 Sept. 2003, 16 April 2004.

29 *Pakana News*, no. 54, 2004–7.

30 *Mercury*, 26, 27 July 2002.

31 ibid., 16 April, 27 May, 16 June, 29 Oct., 11 Nov. 2004.

32 ibid., 16, 22, 23 March 2005.

33 ibid., 24 March 2005.

34 ibid., 24, 25 March 2005.

35 *Examiner*, 11 May 2005; *Mercury*, 11 May 2005.

36 *Mercury*, 11 May 2005.

37 ibid., 12 May 2005.

38 ibid.; *Examiner*, 11 May 2005.

39 *Mercury*, 15, 17, 18 June 2005.

40 *Bleathman v Taylor*, 13.

41 *Mercury*, 25 June 2009.

42 See <www.dpac.tas.gov.au/divisions.cdd/oaa/eligibility_policy> accessed 15 July 2009.

43 *Sunday Tasmanian*, 6 Jan. 2002.

44 ibid.; *Mercury*, 1 June 2002.

45 *Sunday Tasmanian*, 6 Jan. 2002; *Pakana News*, April 2002; *Mercury*, 1 June 2002.

46 *Sunday Tasmanian*, 6 Jan. 2002; *Mercury*, 14 Feb. 2002.

47 *Pakana News*, Aug. 2002.

48 ibid.

49 *Mercury*, 13, 15 June 2002.

50 ibid., 2 Aug. 2003.

51 *SMH*, 13 July 2009.

52 *Mercury*, 8 March 2008.

53 ibid., 23 Nov. 2006.

54 ibid., 30 Nov. 2006.

55 TPP, *Hansard*, House of Assembly, 21 Nov. 2006, 26–85; *Mercury*, 22 Nov. 2006.

56 Groom, *Report of the Stolen Generations Assessor*, 2.

EPILOGUE

1 *Mercury*, 7 Nov. 2009.

2 ibid., 11 Dec. 2009.

3 ibid., 11 Feb. 2010.

4 *Sunday Tasmanian*, 13, 27 March 2011.

5 Bowdler, "Submission to the Hon. David O'Byrne', 2.

6 ibid.

7 ibid.

Bibliography

ARCHIVAL AND GOVERNMENTAL MANUSCRIPT COLLECTIONS

Archives Office of New South Wales, Sydney

2/8130   Col. Sec., Appendix A: Special Bundles, 1794–1825, Van Diemen's Land, 1807–16. Remarks on the Country and Settlements Formed in Van Diemen's Land, 1809.

Cape Barren School, Cape Barren Island, Tasmania (CBS)

Cape Barren Island School and Punishment Book, 19 June 1916, 3 Nov. 1918.

Flinders Municipality, Council Chambers, Whitemark, Flinders Island, Tasmania (FM)

Flinders Council Minute Book, 26 Feb. 1908, 2 June 1910, 8 Feb., 7 June, 5 July, 11 Oct. 1930, 17 Jan. 1931.

Mitchell Library, State Library of New South Wales, Sydney (SLNSW ML)
Official sources

A1205   Despatches to the Governor of New South Wales, vol. 16, 1829.

A1219   Despatches to the Governor of New South Wales, vol. 30, 1838.

A1352   Orders and Proclamations of Lieutenant-Governor Sorell, 1817–22.

BT   Bonwick Transcripts, series 1, vol. 4, box 52, 1268–74.

C190   Van Diemen's Land, Register of Deaths, 1803–20.

Other sources

A316   Gunn Papers.

A612   Tasmanian Aborigines.

A860   Rowland Hassall Papers, vol. 2, part 1.

A1055/3   Thomas Scott, Sketches and Plans, 1820 and following years.

A1248/2   Writing Notes and Correspondence of E.W. Stephens.

A2170   Arthur Papers, vols 9, 28.

A7022–92   Robinson Papers, vols 24, 50, 67.

MSS3597   Flinders Island Papers.

Public Record Office, London (PRO)

CO 201/35   Collins to Colonial Office, 27 Dec. 1802.

CO 280/93   Despatches, Jan.–March 1838.

CO 280/133   Despatches, July–Aug. 1841.

CO 280/195   Despatches, July–Oct. 1846.

CO 280/215   Despatches, 5–7 Dec. 1847.

Tasmanian Archive and Heritage Office, Hobart (TAHO)
Chief Secretary's Department (CSD)

4/77/231   Correspondence with Royal Society of Tasmania, 1864.

7/26/215   Correspondence Relating to Truganini.

7/33/450   Burial of Truganini, 1876.

7/45/833   Du Cane to Ministers, 14 Aug. 1871.

10/31/488   Burial of Truganini, 1876.

13/6/168   Correspondence with Malcolm Collis to Chairman of Board of Education, 1 Aug. 1881.

22/336/104/37   A.W. Burbury, 'Report on the condition of the half castes at Cape Barren Island Reservation', 25 Sept. 1929.

22/416/104/10   Ministerial Memo, Minister for Lands and Works, 26 Feb. 1937.

22/531/104   Correspondence between the Commonwealth Statistician, Roland Wilson, and CSD, 6, 14 June, 18, 23 Sept. 1946.

Colonial Secretary's Office (CSO)

1/316/7578/1   Miscellaneous Correspondence and Reports, 1824–31, Relating to Atrocities Committed by the Aborigines.

1/317/7578/2   Reports by G.A. Robinson.

1/318/7578/3   Reports by G.A. Robinson.

1/319/7578/4   Papers Relating to the Aborigines Committee.

1/320/7578/5   Reports by Police Magistrates *re* Roving Parties.

1/321/7578/6   Applications for Position of Storekeeper at Bruny Island, 1829; Applications to Join Parties in Pursuit of Aborigines; Applications for Indulgences and Rewards; Letters from John Parish.

1/323/7578/8   Jackson's Reports on the Islands in the Straits; Suggestion *re* Capture of Aborigines; Answers to Questions Circulated by Aborigines Committee.

1/327/7578/12   Papers Relating to Sydney Aborigines; the Eligibility of Bruny Island for an Aboriginal Establishment; the Two Aboriginal Boys Held by Batman.

1/329/7578/14   Papers Relating to the Roving Parties and to the Line.

1/330/7578/15   Correspondence with Major Abbott, Edward Curr (*re* Goldie Affair), Gilbert Robertson, and Others; Reports on the Killing of Aborigines and Captured; Some Flinders Island Papers.

1/331/7578/16   Papers *re* Gilbert Robertson, 1828–31.

1/332/7578/17   Minutes of the Aborigines Committee.

1/740

8/157/1166   Papers Relating to Flinders Island, 1842–43.

11/27/658   Report of Lieutenant Matthew Friend on the Flinders Island Aboriginal Establishment, 31 Oct. 1846.

24/66   Report of the Surveyor-General on the Islands of Bass Strait, 1849.

24/93/3033   Correspondence by Col. Sec. to Denison, Jan. 1850.

24/284/6314   Milligan and Oyster Cove, 1854.

Education Department (ED)

3713/1077 110/335, 110/732–733   Correspondence Relating to the Education of the Children at Cape Barren Island, 1890–1901.

General Index (GI)

4/1692	Oyster Cove Visitors' Book, 1858–66.
CBI file C.I.A.	Booth, 'The half castes of the Furneaux Islands', Feb. 1959 (typescript report to the Bishop of Tasmania).
LSD, no. 11	Journal of Charles Grimes (James Meehan).
NS 65	Bedford papers
NS 323/1	Diary of Adam Amos.
NS 373/11	Register of Services, Church of the Epiphany, Cape Barren Island, 1889–1906.
VDL 341	Diary and Field Book of Henry Hellyer.

Governor's Office (GO)

33/7	Governor's Office, Internal Correspondence, 1824–30.
52/2	Governor's Office, in Letters, 1823–26.

Lands and Survey Department (LSD)

1/51/32	Surveyor-General to Col. Sec., 17 Feb. 1868, and Other Papers.
1/51/33	Report of Surveyor-General Power, Sept.–Oct. 1854.
1/51/52	Remarks on Bass Strait Islands by John Thomas to the Surveyor-General, Sept. 1861.
1/51/459	
2/4/54	Petition to Governor, Dec. 1879.
17/1	
51 [1]	Report of Dr F. Gaha to Secretary of Department of Lands, June 1930.
643/30	Correspondence File, 1913–30 (including folio 1646/22).

Premier's Department (PD)

1/224/225   Cape Barren Island, 1910.

University of Tasmania (U. Tas.)

Bladon Papers, U. Tas. Library, 8/RS/190/D34.

Minutes of the Conference of Cape Barren Islanders, Launceston, 13–14 Aug. 1971, Abschol Archives.

Montgomery Papers, papers relating to Cape Barren Island, Christ College, BC 46 CBI.

Newcombe, Ken: 'Their barren existence' (typescript). Hobart, 1970.

Stephens Papers, U. Tas. Library.

COURT REPORTS

Bleathman v Taylor [2007] TASSC 82 (8 November 2007).

Mabo v Queensland (no. 2) ('Mabo Case') HCA 23; (1992) 175 CLR 1 (3 June 1992).

Edwina Shaw & Anor v Charles Wolf & Ors [1998] FCA 389 (20 April 1998).

In the Matter of The Aboriginal Land Act 1995 and In The Matter of Marianne Watson (No. 2) [2001] TASSC 105 (27 August 2001).

Patmore & Ors v Independent Indigenous Advisory Committee [2002] AATA 962 (October 2002).

PARLIAMENTARY PAPERS AND ACTS
Great Britain, 19th Century House of Commons Sessional Papers (BPP)

'Aboriginal tribes', vol. 44, no. 617, 1834.

'Aborigines (Australian colonies)', vol. 34, no. 627, 1844.

'Australian Aborigines', vol. 34, no. 526, 1839.

'Papers relating to His Majesty's settlements at New South Wales, 1811–1814', vol. 18, no. 450, 1816.

'Report of the commissioner of inquiry on the state of the agriculture and trade in the colony of New South Wales', vol. 10, no. 136, 1823.

'Report from the Select Committee on Aborigines (British settlements)', vol. 7, no. 425, 1837.

'Van Diemen's Land', vol. 19, no. 259, 1831.

Tasmania (TPP)

Acts

Aboriginal Lands Act 1995 (No. 98 of 1995).

Aboriginal Lands Amendment Act (No. 2) 2005 (No. 25 of 2005).

Cape Barren Island Reserve Act 1912.

Cape Barren Island Reserve Act 1945.

Expiration of Cape Barren Reserve Act 1945, 1951.

Hansard

House of Assembly: 15 Sept. 1994, 1–17; 13 Aug. 1997, 35–86; 21 Nov. 2006, 26–85.

Legislative Council: 12 July 1991, 181–2; 27 April 1994, 1–82; 16 June 2005, 1–48.

Journals & Papers

'Half-caste Islanders in Bass Straits' (T. Reibey), Legislative Council, vol. 9, no. 48, 1863.

'Letter from the Venerable Archdeacon Reibey, on the subject of the half-caste Islanders in the Straits', Legislative Council, vol. 7, no. 17, 1862.

'Report of the Aboriginal Affairs Study Group of Tasmania', Parliament, vol. 199, no. 94, 1978.

'Report of the committee appointed by the state government to examine several matters concerned with the future development of Flinders Island', Parliament, vol. 179, no. 15, 1968.

'Report of the Joint Committee of the House of Assembly and Legislative Council appointed to enquire into matters connected with the Flinders Island Municipality', Parliament, vol. 139, no. 22, 1948.

'Report of the Select Committee appointed 29 October 1924, to inquire into and report upon the best means of dealing with the half-caste problem on the Furneaux Group of Islands', Parliament, vol. 91, no. 48, 1924–25.

'Report of the secretary for Lands 1937–38', Parliament, vol. 119, no. 13, 1938.

'Report of the secretary for Lands and Surveyor-General's Department 1944', Parliament, vol. 131, no. 10, 1944–45.

'Report upon the state of the islands, the condition and mode of living of the half-castes, the existing methods of regulating the reserves, and suggesting lines for future administration' (J.E.C. Lord), Parliament, vol. 59, no. 57, 1908.

PERSONAL COMMUNICATIONS

Cameron, Patsy: personal communication, 8 July 2010; email to author, 17 Dec. 2010

Esdaile, Charles: email to author, 18 June 2010.

Mansell, Sarah (Mrs): personal communication, 30 July 1973.

McGowan, Angela: personal communication, 19 Jan. 2010.

Residents at Deloraine: interview by the author, 18 March 2006.

THESES

Hart, Philip R: 'The Church of England in Tasmania under Bishop Montgomery', MA thesis, U. Tas., 1963.

Skira, Irynej: 'Tasmanian Aborigines and muttonbirding: a historical examination', PhD thesis, U. Tas., 1993.

TYPESCRIPT MATERIAL

Bowdler, Sandra: 'Submission to the Hon. David O'Byrne, minister for the Environment, Parks and Heritage'. Perth, 22 Oct. 2010, copy in possession of the author.

Chobanian, Connie: 'Cape Barren'. Sydney: ABC, 1971.

'Comments on recommendations of the Aboriginal Affairs Study Group', TAC, 11 Dec. 1978, copy in possession of the author.

Department of Premier and Cabinet: 'Report of the Aboriginal forum held on 21 May 1994', Hobart, 1994.

Groom, Ray: 'Tasmanian Aboriginal people: a step towards full recognition and appreciation', paper presented to the meeting with Aboriginal communities in Launceston, 16 Dec. 1993.

King, Brian: 'Barren future'. *Four Corners*. Sydney: ABC, 18 May 1971.

Mansell, Michael: 'Aboriginal Provisional Government', unpub. paper, TAC, n.d.

Wagstaff, P., Gibson, J. and Manning, J.: 'Cape Barren Island'. Social Science Research Council research file: Canberra, 1966.

NEWSPAPERS AND PERIODICALS

Aboriginal Treaty Newsletter, Sept. 1982.

Adelaide Advertiser, 20 Nov., 18 Dec. 1982.

Advertiser, 9 April 1988.

Advocate (Burnie), 17 Jan. 1984, 2 Sept. 1987, 18 June 1991, 1993, May 1994, 14 Oct. 1999.

The Age, 11 April 1970, 23 Dec. 1982, 8 June 1983, April, May 1987, 30 April 1988.

Asiatic Journal, Sept. 1820.

The Australian, 2 March, 6 April 1984, 5 Oct. 1985, 7 April 1988, 18 Oct. 1995, 27 May 1997, 14, 17, 28–29 Dec. 2002, 6, 10, 13 Jan., 7 May 2003.

Australian Financial Review, 28 Feb. 31 Oct. 2003.

Border Morning Mail, 3 Sept. 1987.

The Bulletin, 19 May 1987.

Canberra Times, 12 April 1984, 31 May 1987, 7 April 1988.

Church News, April 1871, Aug., Dec. 1891, Aug. 1894.

Circular Head Chronicle, 16 Sept. 1992.

Colonial Advocate, 1 May 1828, 1 April 1830.

Colonial Times, 1826–31.

The Courier, 24 March, 28 April 1837.

Courier Mail, 18 Aug. 2001.

Daily Telegraph (Sydney), 23 Dec. 1982, 28 April 1987, 21 Dec. 2002.

Examiner (Launceston), 2 Oct. 1847, 6 Feb. 1876, 8 March 1884, 27 Aug. 1902, 12 Jan. 1911, 3 Oct. 1936, Nov., Dec. 1947, Aug., Sept. 1968, 5 April 1984, April, 9 Oct. 1987, 20 July 1991, 22 May 1992, 1993, 1999, Sept. 2000, 11 May 2005.

Herald-Sun (Melbourne), 23 Dec. 2002.

Hobart Town Advertiser, Dec. 1847.

Hobart Town Courier, 1827–31.

Hobart Town Gazette, 1817–19, 1823–27.

Launceston Advertiser, 1829, Sept. 1830.

Manning River Times, 6 April 1988.

Mercury (Hobart), 1869, May 1876, 27 Feb. 1905, 21 Nov. 1911, 13 Sept. 1912, 1968, 12 July 1969, 1 May 1976, 3 April 1978, 1982–93 (discontinuous), 3 June, 11 Dec. 1995, Aug., Nov. 1997, April, Oct. 1998, March, Oct. 1999, 5 July 2000, March 2001, 2002, Aug., Sept. 2003, 2004, March, May, June 2005, Nov. 2006, 8 March 2008, 25 June 2009.

Northern Territory News, 9 April 1988.

Pakana News (TAC, Hobart), 2002, 2003, 2004–7.

Pugganna News (TAC, Hobart), June, Sept. 1987.

Sunday Examiner, 15 Nov. 1987, 30 Aug. 1992.

Sunday Tasmanian, 11 April 1999, 6 Jan., 16 June 2002.

Sydney Gazette, 18 March, 2 Sept. 1804.

Sydney Morning Herald, 29 Dec. 1982, June, July 1983, 2 May 1987, 4 July 2001, 19, 24 Dec. 2002, 13 July 2009.

The Tasmanian, 16 Nov. 1827, 1828, 1830, 1831.

Tasmanian Church Chronicle, 6 March 1852.

Tasmanian Government Gazette, 8 April 1870, 30 April 1872, 15 March 1881, 15 Dec. 1891.

Tasmanian Review and Register, 1 April 1830.

Togatus (Tasmanian University Union), vol. 41, no. 6, May 1970.

Tribune (Sydney), 20 May 1987.

Van Diemen's Land Intelligencer, 1 May 1828.

The Weekly Examiner, 14 Dec. 1878.

West Australian, 6 April 1988.

MEDIA RELEASES, TASMANIA

Bacon, Jim, 28 Feb., 12 Oct. 1999, 13 Sept. 2000.

Cleary, John, 27 July 1992.

Groom, Ray, 9 June 1993, 21 May 1994.

Napier, Sue, 12, 13 Oct. 1999.

TV PROGRAMS

'The last Tasmanian', *Monday Conference*, ABC TV, 4 Sept 1978.

MONOGRAPHS, CHAPTERS, JOURNAL AND PERIODICAL ARTICLES, REPORTS, REFERENCE WORKS AND CONFERENCE PROCEEDINGS

Allen, Jim: 'Aborigines and archaeologists in Tasmania in 1983', *Australian Archaeology*, vol. 16, 1983, 7–10.

Allen, Jim and Jones, Rhys: 'Oyster Cove: archaeological traces of the last Tasmanians and notes on the criteria for the authentication of flaked glass artifacts', *Papers and Proceedings of the Royal Society of Tasmania*, vol. 114, 1980, 225–33.

Anderson, Ian: 'Re-claiming Tru-ger-nan-ner: de-colonising the symbol', *Art Monthly Australia*, no. 66, Dec. 1993–Feb. 1994, 10–14.

——'Re-claiming TRU-GER-NAN-NER: decolonising the symbol', in Penny van Toorn and David English (eds), *Speaking Positions: Aboriginality, Gender and Ethnicity in Australian Cultural Studies*, Melbourne: Department of Humanities, Victoria University of Technology, 1995, 31–42.

Atkinson, Alan: *The Europeans in Australia: A History*, vol. 1, Oxford: Oxford University Press, 1998.

Attwood, Bain: *Telling the Truth about Aboriginal History*, Crows Nest, NSW: Allen & Unwin, 2005.

Australian Human Rights and Equal Opportunity Commission: *Bringing Them Home: Report of the National Inquiry into the Separation of Aboriginal and Torres Strait Islander Children from Their Families*, Sydney: Sterling Press, 1997.

Backhouse, James: *A Narrative of a Visit to the Australian Colonies*, London: Hamilton, Adams and Co., 1843.

Banner, Stuart: 'Why *terra nullius*? Anthropology and property law in early Australia', *Law and History Review*, vol. 23, no.1, spring 2005, 95–131.

——*Possessing the Pacific: Land Settlers and Indigenous People from Australia to Alaska*, Cambridge, Mass.: Harvard University Press, 2007.

Basedow, Herbert: 'Relic of the lost Tasmanian race: obituary notice of Mary Seymour', *Man*, 14, 1914, 161–2.

Belich, James: *Making Peoples: A History of the New Zealanders from Polynesian Settlement to the End of the Nineteenth Century*, Auckland: Penguin Books New Zealand, 2007.

Bell, J.H: 'Some demographic and cultural characteristics of the La Perouse Aborigines', *Mankind*, vol. 5, no. 10, 1962, 425–38.

Benton, Lauren: *Law and Colonial Cultures: Legal Regimes in World History, 1400–1900*, Cambridge: Cambridge University Press, 2002.

Betts, T: *An Account of the Colony of Van Diemen's Land*, Calcutta: Baptist Mission Press, 1830.

Birmingham, Judy: *Wybalenna: The Archaeology of Cultural Accommodation in Nineteenth Century Tasmania*, Sydney: The Australian Society for Historical Archaeology, 1992.

Blackburn, Kevin: 'Imagining Aboriginal nations: early nineteenth century evangelicals on the Australian frontier and the "nation" concept', *Australian Journal of Politics and History*, vol. 48, no. 2, 2002, 174–92.

Bonwick, James: *The Last of the Tasmanians; or, The Black War in Van Diemen's Land*, London: Sampson Low, Son, & Marston, 1870 [facsimile edition, Adelaide: South Australian Libraries Board, 1969].

Bowden, K.M.: *Captain James Kelly of Hobart Town*, Carlton, Vic: Melbourne University Press, 1964.

Bowen, Peter: 'Issues of Aboriginal identity', *Law Letter*, spring 2006, 31–3.

Boyce, James, 'Fantasy island', in Robert Manne (ed.), *Whitewash: On Keith Windschuttle's Fabrication of Aboriginal History*, Melbourne: Black Inc., 2003, 17–80.

——*Van Diemen's Land*, Melbourne: Black Inc., 2008.

Brantlinger, Patrick: *Dark Vanishings: Discourses on the Extinction of Primitive Races, 1800–1930*, Ithaca and London: Cornell University Press, 2003.

Breen, Shayne, 'Human agency, historical inevitability and moral culpability: rewriting black–white history in the wake of Native Title', *Aboriginal History*, vol. 20, 1996, 108–32.

——*Contested Places: Tasmania's Northern Districts from Ancient Times to 1900*, Hobart: Centre for Tasmanian Historical Studies, 2001.

——'Re-inventing social evolution', in Robert Manne (ed.), *Whitewash: On Keith Windschuttle's Fabrication of Aboriginal History*, Melbourne: Black Inc., 2003, 139–59.

——'Lucy Beeton', in Chris Cunneen (ed.), *Australian Dictionary of Biography Supplement 1580–1980*, Carlton, Vic.: Melbourne University Press, 2005, 24–5.

Breen, Shayne and Summers, Dyan: *Aboriginal Connections with Launceston Places*, Launceston: Launceston City Council, 2006.

Bridges, Roy: *That Yesterday Was Home*, Sydney: Australasian Publishing Company, 1948.

Broadfoot, John: 'An unexpected visit to Flinders Island in Bass Strait', *Chambers' Edinburgh Journal*, 20 Sept. 1845, 187–9.

Broome, Richard: 'The struggle for Australia: Aboriginal–European warfare 1770–1930', in Michael McKernan and Margaret Browne (eds), *Australia: Two Centuries of War and Peace*, Canberra and Sydney: Australian War Memorial and Allen & Unwin, 1988.

——'The statistics of frontier conflict', in Bain Attwood and S.G. Foster (eds), *Frontier Conflict: The Australian Experience*, Canberra: National Museum of Australia, 2003.

——*Aboriginal Victorians: A History since 1800*, Crows Nest, NSW: Allen & Unwin, 2005.

Brown, Steve: *Aboriginal Archaeological Sites in Eastern Tasmania: A Cultural Resource Management Statement*, Hobart: Department of Parks, Wildlife and Heritage, 1991.

Brownrigg, M.B.: *The Cruise of the Freak*, Launceston: J.S.V. Turner, 1872.

Bryden, William: *The Story of Tasmanian Aboriginals*, Hobart: Tasmanian Museum, 1960.

Butlin, N.B.: *Our Original Aggression: Aboriginal Populations of South Eastern Australia 1788–1850*, North Sydney: Allen & Unwin, 1983.

Calder, Graeme: *Levee, Line and Martial Law: A History of the Dispossession of the Mairremmener People of Van Diemen's Land 1803–1832*, Launceston: Fullers Bookshop, 2010.

Calder, James Erskine: 'Some account of the country lying between Lake St Clair and Macquarie Harbour', *Tasmanian Journal of Natural Science*, vol. 3, no. 6, 1849, 415–29.

——*Some Account of the Wars, Extirpation, Habits, etc, of the Native Tribes of Tasmania*, Hobart: Henn & Co., 1875 [facsimile edition, Hobart: Cox, Kay, 1972].

Cameron, Patsy: *Grease and Ochre: The Blending of Two Cultures at the Colonial Sea Frontier*, Launceston: Fullers Bookshop, 2011.

Campbell, Judy: *Invisible Invaders: Smallpox and Other Diseases in Aboriginal Australia 1780–1880*, Melbourne: Melbourne University Press, 2002.

Clark, Julia: *The Aboriginal People in Tasmania*, 2nd edn, Hobart: Tasmanian Museum and Art Gallery, 1988.

Coleman, Peter: 'The Windschuttle thesis', *Quadrant*, vol. 46, no. 12, Dec. 2002, 65–6.

Collins, David: *An Account of the English Colony in New South Wales*, ed. Brian Fletcher, Sydney: Angus & Robertson, 1975 [first published 1798, 1802].

Connor, John: *The Australian Frontier Wars 1788–1838*, Sydney: UNSW Press, 2002.

——'British frontier warfare logistics and the "Black Line"', Van Diemen's Land (Tasmania), 1830', *War in History*, vol. 9, no. 2, 2002, 143–58.

——'The frontier war that never was', in Craig Stockings (ed.), *Zombie Myths in Australian Military History*, Sydney: New South Books, 2010, 10–28.

Cosgrove, Richard: *Aboriginal Economy and Settlement in the Tasmanian Central Highlands*, Hobart: National Parks and Wildlife Service, 1984.

Cove, John J.: *What the Bones Say: Tasmanian Aborigines, Science and Domination*, Ottawa: Carleton University Press, 1995.

Cox, Robert: *Steps to the Scaffold: The Untold Story of Tasmania's Black Bushrangers*, Pawleena, Tas: Cornhill Publishing, 2004.

Crawford, Justice, Ellis, W.F. and Stancombe, G.H. (eds): *The Diaries of John Helder Wedge 1824–1835*, Hobart: Royal Society of Tasmania, 1962.

Crowther, W.E.L.H.: 'The final phase of the extinct Tasmanian race 1847–1876', *Records of the Queen Victoria Museum*, new series, no. 49, 1974, 1–30.

Cumpston, J.S.: *The Furneaux Group, Bass Strait*, Canberra: Roebuck Books, 1972.

Curthoys, Ann: 'Genocide in Tasmania: the history of an idea' in A. Dirk Moses (ed.), *Empire, Colony, Genocide: Conquest, Occupation and Subaltern Resistance in World History*, New York: Berghanh Books, 2008.

Curthoys, Ann, Genovese, Anne and Reilly, Alexander: *Rights and Redemption: History, Law and Indigenous People*, Sydney: UNSW Press, 2008.

Dammery, Sally: *Walter George Arthur: A Free Tasmanian?*, Melbourne: Monash Publications in History, 2001.

——'Walter George Arthur: a health profile of a 19th century Van Diemen's Land Aboriginal man', *Health & History*, vol. 4, no. 2, 2002, 80–92.

Darwin, Charles: *Narrative of the Surveying Voyages of His Majesty's Ships Adventure and Beagle between the Year 1826 and 1836, Describing Their Examination of the Southern Shores of South America, and the Beagle's Circumnavigation of the Globe, Journal and Remarks 1832–1836*, London: Henry Colburn, 1839.

Davies, J.L. (ed.): *Atlas of Tasmania*, Hobart: Department of Lands and Surveys, 1965.

Davies, R.H.: 'On the Aborigines of Van Diemen's Land', *Tasmanian Journal of Natural Science*, vol. 2, March 1846, 409–20.

Davies, Suzanne: 'Aborigines, murder and the criminal law in early Port Phillip, 1841–1851', *Historical Studies*, vol. 22, no. 88, April 1987, 313–35.

Davis, Joseph Barnard: 'On the osteology and peculiarities of the Tasmanians, a race of man recently become extinct', *Natururkundige Vehandelingen der Hollandcshe Maatschappij der Wetenschappen*, vol. 2, no. 4, 1874, 1–14.

Delano, Amasa: *A Narrative of Voyages and Travels*, Boston: E.G. House, 1817.

Denison, William: *Varieties of Vice-Regal Life*, vol. 1, London: Longmans, Green and Co., 1870.

Dixon, James: *Narrative of a Voyage to New South Wales and Van Diemen's Land, in the Ship Skelton, during the Year 1820*, Hobart: Melanie Publications, 1822 [facsimile edition, printed for John Anderson, 1984].

Dennis, Rutledge M.: 'Social Darwinism, scientific racism, and the metaphysics of race', *Journal of Negro Education*, vol. 64, no. 3, summer 1995, 243–52.

Dow, G. and Dow, H.: *Landfall in Van Diemen's Land: The Steel's Quest for Greener Pastures*, Melbourne: Footprint, 1990.

Dunnett, Greg: *A Survey and Assessment of Aboriginal Archaeological Sites in the Northern Region of Tasmania*, Hobart: National Parks and Wildlife Service, 1994.

Duyker, Edward: *An Officer of the Blue: Marc-Joseph Marion Dufresne, South Sea Explorer, 1724–1772*, Carlton, Vic: Melbourne University Press, 1994.

Evans, Raymond: 'The country has another past: Queensland and the history wars', in Frances Peters-Little, Ann Curthoys and John Docker (eds), *Passionate Histories: Myth, Memory & Indigenous Australia*, Canberra: ANU E Press and Aboriginal History Inc., 2010, 9–38.

Fawkner, John Pascoe: *Reminiscences of Early Hobart Town 1804–1810*, Malvern, Vic.: The Banks Society, 2007.

Fels, Marie: 'Culture contact in the County of Buckinghamshire, Van Diemen's Land, 1803–11', *Papers and Proceedings, Tasmanian Historical Research Association*, vol. 29, no. 2, 1982, 47–68.

Fenton, James: *A History of Tasmania from Its Discovery in 1642 to the Present Time*, Hobart: J. Walch and Sons, 1884.

Finlason, W.R.: *Commentaries upon Martial Law with Special Reference to Its Regulations and Restraint*, London: Stevens & Sons, 1867.

Ford, Lisa: *Settler Sovereignty: Jurisdiction and Indigenous People in America and Australia 1788–1836*, Cambridge, Mass.: Harvard University Press, 2010.

George, James: 'Extracts from a diary belonging to James George', *Oatlands District Historical Society Chronicle*, no. 2, 2002, 10–20.

Giblin, Robert W.: *The Early History of Tasmania*, vol. 2, 1804–28, Carlton, Vic.: Melbourne University Press, 1939.

Groom, Ray: *Report of the Stolen Generations Assessor*, Hobart: Department of Premier and Cabinet, 2008.

Hainsworth, D.R.: 'Iron men in wooden ships: the Sydney sealers 1800–1820', *Labour History*, no. 13, Nov. 1967, 19–26.

Hansen, David: *John Glover and the Colonial Picturesque*, Hobart, Tasmanian Museum and Art Gallery, 2004.

Hartwell, R.M.: *The Economic Development of Van Diemen's Land 1829–1850*, Carlton, Vic.: Melbourne University Press, 1954.

Hiatt, Betty: 'The food quest and the economy of the Tasmanian Aborigines', *Oceania*, vol. 38, no. 2, 1967, 99–133; no. 3, 1968, 190–219.

HRA, series I: *Governor's Despatches to and from England, 1788–1848*, vols iv, v, xii, ed. Frederick Watson, Sydney: Government Printer, 1914–25.

HRA, series III: *Despatches and Papers Relating to the Settlement of the States*, vols i–vii, ed. Frederick Watson, Sydney: Government Printer, 1921–23; vols viii–x, ed. Peter Chapman, Melbourne: Melbourne University Press, 1996–2000.

Historical Records of New South Wales, vol. 5: *King, 1803, 1804, 1805*, ed. F.M. Bladen, Mona Vale, NSW: Lansdowne Slattery & Co., 1979.

Hobler, G.: *The Diaries of Pioneer George Hobler, October 6, 1800–December 13, 1882*, Sydney: C. & H. Reproductions, 1992.

Hull, H.M.: *Royal Kalendar, and Guide to Tasmania for 1859*, Hobart: William Fletcher, 1859.

Jeanneret, Henry: *Vindication of a Colonial Magistrate*, London: Hope and Co., 1854.

Jeffreys, Charles: *Van Diemen's Land: Geographical and Descriptive Delineations of the Island of Van Diemen's Land*, London: J.M. Richardson, 1820.

Jones, Rhys: 'Tasmanian Aborigines and dogs', *Mankind*, vol. 7, no. 4, 1970, 256–71.

——'Tasmanian tribes', Appendix in Norman B. Tindale, *Aboriginal Tribes of Australia: Their Terrain, Environmental Controls, Distribution, Limits and Proper Names*, Canberra: Australian National University Press, 1974, 317–54.

——'The Tasmanian paradox', in R.V.S. Wright (ed.), *Stone Tools as Cultural Markers: Change, Evolution and Complexity*, Canberra: Australian Institute of Aboriginal Studies, 1977, 189–204.

Kee, Sue: *Midlands Aboriginal Archaeological Site Survey*, Hobart: Department of Parks, Wildlife and Heritage, 1990.

—— *Aboriginal Archaeological Sites in North East Tasmania*, Hobart: National Parks and Wildlife Service, 1991.

Kercher, Bruce: *An Unruly Child: A History of Law in Australia*, St Leonards, NSW: Allen & Unwin, 1995.

Kiernan, Ben: *Blood and Soil: A World History of Genocide and Extermination from Sparta to Darfur*, New Haven and London: Yale University Press, 2007.

King, Jonathan: *'In the Beginning . . .' The Story of the Creation of Australia from the Original Writings*, South Melbourne: Macmillan Australia, 1985.

Lambeck, Kurt, et al., 'Sea level change through the last glacial cycle', *Science*, vol. 292, 27 April 2001, 679–86.

Langford, R.F.: 'Our heritage—your playground', *Australian Archaeology*, vol. 16, 1983, 1–6.

Lennox, Geoff: 'The Van Diemen's Land Company and the Tasmanian Aborigines: a reappraisal', *Papers and Proceedings, Tasmanian Historical Research Association*, vol. 37, no. 4, 1990, 165–208.

Levy, M.C.I.: *Governor George Arthur: A Colonial Benevolent Despot*, Melbourne: Georgian House, 1953.

Lippmann, Lorna: *A Somewhat Startled Realisation*, Canberra: Office of Community Relations, Australian Government Publishing Service, 1978.

Lourandos, Harry: *Continent of Hunter Gatherers: New Perspectives in Australian Prehistory*, Cambridge: Cambridge University Press, 1997.

MacDonald, Helen: *Human Remains: Episodes in Human Dissection*, Melbourne: Melbourne University Press, 2005.

Macfarlane, Ingereth: *A Regional Survey of Archaeological Sites in North West Tasmania*, Hobart: Department of Parks, Wildlife and Heritage, 1991.

Madley, Benjamin: 'From terror to genocide: Britain's Tasmanian penal colony and Australia's history wars', *Journal of British Studies*, vol. 47, Jan. 2008, 77–106.

Mallett, Molly: *My Past—Their Future: Stories from Cape Barren Island*, Hobart: Blubber Head Press in association with Riawunna, Centre for Aboriginal Education, 2001.

Manderson, Desmond: 'Not yet: Aboriginal people and the deferral of the rule of law', *Arena Journal*, nos 29/30, 2008, 219–72.

Mann, Barbara Alice: *George Washington's War on Native America*, Lincoln and London: University of Nebraska Press, 2008.

Mansell, Michael: 'Land rights for Tasmania's Aborigines', *Arena*, no. 50, 1978, 92–7.

——*Aboriginal Land Rights in Tasmania*, Launceston: TAC, 1986.

Maxwell-Stewart, Hamish: 'Competition and conflict on the forgotten frontier', *History Australia*, vol. 6, no. 3, Dec. 2009, 1–26.

McFarlane, Ian: 'Cape Grim', in Robert Manne (ed.), *Whitewash: On Keith Windschuttle's Fabrication of Aboriginal History*, Melbourne: Black Inc., 2003, 277–98.

——*Beyond Awakening: The Aboriginal Tribes of North West Tasmania*, Hobart: Fullers Bookshop, 2008.

——'NJB Plomley's contribution to north-west Tasmanian regional history', in Anna Johnston and Mitchell Rolls (eds), *Reading Robinson: Companion Essays to Friendly Mission*, Hobart: Quintus Publishing, 2008, 127–41.

McGowan, Angela: *Archaeological Investigations at Risdon Cove Historic Site 1978–1980*, Occasional paper no. 10, Hobart: National Parks & Wildlife Service, 1985.

McKay, Anne (ed.): *Journals of the Land Commissioners for Van Diemen's Land, 1826–28*, Hobart: U. Tas. in conjunction with the Tasmanian Historical Research Association, 1962.

McMahon, J.F.: 'The British Army: its role in counter-insurgency in the Black War in Van Diemen's Land', *Tasmanian Historical Studies*, vol. 5, no. 1, 1995–96, 56–63.

McRae, M.D.: 'Port Davey and the South West', *Papers and Proceedings, Tasmanian Historical Research Association*, vol. 8, 1960, 46–50.

Melville, Henry: *The History of Van Diemen's Land from the Year 1824 to 1835, Inclusive during the Administration of Lieutenant-Governor George Arthur*, ed. George Mackaness, Sydney: Horwitz–Grahame, 1965.

Milligan, Joseph: 'On the dialects and languages of the Aboriginal tribes of Tasmania, and on their manners and customs', *Journals and Papers, Legislative Council of Tasmania*, 1856, paper 7.

Reproduced in Robert Brough Smyth, *The Aborigines of Victoria with Notes Relating to the Habits of the Natives of Other Parts of Australia and Tasmania*, Melbourne: Government Printer, 1876 (facsimile edition, Melbourne: John Currey, O'Neill, 1972).

——'On the dialects and languages of the Aboriginal tribes of Tasmania, and on their manners and customs', *Papers and Proceedings, Royal Society of Tasmania*, vol. 3, 1859, 275–82.

Mollison, B.C.: *The Tasmanian Aborigines: Tasmanian Aboriginal Genealogies*, vol. 3, Hobart: Psychology Department, U. Tas., 1977.

Morgan, Sharon: *Land Settlement in Early Tasmania: Creating an Antipodean England*, Cambridge: Cambridge University Press, 1992.

Murray, Tim and Williamson, Christine: 'Archaeology and history', in Robert Manne (ed.), *Whitewash: On Keith Windschuttle's Fabrication of Aboriginal History*, Melbourne: Black Inc., 2003, 311–33.

Murray-Smith, Stephen: 'Beyond the pale: the Islander community of Bass Strait in the 19th century', *Papers and Proceedings, Tasmanian Historical Research Association*, vol. 20, no. 4, Dec. 1973, 167–200.

Napier, Charles James: *Colonization Particularly in Southern Australia with Some Remarks on Small Farms and Overpopulation*, Reprints of Economics Classics, New York: Augustus M. Kelly, Publishers, 1969 [first published 1835].

Needham, J.S.: 'Cape Barren Island', *ABM Review*, vol. 17, 1931, 171–2.

Nicholls, Mary (ed.): *The Diary of the Reverend Robert Knopwood 1803–1838*, Hobart: Tasmanian Historical Research Association, 1977.

Nixon, Francis Russell: *The Cruise of the Beacon*, London: Bell & Daldy, 1857.

Pagden, Anthony: *Lords of All the World: Ideologies of Empire in Spain, Britain and France c. 1500–1800*, New Haven and London: Yale University Press, 1995.

Pardoe, Colin: 'Population genetics and population size in prehistoric Tasmania', *Australian Archaeology*, no. 22, 1986, 1–6.

——'Isolation and evolution in Tasmania', *Current Anthropology*, vol. 32, Feb. 1991, 1–12.

Parry, Naomi: '"Hanging no good for black fellow": looking to the life of Musquito', in Ingereth Macfarlane and Mark Hannah (eds), *Transgressions: Critical Australian Indigenous Histories*, Canberra: ANU E Press, 2007, 153–76.

Penn, Nigel: *The Forgotten Frontier: Colonist and Khoisan on the Cape's Northern Frontier in the 18th Century*, Cape Town: Double Story Books, 2005.

Phillips, Susan Burton: 'Reconstructing the rules for the land rights contest', in *Essays on the Mabo Decision*, Sydney: Law Book Co., 1993.

Plomley, Norman James Brian: *An Annotated Bibliography of the Tasmanian Aborigines*, Occasional paper no. 28, London: Royal Anthropological Institute of Great Britain & Ireland, 1969.

——*The Aboriginal/Settler Clash in Van Diemen's Land 1803–1831*, Launceston: Queen Victoria Museum and Art Gallery, 1992.

——*The Tasmanian Aborigines*, Launceston: Plomley Foundation, 1993.

——'The Aboriginal tribes in Tasmania', Appendix 5 in Norman James Brian Plomley (ed.), *Friendly Mission: The Tasmanian Journals of George Augustus Robinson 1829–1834*, 2nd edn, Launceston and Hobart: Queen Victoria Museum & Art Gallery and Quintus Publishing, 2008, 1006–13.

——*The Westlake Papers: Records of Interviews in Tasmania by Ernest Westlake, 1908–1910*, Occasional paper no. 4, Launceston: Queen Victoria Museum & Art Gallery, n.d.

——(ed.):*Weep in Silence: A History of the Flinders Island Aboriginal Settlement*, Hobart: Blubber Head Press, 1987.

——(ed.): *Jorgen Jorgenson and the Aborigines of Van Diemen's Land*, Hobart: Blubber Head Press, 1991.

——(ed.): *Friendly Mission: The Tasmanian Journals of George Augustus Robinson 1829–1834*, 2nd edn, Launceston and Hobart: Queen Victoria Museum & Art Gallery and Quintus Publishing, 2008.

——and Henley, Kristen Anne: *The Sealers of Bass Strait and the Cape Barren Island Community*, Hobart: Blubber Head Press, 1990.

Pybus, Cassandra: *Community of Thieves*, Melbourne: William Heinemann Australia, 1991.

——'Robinson and Robertson', in Robert Manne (ed.), *Whitewash: On Keith Windschuttle's Fabrication of Aboriginal History*, Melbourne: Black Inc., 2003, 258–76.

Rae-Ellis, Vivienne: *Trucanini: Queen or Traitor?*, Canberra: Australian Institute of Aboriginal Studies, 1981.

——*Black Robinson: Protector of the Aborigines*, Melbourne: Melbourne University Press, 1988.

Randriamahefa, Kerry: *Aborigines in Tasmanian Schools*, Research Study no. 144, Hobart: Education Department of Tasmania Research Branch, April 1979.

Reece, R.H.W.: *Aborigines and Colonists: Aborigines and Colonial Society in New South Wales in the 1830s and 1840s*, Sydney: Sydney University Press, 1974.

Reynolds, Barrie: 'Walter Edmund Roth', in Geoffrey Serle (ed.), *Australian Dictionary of Biography*, vol. 11, Melbourne: Melbourne University Press, 1988, 463–4.

Reynolds, Henry: *The Other Side of the Frontier*, Ringwood, Vic.: Penguin Books Australia, 1982.

——*Frontier: Aborigines, Settlers and Land*, North Sydney: Allen & Unwin Australia, 1987.

——*Fate of a Free People: A Radical Re-Examination of the Tasmanian Wars*, Ringwood, Vic.: Penguin Australia, 1995.

——*An Indelible Stain? The Question of Genocide in Australia's History*, Ringwood, Vic.: Viking, 2001.

Ritchie, John: *Punishment and Profit: The Report of Commissioner John Bigge on the Colonies of New South Wales and Van Diemen's Land 1822–1823; Their Origins, Nature and Significance*, Melbourne: William Heinemann Australia, 1970.

Robson, Lloyd: *A History of Tasmania*, vol. 1, Melbourne: Oxford University Press, 1983.

Rose, Michael (ed.): *For the Record: 160 Years of Aboriginal Print Journalism*, St Leonards, NSW: Allen & Unwin, 1996.

Roth, Henry Ling: *The Aborigines of Tasmania*, 2nd edn, Halifax: F. King & Sons, 1899.

Rowley, C.D.: *The Destruction of Aboriginal Society*, Canberra: ANU Press, 1970.

Rutledge, Martha: 'Charles Edward Jeanneret', in Bede Nairn, Geoffrey Serle and Russel Ward (eds), *Australian Dictionary of Biography*, vol. 4, Melbourne: Melbourne University Press, 1972, 472–3.

Ryan, Lyndall: *The Aboriginal Tasmanians*, St Lucia, Qld: University of Queensland Press, 1981.

——*The Aboriginal Tasmanians*, Vancouver: University of British Columbia Press, 1981.

——*The Aboriginal Tasmanians*, paperback edition, St Lucia, Qld: University of Queensland Press, 1982.

——'The survivors: Tasmanian Aboriginals and the Bicentennial', *Island*, vol. 32, spring 1987, 52–9.

——*The Aboriginal Tasmanians*, 2nd edn, St Leonards: Allen & Unwin, 1996.

——'The struggle for Trukanini 1830–1997', *Papers and Proceedings*, *Tasmanian Historical Research Association*, vol. 44, no. 3, Sept. 1997, 153–73.

——'Who is the fabricator?', in Robert Manne (ed.), *Whitewash: On Keith Windschuttle's Fabrication of Aboriginal History*, Melbourne: Black Inc., 2003, 230–57.

——'Massacre in Tasmania: how do we know?', *Australia and New Zealand Law and History Journal*, vol. 6, 2006, <http://www.anzlhsejournal.auckland.ac.nz/pdfs_2006/Paper_6_Ryan.pdf> (accessed 20 Sept. 2008).

——'List of multiple killings of Aborigines in Tasmania: 1804–1835', in Jacques Semelin (ed.), *Online Encyclopaedia of Mass Violence*, Paris, 2008, <http://www.massviolence.org/List-of-multiple-killings-of-Aborigines-in-Tasmania-1804> (accessed 29 Sept. 2009).

——'Massacre in the Black War in Tasmania 1823–1834: a case study of the Meander River region, June 1827', *Journal of Genocide Research*, vol. 10, no. 4, Dec. 2008, 479–99.

——'Settler massacres on the Port Phillip frontier, 1836–1851', *Journal of Australian Studies*, vol. 34, no. 3, Sept. 2010, 257–73.

——'"Hard evidence": the debate about massacre in the Black War in Tasmania', in Frances Peters-Little, Ann Curthoys and John Docker (eds), *Passionate Histories: Myth, Memory and Indigenous Australia*, Canberra: ANU E Press and Aboriginal History Incorporated, 2010, 39–50.

Sagona, A.G.: 'The quest for red gold', in Antonio Sagona (ed.), *Bruising the Red Earth: Ochre Mining and Ritual in Aboriginal Tasmania*, Melbourne: Melbourne University Press, 1994, 8–38.

Sagona, Claudia: *An Annotated Bibliography of the Tasmanian Aborigines 1970–1987*, Melbourne: Art School Press, Chisholm Institute of Technology, 1989.

Sanders, Will: *The Tasmanian Electoral Roll Trial in the 2002 ATSIC Elections*, Paper no. 245/2003, Canberra: Centre for Aboriginal Economic Policy Research, ANU, 2003.

Schaffer, Irene and McKay, Thelma: *Profiles of Norfolk Islanders to Van Diemen's Land. H.M.S. Porpoise 1807–8*, vol. 2, part 2, Hobart: self-published, 1990.

Scott, Peter: 'Land settlement', in J.L. Davies (ed.), *Atlas of Tasmania*, Hobart: Department of Lands and Surveys, 1965, 43.

Semelin, Jacques: 'In consideration of massacres', *Journal of Genocide Research*, vol. 3, no. 3, 2001, 377–89.

——'From massacre to the genocidal process', *International Social Science Journal*, vol. 54, no. 174, Dec. 2002, 433–42.

——'Towards a vocabulary of massacre and genocide', *Journal of Genocide Research*, vol. 5, no. 2, 2003, 193–210.

Serventy, D.L.: 'Mutton-birding', in *Bass Strait: Australia's Last Frontier*, Sydney: Australian Broadcasting Commission, 1969, 53–60.

Shaw, A.G.L.: 'Sir George Arthur (1784–1854)', in Douglas Pike (ed.), *Australian Dictionary of Biography*, vol. 1, Melbourne: Melbourne University Press, 1966, 32–8.

——*Sir George Arthur, Bart, 1784–1854: Superintendent of British Honduras, Lieutenant-Governor of Van Diemen's Land and of Upper Canada, Governor of the Bombay Presidency*, Melbourne: Melbourne University Press, 1980.

Shelton, D.C. (ed.): *The Parramore Letters*, Epping, NSW: privately published, 1993.

Skira, Irynej: 'Aboriginals in Tasmania: living on Cape Barren Island in the twentieth century', *Papers and Proceedings, Tasmanian Historical Research Association*, vol. 44, no. 3, 1997, 187–201.

Standfield, Rachel: ' "These unoffending people": myth, history and the idea of Aboriginal resistance in David Collins' *Account of the English Colony of New South Wales*', in Frances Peters-Little, Ann Curthoys and John Docker, (eds), *Passionate Histories: Myth, Memory and Indigenous Australia*, Canberra: ANU E Press and Aboriginal History Incorporated, 2010, 123–40.

Stockton, Jim: 'The prehistoric population of northwest Tasmania', *Australian Archaeology*, vol. 17, 1983, 67–78.

Stoddart, Emily: *The Freycinet Line, 1831: Tasmanian History and the Freycinet Peninsula*, Coles Bay: Freycinet Experience Pty Ltd, 2003.

Stokes, John Lort: *Discoveries in Australia: With an Account of the Coasts and Rivers Explored and Surveyed during the Voyage of HMS Beagle in the Years 1837–1843*, vol. 2, London: T. & W. Boone, 1846.

TAC: *Oyster Cove*, Hobart: TAC, 1985.

——*Land Rights in Tasmania*, Hobart: TAC, n.d.

Tardif, Phillip John: *John Bowen's Hobart: The Beginning of European Settlement in Tasmania*, Sandy Bay, Tas.: Tasmanian Historical Research Association, 2003.

——'Risdon Cove', in Robert Manne (ed.), *Whitewash: On Keith Windschuttle's Fabrication of Aboriginal History*, Melbourne: Black Inc., 2003, 218–24.

Taylor, John Albert: *A Study of the Palawa (Tasmanian Aboriginal) Place Names*, Launceston: Uniprint, 2007.

Taylor, Rebe: *Unearthed: The Aboriginal Tasmanians of Kangaroo Island*, Adelaide: Wakefield Press, 2002.

——'The polemics of eating fish in Tasmania: the historical evidence revisited', *Aboriginal History*, vol. 31, 2007, 1–26.

——'The polemics of making fire in Tasmania: the historical evidence revisited', *Aboriginal History*, vol. 32, 2008, 1–27.

Thorpe, Bill: 'Aborigines, settlers and the fauna war in colonial Queensland: the "Warroo Battue" of 1877', *Journal of Australian Studies*, no. 19, 1986, 21–30.

Tindale, N.B.: 'Tasmanian Aborigines on Kangaroo Island, South Australia', *Records of the South Australia Museum*, vol. 6, 1937, 29–37.

——'Results of the Harvard–Adelaide Universities Anthropological Expedition, 1938–1939. Growth of a people: formation and development of a hybrid aboriginal and white stock on the islands of Bass Strait, Tasmania, 1815–1949', *Records of the Queen Victoria Museum*, vol. 2, 1953, 1–64.

Turnbull, Clive: *Black War: The Extermination of the Tasmanian Aborigines*, Melbourne: Lansdowne Press, 1965 [first published Melbourne: F.W. Cheshire, 1948].

Tyler, Edward B.: *Researches into the Early History of Mankind and the Development of Civilisation*, 3rd edn, London: J. Murray, 1878.

——'On the Tasmanian Aborigines as representatives of paleolithic man', *Journal of the Anthropological Institute*, vol. 23, 1894, 141–54.

Vallance, T.G., Moore, D.T. and Groves, E.W.: *Nature's Investigator: The Diary of Robert Brown in Australia 1801–1805*, Canberra: Australian Biological Resources Study, 2001.

Vamplew, Wray (ed.): *Australians: Historical Statistics*, Sydney: Fairfax, Syme & Weldon Associates, 1987.

Vanderwal, Ronald L. and Horton, David: *Coastal Southwest Tasmania: The Prehistory of Louisa Bay and Maatsuyker Island*, Terra Australis no. 9, Canberra: Department of Prehistory, Research School of Pacific Studies, Australian National University, 1984.

Van Toorn, Penny: *Writing Never Arrives Naked: Early Aboriginal Cultures and Writing in Australia*, Canberra: Aboriginal Studies Press, 2006.

Vattel, Emmerich de: *Droit des Gens ou Principes de la Loi Naturelle*, 1758 edn. [*Law of Nations or the Principles of Natural Law*] (electronic source), Carnegie: Institute of Washington, 1916.

Victorian Aboriginal Group: *29th Annual Report*, Melbourne: Victorian Aboriginal Group, 1958.

Walker, James Backhouse: *Early Tasmania: Papers Read before the Royal Society of Tasmania during the Years 1888 to 1899*, Hobart: Government Printer, 1973.

Webb, Stephen: *Paleopathology of Aboriginal Australians*, Cambridge: Cambridge University Press, 1990.

Wentworth, William Charles: *Statistical, Historical, and Political Description of the Colony of New South Wales, and Its Dependent Settlements in Van Diemen's Land*, London: G. and W.B. Whittaker, 1819.

West, Ida: *Pride against Prejudice: Reminiscences of a Tasmanian Aborigine*, Canberra: Australian Institute of Aboriginal Studies, 1984.

——'Truganni', in David Horton (ed.), *The Encylopaedia of Aboriginal Australia*, vol. 2, Canberra: Aboriginal Studies Press, 1994, 1104–5.

West, John: *The History of Tasmania*, ed. A.G.L. Shaw, Sydney: Angus & Robertson in association with the Royal Australia Historical Society, 1971.

White, John: *Land Rights for Tasmanian Aborigines: A Discussion Paper*, Hobart: Government of Tasmania, 1990.

Windschuttle, Keith: *The Fabrication of Aboriginal History*, vol. One, *Van Dieman's Land 1803–1847*, Sydney: Macleay Press, 2002.

Wolfe, Patrick: 'Land, labor and difference: elementary structures of race', *American Historical Review*, vol. 106, no. 3, June 2001, 866–905.

——'Settler colonialism and the elimination of the native', *Journal of Genocide Research*, vol. 8, no. 4, 2006, 387–409.

Index

Note: Page numbers in *italics* denote illustrations

Printed in Great Britain
by Amazon